D0539039

THE PERFECT MILE

OTHER BOOKS BY NEAL BASCOMB

Higher: A Historic Race to the Sky and *The Making of a City*

THE
PERFECT MILE

Three Athletes. One Goal.
And less than Four Minutes to achieve it.

Neal Bascomb

CollinsWillow
An Imprint of HarperCollins*Publishers*

First published in Great Britain in 2004 by
CollinsWillow an imprint of HarperCollins*Publishers* London

1 3 5 7 9 8 6 4 2

A CIP catalogue record for this book is
available from the British Library

The HarperCollins website address is:
http://www.fireandwater.com/www.harpercollins.co.uk

ISBN 0-00-717373-3

Set in Linotype Minion with Giovanni Book display by
Rowland Phototypesetting Ltd, Bury St Edmunds, Suffolk
Printed and bound in Great Britain by
Clays Ltd, St Ives plc

Picture acknowledgements
AP p8 (top); **Bettman/CORBIS** p1 (top), p3 (top), p6 (top),
p8 (bottom); **Duke D'Ambra, courtesy of Wes Santee** p2
(bottom), p3 (bottom), p5 (top); **Fairfax Photos** p2 (middle);
Frank Scherschel/Time Life Pictures/Getty Images p1 (middle);
Herald & Weekly Times, Ltd p2 (top); **Hulton Archive/
Getty Images** p4 (top), p5 (bottom); **Lisa Larsen/Time
Life Pictures/Getty Images** p5 (middle); **Ralph Morse/Time Life
Pictures/Getty Images** p7 (top); **Leonard McCombe/Time
Life Pictures/Getty Images** p1 (bottom); **George Silk/Time Life
Pictures/Getty Images** p6 (bottom), p7 (bottom); **Jimmy
Sime/Central Press/Hulton Archive/Getty Images** p4 (bottom).

CONTENTS

Prologue   1

PART I
A Reason to Run   5

PART II
The Barrier   85

PART III
The Perfect Mile   229
Epilogue   301

Acknowledgements   319
Author's Note   321
References   323
Index   369

PROLOGUE

'How did he know he would not die?' a Frenchman asked of the first runner to break the four-minute mile. Half a century ago the ambition to achieve that goal equalled scaling Everest or sailing alone around the world. Most people considered running four laps of the track in four minutes to be beyond the limits of human speed. It was foolhardy and possibly dangerous to attempt. Some thought that rather than a lifetime of glory, honour, and fortune, a hearse would be waiting for the first man to accomplish the feat.

The four-minute mile: this was the barrier, both physical and psychological, that begged to be broken. The number had a certain mathematical elegance. As one writer explained, the figure 'seemed so perfectly round – four laps, four quarter miles, four-point-oh-oh minutes – that it seemed God himself had established it as man's limit'. Under four minutes: the place had the mysterious and heroic resonance of reaching sport's Valhalla. For decades the world's best middle-distance runners tried and failed. They came to within a second or so, but that was as close as they were able to get. Attempt after spirited attempt proved futile. Each effort was like a stone added to a wall that looked increasingly impossible to breach.

1

The four-minute mile had a fascination beyond its mathematical roundness and assumed impossibility. Running the mile was an art form in itself. The distance, unlike the 100-yard sprint or marathon, required a balance of speed and stamina. The person to break that barrier would have to be fast, diligently trained, and supremely aware of his body, so that he would cross the finish line just at the point of complete exhaustion. Further, the four-minute mile had to be won alone. There could be no team-mates to blame, no coach during half-time to inspire a comeback. One might hide behind the excuses of cold weather, an unkind wind, a slow track, or jostling competition, but ultimately, these obstacles had to be defied. Winning a foot race, particularly one waged against the clock, was a battle with oneself, over oneself.

In August 1952 the battle commenced. Three young men in their early twenties set out to be the first to break the barrier. One of them was Wes Santee, the 'Dizzy Dean of the Cinders'. Santee was a natural athlete, the son of a Kansas ranch hand, born to run fast. He amazed crowds with his running feats, basked in the publicity, and was the first to announce his intention of running the mile in four minutes. 'He just flat believed he was better than anybody else,' said one sportswriter. Few knew that running was his escape from a brutal childhood.

Then there was John Landy, the Australian who trained harder than anyone else and had the weight of a nation's expectations on his shoulders. The mile for Landy was more aesthetic achievement than foot race. He said, 'I'd rather lose a 3:58 mile than win one in 4:10.' Landy ran night and day, across fields, through woods, up sand dunes, along the beach in knee-deep surf. Running revealed to him a self-discipline he never knew he possessed.

And finally there was Roger Bannister, the English medical student who epitomised the ideal of the amateur athlete in a world being overrun by professionals and the commercialisation of sport. For Bannister the four-minute mile was 'a challenge of the human spirit', but one to be realised with a calculated plan. It required scientific experiments, the wisdom of a man who knew great suffering, and a magnificent finishing kick.

All three runners endured thousands of hours of training to shape their bodies and minds. They ran more miles in a year than many of us walk in a lifetime. They spent a large part of their youths struggling for breath. They trained week after week to the point of collapse, all to shave off a second, maybe two, during a mile race – the time it takes to snap one's fingers and register the sound. There were sleepless nights, training sessions in rain, sleet, snow, and scorching heat. There were times when they wanted to go out for a beer or a date yet knew they couldn't. They understood that life was somehow different for them, that idle happiness would elude them. If they weren't training or racing or gathering the will required for these, they were trying not to think about training and racing at all.

In 1953 and 1954, as Santee, Landy, and Bannister attacked the four-minute barrier, getting closer with every passing month, their stories were splashed across the front pages of newspapers around the world, alongside headlines of the Korean War, the atomic arms race, Queen Elizabeth's coronation, and Edmund Hillary's climb towards the world's rooftop. Their performances outdrew golf majors, Ashes Tests, horse derbies, football and rugby matches, and baseball pennant races. Stanley Matthews, Ben Hogan, Rocky Marciano, Mike Hawthorn and Surrey County Cricket Club were often in the shadows of the three runners, whose achievements attracted media attention to athletics that has never been equalled. For weeks in advance of every race the headlines heralded an impending break in the barrier: 'Landy Likely to Achieve Impossible!'; 'Bannister Gets Chance of 4-Minute Mile!'; 'Santee Admits Getting Closer to Phantom Mile'. Articles dissected track conditions and the latest weather forecasts. Millions around the world followed every attempt. Whenever any of the runners failed – and there were many failures – he was criticised for coming up short, for not having what it took. Each such episode only motivated the others to try harder.

They fought on, reluctant heroes whose ambition was fuelled by a desire to achieve the goal and to be the best. They had fame, undeniably, but of the three men only Santee enjoyed the publicity, and that proved to be more of a burden than an advantage. As for riches, financial reward was hardly a factor. They were all amateurs. They had to scrape around for pocket change, relying on their hosts at races for decent room and board. The prize for winning a meet was usually a watch or a small trophy. At that time, the dawn of television, when amateur sport was losing its innocence to the new spirit of win-at-any-cost, these three strove only for the sake of the attempt. The reward was in the effort.

After four soul-crushing laps around the track, one of the three finally breasted the tape in 3:59.4, but the race did not end there. The barrier was broken, and a media maelstrom descended on the victor, yet the ultimate question remained: who would be the best when they toed the starting line together?

The answer came in the perfect mile, a race no longer fought against the clock, rather against one another. It was won with a terrific burst around the final bend in front of an audience that spanned the globe.

If sport, as a chronicler of this battle once said, is a 'tapestry of alternating triumph and tragedy', then the first thread of this story begins with tragedy. It occurred in a race 120 yards short of a mile, at the Olympic 1,500m final in Helsinki, Finland, almost two years to the day before the greatest of triumphs.

I

A REASON TO RUN

1

I have now learned better than to have my races dictated by the public and the press, so I did not throw away a certain championship merely to amuse the crowd and be spectacular.

Jack Lovelock, 1,500m gold medallist, 1936 Olympics

On 16 July 1952 at Motspur Park, south London, two men were running around a black cinder track in singlets and shorts. The stands were empty, and only a scattering of people watched former Cambridge miler Ronnie Williams as he tried to stay even with Roger Bannister, who was tearing down the straight. It was inadequate to describe Bannister as simply 'running': eating up yards at a rate of seven per second, he was moving too fast to call it running. His pacesetter for the first half of the time trial, Chris Chataway, had been exhausted, and the only reason Williams hadn't folded was that all he needed to do was maintain the pace for a lap and a half. What most distinguished Bannister was his stride. *Daily Mail* journalist Terry O'Connor tried to describe it: 'Bannister had terrific grace, a terrific long stride, he seemed to ooze power. It was as if the Greeks had come back and brought to show you what the true Olympic runner was like.'

Bannister was tall – six foot one – and slender of limb. He had a chest like an engine block and long arms that moved like pistons. He flowed over the track, the very picture of economy of motion. Some said he could have walked a tightrope as easily, so balanced and even was his foot placement. There was no jarring shift of gears when he accelerated, as he did in the last stage of the three-quarter-mile time trial, only a quiet, even increase in tempo. Bannister loved that moment of acceleration at the end of a race, when he drew upon the strength of leg, lung, and will to surge ahead. Yes, Bannister ran, but it was so much more than that.

As he sped to the finish with Williams at his heels, Bannister's friend Norris McWhirter prepared to take the time on the sidelines. He held his thumb firmly on the stopwatch button, knowing that because of the thumb's fleshiness, having it poised only lightly added a tenth of a second at least. Bannister shot across the finish; McWhirter punched the button. When he read the time, he gasped.

Norris and his twin brother Ross had been close to Bannister since their days at Oxford University. They were three years older than the miler, having served in the Royal Navy during the Second World War, but they had been Blues together in the university's athletic club. Norris had always known there was something special about Roger. Once, during an Italian tour with the Achilles Club (the combined Oxford and Cambridge athletic club), which Bannister had dominated, McWhirter had looked over with amazement at his friend sleeping on the floor of a train heading to Florence and thought, 'There lies the body that perhaps one day will prove itself to possess a known physical ability beyond that of any of the one billion other men on earth.' Sure enough, as McWhirter stared down at his stopwatch that July afternoon, he could hardly believe the time: Bannister had run three-quarters of a mile in 2:52.9, four seconds faster than the world record held by the great Swedish miler Arne Andersson.

After gathering his breath, Bannister walked over to see what the stopwatch read. Cinders clung to his running spikes. At the time, athletics shoes were simply a couple of pieces of thin leather that moulded themselves so tightly to the feet when the laces were drawn that one could see the ridges of the toes. The soles were embedded with six or more half-inch-long steel spikes for traction. Running surfaces, too, had advanced very little over the years. They were mostly oval dirt strips layered on top with ash cinders that were taken from boilers at coal-fired electricity plants. Track quality depended on how well the cinders were maintained, since in the sun they became loose and tended to blow away, and when it rained the track turned to muck. Motspur Park's track benefited from the country's best groundskeeper, and it was one of the fastest, which was why Bannister had chosen it for this time trial.

He always ran a three-quarter-mile trial before a race to fix in his mind his fitness level and pace judgement. This trial was particularly important because in ten days' time, given that he qualified in the heats, he would run the race he had dedicated the past two years to winning: the Olympic 1,500m final. A good time this afternoon was crucial for his confidence.

'Two fifty-two nine,' McWhirter said.

Bannister was taken aback. Williams and Chataway were just as incredulous. The time had to be wrong.

'At least, Norris, you could have brought a watch we could rely on,' Bannister said.

McWhirter was cross at such a suggestion. But he knew one way to make sure his stopwatch was accurate. He dashed to the telephone booth near the concrete stadium stands, put in a penny coin, and dialled the letters T-I-M. The phone rang dully before a disembodied voice came on to the line, tonelessly saying, 'And on the third stroke, the time will be two thirty-two and ten seconds – bip–bip–bip – and on the third stroke, the time will be two thirty-two and twenty seconds – bip–bip–bip . . .' Norris checked his stopwatch: it was accurate.

After McWhirter returned and confirmed the result to the others, they agreed that Bannister was certain of a very good show in Helsinki. They dared not predict a gold medal, but they knew that Bannister considered a three-minute three-quarter mile the measure of top racing shape. He was now seven seconds under this benchmark. All of his training for the last two years had been focused on reaching his peak at exactly this moment – and what a peak it was. He was in a class by himself. The critics – coaches and newspaper columnists – who had condemned him for following his own training schedule and not running in enough pre-Olympic races would soon be silenced.

There was, however, a complication, which McWhirter had yet to tell Bannister. As a journalist for the *Star*, McWhirter kept his ear to the ground for any breaking news, and he had recently heard something very troubling from British Olympic official Harold Abrahams. Because of the increased number of entrants, a semi-final had been added to the 1,500m contest. In Helsinki, Bannister would have to run not only a first-round heat, but also a semi-final before reaching the final.

The four men bundled into McWhirter's black Humber and headed back to the city for the afternoon.

When Bannister was not racing around the track, where he looked invincible, the 23-year-old appeared slighter. In trousers and a shirt, his long corded muscles were no longer visible, and it was his face one noticed. His long cheekbones, fair complexion, and haphazard flop of straw-coloured hair across the forehead gave him an earnest expression that turned boyish when he smiled. However, there was quiet aggression in his eyes. They looked at you as if he was sizing you up.

As Norris McWhirter turned out of the park, he finally said, 'Roger . . . they put in a semi-final.'

They all knew what he meant: three races in three days. Bannister had trained for two races, not three. Three required a significantly higher level of stamina; Bannister had concentrated on speed work. With two prior races, the nervous energy he relied on would be exhausted by the final – if he made the final. It was as if he were a marksman who had precisely calibrated the distance to his target, then found that his target had been moved out of range. Now it was too late to readjust the sights.

Bannister looked out the window, saying nothing. Away from Motspur Park with its trees and long stretches of open green fields, the roads were choked with exhaust fumes and bordered by drab houses and abandoned lots overgrown with weeds. The closer they got to London, the more they could see of the war's destruction, the craters and bombed-out walls that had yet to be bulldozed and rebuilt. A fine layer of soot clouded the windows and greyed the rooftops.

The young miler didn't complain to his friends, although they knew he was burdened by the fact that he was Britain's great hope for the 1952 Olympics. He was to be the hero of a country in desperate need of a hero.

To pin the hopes of a nation on the singlet of one athlete seemed to invite disaster, but Britain at that time was desperate to win at something. So much had gone wrong for so long that many questioned their country's standing in the world. Their very way of life had come to seem precarious. 'It is gone,' wrote James Morris of his country in the 1950s. 'Empire, forelock, channel and all . . . the world has overtaken [us]. We are getting out of date, like incipient dodos. We have reached, none too soon, one of those immense shifts in the rhythm of a nation's history which occur when the momentum of old success is running out at last.' The First World War had put an end to Britain's economic and military might. The depression of the 1930s slowly drained the country's reserves, and its grasp on India started to slip. Britain moved reluctantly into the Second World War, knowing it couldn't stand alone against Hitler's armies. Once the British joined the fight, they had to throw everything into the effort to keep the Nazis from overrunning them. When the war was over they discovered, like the Blitz survivors who emerged onto the street after the sirens had died away, that they were alive, but that they had grim days ahead of them.

Grim days they were. Britain owed £3 billion, principally to the United States, and the sum was growing. Exports had dried up, in large part because half of the country's merchant fleet had been sunk. Returning soldiers found rubble where their homes had once stood. Finding work was hard, finding a place to live harder. Shop windows remained boarded up. Smog from coal fires deadened the air. Trash littered the alleys. There were queues for even the most basic staples, and when one got to the front of the line, a ration card was required for bread (three and a half pounds per person per week), eggs (one per week), and everything else (which wasn't much). Children needed ration books to buy their sweets. Trains were overcrowded, hours off schedule, and good luck finding a taxi. If this was victory, asked a journalist, why was it 'we still bathed in water that wouldn't come over your knees unless you flattened them?'

And the blows kept falling. The winter of 1946–7, the century's worst, brought the country to a standstill. Blizzards and power outages ushered in what the Chancellor of the Exchequer called the 'Annus Horrendus'. It was so cold that the hands of Big Ben iced up, as if time itself had stopped. Spring brought severe flooding, and summer witnessed extremely high temperatures. To add to the misery, there was a polio scare.

Throughout the next five years, 'austerity' remained the reality, despite numerous attempts to put the country back in order. Key industries were nationalised, and thousands of dreary prefabricated houses were built for the homeless. In 1951 the Festival of Britain was staged to brighten what critic Cyril Connolly deemed 'the largest, saddest and dirtiest of the great cities, with its miles of unpainted half-inhabited houses, its chopless chop-houses, its beer-less beer pubs ... its crowds mooning around the stained green wicker of the cafeterias in their shabby raincoats, under a sky permanently dull and lowering like a metal dish-cover'. The festival, though a nice party, was an obvious attempt to gloss over people's exhaustion after years of hardship. Those who were particularly bitter said that the festival's soaring Skylon was 'just like Britain', standing there without support. To cap it all, on 6 February 1952 London newspapers rolled off the presses with black-bordered pages: the king was dead. Crowds wearing black armbands waited in lines miles long to see George VI lying in state in Westminster

Abbey. As they entered the hall, only the sounds of footsteps and weeping were heard. A great age had passed.

The ideals of that bygone age – *esprit de corps*, self-control, dignity, tireless effort, fair play, and discipline – were often credited to the country's long sporting tradition. It was said that throughout the empire's history, 'England has owed her sovereignty to her sports.' Yet even in sport she had recently faltered. The 1948 Olympic Games in London had begun badly when the Olympic flame was accidentally snuffed out on reaching England from Greece. America (the 'United, Euphoric, You-name-it-they-had-it States' as writer Peter Lewis put it) dominated the games, winning thirty-eight gold medals to Britain's three. After that the country had to learn the sour lesson of being a 'good loser' in everything from football and cricket to rugby, boxing, tennis, golf, athletics, even swimming the Channel. It looked as though the quintessential English amateur – one who played his sport solely for the enjoyment of the effort and never at the cost of a complete life – simply couldn't handle the competition. He now looked outdated, inadequate, and tired. For a country that considered its sporting prowess symbolic of its place in the world, this was a distressing situation.

Roger Bannister, born into the last generation of the age that ended with George VI's death, typified the gentleman amateur. He didn't come from a family with a long athletic tradition, nor one in which it was assumed he would go to Oxford, as he did, to study medicine and spend late afternoons at Vincent's, the club whose hundred members represented the university's elite.

His father, Ralph, was the youngest of eleven children raised in Lancashire, the heart of the English cotton industry and an area often hit by depression. Ralph left home at 15, took the British Civil Service exams, qualified as a low-level clerk, and moved to London. Over a decade later, after working earnestly within the government bureaucracy, he felt settled enough to marry. He met his wife Alice on a visit back to Lancashire, and on 23 March 1929 she gave birth to their first son and second child, Roger Gilbert. The family lived in a modest home in Harrow, north-west London. Forced to abandon their education before reaching university (his mother had worked in a cotton mill), Roger's parents valued books and learning above everything else. All Roger knew of his father's athletic interests was that he had once won his school mile and then fainted. Only later in life did he learn that his father carried the gold medal from that race on his watch chain.

Bannister discovered the joy of running on his own while playing on the beach. 'I was startled and frightened,' he later wrote of his sudden movement forward on the sand in bare feet. 'I glanced round uneasily to see if anyone was watching. A few more steps – self-consciously . . . the earth seemed almost to move with me. I was running now, and a fresh rhythm entered my body.' Apart from an early passion for moving quickly, nothing out of the ordinary marked his early childhood. He spent the years largely alone, building models, imagining heroic adventures, and dodging neighbourhood bullies, like many boys his age.

When he was 10 this world was broken; an air-raid siren sent him scrambling back to his house with a model boat secured under his arm. The Luftwaffe didn't come that time, but soon they would. His family evacuated to Bath, but no place was safe. One night, when the sirens sounded and the family took refuge underneath the basement stairs of their new house, a thundering explosion shook the walls. The roof caved in around them, and the Bannister family had to escape to the woods for shelter.

Although the war continued to intrude on their daily lives, mostly in the form of ration books and blacked-out windows, Roger had other problems. As an awkward, serious-minded 12-year-old who was prone to nervous headaches, he had trouble fitting in among the many strangers at his new school in Bath. He won acceptance by winning the annual cross-country race. The year before, after he had finished eighteenth, his house captain had advised him to train, which Bannister had done by running the two-and-a-half-mile course at top speed a couple of times a week. The night before the race the following year he was restless, thinking about how he would chase the 'third form giant' who was the favourite. The next day Bannister eyed his rival, noting his cockiness and general state of unfitness. When the race started, he ran head down and came in first. His friends' surprise would have been trophy enough, but somehow this race seemed to right the imbalance in his life as well. Soon he was able to pursue his studies, as well as interests in acting, music, and archaeology, without feeling at risk of being an outcast – as long as he kept winning races. Possessed of a passion for running, a surfeit of energy, and a preternatural ability to push himself, he won virtually all of them, usually wheezing for breath by the end.

Before he left Bath to attend the University College School in London, the headmaster warned, 'You'll be dead before you're 21 if you go on at this rate.' His new school had little regard for running, and Bannister struggled to find his place once again. He was miserable. He tried rugby but wasn't stocky or quick enough; he tried rowing but was placed on the third eight. After a year he wanted out, so at 16 he sat for the Cambridge University entrance exam. At 17 he chose to take a scholarship to Exeter College, Oxford, since Cambridge had put him off for a year. He never had a problem knowing what he wanted.

Bannister intended to study to become a doctor, but he knew he needed a way not only to fit in but to excel among his fellow students, most of whom, in 1946, were eight years older than he, having deferred placement because of the war. A schoolboy among ex-majors and brigadiers, he realised that running was his best chance to distinguish himself. The year before, his father had taken him to see the gutsy, diminutive English miler Sydney Wooderson take on the six-foot giant Arne Andersson at the first international athletics competition since the war's end. White City stadium, located in west London, was bedlam as Andersson narrowly beat Wooderson. 'If there was a moment when things began, that was it for me,' Bannister later said. In a foot race, unlike other sports, greatness could be won with sheer heart. He sensed he had plenty of that.

Before he even unpacked his bags at Oxford, Bannister sought out athletes at the track. He found no one there, but discovered a notice on a college bulletin board for the University Athletic Club. He promptly mailed a guinea to join but received no response. He decided to go running on the track anyway, even though one of the groundskeepers advised, 'I'm afraid that you'll never be any good. You just haven't got the strength or the build for it.' Apparently the groundskeeper thought everyone needed to look like Jack Lovelock, the famous Oxford miler: short, compact, with thick, powerful legs. The long-limbed, almost ungainly Bannister persisted nonetheless. Three weeks later, having finally received his membership card, he entered the Freshman's Sport mile wearing an oil-spotted jersey from his rowing days. He thought it best to lead from the start – a strategy he would afterwards discard – and finished the race in second place with a time of 4:52. After the race, the secretary of the British Olympic Association advised him, 'Stop bouncing, and you'll knock twenty seconds off.' Bannister had never before worn running spikes, and their grip on the track had made him, as he later described, 'over-stride in a series of kangaroo-like bounds'.

The cruel winter of 1946–7, with its ten-foot snowdrifts, meant that someone had to shovel out a path on the track so the athletes could train; Bannister took to the yeoman's task, and for his effort won a third-string spot in the Oxford versus Cambridge mile race on 22 March 1947. On that dreary spring day, on the very track at White City where he had watched Wooderson compete, Bannister discovered his true gift for running. He stepped up to the mark feeling the pressure to run well against his university's arch rival. From the start Bannister held back, letting the others set the pace. The track was wet, and the front of his singlet was spotted black with cinder ash kicked up by the runners ahead of him. After the bell for the final lap, Bannister was exhausted but still close enough to the leaders to finish respectably. All of a sudden, though, he was overwhelmed by a feeling that he just had to win. It was instinct, a 'crazy desire to overtake the whole field', as he later explained. Through a cold, high wind on the back straight, he increased the tempo of his stride, and to everyone's shock, team-mates and competitors alike, he surged past on the outside. In the effort inspired by the confluence of body and will, he felt more alive than ever before. He pushed through the tape twenty yards ahead of the others in 4:30.8. It wasn't the time that mattered, rather the rush of passing the field with his long, devouring stride. This was ecstasy, and it was the first time Bannister knew for sure there was something remarkable in the way he ran – and something remarkable in the feeling that went with it.

After the race he met Jack Lovelock, the gold medallist in the 1,500m at the 1936 Olympics and the former world record holder in the mile. 'You mean *the* Jack Lovelock,' Bannister said on being introduced. Lovelock was a national hero, Exeter graduate, doctor, and blessed with tremendous speed. It didn't take much insight on his part to see in Bannister the potential resurrection of British athletics.

Bannister didn't disappoint. On 5 June he clocked a 4:24.6 mile, beating the time set by his hero Wooderson when he was the same age, 18. In the summer Bannister travelled with the English team on its first post-war international tour, putting in several good runs. In November he was selected as a 'possible' for the 1948 Olympics, then turned down the invitation. He wasn't ready, he decided, to some criticism.

It was in his nature to listen to his own counsel, not that of others. He had taken a coach, Bill Thomas, who had once trained Lovelock, but Bannister soon became disgruntled with him. Thomas attended to Bannister on the track while wearing a bowler hat, suit and waistcoat. He barked instructions at the miler on how to hold his arms or how many laps to run during training. When the young miler asked for the reasoning behind the lessons, Thomas simply replied, 'Well, you do this because I'm the coach and I tell you.' When Bannister ran a trial and enquired about his time, Thomas said, 'Oh, don't worry about that.' Soon Bannister dropped him, preferring to discover for himself how to improve his performances.

The next year he became Oxford Athletic Club secretary, then quickly its president. He won the Oxford versus Cambridge meet for the second year; he competed in the Amateur Athletic Association (AAA) championships in the summer, learning the ropes of first-class competition. Increasingly the newspapers headlined his name. He even saved the day at the opening ceremony for the Olympics when it was discovered that the British team hadn't been given a flag with which to march into the stadium. Bannister found the back-up flag, smashing the window of the commandant's car with a brick to retrieve it.

Four years later, he intended to save the British team's honour again.

Roger Bannister's preparations for the Helsinki Games began in the autumn of 1950. He had spent the two previous years studying medicine, soaking up university life, hitch-hiking from Paris to Italy, and going on running tours to America, Greece, and Finland. His body filled out. He won some races and lost others but, importantly, he turned himself from an inexperienced, weedy kid into a young man who clearly understood that Oxford and running had opened up worlds to him that otherwise would have remained closed. He was ready to make his Olympic bid, and afterwards to put away his racing spikes for a life devoted to medicine.

Bannister's plan was to spend one year competing against the best international middle-distance runners in the world, learning their strengths and weaknesses and acclimatising to different environments. Then, in the year before the Games, he would focus exclusively on training to his peak, running in only a few races so as not to take off his edge. The plan was entirely his own. Having spoken to Lovelock about his preparations for the 1936 Olympics, Bannister felt he needed no other guidance.

First he flew to New Zealand over Christmas for the Centennial Games, where he beat the European 1,500m champion Willi Slijkhuis and the Australian mile champion Don Macmillan, both of whom he was likely to face in Helsinki. His mile time was down to 4:09.9, a reduction of more than forty seconds from his first Oxford race three years earlier. While in New Zealand he visited the small village school Lovelock had attended, noticing that the sapling given to the Olympic gold medal winner had now grown into an oak tree. The symbolism wasn't lost on him. Back in England Bannister continued his fellowship in medicine through the spring of 1951 at Oxford, where he investigated the limits of human endurance and chatted with such distinguished lecturers as J. R. R. Tolkien and C. S. Lewis. He then flew to Philadelphia to compete in the Benjamin Franklin Mile, the premier American event in middle-distance running. The press fawned over this foil to the American athlete, commenting on his travelling alone to the event: 'No manager, no trainer, no masseur, no friends! He's nuts – or he's good.' In front of forty thousand American fans, Bannister crushed the country's two best milers in a time of 4:08.3. The *New York Herald Tribune* described him as the 'worthy successor to Jack Lovelock'. The *New York Times* quoted one track official as saying, 'He's young, strong and fast. There's no telling what he can do.'

The race brought Bannister acclaim back home. To beat the Americans on their own turf earned one the status of a national hero. When he followed with summer victories at the British Games and the AAA championships, it seemed track officials and the press were ready to award him the Olympic gold medal right then and there. They praised his training as 'exceptional', an 'object lesson'. Of his long, fluid stride, the British press gushed that it was 'immaculate' and 'amazing'. He left rivals standing; he was a 'will-o'-the-wisp' on the track. After a race that left the crowd laughing at how effortlessly Bannister had won, a British official predicted, 'Anyone who beats him in the Olympics at Helsinki will have to fly.'

Then the positive press turned quickly to the negative. Following his own plan, Bannister stopped running mile races at summer's end. Tired from competition, he felt he had learned all he needed during the year and should now dedicate himself to training. When he chose to run the half-mile in an international meet, the papers attacked: 'Go Back to Your Own Distance, Roger'. This was only the beginning of the criticism, but Bannister remained focused on his goal.

To escape the attention, he journeyed to Scotland to hike and sleep under the stars for two weeks. One late afternoon, after swimming in a lake, he began to jog around to ease his chill. Soon enough he found himself running for the sheer exhilaration of it, across the moor and towards the coast. The sky was filled with crimson clouds, and as he ran, a light rain started to fall. With the sun still warming his back, a rainbow appeared in front of him, and he seemed to run towards it. Along the coast the rhythm of the water breaking against the rocks eased him, and he circled back to where he had begun. Cool, wet air filled his lungs. Running into the sun now, he had trouble seeing the ground underneath his feet, but still he rushed forward, alive with the movement. Finally spent as the sun disappeared from the horizon, he tumbled down a slight hill and rested on his back, his feet bleeding but feeling rejuvenated. He had needed to reconnect to the joy of running, away from the tyranny of the track.

Throughout the winter of 1951–2, Bannister immersed himself into his first year of medical school at St Mary's Hospital in London, learning the basics of taking a patient history and working the wards. He was, by the way, also training for the Olympics. By the spring he had developed his stamina and began speed work on the track. When he announced that he wouldn't defend his British mile championship, the athletics community objected. It was unthinkable. He had obligations to amateur sport; he had to prove he deserved his Olympic spot; he must take a coach now; he couldn't duck his British rivals. Bannister made no big press announcements defending his reasons, he simply stuck to his plan, trusting it. As isolating as this plan was, so far it had taken him exactly where he wanted – so far. Meanwhile, most other athletes trained under the guidance and direction of the British amateur athletics officials.

On 28 May 1952, Bannister clocked a 1:53 half-mile at Motspur Park with his 'space-eating stride'. Ten days later he entered the mile at the Inter-Hospitals Meet and won by 150 yards. Maybe he knew what he was doing. The press turned to writing that he would silence his critics at Helsinki and that his training was 'well-advanced'. Compared to those of the top international 1,500m men, his times were sufficient. His 'pulverizing last lap' would likely win the day. Even L. A. Montague, the *Manchester Guardian*'s esteemed athletics correspondent, trotted out to explain that Bannister was the 'more sensitive, often more intelligent, runner who burns himself up in giving of his best in a great race'. Bannister was Britain's best chance at the gold medal, and Montague wondered, 'Do [critics] really think that they suddenly know more about him than he knows himself?'

Although he lost an 800m race at White City stadium in early July, the headlines exclaimed, 'Don't worry about Bannister's defeat – he knows what he is doing!' Ably assisted by the press, Bannister had painted himself into a corner. He was favoured to bring back gold by everyone from the head of the AAA to revered newspaper columnists – and, by association, by his countrymen as well. Of course, there weren't going to be any scapegoats if he failed. 'No alibis,' as Bannister said himself. 'Victory at Helsinki was the only way out.' A part of him suspected that he had manoeuvred himself into this tight position on purpose. Come the Olympic final, he would have an expectant crowd, the rush of competition, two years of dedicated training, the expectation that it was his last race before retirement, and nobody to blame but himself if he lost. *This* was motivation.

By 17 July most of the British Olympic team had left for Finland, team manager Jack Crump declaring upon arrival in Helsinki, 'We will not let Britain down.' But, though he would have to join the team soon, Bannister was still in London. Like a few other athletes, he wanted to avoid the media frenzy in the prelude to the Games, and the inevitable waiting around, worrying about upcoming events. His friend Chris Chataway, the 5,000m hopeful, had also delayed his departure. The two scoured London for dark goggles to curtain the twenty-one hours of Scandinavian daylight. Given that one rarely saw the sun in London, it proved a difficult search. Bannister also sought out a morning newspaper.

It didn't take him long to find a story headline – 'Semi-Finals for the Olympic 1,500 Metres' – that confirmed what Norris McWhirter had told him the day before about the added heat. 'I could hardly believe it,' Bannister later explained. 'In just the length of time it took to read those few words the bottom had fallen out of my hopes.' Worse, he had drawn a tough eliminating heat in the first round.

As he went about his day in the smog-choked London streets, the crisp air and fast tracks he expected to enjoy in Helsinki seemed threateningly close at hand. One could hardly have blamed him had he not wanted to go at all.

2

The essential thing in life is not so much conquering as fighting well.

Baron de Coubertin, founder of the
modern Olympic Games

In the narrow concrete tunnel, Wes Santee stuck to his position in the seven-man line, waiting to move forward as the first of the American team marched into Helsinki's Olympic Stadium through the Marathon Gate. The applause from the stands reverberated in the tunnel, sounding as if the whole of mankind had come to watch the opening ceremony parade. Santee, his feet more accustomed to cowboy boots or track spikes, stepped ahead in white patent leather shoes. His outfit was a departure from his typical attire of Western shirts and jeans. Like the rest of his team-mates, he wore a dark flannel jacket with silver buttons, grey flannel slacks, and a poplin hat whose brim he had folded to make it look more like a cowboy hat.

The 20-year-old University of Kansas sophomore towered over most of those around him. At six foot one inch, with much of that height in his legs, he looked the clean-cut American athlete, buzz cut included. His shoulders were wide, and he bristled with energy. His face easily lit with a smile, and he almost always said what he thought, with a Midwestern twang. One had the sense that he wore his emotions out in the open, but that this vulnerability had a limit buttressed with steel.

That afternoon of 19 July 1952, he was nothing but a bundle of nervous anticipation as he moved towards the tunnel's mouth. Rain streaked across the opening. He peered past it into the stadium, where hundreds of athletes circled the track. They were dressed in a kaleidoscope of colours and styles: pink turbans, flower-patterned shirts, green and gold blazers, black raincoats, orange hats. It was impossible to tell where each team was from because all the flag inscriptions were in Finnish. Santee could not even pronounce the translation for the United States: *Yhdysvaltain*. The Soviets were already settled on the infield, wearing their cream suits and maroon ties, lined up as neatly as an army regiment. It was their first Olympics since 1912, and they had made no secret of the fact that they were out to beat the Americans.

Finally Santee cleared the tunnel and moved in file towards the track, his head swivelling about to take in the three-tiered stadium and its seventy thousand spectators. It was an awesome sight, like nothing he had ever witnessed. So many people from so many places, charged with excitement and speaking so many different languages. And they had all come this afternoon simply to watch them march around the track, not even to see them compete. On an electric signboard, the likes of which Santee had seen only a few times, were the words *Citius, Altius, Fortius* – Faster, Higher, Stronger. He had made it. He was an Olympic athlete representing his country.

After marching around the mud-soaked track, he followed the row of athletes to his spot on the infield for the ceremony's beginning. He felt as if his eyes weren't wide enough to take in everything happening around him. This was a long way from Ashland, the farming town deep in the south-western part of Kansas where he was raised. The size of the Helsinki stadium alone was enough to marvel at. He remembered arriving at the University of Kansas for the first time and going to the big auditorium for freshman orientation. He'd been with his team-mate Lloyd Koby, who also came from the kind of small town where electricity was just on its way in and a rooster's crow was the only wake-up call one knew. Koby had looked across the numerous tiers of seats, gauged the height of the rafters, turned to Santee, and said, 'Boy, this building would hold a lot of hay.' It was not so much a joke as the only context they knew. But that auditorium was nothing compared to this place, its steep concrete stands seeming to reach the sky.

At a rostrum on the track in front of Santee, the chairman of the organising committee began to speak, first in Finnish, then in Swedish, French, and English, about the Herculean efforts that had gone into these Games. His countrymen had cleared forests, put up hundreds of new buildings of stucco, granite, and steel, enlisted thousands of volunteers, and opened their homes to strangers from around the globe. The stadium in which the opening ceremony was taking place had been the chief target of Russian bombers at the start of the Second World War because of its symbolic value. Now it was once again alive with people, anxious for the competition to commence.

The chairman finished his speech by introducing Finland's president, who stood at the microphone and announced, 'I declare the Fifteenth Olympic Games open!' To the sound of trumpets, the Olympic flag with its five interlocking circles was raised on the stadium flagpole. Then a twenty-one-gun salute boomed. As its echo dissipated, 2,500 quaking pigeons were released from their boxes to swoop and pivot in the air. Santee looked skyward as the birds escaped one by one, carrying the message that the Olympics had begun.

Before the last of them soared away, the scoreboard went blank, and then appeared the words: 'The Olympic Torch is being brought into the Stadium by ... P-A-A-V-O N-U-R-M-I.' Pandemonium ensued. Santee had passed the bronze statue of Nurmi at the stadium entrance and had seen his classic figure on posters wallpapered throughout Helsinki, but few had expected to see the man himself. Peerless Paavo, the Phantom Finn, the Ace of Abo. Nurmi was a national hero in Finland, the godfather of modern athletics. At one time he owned every record from 10,000m down to 1,500m. At the

1924 Paris Olympics he claimed three gold medals in less than two days. Put simply, he was the greatest. Now bald-headed, slight of stature, and 55 years old, Nurmi ran into the stadium in a blue singlet with the torch in his right hand, his stride as graceful and effortless as ever. Photographers manoeuvred into position. The athletes, Santee included, broke ranks, storming to the track side to catch a glimpse of the unconquerable man.

The fire leaping from the birch torch Nurmi held had been lit in Olympia, Greece, on 25 June and had since weathered a five-thousand-mile journey across land and water. When Nurmi finished his run around the track, as athletes and spectators alike jostled one another to get a better look, he passed the flame to a quartet of athletes at the base of the 220-foot-tall white tower at the stadium's south end. While they ascended the tower, at the top of which another Finnish champion, Hannes Kolehmainen, waited, a white-robed choir stood to sing. The stadium was reverently silent. Kolehmainen took the torch and tilted it to light the Olympic flame, which would burn until the Games ended.

Santee and the other athletes returned to their places in the field. From a distance each team looked uniform, its athletes dressed in matching outfits and standing side by side. On closer inspection, they were an odd assembly of men and women: stocky wrestlers, tall sprinters, wide-shouldered shot-putters, cauliflower-eared boxers, miniature gymnasts, crooked-legged horsemen, and weather-beaten yachtsmen – all with their own ambitions for victory in the days ahead. As Santee stood in the middle of this medley of people, looking at the Olympic flame and hearing the jumble of voices all around him, the strangeness of the scene overwhelmed him. He had been overseas only one other time. Except for travelling to athletics meets, he had never left the state of Kansas. Now he was in this enormous amphitheatre in a country where night lasted only a few hours. He didn't have his coach with him. He had few friends among the athletes. He had rarely faced international competition. He was scheduled to run in the 5,000m even though the 1,500m was his best distance. Filled with these thoughts, Santee gulped. The tightness in his throat felt like a stone. Indeed, he was a long way from Kansas now.

Had his father had his way, in the summer of 1952 Wes would still have been pitching hay, fixing fence posts, and ploughing fields back in Ashland. Most fathers want their sons to have a better life, but Wes Santee didn't have such a dad.

David Santee was born in Ohio in the late 1800s. He lived a helter-skelter childhood, never advancing past the second grade (for 7- to 8-year-olds). He was a keen braggart and adept at the harmonica, but his only employable skill was hard labour. Over six feet tall and weighing 220lb, he had the size for it. His cousin married a ranch owner named Molyneux in western Kansas, and David Santee went out to work the eight thousand acres as a hired hand. He met Ethel Benton, a tall, gentle woman who had studied to be a teacher, on a blind date. They were soon married, and shortly afterwards expecting the first of three children. On 25 March 1932, the town doctor was called to the ranch to deliver Wes Santee. He came into the world kicking.

Santee was raised on the Molyneux cattle and wheat ranch five miles outside Ashland. It was practically a pioneer's existence, with an outhouse, no running water, no electricity. If you wanted to listen to the radio, you had to hook it up to the car battery. Farm life was vulnerable to the often cruel hand of nature. The Santees lived through the drought of the Dust Bowl years, when sand squeezed through every crack in the house and made the sky so dark that the chickens went to roost in mid-afternoon. They survived tornados and storms of grasshoppers that ate everything they could chew, including the handle of a pitchfork left out against a fence post. In good times and bad, Mr Molyneux ruled the ranch. He liked the Santee boy's spirit and was more a father to Wes than his own ever was. Molyneux was a successful rancher and businessman; he owned Ashland's dry goods store and enjoyed taking the boy into town to buy him a double-dip ice cream cone at the drugstore. But Molyneux died when Wes was in the fourth grade, and by the age of 10 his happy childhood had ended abruptly. From that point on he was his father's property, suffering his bad temper while working a man's day on the ranch. His only freedom was running.

For Santee, running was play. He ran everywhere. 'I just don't like to fiddle around,' he said. 'If I was told to get the hoe, I'd run to get it. If I had to go to the barn, I'd run.' The only bus in town was a flat-bed truck, so instead of riding, Santee ran the five miles to school. When he returned in the early afternoon, he ran from his house into the fields to help with the ploughing or to corral one of the four hundred head of cattle. At dusk, when his father called it a day, an exhausted Santee didn't walk home for supper, he ran – fast, wearing his cowboy boots. As the distance from his father lengthened, a weight lifted from his shoulders, and by the time he had washed up and changed clothes he was as fresh as if he hadn't worked at all.

Later, when a remark, a look, or seemingly nothing at all set off his father's rage, this freshness was torn from Wes. He took the brunt of his father's anger, saving his younger brother Henry, who suffered from rickets as a child, and his younger sister Ina May from the worst of it. David Santee dispensed his cruelty with forearm, fist, rawhide buggy whip, or whatever else was at hand. Once it was a hammer. Wes considered himself lucky that his old man didn't drink or the situation could have been really bad. Some sons of abusive fathers want to become big enough to fight back; Santee wanted to become fast enough to get away.

Very early on he recognised that he had a gift for running. He was never very good in the sprint, but if the game was to run around the block twice, he always won. In eighth grade, when Wes was in his early teens, the high-school coach came down to evaluate which kids were good at which sports. That was how a small town developed its athletes. The coach threw out a football to see who threw or kicked it the furthest, threw out a basketball to see who made a couple of jump shots. Then he told Santee and the other twenty kids in his class to run to the grain elevator. Within a few hundred yards Santee was all alone and knew he had the others whipped. This was 'duck soup' he said to himself as he ran to the grain elevator and back and took a shower before the others had returned. Most walked half the distance.

When a new kid named Jack Brown, who was rumoured to be quite a runner, arrived in town, the townspeople urged Santee to race him. The first day of his freshman year, Santee joined Brown at the starting line of the half-mile track used for horse races and almost lapped him by the finish. It felt good to be better than everybody else at something. What had started as a combination of fun – running to chase mice or the tractor – and a means to escape his father's clutches had now become a way to excel. Each race he won bolstered his pride.

J. Allen Murray was there to help him on this path. Murray was Ashland's high-school track and field coach (as well as history teacher and basketball/football coach). He believed Santee could be the next Glenn Cunningham, the most famous United States middle-distance runner and a Kansas native. The problem was that Santee barely had enough time for classes, let alone running, because his father wanted him home to work. Murray told Wes that if he didn't have time to train, he should just continue to run everywhere he went. That was fine with Santee.

Finally the time came for his first track meet. Scheduled for a Saturday, the meet was delayed until Monday because of a thunderstorm. Unfortunately, Santee worked on Mondays, and he knew his father would object to losing an afternoon of his free labour. Murray told him he would take care of it. The next evening he walked up the steps to the Santees' house. He had invited himself to dinner. Wes's father normally greeted visitors with a .22-calibre pistol and an offer of five minutes to get off his property. This time David Santee at least pushed open the door, but his hospitality ended there. Through dinner and dessert, Coach Murray explained to Wes's parents why they should allow their son to attend the meet – how it was good for the boy to be challenged in competition. David Santee didn't utter a word the entire evening: not a yes, not a no. Murray left without an answer, and Wes disappeared into the fields afterwards. Alone in the dark, he clawed at the dirt and grass, wondering how he would ever get out of this place. If he hadn't learned to hate his father before this night, he did so now.

The next day Coach Murray told him to get up early on Monday to do his chores; he would pick him up at seven o'clock. Santee rose at four, hauled feed, milked the cows, and did everything required of him before his coach arrived. David Santee was working in the fields and thought his son had simply left for school. It was the first time Wes had left the county, and although he was the youngest in the mile race, unaware of competition tactics and scared after having disobeyed his father, he placed third. He was awarded a red ribbon and could barely stand still with the excitement. But then he had to go home. When he entered the house, his father was sitting at the table. From the grim look on his face he obviously knew that Wes had gone to the meet.

'I won third place,' Wes said with sheepish excitement.

'If you have time to miss school and do all this' – his father bit off each word – 'then you have time to get all the rest of the ploughing done.'

For some eighteen hours, Wes Santee sat on the tractor, plough-ing miles of fields without a break for lunch, and certainly not for school. His throat burned from thirst, his spine ached from the jarring movements of the tractor on uneven terrain, and his hands were rubbed raw from gripping the wheel. Working from dawn until ten o'clock at night, Wes finished two days of ploughing in one. As a man who spent most of his youth labouring on the farm, he would remember that day as the hardest he had ever endured. When he finally returned to school, Murray asked if he was all right. Santee nodded. Murray then asked him if he wanted to go to the next meet in Mead, Kansas. Santee said yes.

After Wes left, Murray called the ranch to say one thing to Santee's father: 'I want you to bring your truck in and haul some kids to Mead.' David Santee didn't reply, but the tone in Coach Murray's voice made him understand that he didn't have a choice in the matter. Like most bullies, David Santee folded when someone finally stood up to him. The next week he showed up on time with his truck, and though it angered him that his son was wasting time that would be better spent on the ranch, he never got in the way of Wes's running again.

Over the next four years, Wes Santee scorched around tracks throughout Kansas. He won two state mile championships, broke Glenn Cunningham's state high-school record, became the favourite son of Ashland, and was targeted by college track recruiters from coast to coast. He had found his way out, and now there was nothing that could stand in his way. He trained as much as possible, studied hard to keep his grades up, and decided not to let things get too far with his high-school girlfriend because recruiters were not interested in athletes with wives or children. Shutting himself down with her was not easy, but he had to get out of Ashland.

When Bill Easton, the University of Kansas track and field coach, offered him a scholarship in 1949, Santee accepted. Over the previous two years Easton had won his confidence, probably because he was everything Santee's father was not: he wore a coat and tie, spoke intelligently, won friends easily, and backed up his words with action. Under Easton's guidance and encouragement, the KU track team had become one of the country's best.

The summer before he left for college, Wes had his last confrontation with his father. While he dug yet another six-foot-deep hole in the hard ground for the soon-to-arrive electricity poles, his father started pounding on his back with his fists because he was digging too slowly. That was it. The 17-year-old, his shirt soaked with sweat and hands blistered from the work, stormed back to the house, informed his mother he was leaving, and said goodbye to Henry and Ina May. In the stable, he saddled Bess, the horse his father had given him, and put a halter on a second mare, which Wes had yet to name (a local farmer had given her to Wes in exchange for breaking some horses). He then led his two horses towards the front gate, a cloud of dust from their hooves trailing behind them.

Suddenly, his father appeared from behind the barn and blocked his way. 'You're not taking that horse anywhere,' he said, gesturing towards Bess.

Sensing the coiled violence in the rigid way his father stood in front of him, Wes grimly said 'Okay' and unstrapped his saddle from Bess. He then threw it over the other horse, which had never been ridden before, and led her through the gate, leaving his father without a goodbye. When he was two hundred yards away, Santee carefully hoisted himself up on the horse and rode into town. He stayed with a friend who owned the local ice plant and had once told him that he could stay with him if things ever got too bad at the ranch. Santee lived there until college began.

In Lawrence, Santee fell under the protection of Bill Easton. The coach invited the youth, who had almost nothing with him but the clothes on his back, to stay at his house until his dormitory was ready. Santee might have been bold-talking and powerful, but he needed someone to care for him. The first morning, over a breakfast of bacon and eggs, Easton told Santee that he needed to set a good example and help lead the team. Easton spoke to him like an equal, and Santee listened.

Coach Murray had given him the opportunity to run; Coach Easton showed Santee how to turn his raw talent as a runner into greatness. It had little to do with changing his short, clipped stride, which had become ingrained in his youth while running along plough furrows and through pastures where a long stride would have been dangerous on the uneven terrain. Santee did not bring his arms back in a normal long arc, nor drive to the extreme with his kicking foot like most distance runners. Instead he had the quick arm swing and knee action of a sprinter. But with his native speed, coordination, long legs, strong shoulders, and ability to relax, he was able to sustain this sprinter style over long distances. Easton was convinced that reshaping his stride into a more classical motion would do more harm than good, so he taught Santee to harness his power through training, pace judgement, and focus. Soon enough, seniors on his team were struggling to keep up with him in practice and competition.

Led by Santee, the freshman squad won the Big Seven cross-country and indoor championships – the league that comprised the biggest and best colleges in sport in the Midwest, namely Kansas State, Iowa State, University of Missouri, University of Colorado, University of Nebraska and University of Oklahoma alongside University of Kansas. Santee set the national collegiate two-mile record in 9:21.6 and began to win headlines as the 'long-legged loper' who would 'play havoc' with most, if not all, of Glenn Cunningham's records by the time he was finished. In the spring of 1951, at the Amateur Athletic Union (AAU) championships, he took seventeen seconds off the 5,000m record in the junior division, and the next day he placed second in the senior division. By the end of his freshman year, his mile time hovered in the four-minute teens (4:15, 4:16, 4:17). That summer he earned a spot on an AAU-sponsored tour to Japan and found himself running in Osaka, Sapporo, and Tokyo. There he met the American half-miler Mal Whitfield who had won two gold medals at the 1948 Olympic Games. While some athletes were hesitant to share a hotel room with the black track star, Santee gladly jumped at the opportunity. Whitfield taught the young miler to make sure to keep his toes pointed straight ahead when striding, so as not to lose even a quarter inch of distance with each stride. He also explained to Wes that a miler had the time and physical reserves to make only one offensive and one defensive move in the course of a race. When Santee returned to Kansas in August, he felt certain he was ready for more international competition. He announced to local reporters, 'I want to make the Olympic team and go to Helsinki, Finland.'

In his second, or sophomore, year this 'sinewy-legged human jet', as one reporter described Santee, proved that he was on his way. Some began to compare him to Emil Zatopek, the Czech star who ran everything from the mile to the marathon at world-class levels. This was the level of enthusiasm Santee generated on and off the track. He loved racing in front of large crowds and never tired. His talent just barely outmeasured his confidence. On a flight to one meet, a Kansas Jayhawks team-mate held out a newspaper article to show Wes. 'Look what it says here . . . [Santee's college competitor] Billy [Herd] hasn't been beaten in any kind of a race for almost two years. That includes relay carries . . . He's gobbled up some pretty good boys too, Wes.'

Santee stretched his boots out into the aisle. 'Yeah, he's a good boy. But he hasn't tried to digest me yet.'

In two-mile races during his sophomore year, Santee lapped his competitors. In cross-country meets he was slipping into his sweats before other runners had finished. During the indoor season he set record after record in the mile, leading his team to a host of dual meet victories. It was almost too easy. On campus he ran from class to class, and professors set their watches by the precise time at which he started his training sessions.

In April 1952 at the Drake University Relays in Des Moines, Iowa, one of the year's most important outdoor track meets, Santee anchored the four-mile relay for his team. When the baton was passed to him, Georgetown's Joe LaPierre was some sixty yards ahead. Santee blazed three 62-second quarter-miles, yet had trouble gaining ground because LaPierre was running brilliantly himself. As Santee sped into the first turn of the last lap, Easton yelled out, 'He's wilting in the sun!' Santee was finally gaining. Stride after stride he closed the gap. When he burst through the tape yards ahead of LaPierre, setting a national collegiate mile record in 4:06.8, Wes Santee had officially arrived. 'Santee's not human,' said the Georgetown coach. The Des Moines Register quipped, 'Santee stuck out above every other athlete like the Aleutian Islands into the Bering

Sea.' The national papers picked up the best quote, from the Drake coach: 'Santee is the greatest prospect for the four-minute mile America has yet produced. He not only has the physical qualifications, but the mental and spiritual as well.'

But first Santee turned his sights to the Olympics. As holder of national titles in the 1,500m and the 5,000m, he by right qualified for the American trial in each. In mid-June he went to California with Easton to spend a week training. They decided together that he should participate in both trials. 'I just want to make the Olympic team,' he told his coach. 'Time or race isn't important.' On 27 June, at the Los Angeles Memorial Coliseum, Santee placed second in the 5,000m trial, guaranteeing a trip to Helsinki. That night he dined on his customary steak and potato dinner and enjoyed quiet conversation with Easton back at the hotel. The next day, braving one of the coldest June days in Los Angeles history, he readied himself for the 1,500m trial in front of forty-two thousand spectators. Santee looked around for Easton, but couldn't find him. A whistle was blown, the race called, and Santee approached the starting line alongside milers Bob McMillen and Warren Druetzler, both of whom he was sure he could beat. In the programme listing the qualifiers for the 3.40 p.m. race, Santee was predicted to 'win as he pleases – he has all year'. He was revved to go.

Suddenly, two AAU officials grabbed his arm and shuffled him off the track before he could protest. 'Wes, they're not going to let you run,' one official said.

'What do you mean?' Santee asked, shrugging off their hold on him. 'What's going on?'

Out of the corner of his eye he saw Easton running across the field. Though wearing a jacket, tie, and dress shoes, he was moving fast.

The race starter called, 'Runners to your mark!' and then the gun fired. Santee watched helplessly as the trial started without him.

Easton finally made it to his side. 'Wes, I'm sorry. We've been in a meeting for over an hour and they're saying you're not good enough to run both races, and they won't let you drop out of the 5,000 to run the 1,500.'

This wasn't right. Only the previous week he had run the third fastest 1,500m time in AAU history: 3:49.3. It was the fastest time by an American in years. Santee welled with anger, and with balled fists looked ready to act out his frustration.

Easton pulled him to one side. The coach had the stocky build of a wrestler, and even then, in his late forties with a fleshy, oval face, he looked capable of stopping this tall athlete if necessary. His voice was calm. 'They told me you were only 19 [sic] – not good enough to run the 5,000 against Zatopek followed up with the 1,500. I told them we don't particularly want to run the 5,000; we want to run the 1,500. Their only response was, "You qualified for that, and you have to stay with it."'

There was nothing to be done. Easton knew that no Olympic rule forbade an athlete from participating in two events. If he qualified, he qualified. Those were the rules, but the AAU ran the show, and if a rule interfered with what the AAU wanted, its leader either ignored the rule or changed it. This was the first time, yet unfortunately not the last, that the AAU would stand in Santee's way. Yes, he was off to Helsinki to race in the 5,000m, but his best chance of coming home with a medal was in the 1,500m.

The three weeks between the trial and the opening ceremony in Helsinki was a whirlwind. Santee nearly died on a flight from Los Angeles to St Louis when the plane carrying America's Olympic athletes went into a tailspin and passengers were thrown from their seats. When the plane finally righted itself, the preacher and pole-vaulter Bob Richards walked down the aisle asking for confessions. After a long layover in St Louis, they arrived in New York. Santee participated in the national TV show *Blind Date*, hosted by Arlene Francis, as well as the first Olympic telethon with Bob Hope and Bing Crosby. He ran in an exhibition three-quarter-mile race on Randall's Island and set a new American record of 2:58.3, not to mention leaving the Olympic 1,500m qualifiers far behind. The effort was born of frustration: to show the AAU officials his speed and prove their decision wrong. After a flurry of press interviews, he flew from New York to Newfoundland, then to London and, finally, to Helsinki. By the time Santee arrived in Finland he was a jumble of excitement, jet lag, hope, aggravation, patriotism, fear, and confusion – a very different cocktail of emotions from what he needed to perform at his best.

But there he was at the opening ceremony, right in the middle of it all and wanting to prove he deserved to stand side by side with the best runners in the world. When the ceremony ended, the 5,870 athletes from sixty-seven nations filed out of the stadium, soaked and cold. Santee had only a few more days to pull himself together for his qualifying round. His legs had never failed him before, and no matter the obstacle or his state of mind, he expected them to see him through once again.

3

To be great, one does not have to be mad, but definitely it
helps.

Percy Cerutty, Australian athletics coach

All was quiet in Kapyla, the Olympic village in a forest of pine trees
twenty miles outside Helsinki. John Landy and three of his four
room-mates – Les Perry, Don Macmillan, and Bob Prentice – lay
in their iron-framed beds. The Arctic twilight crept in around the
edges of the window, the sheets were as coarse as burlap, and
the piles of track clothes and shoes reeked, but the Australians were
resting easily, exhausted from being thousands of miles from home
and trying to prepare for the most important athletics competition
of their lives. In the days before an Olympian's event, he felt as if
he were looking over the edge of a cliff; the nerves, upset stomach,
and general unease took a lot out of an athlete. The anticipation
was almost as trying as the event itself. Sleep was the only relief on
offer, if one could finally fall asleep.

'Wake up! Wake up! You don't need all this sleep!' Percy Cerutty
yelled as he burst into the room, swinging the door wide open and
switching on the lights.

'Bloody hell, Percy!' groaned one of his athletes. 'Thanks for
waking us.'

'You blokes don't need all this sleep,' their coach shouted back.
At 57, Cerutty was a whirling dervish, a short, fit man with a flowing
white mane of hair, goatee, toffee-coloured face, blue eyes, and the

kind of voice that could wake the dead when raised. It was often raised.

'All *what* sleep?' his athletes retorted.

'Ah, you're hiding in here. You're avoiding reality!' Cerutty bounced around the floor, kicking up little wakes of cement dust. 'The world is gathered here just outside that doorway, and all you fellas can think of is sleep. Sleep won't get you anywhere.' He was really getting going now. When Cerutty started a rant, he went on for a while. They had to stop him.

It might have been a single voice, but it was their collective annoyance that finally said, 'Look, shut the hell up, Percy. It's all right for you to wander around grandstanding, but we're the ones who have to run. You've been carrying on non-stop since we got here, when all we're trying to do is prepare to race. You're supposed to be here to help us.' Les Perry had to face the mighty Emil Zatopek; Bob Prentice would run a marathon; and Macmillan and Landy would toe the line with the greatest field of middle-distance runners in Olympic history. Cerutty had chosen to crash with his protégés, whether they liked it or not. They had been patient with him, but now he would have to excuse them for finally taking a stand against his antics.

After the athletes had joined him in London on 20 June (as an unofficial, non-sponsored coach, Cerutty had had to pay his own way and could afford the journey from Australia only by slow boat) for a series of pre-Olympic races, Cerutty had provoked incident after incident. They knew he needed to attract attention to promote his coaching techniques, but at what cost? Prancing around Motspur Park wearing only a pair of white shorts, he'd heckled other runners. At White City he had walked up to Roger Bannister, close enough to feel his breath, and said, 'So, you're Bannister . . . We've come to *do* you.' He had showboated to the journalists, too. 'Others can run faster,' he'd boasted, 'but none can run harder than I.' He was dragged off screaming from one meet because he wouldn't leave the track. On arriving in Helsinki, Cerutty had made a beeline to visit Paavo Nurmi without an invitation, and he had stayed so late with Zatopek that the Czech runner was forced to offer his bed to the Australian coach and sleep in the woods himself. His athletes were used to him, but couldn't he have left his eccentricities in Australia? This was the Olympics. Enough was enough.

While Cerutty scrambled about the room, Landy and the others shielded their eyes from the light. Earlier that evening, Landy had scaled the fence surrounding the Olympic training arena to get in some extra training, so he was particularly tired. Compared to Don Macmillan, the miler in the bed next to him, who had long legs and a powerful chest, Landy was small. His 150lb were stretched over a narrow five-foot-eleven-inch frame, and with his quiet voice, soft brown eyes, and shag of curly hair, he hardly stood out in a room. Yet he had a strong presence. In part it was because of his intelligence, which was lively, well rounded, and quick. He also possessed a deep and infectious laugh. But mostly it was an intangible quality that people noticed, a feeling that Landy possessed a reservoir of calm, uncompromising will. In conversation with him, one immediately had the sense that he would be a rock in a storm, and that a friendship with him would endure.

Although Landy had been last on the list to make the Australian team, an honour that earned him a chance to compete but not the funds to make the trip, he had done very well in the six weeks since leaving Melbourne. In London he had placed second in the British AAA championship mile race – a surprise to himself and everybody else in the White City stadium. He'd followed that race with meets in Belfast, Glasgow, Middlesbrough, and another in London. Back home in Australia the press began to pay attention, commenting on his 'paralyzing burst' and how many experts 'had not seen a runner over the last fifteen years with such relaxation, smoothness, and style'. He had even set a new two-mile record with a time of 8:54, a feat that resulted in his inclusion in the 5,000m heats on top of the

1,500m. It also improved the odds posted on him to bring back a medal. Now he just needed some sleep.

Landy and his three friends knew they owed their presence in Helsinki mainly to Cerutty, this madcap little man with his strange ideas about pushing oneself to the limit. After all, they were Cerutty's gang. Unfortunately, enlightenment came at a cost.

To develop four Australian distance runners to Olympic standards had taken more than a sleep-deprivation regime. Unlike Finland, Australia wasn't a country known for investing either attention or dollars in athletics. The six state amateur athletic associations ran perpetually in the red. Training methods were years behind European and American advances. Some Australians even thought too much exercise was bad for one's health. As an athlete from the 1950s put it, 'Runners were oddities; long-distance runners were very peculiar people; and those who ran the marathon were crazy.' The country had a long tradition in track and field, but it was marked by neglect, a focus on gambling in professional foot races, lackadaisical training, a dearth of talent, and very little international success. Spectators and athletes alike had to pay at the gate, yet the expense of running meets consistently fell short of revenues. In promoter's jargon, the sport 'didn't sell'.

Facilities for training and events were lacking as well. Australia, nearly the size of the continental United States, had only two standard athletics fields. One of those was in Melbourne, Landy's hometown, but as Joseph Galli, a cigar-chomping, omnipresent athletics reporter of the time, wrote, 'Olympic Park [was] a depressing shambles – lank grass covers the earth banking, dressing rooms are dirty and primitive, and the burnt-out stand remains as mute testimony of the unwillingness of Government and civic leaders to give amateur athletes the small, permanent stadium they need for the future.' The track itself was a disaster; runners would have posted better times circling a potholed city block through rush-hour traffic.

This is not to say that Australia cared little for sport in general: among sport-crazed nations, it reached the height of bedlam. Early in their history, Australians had imported the English love of sport, and over the years had taken it to an entirely different level. It has been noted that for every thirty words in the Australian language, one has to do with sport. In the early 1950s a *Saturday Evening Post* correspondent explained how the country's sports heroes were accorded a respect greater than that given to 'ministers of State or Gospel', and their fans were among the world's most avid. Total attendance in the minor rounds of Australian football matches typically reached over two million spectators. And when one of their great athletes died, he or she was accorded all the trappings of a state funeral. On the international stage Australians couldn't claim military might, economic superiority, cultural influence, political power, or historical greatness, but they could make their country known in the sporting arena. Success there fostered pride that was wanting in a nation built by convicts and gold prospectors. In cricket and football, tennis and swimming, Australians were respected, but in athletics much less so. And in distance running, not at all.

Young men such as John Landy needed to be convinced to take up running seriously; for most it was just something one played at. Born on 12 April 1930, Landy showed early promise by winning the sprint race at Malvern Grammar School's annual sports meeting. When his proud father Gordon, who had been a fine footballer in his day, turned to his wife Elva and said that one day John would be a 'world champion', she laughed. He was only 6.

Landy enjoyed a comfortable childhood. His family lived in a gracious, five-bedroom house in East Malvern, an upmarket suburb a few miles south-east of Melbourne, a city of one and a half million born during the Gold Rush. The Landy family dated back to the mid-nineteenth-century influx of immigrants from England and Ireland. Along with his two brothers and two sisters, John was loved and supported by his parents, who were neither too strict nor too lenient. His father, a disciplined man, well respected in the community, was a successful accountant and served on the Melbourne Cricket Club board. His mother had a great interest in history and literature. The children attended private schools and were urged to pursue their own interests. They holidayed in Dromana, a seaside town outside Melbourne. If one asked about the Landy family, the response was that they were 'good people'.

The young John Landy was more interested in butterfly collecting than in running. When he was 10 years old, he met a local beetle specialist who introduced him to entomology. With three other local kids, Landy often rode his bike twenty miles into the bush to chase after butterflies with a net and a pair of fast legs. At home he would carefully secure his latest find on a mounting board and add the creature's taxonomic classification for identification.

Only when Landy was 14 and entered Geelong Grammar, an elite boarding school outside the city where the 'prefects whack[ed] the boys', that he began to distinguish himself in sport. It was the height of the war in the Pacific, and his father was away from Melbourne handling logistics for the air force. John was part of a group called the Philistines, boys who, as he described it, weren't regarded as 'intellectual powerhouses' but who knew their way around the playing fields. Like the others, Landy preferred Australian Rules football, and he excelled by being quick on his feet and a fierce competitor. In the off-season Landy proved pretty good at athletics events, too. In his final year at Geelong he won the school cross-country, 440-yard, 880-yard, and one-mile track titles – a clean sweep. He then claimed the All Public Schools mile championship in a time of 4:43.8. That was impressive, but two years earlier at the same championship Don Macmillan had posted a time better by seventeen seconds, so not much attention was paid to Landy's future as a miler outside the small circle of devoted Australian running fans. Still, a handful of people were watching Landy's efforts on the track.

When he enrolled at Melbourne University to take his degree in agricultural science, Landy continued to dabble in running, but he considered his prospects limited. He had a good head for numbers, was aware of the times of Australian and international stars, and given his progress to date he thought his best time in the mile would be 4:20. In whatever sport he pursued, he wanted to be the best, and running laps around the track didn't appear to repay the effort involved, particularly as he began to lose more races than he won. During his second year in college, one spent 120 miles north-east of the city to learn the more practical side of agricultural science (mending fences, driving tractors, tending to sheep and cattle), Landy won the Hanlon 'best and fairest' footballer trophy, a distinguished prize. While there, he didn't win any foot races. More than ever, playing half centre half back looked to be the right choice for his undergraduate sporting activities. He liked being part of a team as well. Like many Australian athletes before him who had great potential, he was losing interest in running as a result of a lack of encouragement and insightful training.

But in late 1950, everything changed. Like many Geelong students, Landy had joined the school's athletic club after graduation in order to participate in meets. The club captain, marathoner Gordon Hall, had advised him to alternate days of cross-country and sprint running. He took that advice. After a race at Olympic Park, however, Hall approached him and said, 'You're not fit.' He suggested Landy speak to his own coach, Percy Cerutty, who was a fixture at Olympic Park; to find him, all one had to do was listen for his piercing voice. The two went to see Cerutty, and Hall introduced Landy, who, though not exceptionally tall, towered over the bantamweight 116lb coach.

Cerutty stroked his chin and finally said, 'Never heard of you.'

The coach liked to press an athlete's buttons in order to gauge his reaction and strength of will. Usually he invaded a young man's space in the process, setting him further on edge. Landy fell for the bait, commenting that he was truly a footballer and only played at running. That attitude was anathema to Cerutty, who demanded 100 per cent commitment from his athletes. Before the conversation had barely begun, Cerutty was walking away. Nonetheless, he told Landy that if he was interested in learning how to run, seriously interested, then he should come by the house in South Yarra for another talk. They didn't set a date.

Cerutty knew what he was doing; an athlete needed to choose to be taught. Only when Landy went to him could Cerutty show him what he would gain by listening to him. He had already recruited two of Australia's brightest young stars and helped them to achieve astounding results.

The first was Les Perry, the 'Mighty Atom', as some called him, because of his short stature and indefatigable energy. Perry had first caught the Cerutty show at an annual professional foot race known as the Stawell Gift. On the infield, Cerutty was waving his arms about while explaining to a crowd how he had just run seventeen miles to the nearest mountain range and back. 'Endurance? You've only got to get out there and do it. Face up to it: man was meant to run.' A year later, upset at his progress in running, Perry answered an advertisement Cerutty had posted in the local Melbourne paper. He went to the house in South Yarra, and over the course of the afternoon Cerutty lifted weights and ran around the house ranting about prehistoric man and the survival of the fittest. But his ideas on fitness made sense. Perry enlisted his help, then urged his friend Don Macmillan to see him as well.

When Macmillan, one of the most naturally gifted milers to appear on the Australian scene for years, showed up at Cerutty's door on a Sunday morning, he was in a terrible state. He was failing his exams, having trouble finding time to train, and worried about his direction in life. Cerutty sat him down to talk about books, to discuss the Bible, and to argue philosophy. Then he gave Macmillan an ultimatum: 'If you want to come work with me, be part of my gang, I'll tell you straight out, I'm not interested in failures. You have to pass all your exams. That bit's up to you, but if you want, I'll tell you how to do it.' He gave Macmillan an hour-by-hour schedule, directing him when to get up, drink his tea, run, study, take a shower, eat, run again, read the paper, and go to bed. Within a few months, Macmillan had passed his exams and won the Australian mile title in record time. At that same championship Les Perry came in first in the three-mile race.

When John Landy decided to make his way to South Yarra, Cerutty's reputation was well established. As he led Landy up the stairs to his study overlooking Melbourne's botanical gardens, the coach paused and, with a befuddled look, asked, 'What did you say your name was? Landy? Gordon Hall told me you won the Combined Public Schools mile last year, and I always study the results . . . What was the time you ran?'

'About 4:44 . . .'

'I have never heard the name,' Cerutty said, looking him straight in the eye. He sensed that Landy would resist taking direction. 'It seems to me, young man, it is time you put the name of Landy on the world map.'

In a study measuring seven feet by seven feet and crowded with books, cherry red velvet couches, dumbbells, a decanter of port, a typewriter, and a hodgepodge of papers and magazines, Landy sat in silence as Cerutty dispelled the notion that Landy would burn out or, worse, harm himself if he trained too much. The 'human organism' was built to handle stress, he said; the body actually welcomed it. Through continuous effort, superior fitness was guaranteed. Look at the rigorous training of Emil Zatopek or the Finnish runners Arne Andersson and Gundar Haegg, he told Landy. Look at Percy Cerutty.

Landy was fired by his ideas. Nobody had ever spoken to him in this way. He told Cerutty that he would train with him. When Landy left, Cerutty simply noted on a card the young man's date of birth and the mile time of 4:43.8 he had run in the 1948 Victorian Public Schools Championship. He filed it away in his athletics card catalogue, unaware that it was John Landy who would launch him into the international arena as a coach.

It took three weeks of hard training and a few lessons on running

style for Landy to realise results. On 20 January 1951, he dropped
his mile time by six seconds. Cerutty then gave Landy a training outline and sent him out on his own, never enquiring as to whether
or not the young runner was following his guidance. And Landy
did not feel the need to offer the information himself. The proof was
in his performances. Two months later, after upper body strength-
ening with dumbbells and hundreds of miles of conditioning work,
his time was down another ten seconds. On 22 May he ran a 4:16
mile, an extraordinary improvement. It was the first time Landy
thought he might have a shot at the Olympics, though the qualifying
time was 4:10. This 'Conditioner of Men', as the brass plate outside
Cerutty's house read, had discovered his greatest athlete yet. Landy
had natural coordination, very strong leg muscles, and most importantly, he could sustain punishing levels of training. In this last
respect, coach and athlete were much alike.

Almost from the day he was born in 1895, Percy Cerutty was a
sickly child. His father was an alcoholic and his mother barely kept
her son from malnourishment. Cerutty was plagued by pneumonia;
his lungs barely functioned. Much of his youth was spent reading.
He was continually nursed to health by his mother and sisters.
At 15, when he took a job as a telegraph messenger boy, he had to
ride his bicycle many miles into the suburbs, and he found that
he enjoyed this. At 18 he won his first foot race. By the age of 21
he was experiencing brutal headaches that blurred his vision and
made him vomit, yet he still raced, posting his best mile time of
4:34, just behind the fastest middle-distance runner in Australia at
that time.

After he married and took up a career as a telephone techni-
cian, however, he hung up his racing shoes for the serious business
of adult life. But soon the dreariness of that life began to sap his
strength; he took to smoking and inactivity. The migraines
worsened, his health deteriorated, and depression overpowered
him. One day, at the age of 39, he stumbled into an empty church

with tears pouring from his eyes. He had reached rock bottom. He was thin and weak with no hope but an early death.

His doctor recommended a six-month leave from the telephone company and gave Cerutty one prescription: 'I can't heal you with medicines, Percy . . . You have to save yourself. If you want to do anything about yourself, you'll get off that bed under your own will and spirit.' Cerutty took that advice seriously. He restricted his diet to raw foods and quit smoking. Perhaps most importantly, he started reading. He devoured everything from poetry to religious texts, weightlifting advice, Eastern philosophy, scientific treatises, and long-distance training guides. He developed a new approach to life, one unencumbered by fear and defined by exerting himself fully – physically, intellectually, and spiritually.

Mostly, though, he exercised. He lifted weights. He joined a walking club and began to take longer and longer hikes through the bush. Within a year he had completed a seventy-mile hike, to his wife's shock. The outdoors exhilarated him. It was not long until he started to run again, and he ran constantly. Soon his body was transformed into that of a much younger man. In 1942, at 47, he showed up at the Malvern Harriers locker room and announced, 'I've come down to have a run with you. I used to be a member here.' Gone were the migraines, rheumatism, and spells of depression. The road hadn't been easy though. When Cerutty had first begun exercising, he would return home on the brink of total collapse, his heart racing. He could hardly push open the front door. He would lie down on the floor, eyes glued to the ceiling as his breathing and heart rate gradually returned to normal. But he learned to appreciate the torture his body endured because he always recovered and returned stronger the next day. 'Thrust against pain. Pain is the purifier,' he said.

Within a year of joining the Harriers, he was regularly clocking mid-four-minute miles. Then came the marathons, 100-mile races in twenty-four hours, 200 miles in forty-eight hours. Such feats by a man of his age brought attention, and Cerutty adored it. He also welcomed the chance to expound his theories. As he codified his philosophy of training and life in the late 1940s, athletes were beginning to pay heed. In 1946 Cerutty purchased three acres in Portsea, a town south of Melbourne on the easternmost point of Port Philip Bay. There he began to build a ten-by-fourteen-foot hut and a larger shack out of lumber dismantled from shipping boxes. He would be a teacher.

By Christmas 1951, when John Landy walked up to the gate for his first and only visit to the Portsea property, Cerutty's buildings and philosophy were complete. He didn't train athletes; he guided 'Stotans'.

The gate to the property was shut. Unlike the rest of the athletes at the camp, Landy had come down to Portsea on his own for the ten-day training session. His parents were circumspect about Cerutty, particularly because of his outlandish antics, but their son's improvement as an athlete was undeniable, so they didn't object to the trip. Seeing no lights on, Landy realised it was too late to catch anybody awake. He had brought a sleeping bag and, not wanting to disturb anyone, he found a hollow to sleep in. Because of the chill in the air, he donned every item of spare clothing he had brought, including his football socks, before slipping into his bag. He was all right until rain began to pelt his bag. Then it turned into a downpour. Shaking, wet to the bone, he stuck it out. By first light the hollow had turned into a streambed, and Landy stumbled into the camp, half in shock from the cold. The Portsea training had begun.

In the year since Landy had first called on Cerutty, he had paid close attention to the coach's direction. He had paid ten shillings for lessons on how to move his arms and how to run like a rooster, clawing at the air. He had strengthened his upper body by lifting dumbbells. He had participated in running sessions on a two-and-a-half-mile horse path named the Tan (after the four-inch layer of tree bark discarded from tanneries, which cushioned the dirt), and bounded up and down Anderson Street Hill with the others under Cerutty's watchful eye. Their runs provoked gasps from the Melbourne residents nearby. They couldn't understand what these young men, hounded by a shirtless older man, were doing. Running for exercise was odd in and of itself, but a group doing so through the botanical gardens carrying bamboo poles in each arm and shrieking like banshees as Cerutty called to them to run like 'primitive man' was pure scandal.

What Cerutty had in mind for the ten-day training camp in Portsea would definitely have been beyond the observers' comprehension. Landy was sceptical as well, yet there he was. By following Cerutty's gruelling regimen, Landy hoped to win a spot on the Olympic team.

Before breakfast the men ran the Hall Circuit, a course that threaded through tea trees, up hills, down steep slopes, and across sand dunes for one mile and 283 yards; the runners were timed and pitted against one another with handicaps and a three-pence bet apiece. The winner won the pot, and Cerutty didn't hesitate to direct runners around the wrong bend so that he could claim the prize himself. Sometimes he clocked their runs and badgered them to go faster, questioning their manhood or dedication, often both. He ridiculed and taunted them mercilessly, particularly Landy, whom he thought needed toughening up. 'Move your bloody arms!' he would shout. 'Too slow! Too slow! . . . Come on, you lazy bastards! You're hopeless bloody dogs! Children could run faster than that!'

Other training sessions were held on nearby golf courses, where Cerutty had his charges accelerate up hills to achieve the kind of energy explosion they needed in a race. They ran up sand dunes for the same effect, an exercise Landy particularly disliked. He preferred the rhythmic flow of running on flat ground. For resistance training they sprinted along the beach in knee-deep surf. When not running, they swam, surfed or hiked along the coast. They were always in a state of movement until Cerutty stopped to give a lecture on the

grass beside the 300-metre Portsea Oval. There he taught his Stotan
– part Stoic, part Spartan – philosophy. Cerutty had coined the term
and its requirements:

1. Realization that, as Wordsworth the poet says, 'Life is real, life is
   earnest,' which denotes there is no time for wasteful ideas and
   pursuits.
2. In place of wasteful hobbies there commences a period of supervised and systematic physical training, together with instruction
   in the art of living fully. This replaces previously undirected life.
3. Swimming will be done all the year round … This especially
   strengthens the will and builds resistance to quitting the task
   ahead.
4. The cessation of late hours. Amusements both social and entertaining should be reduced to a minimum, and then only in the
   nature of relaxation from strenuous work.

Cerutty delivered this philosophy along with quotes from Plato,
Buddha, Jesus, Freud, Einstein, and St Francis of Assisi, among
others. He stressed the importance of yoga, non-conformity, a diet
of oats, the study of nature and animals, and running barefoot to
connect with the Earth. There were also the impromptu lessons after
meals, like the time when Cerutty lectured them on warming up. A
cat was sitting on a ledge outside one of the huts when their coach
snuck over and emptied a bucket of water over it. The cat leapt away
and disappeared in a flash. Cerutty then expounded, 'There. Did the
cat do stretches? Did the cat jog around? Did the cat do knee bends?
Did the cat have a tracksuit on before racing? No, the cat just got up
and went. No more warming up. Forget it.'

For Landy, the son of an accountant and the product of private
schools, this was wild stuff. He laughed off most of it, but there was
wisdom in what Cerutty said about training hard. The body had
amazing limits that most people never tested; Cerutty drove Landy
to try. He had helped bring out a discipline and focus the young

runner never suspected he had. This ability had been dormant, but now it revealed itself. The other athletes at Portsea were impressed by Landy's discipline. During hard runs that seemed to last for ever, they also began to realise they could never match it.

There was no sense of jealousy, however. In fact Landy took away from this time with Cerutty more than important lessons. He had won a tightly knit group of friends at Portsea, among them Perry and Macmillan as well as three-milers Geoff Warren and Trevor Robbins. The hard training and rustic setting combined to create a sort of boot camp, one that drew the athletes together. Landy, Robbins, Warren and two others bunked in the 'ski hut', which was a modified wooden container originally used to import Volkswagen cars. The first night Landy stayed there he had a bad dream about trying to get out of a hole. The nightmare was so vivid that he literally clawed his way out of his top bunk and crashed to the floor. The next night he agreed to be roped into his bed. Meanwhile, Perry and Macmillan, the two more established Stotans, were stay-ing with Cerutty in an old cabin nicknamed after the luxury hotel, 'Menzies', because of its superior accommodation. One morning after a particularly cold night, Landy approached Macmillan and explained, 'It's pretty tough out here. Nobody will get up and get the breakfast. If you do and get everything out and ready, the second you turn your back, suddenly all these vultures' – and Landy then jokingly mimicked a vulture poised to strike with its claws – 'and little monkeys come down and eat it all up and go back up to their bunks, and yours is gone.' By the end of the story, he had Macmillan in hysterics. With each such episode at Portsea, the others liked Landy more and more.

By the tenth day of camp, the gang of runners had bonded. They were both exhausted and inspired. Cerutty came away with a better understanding of what made his runners tick. Of Landy he wrote, 'He undervalues himself, his achievements, and his possibilities, merely because he measures himself not against mediocrity but against the highest levels . . . Courage and desire to excel without undue display of effort, much less suffering, causes him to run well within himself... What his highest potential level is I can only guess at.' Though Cerutty thought it unlikely that Landy would ever become a true Stotan, they both knew who had set him on the path to athletic greatness.

On 12 January 1952, in Melbourne, Landy set out to break 4:10 in the mile, the time established by the Australian Olympic organisers to qualify for Helsinki. Without 'Big Mac' Macmillan to push him, Landy led from the start, pushing harder than ever before, but he crossed the finish line a second short. 'It is bad luck,' he said after the race. 'I don't suppose there will be enough finance to send us both [Macmillan and Landy] to the Olympics.' He swallowed his disappointment, and only a few hours later ran a 3,000m race in 8:53, breaking the Australian open record. The training at Portsea had increased his endurance, but not his speed over shorter distances. Two weeks later in Sydney he beat Macmillan by inches, but again the time was too slow to qualify.

By the cut-off date for selection, Macmillan and Landy had both run the qualifying time in the 1,500m, but only Macmillan had run the requisite speed for the mile. When the list of sponsored Olympic team members was published in March, Landy's name was missing. There was a loophole, however. If Landy and a few others could come up with $A750 each, they could join the team. It was a lot of money, a year's wages for some, and the Geelong Guild Athletic Club rallied to raise it for Landy. They held Saturday night dances and 'chook' raffles, which awarded the winner a dressed hen. With a lot of work and good intentions, the club members raised most of the money, but they were still $A250 short. Landy's father made up the difference. His son was going to the Olympics. John heard the news while driving a tractor on his family farm on the South Gippsland coast, 130 miles south-east of Melbourne. He had only eight weeks to train.

Before Landy left for Europe, Joseph Galli published an article in a magazine by the name of *Sports Novels* whose title mirrored what many were thinking: 'Victorian John Landy May Soon Become Our Greatest Middle-Distance Runner'. It was the reason so much effort had been made to send him. Landy was quoted thanking Cerutty for his guidance, and then the miler made a prediction, not of future success but rather of his untapped potential: 'I don't know just what my body can stand up to,' he said – not yet.

At Kapyla Village in Helsinki, Cerutty finally quieted down. Landy lay in bed, uncertain as to how he would stack up against the world's best. He had made great strides in his development and had run well in England, but still he was unsure. And he was very sensitive to the fact that he owed his Olympic ticket to the generosity of family and friends. He felt pressure to live up to the efforts they had made to get him there in the first place. Yet each day he spent on the track, observing the speed and fluid style of other athletes, his confidence in his ability to compete against them weakened. His coach might have believed he had the greatest insight into running and training, but Landy knew these Europeans and Americans had pretty good ideas of their own about what it took to be world class. He knew he would soon find out how good.

4

If you can meet with Triumph and Disaster
And treat those two impostors just the same . . .
If you can fill the unforgiving minute
With sixty seconds' worth of distance run,
Yours is the Earth and everything that's in it,
And – which is more – you'll be a Man, my son!
Rudyard Kipling, 'If . . .'

The rain during the opening ceremony left the red brick-dust track a soupy mess. During the night, Finnish groundskeepers spread petrol over it and lit hundreds of small fires to burn off the water. Smoke billowed into the sky over the stadium and its acrid scent permeated the surrounding streets. By dawn on Sunday, 20 July, the track had dried, and it was levelled and smoothed out by concrete rollers before the first athletes arrived.

Wes Santee woke up in his room unsure of what to do. Throughout the morning, tens of thousands of people descended on the stadium. Scores of athletes, many of whom represented countries that had been at war a few years earlier, milled about the Olympic Village, passing the time between training sessions, meals, and their competitions. Santee dared not step outside Kapyla, certain he would get lost or run into trouble. He was one of the youngest members of the USA track and field team. It was his first Olympics, and for the life of him he could not find out what he needed to know. When was he competing? Against whom? And when could he train? Remarkably, this fundamental information proved elusive. Everyone had their own races to worry about, and for an Olympics that was being built up as a contest for national pride, particularly between the Americans and the Soviets, Santee was beginning to realise that this did not necessarily mean team leadership and cooperation were priorities.

He was left to fend for himself, a situation that was utterly foreign to him. At the University of Kansas, he was used to being surrounded by team-mates who looked after one another. He was also used to having his coach tell him when to arrive for practice, who he was competing against the next weekend, how to run the race, what to eat beforehand, when to arrive at the stadium, and where he was allowed to warm up. This management of the details allowed him to concentrate on the one thing he had supreme confidence in: his running. As a member of the United States Olympic team, however, directions to the dining hall and bedroom were about the most useful bits of information he had been given. He felt alone and, as the Games commenced, increasingly panicked. The pit in his stomach came less from thoughts of his upcoming race than from how he was going to find out when it was scheduled to take place.

After a day spent scrambling about trying to track down team officials, he cornered a few older American athletes who had a schedule of events and listings about who was competing in which heats. Santee was scheduled to run in the 5,000m qualifying round on 22 July at five o'clock, and yes, there would be an announcer calling out the lap times so that he knew the pace he was running. As far as what kind of competitors he was going to face and whether it would be a slow or fast race, they had no idea. It was quite certain, however, that as part of the American team, which had won half of all the track and field gold medals presented in 1948, Santee was expected to win. Late that afternoon when he went to work out on the training track, he was the only American to neglect to wear his 'U.S.A.–Helsinki–1952' jersey, instead choosing to appear in his orange-red pants and blue University of Kansas jersey. He wanted to win for his country as much as anyone, but at that moment he felt a lot more comfortable in his KU colours.

On the first day of the Olympics, Czech star Emil Zatopek stormed to victory in the 10,000m, beating British hopeful Gordon Pirie to win the first of what many assumed would be two gold medals. The United States captured its first track and field gold thanks to high-jumper Walter Davis, the six-foot-eight-inch Texan who set a new Olympic record in the process. The Soviets countered by sweeping the women's discus. The second day of events saw an American stranglehold on the track and in the field; the Soviets ruled gymnastics. By the third day, newspapers around the world headlined the points table: the US was in first position, the USSR second, and Czechoslovakia third. Great Britain ranked fourth, and had yet to capture a gold. As promised, the fifteenth Olympiad was shaping into a battle between the United States and the Soviets.

National pride had always played a role in the Olympics, but never as much as it did in the 1952 Games. In the four years leading up to Helsinki, the Soviets had 'mobilized to win the Olympic War', as *Life* magazine put it. They had combed the countryside for athletes, hired hundreds of coaches, and poured billions of roubles into training programmes and stadia construction. No effort was spared. In Helsinki, Russia (along with Eastern bloc countries Poland, Bulgaria, Hungary, Romania, and Czechoslovakia) demanded separate 'Reds Only' housing and training quarters, and they afforded their athletes every luxury including platters of caviar and smoked salmon. In their camp in Otaniemi, they hung a huge portrait of Stalin over the entrance and erected a wooden scoreboard to post their points totals. The Cold War, which was developing on the Korean peninsula and through the atomic arms race, had entered the sporting arena with a decided chill.

The United States was equally focused on winning. And when it came to preparations they were hardly lacking. After all, the team was primarily composed of scholarship-funded college athletes who had devoted endless hours to training under the guidance of full-time coaches. One needed only to look at the jugs of vitamins available for 'Americans Only' in the Kapyla dining halls to appreciate the special treatment they enjoyed. Many complained that countries such as Britain, who had invented the idea of the amateur athlete, didn't stand a chance in the face of what amounted to a 'professional' approach to sport. Rightly or wrongly, sport was changing, and Helsinki marked a symbolic shifting point. The only remaining question was who would win this particular match-up, and by what margin.

Santee had a front seat to this battle, particularly since one of the greatest rivalries between the two countries was in basketball. Half of the American team comprised University of Kansas players, and Wes was privy to the stories of seven-foot Russian stars and how long they had trained together. But Santee had his own concerns about winning for his country, particularly since the track and field squad was considered one of the big point scorers for the American team.

By Tuesday, 22 July, the day of his qualifying round, Santee had learned little about his race and he desperately wished Bill Easton was there with him. Santee discovered that he could not warm up on the track before the race, which was part of his normal routine, so he jogged around outside the stadium before returning to the locker-room to be called out for his heat. All around him athletes were speaking in unrecognisable languages, and he had no idea who among them he was competing against or what times they usually ran. His biggest fear was falling too far behind the leaders. There was no one to speak to about strategy. And he could not help thinking that he should not even have been in this race. The 1,500m was his best distance; he certainly had much more experience running it. Seldom did a runner, even one as naturally talented as Wes Santee, have the speed and stamina to compete at a world-class level in the 1,500m and the 5,000m. With each minute that passed, his apprehension grew.

When he saw Fred Wilt, the Indiana University alumnus who had competed extensively overseas, Santee hurried across the locker-room to speak to him. Wilt would know what Santee should do.

'I really don't know much,' Wilt said after Santee had told him the names of those in the heat against him. 'Except that Schade guy. He'll probably run a steady, even race. Follow him.'

And with this information, Santee was called to the track for his heat by an Olympic official. He jogged into the stadium, feeling only slightly comforted by this one piece of advice. With Easton, he would have gone over the race on the blackboard in his office at KU, his coach indicating lap times to shoot for, how the other runners traditionally ran, and when to move with the pack or ahead of it. His race was literally drawn out for him in chalk. Only when Santee approached the starting line did he notice the German ace Herbert Schade. Except for the Canadian runner Ferguson, the rest of the field was a mystery. What if the German started out too fast or too slow? What was the best time he was capable of running? There were tens of questions he needed answered and only seconds before the race started. By the time the athletes were called to their marks, Santee felt overwhelmed. This was the Olympics. He was representing his country, and, perhaps more importantly, Kansas. He had to do well, yet he felt displaced, as if he had been blindfolded, led out into a dark field, and left alone to find his way out.

Soon enough the starting gun fired, and Santee was running. Into the first turn, he was in a good position behind Schade, right where he wanted to be. The first lap went well; Schade led, Santee kept back by several runners, but stayed close enough. By the third lap, Santee and the German were alone. The others had fallen back on the pace. Halfway through the race, Santee sensed his legs tiring, but he held on to second position. At the 3,000-metre mark he heard Schade's time called – 8:23 – and then his own, two seconds slower. It was too fast. The best he had run this distance was 8:44, and he was 150 yards ahead of that pace. Santee began to lose confidence. He couldn't maintain this kind of speed. What he should have known before this point in the race was that the German was using this heat to show how fast he was to Czechoslovakia's Zatopek and France's Mimoun, both of whom were in separate heats and would likely prove his stiffest competition in the final. An Olympic record would be broken if Schade continued at this pace, and he meant to continue.

Half a lap later, Santee lost momentum. His arms and legs leadened; his chest couldn't bring in enough breath. His pace slackened. By 4,000 metres he hardly felt like he was moving, the sensation more like running through water than over a track. Everything seemed to be happening in slow motion. He couldn't drive his legs. Runner after runner passed him and there was nothing he could do, even had he been suddenly infused with all the will power in the world. His body had given out. He finished at a dismally slow pace, thirteenth overall, in a time of 15:10.4 – the worst showing at this distance of his career.

As he put on his sweatsuit, Santee was exhausted physically, but the fear and dread before the race had taken an even greater toll. Emotionally he was a wasteland. He didn't want to speak to anybody. He was embarrassed when he left the stadium, wanting to hole up in his room until they flew out of Helsinki. As he later said, 'Not only did I lose, I wasn't even in the race.' For an athlete who had seldom known defeat, particularly on this scale, this was agony. It was like the loss of a first love. His heart literally ached.

Sitting in the stands at the Olympic Stadium on 24 July, Landy did not like his chances in the 1,500m set to take place in less than hour. He was in the fourth, and probably most difficult, heat in the qualifying round. Only the top four finishers in his race moved forward to the semi-final, and his eight-man heat included French and Yugoslav champions El Mabrouk and Otenhajmer, as well as America's Bob McMillen and England's Roger Bannister, the latter of whom Landy had met briefly while competing in London. Landy knew that his best time in the distance (3:52.8) was several seconds slower than his competitors, plus he was much more accustomed to running a mile than 1,500m.

Although only 120 yards shorter than the mile, the 1,500m was an awkward race. Standard European tracks, Helsinki included, were 400 metres in length, meaning that runners competed over three and three-quarter laps. Landy disliked the race, as he later explained: 'There's nothing graceful about it. You don't start where you finish, it's ugly.' The split times were difficult to understand, and given the incomplete first lap, he found it hard to get into his rhythm.

At that moment, however, Landy was more interested in watching the 5,000m final, which was about to start. He had failed to qualify for the longer event, finishing over thirty seconds behind the winner of his heat, Alain Mimoun, in tenth position overall. It was a poor showing, but his personal best, achieved in early February, had been only two seconds faster. He had to settle for watching his friend and countryman Les Perry try to take home a medal in an event featuring the 'human locomotive' Emil Zatopek, former gold medal winner Gaston Reiff, new Olympic record holder Herbert Schade, and English up-and-comer Chris Chataway, as well as the fearsome French-Algerian Mimoun. It promised to be a must-see battle.

When the gun went off, the red-headed Chataway moved into an early lead, at the head of the pack for the first lap, with Schade behind him and Perry in the middle of the pack. The Australian team cheered on the 'Mighty Atom', but by the end of the third lap, with the first four runners averaging sixty-seven seconds per lap, Perry looked like a minor player on a great stage. Soon enough, Zatopek was setting the pace. The very sight of the 30-year-old Czech army major was frightening. His bony five-foot-eight-inch frame sped down the track in an unrhythmic mess of arms and legs. His head rolled back and forth as he ran; his tongue protruded from his mouth; his face contorted as if, one sportswriter noted, he was experiencing an 'apoplectic fit'. Yet the runners knew he was fitter than they were, and Zatopek did not hesitate to inform them of the matter, mid-race. While his competitors gasped for air, the Czech considered it a good time for a conversation. During his 10,000m final, in which he'd broken his own world record, Zatopek had run alongside the Russian Anoufriev, who had set a rapid early pace, and admonished him on the dangers of going out too fast. As Zatopek blazed into the lead in the 5,000m final, he yelled back at Schade in German, 'Herbert, do two laps with me!'

Two thousand metres from the finish, the tactical race began. Schade, answering Zatopek's taunt, burst into the lead, with Chataway and Reiff staying close behind. Zatopek faded. Then Pirie picked up his tempo, shifting easily past the Czech and the rest of the field. Schade quickly regained first position, pushing Pirie aside, then Mimoun started to make his move. With just over a lap to go it was Schade, Chataway, Mimoun, Zatopek and Pirie. At the bell, Zatopek kicked. From the stands the spectators could almost feel the excruciating effort required of him to make the move. But it was to no advantage. Chataway cruised past him a hundred metres down the track with Schade and Mimoun breathing down his neck. Zatopek trailed in fourth position, looking altogether finished. Schade then regained the lead, only to have Chataway steal it right back at the final turn.

'ZAT-O-PEK! ZAT-O-PEK! ZAT-O-PEK!' The cry erupted from the stands. The crowd was on its feet. Face twisted, mouth gaping, arms flailing, eyes open wide, Zatopek found another spurt. Suddenly Chataway caught the track's edge with his foot and went crashing onto the red brick surface, churning up a cloud of dust behind him. Mimoun and Schade attempted to hold off Zatopek as he drove around the turn, but there was nothing they could do to keep him from victory. The crowd boomed again when the Czech sprinted down the straight. Every step looked like it would be his last, yet somehow he found a way to continue forward. He snapped the tape with a new Olympic record time, with Mimoun second, Schade third, Reiff fourth, Chataway fifth (after picking himself up off the track), and Perry in an exhausted sixth place.

Announcers, journalists, spectators, and athletes alike understood that they had just witnessed greatness in the form of Emil Zatopek. He had now claimed his second gold medal, and with his participation in the marathon a few days later, a race he had never run, Zatopek was proving he deserved the acclaim of being the finest distance runner since Nurmi. Although Perry had not medalled, he had run his best time, and Landy had to believe that his friend was proud simply to have competed in the same race as his hero Zatopek. Landy himself was impressed by the Czech's tactical skill, but more than that, he had never seen someone with such overpowering physical fitness.

Everyone in the stadium was still revelling in Zatopek's victory when the 1,500m qualifying rounds began. While Landy warmed up with a light jog on the infield, his countryman Don Macmillan placed fourth in his heat, qualifying for the semi-final the next day. Of the runners in the three heats before Landy's who advanced to the next round, all had run better than his fastest 1,500m time. He had his work cut out for him.

Landy stepped up to the line. Three minutes and fifty-seven seconds later, his Olympic hopes were dashed. El Mabrouk came from behind to finish first with a time of 3:55.8, an unexceptional pace. McMillen, Bannister, and the Hungarian Tolgyesi followed him in, with Landy one second behind in fifth position. As Landy later described it, the last hundred metres of the race was a 'mad scramble', but he was too tired in the final straight to overtake Tolgyesi.

The Australian miler was disappointed in himself, regardless of his doubts before the race. He had travelled all this way and failed to make even the semi-finals. He knew the reason, too: since his good runs in England, he had come off his peak, a consequence of incomplete training. Cerutty took his athlete's loss as a personal affront, and after the race he was not exactly comforting to Landy. The exact form of his vitriol is probably best left forgotten, but his coach's general attitude towards Landy, rightly or wrongly, was that he lacked a 'killer instinct'. And worse, throughout the Australian team, which was not performing well except for sprinters Shirley Strickland and Marjorie Jackson, there were grumblings that many athletes had not deserved to make the Olympics in the first place. In fact, the team manager issued a report after returning to Australia that bluntly stated, 'No man or woman should be selected for future Australian teams who is not prepared to undergo a Spartan-like period of self-denial and rigorous training as practiced in other countries.'

Unfair as this attitude was, it stung Landy, who had been one of the last athletes to make the team. However, he refused to wallow in his failure to qualify for the 1,500m or 5,000m finals. He thought there was a lot he could learn while in Helsinki, especially from the athletes who had so far dominated the Games. The chance to observe Zatopek, for one, tempered the disappointment Landy felt.

Long before his 5,000m win and subsequent marathon victory, Zatopek was of interest to Landy. Cerutty often talked of him, and Les Perry idolised him because of his infamously hard training schedule and unrivalled record in distance running. When Perry first arrived in Helsinki, he had put on his tracksuit and run the three miles across to Otaniemi where the Iron Curtain countries were housed. Once past the guards at the gate, he'd found Zatopek down on the track and ran alongside him until he'd mustered the nerve to say, 'I'm Les Perry from Australia.' Zatopek had put his arm around the bespectacled fan and said in English, 'You come from the other village to see me? You honour me! Join me. We will run together.' After working out, they'd had a shower, dinner, and tea, then Zatopek had invited Perry to watch the Bolshoi Ballet performing in the camp. When Perry finally returned to Kapyla, he regaled his room-mates with the experience.

After his 1,500m loss, Landy made it his job to study other athletes at the old track near the stadium where they trained. He spent hours there, mentally noting how they ran and learning about their training methods. Zatopek, to whom Landy later referred as the 'Piped [sic] Piper of Hamelin', fascinated him the most. With a pack of other devotees at the track, Landy followed the Czech as he jogged forward and backward, speaking about running. There was much to take in and a lot to jot down afterwards because Zatopek talked almost as fast as he ran. He happily shared his love for the sport and spoke about how he had achieved so much since taking up running at the age of 19. 'When I was in the 1950 European Championships . . .' he began one story, talking about the race and the athletes he had competed against; 'last year I was doing twenty by 400m in training . . .' he revealed, or 'I ran in the snow in my army boots . . .' The Czech's training methods were clearly based on making running a way of life. He believed in training one's will power in small steps, every day. Discipline was the key. As for style, which he was accused of lacking, he was plainspoken: 'I shall learn to have a better style once they start judging races according to their beauty. So long as it's a question of speed, my attention will be directed to seeing how fast I can cover the ground.'

His three gold medals proved to Landy that Zatopek was on the right track. He wasn't about antics, Eastern philosophy, recriminations, or wild theories – unlike Cerutty, who had Don Macmillan preparing for the 1,500m final by jogging around the track wearing two tracksuits and a towel wrapped around his head. Zatopek had devised schedules and methods of maintaining the balance between speed and endurance throughout the year. Landy liked this analytical approach. Cerutty disliked schedules: he felt they confined the soul. The two men were opposites, and Landy had the intelligence and independence to understand that all he owed his coach were his achievements to date. While in Helsinki, Landy plotted his future.

Roger Bannister was too exhausted to sleep. No amount of tossing, turning, shuffling, or kicking his feet against the sheets would allow him to drop off. Every second and minute brought the 1,500m final closer; every hour a new wave of anxiety swept over him. At 4.30 p.m. the next day he would line up against eleven of the best middle-distance runners in the world. His confidence was torn by having already run two races instead of the one he had expected to run to qualify for the final. He feared he was already beaten.

The past week had brought only restless days and nights. He and his room-mates – sprinter Nicholas Stacey, quarter-miler Alan Dick, and three-miler Chris Chataway – had tried to relieve the constant churning of their thoughts about victory or defeat, and about what would make the difference between the two. Resting on their unkempt beds, they spoke of politics and history, read books, or joked around with one another. One evening, Stacey mounted a wooden box, as if it was an Olympic podium, to accept his imaginary gold medal and offer a congratulatory speech. At other times they discussed their competitors, particularly Zatopek, whom they thought inhuman in ability. 'While he goes for a twenty-mile training run on his only free day,' Chataway said, 'we lie here panting with exhaustion, moaning that the gods are unkind to us, and that we're too intelligent to train hard. It's all nonsense.' Inevitably, the four thought again and again about that second when the starting gun would fire, and whether or not they would prove good enough. Regardless of what happened, they promised one another that once the Olympics had ended they would never put themselves through this torture again.

By the morning of Saturday, 26 July, Bannister was the only one of his room-mates still tense, though he tried not to show it, as far as possible keeping to himself his doubts about being able to win the race. The others had finished their events, nobody in triumph, and Chataway most disastrously, of course, by falling on the final lap of the 5,000m final. Bannister had watched the race, and its conclusion impressed on him how important his finishing kick would be.

Absence of victory was the same story for the entire British team. Just two days of competition remained on the track and in the field and they had won only a handful of medals, not one of them gold. Nor had any British athlete won gold in any of the other events. The British reporter who had said before the Games 'I will eat a pair of spiked shoes if our team doesn't win twelve gold medals' was dangerously close to having a mouthful of leather. Headlines cried out 'Don't Worry, We Are Still in the Fight', yet column after column reported failure and missed chances.

There was one hope left, though: Roger Bannister. Now, more than ever, his countrymen rallied around him. A few days before, the *Daily Mirror* columnist Tom Phillips had compared Bannister to a great racehorse trainer who 'rarely bothered about picking minor honours here and there. If he wished to win a classic race, he got his horse perfectly fit for that day and nearly every time his horse was first past the post.' Phillips concluded, 'I believe Bannister will win and teach some of our other athletes, and the officials and coaches, a lesson in strategy and tactics.'

If confidence could be drawn from the number of column inches guaranteeing his victory, Bannister was a sure thing. Most sports-writers considered him their favourite. But his legs hurt. He hadn't slept soundly in days. He was plagued by worries, both real and otherwise. His qualifying round and semi-final in the previous two days had been brutal. To avoid the jostling and elbowing of a crowded field he'd run both races in the second and third lanes, adding at least twenty yards to each and exhausting himself even more. The semi-final had been especially taxing because there was a fight to the finish that placed him a narrow four-tenths of a second ahead of Jungwirth from Czechoslovakia, who had failed to qualify. Usually Bannister required three or four days of recovery after such a race because of his limited training regime, but now he had been given only twenty-four hours.

In his room, waiting as the minutes ticked past, Bannister knew the 1,500m final would draw the world's attention. He knew the stands would be jammed to capacity. He knew his competitors had also trained for thousands of hours for this day, and that they would strive with every muscle and ounce of will to claim victory. It was impossible not to rehearse the coming race over and over again in his head. How quickly should he start? Should he stay on the inside lane or move to the outside? Where must he be by the third lap? How close to the finish could he start his burst?

When Bannister made his way down the tunnel underneath the stadium that afternoon, he was no less tortured. His face was blanched, his step uncertain. Australian miler Don Macmillan walked alongside him. He was in bad shape as well, dehydrated and soaked with perspiration after the voodoo warm-up imposed by his coach, yet he noticed that Bannister, against whom he had run in New Zealand in 1950, was pale and nervous.

'Good luck, Don,' Bannister said, heading up into the stadium.

'Thanks, Roger,' Macmillan choked out.

The time had come. When the Duke of Edinburgh arrived in the stands, the crowd cheered. The sun even broke through the clouds to honour this signature Olympic race. While the other athletes stretched and jogged around the infield to warm up, Bannister rested on the bench. Chris Brasher, the British steeple-chaser and former president of the Cambridge University Athletic Club, watched from the stands and later described his friend's appearance: 'There was a peculiar loneliness about Roger. He stood apart from the others, looking drawn and white, as if he were about to go into a torture chamber.' Chris Chataway was also in the stands. He had written to his mother the day before to tell her how concerned he was about Bannister's state in the days before his race. As Chataway waited for the race to begin, he worried that his room-mate had already defeated himself in his mind. However, though tense and sapped of energy from two heats, Bannister still felt that he had a chance. Every race was imperfect, and he had always come through in the past.

Once Finnish middle-distance runner Denis Johansson had completed a presumptuous pre-race victory lap, the starter called the race. With the eleven others, Bannister came to the line. The crowd hushed for the gun. He had prepared his whole athletics career for this moment. Suddenly, they were off.

The German Lamers carried the field through the first lap in 57.8 seconds, looking as though he might be pacing for his countryman and the favourite to win, Werner Lueg. Throughout this first lap, Bannister stayed to the inside; he did not have the energy to battle in the middle of the pack. Lamers soon faded, and Lueg took the lead, finishing the second lap at a slower pace in 2:01.4. By this time Bannister had managed to come up through the field and was running in fifth place. At the bell, Lueg was still leading. He finished the third lap in 3:03, still on the slow side given the field's talent. Only three-quarters of a lap to go.

In the radio broadcast booth, BBC announcer Harold Abrahams was worried for Bannister, despite the fact that he was in the right position – third – for making his break. 'He is not running as well as one would hope,' Abrahams said. 'He is looking rather tired.'

In the back straight of the last lap, the race heated up. Two hundred metres from the finish and the whole field was nearly sprinting. Down the straight, Aberg of Sweden and then El Mabrouk of France tried to surge to the head of the pack. Bannister was next, deciding to strike at the same time Lovelock had in the 1936 Olympics final to win the gold.

'Bannister is in third position with 180 metres to go. Bannister fighting magnificently. Bannister now trying to get into the lead.'

This was it, Bannister thought. Although he had suffered nothing but dread since learning of the added semi-final, he was now in the ideal spot to win the gold. He had managed the jostling field, kept with the pace, and avoiding tripping. As he moved into the final turn, now in second place, he called on the full effect of his finishing kick – his most potent weapon. He gave the order to his legs to go, but for the first time in his life his kick wasn't there. When he should have leapt ahead, he stalled. His legs just didn't have the energy. It was a shock. Little Josey Barthel from Luxembourg swept by him, unbelievably, impossibly. Then the American, McMillen, passed him as well. Bannister felt drained and helpless, knowing he had lost.

'Bannister is fading!' Abrahams called into the microphone.

Lueg held strong, stretching his lead by three yards at the end of the turn. Barthel then struck, delivering the finish Bannister wanted for his own. The Luxemburger cruised past Lueg in the final fifty metres with McMillen also coming up fast.

'And it's Barthel wins. Second, the American. Third, Lueg. Fourth, Bannister. Time, 3:45.2.'

It was a new Olympic record, and the surprise upset of the Games. Bannister was so exhausted by the end of the race that he had to hold on to the back of Lueg's singlet to keep from pitching to the track. He hadn't even claimed a bronze. The British team was distraught. Columnists began to sharpen their pencils. This was a betrayal of trust.

Barthel was handed roses, and then he rested on a bench to take off his shoes. The *New Yorker*'s A. J. Liebling observed, 'He had had no trainer and no compatriot with him when he came into the stadium, and he was still alone. It must have been a great solace to him on the night before the race, knowing he had nobody to disappoint.' How different it was for Bannister who, full of emotion, later watched Barthel mount the victory dais and weep tears of joy while Luxembourg's anthem played throughout the stadium. For Bannister, the Helsinki final was a disaster. He told his friend Brasher years later, 'A disaster is something which is shared between you and the public which expects something of you and which you cannot or have not fulfilled.'

As he headed back to the Olympic Village later that afternoon, fending off the press who were preparing to excoriate him for his insufficient preparations, Bannister needed to find a way to overcome what had happened. He couldn't go out a loser. His answer would be to attempt a challenge that had been in the making for a very long time: the four-minute mile. And he would not be alone in the effort.

5

The man who has made the mile record is W. G. George . . .
His time was 4 minutes 12.75 seconds, and the probability is
that this record will never be beaten.

Harry Andrews, 1903

To the furthest limit he searches out.

Job 28:3

Before stopwatches, cinder tracks, and perfect records, man ran for
the purest of reasons: to survive. The saying goes that 'Every morning in Africa, an antelope wakes up. It knows it must outrun the
fastest lion, or it will be killed. Every morning in Africa, a lion wakes
up. It knows it must run faster than the fastest antelope, or it will
starve. It doesn't matter whether you're a lion or an antelope – when
the sun comes up, you'd better be running.' There are few instincts
more natural than the body in full motion as it races across a field or
through the trees. From the beginning, we were all made to run. In
days past, when 'survival of the fittest' meant exactly that, the only
measure of the race was whether the hunted reached safety before
being overtaken. Seconds and tenths of seconds had no meaning.

Sport evolved from this competition to survive. In ancient Egypt,
newly chosen kings went on a ceremonial run, as historian Edward
Sears wrote, that 'symbolized laying claim to his domain and proved
that he was fit enough for the demands of his position'. Thirty years
after the king's coronation, and every three years thereafter, he was
challenged to run the same long distance he had as a young man. If

he failed, he lost his power to rule. Other early societies proved status through skills such as hitting targets with a bow and arrow, lifting heavy rocks, or jumping across streams; but the ability to run faster and further than others remained a dominant standard.

It was fitting that the first event in civilisation's earliest and greatest celebration of sport, the Olympic Games in 776 BC, was a foot race. A Greek citizen named Coroebus sprinted 200 yards across a meadow alongside the river Alpheus and was crowned winner with a garland made from the leaves and twigs of an olive tree. Sporting ability was integral to Greek life, and its people were the first to promote what would later be phrased *mens sana in corpore sano* – the sound mind in a sound body. Ancient Olympic champions were treated like gods, worthy of worship and great odes. The athletes ran their races naked and barefoot, and as the years passed they instituted ten-month training regimes and began to specialise in certain distances. Longer races involved running from one end of the stadium to the other and back, the distances varying from stadium to stadium. Success was recorded by how many victories an athlete had claimed over his fellows, not by their times (crudely measured, in those days, by sundial or water clock).

The Romans favoured gladiator contests over athletics, but they made two important contributions to the story of the four-minute mile: first, they were devoted to statistics and detailed the results of their sporting heroes (namely chariot racers); second, they were the first to come up with the distance of the mile. Roman soldiers calculated their long marches in *mille passus* (*mille*, one thousand; *passus*, a two-step stride). Given that each stride was roughly two feet and five inches – shorter than average because the soldiers carried over fifty pounds of provisions and weapons – the earliest mile translated to roughly 1,611 yards.

In sixteenth-century England, footmen, who travelled long distances by the sides of heavy coaches, steering their masters away from dangerous spots in the road, were the first to race, often at the bidding of their masters. They used the mile-posts, first installed by the ruling Romans, as starting and finishing lines. This tradition developed throughout the seventeenth and eighteenth centuries into village festival 'freak runs', where the competitors ran on stilts or while carrying a load of fish. Endurance contests, whether walking or running, were also popular.

By the nineteenth century, 'pedestrians', as the English runners were known, were running on the roads for cash. Events were often organised by local pubs in order to draw a crowd. Since the mile race was a favourite, it paid to specialise in that distance. The idea of competing for a mile record instead of simply against one's opponent in a particular race evolved gradually from the standardisation of the mile at 1,760 yards, advances in timekeeping, and an early industrial society's passion for quantifying everything in sight. It so happened that a grass track divided into quarter-miles fitted nicely on to a cricket ground or football field, and it was much safer racing there than on increasingly busy roads. Technology, progress, and coincidence had played its part. Now all the mile race needed was a few fast souls.

Running a mile in less than five minutes was considered the breaking point until Scottish landowner Captain Robert Barclay came along. Famous for his cheerful disposition, predilection for lifting heavy objects, and for walking a thousand miles in a thousand hours, Barclay won 500 guineas by posting a 4:50 mile in 1804. Then, in 1825, James Metcalf, 'a tailor by trade, but a pedestrian by profession' who trained by chasing hounds, beat Barclay's time by a margin of twenty seconds. Over the next sixty years, various milers chipped away at the record, second by painful second, the best runners earning championship belts for their efforts. Over time, the stakes wagered rose into the thousands of pounds.

For most of the nineteenth century, the 'gentleman amateur' was absent from this scene. This British public school ideal, favoured by the universities of Oxford and Cambridge, was indeed a noble thought, but the runners guided by subscribing to its strict rules were no match for the best of the professionals. That was until chemistry apprentice Walter George began training seriously and reduced his mile time to 4:18.8 in 1884. As this was just two seconds shy of the record held for the previous eight years by the professional William Cummings, a showdown between the two was inevitable.

To test himself against Cummings, George was forced to forfeit his amateur status, despite having offered his earnings from the races to a hospital charity. After a series of preliminary races where both had a share of the victories, on 23 August 1886 Cummings and George faced off for the 'Mile of the Century'. Twenty-five thousand spectators crowded around a bicycle track to watch George run so fast that he left Cummings unconscious behind him on the last lap. His record of 4:12.8 lasted for three decades and set the stage for Paavo Nurmi to introduce the four-minute mile to the world, establishing an irresistible challenge to athletes that would guarantee their place in history.

It is impossible to know who first uttered the challenge of running the mile in less than four minutes. Reports date back to 1770 of an English runner who made the distance from Charter House Wall to Shoreditch Church in the City of London in this time, but even nineteenth-century historians raised a sceptical eye to the account. In 1915, when American Norman Taber broke George's record by less than two-tenths of a second, the athletics world was not set on fire. It was too slim a difference to warrant much more than a passing remark in the record books. Then, on 23 August 1923, 26-year-old farm engineer Paavo Nurmi from Turku in Finland was drawn into a faster first lap than he would have liked by Swedish miler Edvin Wide. Nurmi, who always ran with a large stopwatch in his hand and preferred an even-paced race, kept up with Wide's fast start. By the third lap Wide had faded, but Nurmi continued the pace. He broke Taber's record by two seconds with a 4:10.4. It was a giant step forward, given how long it had taken Taber to reduce Walter George's mark by just a fraction of a second. Suddenly the mile record was in play again, and when, at the 1924 Paris Olympics, Nurmi won gold medals in the 1,500m and 5,000m in the space of forty-two minutes, he looked capable of anything. Joseph Binks, a noted journalist and former British miler, suggested to Nurmi that the mile barrier was within grasp. Nurmi replied, 'No. Four minutes four seconds, maybe!' Self-deprecation or not, the Finnish miler had put the possibility of a four-minute mile on the table.

Inspired by Nurmi, a new wave of talented milers appeared in the 1930s, and their races packed stadiums around the world. Races at Madison Square Garden rivalled modern-day prize fights. The air was dense with smoke, the crowds rowdy and devoted to their favourite runners, and the stands so close to the track that fans felt the rush of air when the field surged past. The first miler to run four minutes and single digits was Frenchman Jules Ladoumegue. An orphan who first ran in village-to-village races, Ladoumegue competed on pure emotion. Before races he was so agitated that he had to be pulled to the starting line. If a door closed suddenly behind him, he nearly jumped out of his skin. Once running, though, he loved the heat of battle and became a national treasure for his efforts. On 4 October 1931 he took advantage of a windless, sunny Parisian afternoon and the pacemaking of half-miler Rene Morel to reduce the mile record to 4:09.2.

Jack Lovelock, the New Zealand-born but British-adopted miler with a compact frame and keen idea of his abilities and limitations, was the next to lower the record. In his youth he had developed his smooth running style by striding alongside a stone wall while a friend on the opposite side chastised him whenever he saw his head moving up or down. On 15 July 1933 in Princeton, New Jersey, he ran a 4:07.6 while representing Oxford University against the Americans. After the race, the *New York Herald Tribune* praised, 'It was all so easily accomplished, with so little outward evidence of stress and strain, as to make a four-minute mile seem just around the corner.' Lovelock never reduced this time, but his Olympic gold medal in the 1,500m, his epic races against Glenn Cunningham and Sydney Wooderson, and his insight about training and tactics added to his legacy.

With a time of 4:06.8, Lovelock's rival, the American Glenn Cunningham, seized the mile record only eleven months after the New Zealander had claimed it. The 'Kansas Powerhouse' was legend long before he ran the fastest mile in the world. At the age of 7, he and his brother tried to stoke the fire in their small schoolhouse's stove by dousing the coals with kerosene. His brother died as a result of the accident, and Glenn burned his legs almost beyond repair. During recovery he found walking more painful than running, and an athlete was born. Cunningham learned to work around his disability, and at his first inter-varsity mile at the University of Kansas, he exploded on the last lap to beat the field. His running inspired a generation of Kansas farm boys and gave Americans the hope that the four-minute mile could be theirs.

Sydney Wooderson brought the mile record back to England in 1937. Walter George, now 79 years old, was there to see it. At five feet six inches and 126lb, Wooderson was an atypical miler. When he stepped on to the track in his thick glasses and with the meek demeanour of a solicitor's clerk, he looked the underdog. Once running, however, he was an indomitable force. He dealt with his loss to Lovelock at the 1936 Olympics by staging an attempt to beat Cunningham's mile time. On 28 August 1937 at Motspur Park, he arranged for pacemakers from his athletic club to lead him around the first three laps. Using his famed kick, he handled the last lap alone and registered a time of 4:06.4.

Slowly, by investing more and more time and energy in training, milers approached the goal of four laps of the track in four minutes. But six and a half seconds was a long time off, and the small reductions made by the best runners to the record were just that, small reductions. The possibility of seeing 'the other side' of the numerical barrier was looking increasingly uncertain.

When Swedish runners Gundar Haegg and Arne Andersson finished their epic battles by the end of the Second World War, the four-minute mile appeared unattainable. Of the two, Haegg had a more natural, flowing stride, but Andersson trained harder. A year apart in age, they reached their peak at the same time. Separately, they were the finest milers, in terms of fitness and form, possibly ever to have graced the track; racing against each other, they looked to be the best that ever would. Over the course of three and a half years, Haegg and Andersson passed the mile record back and forth to each other:

Date	Runner	Place	Time
1 January 1942	Haegg	Gothenburg, Sweden	4:06.2
7 October 1942	Andersson	Stockholm, Sweden	4:06.2
9 April 1942	Haegg	Stockholm, Sweden	4:04.6
1 January 1943	Andersson	Gothenburg, Sweden	4:02.6
18 July 1944	Andersson	Malmö, Sweden	4:01.6
17 July 1945	Haegg	Malmö, Sweden	4:01.4

Their duels inspired great performances, yet the barrier still stood untouched. Journalists and statisticians tried to convince the athletics world that the record would inevitably be run. They calculated that the average world-class miler could sustain a 7.33-yard-per-second speed (or 15mph). This meant that the difference between Haegg's best time and the four-minute mile was a short twelve yards – less than 1 per cent of the race's total distance. Nothing. But others disagreed, quite publicly as well. Coach Brutus Hamilton, one of the most revered figures in athletics, published 'The Ultimate of Human Effort', listing the perfect records for the javelin, shot-put, 100m, 400m, mile, 5,000m, and 10,000m beyond which man could never go. Hamilton backed up his analysis with detailed statistics, but many would have considered his word final had he simply jotted these 'perfect records' down on a cocktail napkin. Of the question 'Can the mile be run in four minutes flat?' Hamilton wrote, 'Not quite.' The fastest time that would ever be possible, he stated, was 4:01.6. Although Hamilton, who wrote the article in 1935, had by 1945 been disproved by two-tenths of a second, he still found the idea of anyone running faster difficult to imagine.

Many wanted the bogey to go away, including the 1912 Olympic 1,500m champion Colonel Strode-Jackson, who wrote at the height of the Haegg–Andersson struggle, 'When we stop this nonsense of running like a metronome and with the watch always in mind, we will get back to real racing, the triumph of one runner over another. That is what racing was meant to be and what it will be when we get the four-minute myth out of the way.'

Myth or not, twelve yards or many more, the barrier remained, and with each passing year, as runners attempted to break through its walls and failed, the mile barrier grew in notoriety. By 1952, as Frank Deford, one of the finest writers to report on the challenge, pointed out, 'The Poles had been reached, the mouth of the Nile found, the deepest oceans marked, and the wildest jungles trekked, but the distance of the ground that measured a mile continued to resist all efforts to traverse it, on foot, in less than four minutes.'

The 1952 Olympic flame had barely been snuffed out in the Helsinki stadium when the editorials and reviews of the Games began to spin off the presses. Two points were indisputable: the Finns had proved to be fine hosts of the competition, and more records were broken in these Games than in any other Olympics in history.

Fewer than forty-eight hours after the closing ceremony in Helsinki, another competition was held, this time in London's White City stadium, pitting a British Empire team against the United States. The stadium had staged an Olympic Games itself in 1908 and was infamous for setting the official marathon distance at 26 miles, 385 yards (instead of simply 26 miles) so that the race would finish in front of Queen Alexandra's royal box. The stadium was now used for greyhound racing and an assortment of other events, including athletics. The Americans beat the British Empire team, as they had beaten the world a few short days before.

In the four-mile relay, where four runners from each team ran a mile, Roger Bannister earned the Empire team an early lead. But the second member of his team lost this advantage. Running third leg for the Americans, Wes Santee threatened to stretch out a lead for his team too great to overcome, but John Landy, running in the same leg for the Empire team, managed to close on Santee in the final 440. The anchors for each team traded leads, but in the end the Americans won. It was the first time Bannister, Santee, and Landy had competed in the same race. None of the three remembered much of the other, not a conversation, nor an impression of one another's abilities. Yet as these three milers went their separate ways – Bannister back to life at St Mary's Hospital, a short distance away by Tube, and Landy and Santee on long flights to their respective countries – each charted a course in the days ahead that would bring them back together again. It would be a struggle they and tens of millions would never forget.

Santee flew back with an American team flush with victory. Although the Soviets had fought well in their events and had, for a few days, looked like they might actually win the most medals, they hadn't been able to match the strength of the United States track and field team, which won fourteen gold and thirteen silver and bronze. Among his team-mates, Santee was in the minority of those who did not medal. Watching the 1,500m final, knowing he had beaten the second-place finisher Bob McMillen 'every time we had stepped on a track', left him feeling empty and as helpless as a puppet. He was certain he could have won the race had he been given the chance the amateur officials had stolen from him in Los Angeles.

Before heading back to the University of Kansas, Santee went to visit his parents in Ashland for the first time since he had ridden away on that unnamed horse. If he was waiting for his father to say how proud he was of his son, Wes left empty-handed. Either his father simply didn't understand what he had accomplished through his running, or the man just couldn't express any feeling other than bitterness. Either way his silence stung. Over the past two years he had tried to convince his mother to leave his father, but she told Wes that since he had left his father had mended his 'negative ways and stopped being so mean'. Regardless, Wes wanted nothing to do with the man.

Back in Lawrence, Santee sat down with Coach Easton, who did express his pride in Wes. Easton suggested he could learn a great deal from his Olympic experience, but Santee was less philosophical. It was not in his nature to suffer defeat. In his high school senior year he had lost the mile race in the state finals to Bill Tidwell. Although expected to win, particularly since he had in his sophomore and junior years, Santee had refused to be crestfallen. His close friend Don Humphreys had been surprised at his indifference. 'I couldn't understand how you could be up after losing the mile by a stride or two,' he'd remarked to Wes. 'I know Tidwell was a good distance runner, but it never occurred to me that he could beat you.' Santee had explained in a matter-of-fact tone, 'Oh, Tidwell, he's not a miler.' It took a while for Humphrey to understand this response. Then he thought of a football player who gets knocked down in a game and gets right back up and sets out to return the favour. Santee had that killer instinct. As Humphreys later said, 'Guys like that never get whipped in their minds. Even when they get beat, they're not beat.'

In Helsinki, Santee felt he had learned how to fend for himself and compete against the best. He wanted to prove what a big mistake it had been to prevent him from running in the 1,500m; more importantly, he also wanted to show how good he really was. He set his sights on a goal that had always been on the horizon for him: the four-minute mile. In the list of high-school prophecies published when he graduated was the following: 'Wesley Santee has recently broke the world mile record in a time of 3 min., 58.3 sec. And it should stand for many years to come.' Since his win at the Drake Relays the previous spring, the prediction by sportswriters that he was a sure bet for the world mile record had brought the goal closer in sight. His blistering three-quarter-mile run in New York before leaving for the Olympics had made him realise just how close. Only days after returning to campus, Santee marched into the office of the University of Kansas newspaper. He had an announcement to make: Wes Santee was going to be the first to run the four-minute mile. For years he had known he was capable. Now his intention was a matter of public record.

John Landy had a different announcement to make when he landed in Melbourne, but one just as telling. Directly after the British Empire versus United States match, he had boarded a flight to Australia. He had declined to join Macmillan and Perry, who, accompanied by Cerutty, were running in a series of competitions in Scandinavia. Landy needed to get back to his agricultural science studies, which had fallen by the wayside as a result of his efforts to make the Olympic team. And he wanted to start training again. Landy was determined to show that his trip to Helsinki had been worth the time and money it had taken to get him there. This desire to redress his failure to qualify in either of his events, a failure that had been met with what he believed was unwarranted criticism, was also woven into his excitement about the prospect of becoming a faster and stronger runner. He felt he had been given the lessons now – in terms of improving his stride and training methods – to reach this new level. Zatopek and other European middle-distance runners had shown him how.

For his stride, he would be helped by a pair of European track shoes he had bought. Landy wanted nothing more to do with the kangaroo-hide track shoes made in Melbourne, which were designed primarily for sprinting on grass tracks. Therefore, the spikes were built up in the front, so much so that it was awkward to lower the heel of the foot to the ground. They required him to run on his toes. In Helsinki, Landy noticed that the European middle-distancers ran in spikes with flat soles and a heel, and they had a smoother, more relaxed stride. But shoes alone would not change his running style; he would also have to practise the arm and leg action of the Europeans until it became habit.

But, as Zatopek had shown, style was not what separated the Czech from every other distance runner in the world. It was his demanding training, and Landy felt that if achieving fast mile times was mostly a question of working hard, he was willing to make the sacrifice. On the flight back to Australia, he spent many hours rehashing in his notebook the type of training sessions Zatopek had discussed with him and other runners, concocting a plan to achieve for himself the kind of fitness Zatopek had revealed in Helsinki. By doing so, he hoped to beat Don Macmillan's national record in the mile – 4:08.9 – and win the Australian championship in early 1953.

When Landy arrived at Melbourne's airport, journalists herded around the athletes asking for their comments on the Olympics and on the future. Some complained of having travelled too far with too little rest; others denied that they were ready to retire; many defended their achievements or lack thereof. Landy spoke of Emil Zatopek. He explained how the Czech had proved his superiority, earning three gold medals. 'He thoroughly deserved his success because he is the hardest trained athlete in the world,' Landy said. It was obvious to those who knew the young Australian miler that he meant to claim this distinction for himself. Though his goals had nothing yet to do with a four-minute barrier, unwittingly they had set him on its path, and he would soon show that nothing was safe from his determination.

Of the three runners, Bannister suffered the worst for not having lived up to expectations. Save for a horse named Foxhunter whose winning jump came eight minutes before the closing ceremony began, the British would have managed to go the whole Games without a single gold medal. For athletics enthusiasts, this single medal provided little solace. They wanted revenge. The press provided an outlet for their anger. 'Hang out the crepe and lower the flag to half mast,' the *Sunday Express* bellowed. 'Right now I feel like suing British athletes for breach of promise,' the *People* commented. Editorials questioned whether amateurism was dead. Some thought the sooner the British realised this was true, the sooner they would have a fighting chance against the Americans and Soviets. Others defended the ideal, but belittled the athletes for a lack of commitment to excellence. Journalist Hyton Cleaver wrote, 'Britain was failing to win, not because she was paying the price of amateurism but because she had lost the art of being spectacular.'

Bannister was a lightning rod for most of this criticism, and the same journalists who had first condemned then praised his independent training methods had shifted back again. Their vitriol tormented him. Headlines read, 'Bannister Fails!' The *Daily Mirror* hurt the most:

Roger Bannister could have won the 1,500 metres if the A.A.A. had persuaded him to compete regularly in Britain. Instead, they ignored the advice of their chief coach, Mr. Geoffrey Dyson, and allowed Bannister to have only one actual race in a year before going to Helsinki.

He ran like a 'green' three-year-old thoroughbred having its first race in a classic – running all over the track, on the inside, then the outside, accelerating and slowing up before making his final effort, to finish fourth. We heard wonderful stories in Helsinki that Bannister would win because he had done a world-shattering time in a secret trial before leaving. MAYBE HE DID. ANYONE CAN RUN QUICKLY PAST TREES!

Not only did Bannister have to read about how he let down his country, he also had to suffer those who stopped him on the street, demanding to know what had gone wrong. This scrutiny was a difficult thing to bear at the age of 23.

Throughout his life Bannister had sensed that he had a 'greater degree of self-determination' than others, but the Olympics rudely disproved this notion. He was human like everybody else. Ridiculed and defeated, he decided that only an ambition greater than an

Olympic gold could absolve him of what had happened in Helsinki. He couldn't just walk away from running after such a disaster.

Days after returning from Helsinki, Bannister sent letters to miler Brian Hewson and Chris Chataway asking if they would push him in a four-minute-mile attempt – not next year, as they might have expected, but now. He still planned on retiring before the start of his second year of medical school. The Motspur Park time trial had shown he had the legs for a record attempt, and Bannister wanted to silence his critics with an achievement most thought insurmountable. Then they would know what kind of an athlete he was. Even more than answering for his failure, Bannister wanted to capture the four-minute mile to show how one could achieve athletic greatness without the sacrifice of everything else in life. This was the ideal the Greeks had been the first to promote, that the British later advanced, and that the world was ready to discount. The four-minute mile wasn't an end in itself. Rather, it was a challenge Bannister wanted to embrace as a proof of his theorem about sport and life.

But as the summer of 1952 drew to a close, with Bannister exhausted from competitive strain and Chataway and Hewson unable to help him, because of other commitments, this challenge had to wait. Bannister knew that the demands on him at St Mary's would only increase, but retirement from running was out. He had not yet lined up everything he needed for the effort, but he was confident that the moment would come. The four-minute mile had a long history, and it could wait a few more months to be broken.

II

THE BARRIER

6

A man who sets out to become an artist at the mile is something like a man who sets out to discover the most graceful method of being hanged. No matter how logical his plans, he can not carry them out without physical suffering.

Paul O'Neil, *Sports Illustrated*

In Melbourne's Central Park, opposite his East Malvern house, John Landy watched his shadow. As he ran around a blue-stone gravel path in flat-soled sand shoes, he studied the rhythm of his legs and the movement of his arms. He might never catch his shadow, but he could learn from it. Over the course of his run, he balanced the action of his arms and legs. The higher he carried his arms, the more distance he won from his stride. However, the technique he was developing was more complicated than simply swinging his arms out and up as far as possible. If he overextended, he lost equilibrium in his stride and wasted energy. Rather, he was looking for symmetry of form, where his arm action was completely in sync with his knee lift and consequently the drive from his hips. His head needed to remain level, his centre of gravity still, his shoulder muscles relaxed, and his feet landing from heel to toe, nearly flat-footed. And all of this needed to occur effortlessly. Slowly he was shaping his running style into one worthy of an 'Inca courier', as a sportswriter later commented, where he seemed to almost float over the track.

By mid-September 1952, one month after returning to Australia, Landy was fast moving beyond Cerutty's teachings. Cerutty had promoted a low-arm carriage, believing that man should run like a rooster, clawing at the air, or like African warriors who carried spears by their sides over great distances. Landy preferred to mimic the European runners, who had proved themselves superior in style and performance at Helsinki. 'They don't run on their toes like sprinters and paw the track with their spikes as I used to,' Landy said. 'With a higher arm carriage your knees automatically lift and you get a slightly longer stride. But, most important, there is no tension in the leg muscles. When it comes to the final spurt you have so much extra strength to get on your toes and sprint home. Try standing on your toes and feel the tension in your calf and thigh muscles, and see what I mean.' With each passing day his body grew more accustomed to this new style, and he was getting more return for his effort.

And there was a great deal of effort, particularly in the intensity of his training. Landy never wanted to step up to the starting line again unless he was the fittest person on the track. His training sessions required intense dedication, and they were run smarter and harder than any guided by Cerutty. Before Helsinki, his improvements had resulted from a lucky-dip collection of endurance work. Because Cerutty despised schedules he had his gang run until they hurt, and then he pushed them further. This was the crux of his training method. However, running a fast mile required more than simply putting up with pain. Such conditioning worked only to a certain point; middle-distance running was about more than stamina. According to Zatopek, one had to train for speed. Improvement in that area was won by subjecting the body to periods of high stress at a fast pace, while reducing the recovery time between these periods. Zatopek sold this theory of repetition running by dint of his Helsinki success. His theory was now Landy's practice.

The training ideas Landy had scribbled into his notebook had translated into a hard regimen. Through the early Australian spring (while it was moving into autumn in the northern hemisphere), with Cerutty and his running mates still away on tour, Landy ran alone. His agricultural science studies demanded he train at night, once he had finished with his papers and reading. At eleven o'clock, or past midnight, he would slip quietly out of his house, making sure not to wake his parents or four siblings, who had little idea of the extreme effort he was making. Many nights it was difficult to force himself to put on his shoes and get out there. As he put it, 'the mind is always selling the body'. He often rationalised that he was too tired and might better put off the run until the next day, or that he deserved a day off. But then he would convince himself to run at least a few laps. 'It's like a car starting. There's an immense amount of energy you need to start the car, but once you're rolling, it's easy.' Since he had returned from the Olympics, Landy hadn't missed a single training session. This was a pure exercise of will.

On a typical night, Landy walked across the street to Central Park and began a series of alternating fast and slow laps around the 600-yard oval path made of gravel. A few street lights illuminated the make-do track, but even blindfolded he would have known every inch of the way. Alone, the only sound his feet hitting gravel, he concentrated solely on how much faster he could push himself. He didn't carry a watch; his effort was measured by the interplay of exhaustion and recovery. For most of the lap he would maintain a fast, even pace, but not all-out effort. Then he would burst ahead at the end and sprint until his legs felt uneasy below him. Next he reduced his pace to a jog, feeling his breath return and the pain ebb, but only at a pace slow enough so that on the next lap he could repeat the fast, even pace and surge of before. By stressing his legs and lungs to such an extreme point, he was immunising himself against the pain.

An hour and a half into the session, Landy had usually run between eight and twelve 600-yard laps at a pace of roughly ninety seconds each (or a sixty-five-second 440-yard lap). Between each, he jogged a lap of the oval path in four minutes. He repeated these sessions, pushing himself to the limit of his physical abilities, five nights a week. On the remaining two nights in the week he ran seven miles, sometimes more, at a five-and-a-half- to six-minute pace, along the roads leading out of Melbourne. This was to build endurance. Regardless of the weather, sore tendons, blistered feet, or fatigued muscles, Landy trained like this religiously.

It was the stringing together of session after session, without compromise of effort, that most tested his discipline. On a typical day, he left his house by 8 a.m., walking a mile to the Caulfield railway station where he took a train into the city. Occasionally some people remarked on how slowly he walked, but they had no idea of the limits to which he had pushed his body the previous night. At the University of Melbourne, he attended classes on subjects such as soil science, bacteriology, and farm economics, broke for lunch with his classmates, and then attended more lectures until returning to East Malvern to have dinner with his family. Except for drinking a great deal of milk, his diet was utterly normal. He might relax briefly after dinner, but he soon withdrew to his room to study for several hours before sneaking out of the house to train again. Returning back to the house after midnight, he took a shower and collapsed into bed.

In this schedule, there were no spare moments for girlfriends or a social life, much to the dismay of his sisters. There was little time either for a generous night's sleep – six or seven hours at the most. Still Landy persisted, convinced he was on the right path. Of the rigours of training, he told *Track & Field News*, 'The harder, the better.' Of his motivation, he told the *Sydney Morning Herald*, 'I just go out there and work. I've got to punish myself to get anywhere.' Of pain and injury, he told *Sports Illustrated*, 'There is no gray – just black and white . . . If you're hurt enough to limp, you can't run at all. If you aren't, it makes no difference.'

Landy's resolve was extraordinary. It was sustained by a still developing attraction to running. As opposed to playing football, he was the sole master of how well he ran the mile. And the harder he trained, the more control he had over his body to dictate this performance. He might not have noticed the dramatic change in his fitness because he had experienced it slowly, but others certainly did. One weekend afternoon he invited 18-year-old up-and-comer Robbie Morgan-Morris out to train with him. The young runner, who had recently won a cross-country championship, was agog at the opportunity to run with an Olympian. He had seen Landy race against Don Macmillan before Helsinki, but was astonished at what he saw in Central Park. Morris followed Landy for a few laps, but was soon run off his feet. Landy kept going and going, faster and faster. Nobody in all Australia ran this way. Morris thought to himself, 'How fast is this bloke doing this?'

In October, Les Perry returned from his Scandinavian tour. Perry had probably seen Landy run more than any other person. He knew how much his friend had improved under Cerutty, but when he visited Landy at Central Park, he was shell-shocked to see him run so well. His legs and arms were more defined. His running style had been transformed. And the speed . . . Perry, too, tried to keep up with Landy over several laps, but couldn't. 'This is terrific sort of training,' he said. He knew Landy had been disappointed about Helsinki, that it was in his nature to try to right the wrong of not performing at the level some might have expected, but this kind of speed and repetition work was beyond his imagination. 'Is this the sort of thing you've been doing?'

'I've had a bit of a routine,' Landy replied.

Later, Landy told him how he had been following Zatopek's advice. Perry suspected that the Australian athletics community, Cerutty included, was in for a surprise when Landy next took to the track. When their coach tried to lasso Landy back into his fold, the runner was polite but clear. 'I'm taking no more advice from anyone,' he said. 'I simply want to put together the best of what I've seen.'

In the history of athletic training, selecting the best course for how to train, for how long, and at what intensity, was a matter of intuition. Ancient Greek athletes trained by running in every direction save skyward. They skipped, jogged, hopped, and on occasion sprinted while rolling a large hoop in front of them. Their coaches carried forked sticks for motivation. The Greeks understood the importance of increasing exertion over time, but their use of this theory lacked sophistication. Milo of Croton walked every day with a calf in his arms in order to gain strength in his arms and legs slowly as the cow matured. Hellenic runners trained to indefinite four-day schedules called 'tetras': the first day consisted of light exercise; the second, intense effort; the third, rest; and the fourth, moderate exercise. Before competitions they seasoned their meals with special herbs and mushrooms. Aristotle recommended training one's breath by holding it for increasing lengths of time; this improved strength and allowed the body to retain its spirits and humours.

The ancient Romans had their own ideas about how to prepare their athletes, whether gladiator or runner. In early training, their diet was limited to dried figs, boiled grain and fresh cheese. Later, they added meat to their diet, generally pork because, as one Roman advised, 'If they lived but one day on any other food, [they] found their vigour manifestly impaired the next.' They were allowed only small portions of water and were forbidden to engage in sexual intercourse. To familiarise themselves with pain, slaves flogged their backs with rhododendron branches until they bled. They exercised in the open air no matter the weather. They followed these sessions with tepid baths and copious amounts of sleep. The latter was supposed to enliven the athlete and promote muscular strength.

By the seventeenth century, athletes were having their spleens removed to increase their speed, an operation with a one-in-five chance of death. Training techniques looked like they would never move beyond the arcane and bizarre until Captain Barclay of mile fame set down his ideas in writing in 1813. Generations of pedestrians followed his advice. Some of his suggestions, such as purging the body by the use of Glauber salts, eating a breakfast of 'beef-steak or muttonchops under-done, with stale bread and old beer', and lying in bed naked for half an hour after exercise, were nonsensical. However, he also advised a rigorous regime of exercise that started at five o'clock in the morning and lasted throughout the day:

1. Sprint half-mile up a hill.
2. Walk six miles at a moderate pace.
3. Eat breakfast at seven o'clock.
4. Walk six miles at a moderate pace.
5. Lie in bed without clothes for a half-hour at twelve o'clock.
6. Walk four miles.
7. Eat dinner at four o'clock (same meal as breakfast).
8. Sprint half-mile immediately after dinner.
9. Walk six miles at moderate pace.
10. Retire to bed at eight o'clock.

Barclay had scant understanding of why his regime produced results, but it had worked for him, so others suspected they would benefit from it as well. In subsequent years, athletes replaced walking with more running, and both their fitness and speed continued to improve. Barclay's theories had provided a solid foundation.

Nonetheless, in the nineteenth century the general public still believed that too much exercise guaranteed an untimely death. In 1864, *London Society*, a widely read journal of the time, commented in regard to amateur athletics that 'Not all training is good or desirable; very much is unquestionably injurious. The honour of a place in the representative eight of the Universities has been purchased in many instances at the cost of years of life.' Some physicians thought that the heart had a limited number of beats over a lifetime, and that by speeding up the heart rate during exercise was a foolish waste of a very precious resource.

That athletes persisted in their efforts to see what was physically possible was testament to mankind's innate tenacity and desire to succeed. Walter George further stretched boundaries, explaining, 'First, I figured out the time I thought the mile should be run in.

Second, I started testing my theories and particularly my own constitution and capabilities; the result of this study soon convinced me that the then existing records at the distance were by no means good.' His methods included speed drills, running on his toes in place, and extensive walks. Both speed and stamina were gradually built up as knowledge about the human body's limits and possibilities accumulated. In Britain and the United States, athletics manuals espousing the latest techniques began to appear on a regular basis. One, published by an 'athletic instructor' at Harvard in 1904, provided a typical schedule (runners a century later would deem this laughable):

> *Monday* a mile with a fairly good three-quarters and the last quarter easy. *Tuesday* a half mile in about two minutes ten seconds, a rest, and then another easier half mile, sprinting the last hundred yards. *Wednesday* jogging up and down the straightaway, rather quicker than if running a mile, followed by an easy one and one-half miles. *Thursday* a fast half, followed by a rest and an easy three-quarters. *Friday* an easy two miles, sprinting the last hundred yards. *Saturday* a mile trial on time. *Sunday* some walking.

The trials and the errors continued. In 1910, runner Alf Shrubb suggested walking sixteen miles three or four times a week to get in optimum shape. Paavo Nurmi proved that much longer training runs over years would bring further improvements in time. Plus, he was an advocate of even-paced runs, keeping lap times consistent throughout to level out his expenditure of effort. In the late 1920s, marathoner Arthur Newton propagated continuous year-round exercise, including sessions of twenty miles a day. Jack Lovelock believed that hard work was necessary, but that an athlete risked staleness if he ran too many races. To combat this, he espoused 'peak training', building oneself up with stamina, then speed work, and then saving the best for race day. In the 1930s,

German physiologist Dr Gerschler promoted 'interval training', advising athletes to run a fast lap followed by a slow lap on the track. These were timed to ensure strict routine. Zatopek came up with the same idea by himself, but refused to time his runs. Meanwhile, the Swedes, led by Gundar Haegg, believed the key to training rested in 'speed-play', known as 'Fartlek'. This also included fast and slow combinations of running, but always away from the track. With Fartlek, in order for athletes to stay fresh, they needed the joy and freedom of running through forests, up and down hills, judging for themselves when to accelerate and when to hold back. The track should only be visited for races.

Throughout the development of new techniques, doctors and laypeople alike continued to advise against the perils of so much running. In 1927, British physiologist and Nobel laureate Archibald Hill wrote that 'it's not unusual for an athlete to tear a tendon, or to strain a muscle, and not unknown even for him to pull off a piece of a bone by an exceedingly violent effort. We are obviously not far from our limit of safety. If we doubled our speed of movement . . . athletics would become a highly dangerous pastime.' Despite studies proving otherwise, the general belief was that overtraining could permanently damage the heart and other essential organs. Madness was assigned to those who pushed the boundaries of what was possible. Yet athletes continued to push to improve.

Timers, no timers, on the track, in the woods, schedules, no schedules, staleness, peaks, plateaus, stamina versus speed, the Stotan life, long walks, runs of ten miles a week, twenty, thirty, fifty – training had advanced a long way from carrying calves and flogging backs, but not to the point of certainty. By the 1950s, coaches and former athletes had started a cottage industry out of giving (often conflicting) advice; fads were common, and the latest champions were proclaimed to have the perfect method until they were beaten by others. The only sure thing was that the question 'What to do?' had many answers, and every athlete had to find his or her own.

*   *   *

John Landy had found his own way since returning from the Olympics, and he followed it mercilessly. His new running style and Zatopek-inspired routine of running himself into exhaustion promised great returns, yet he had no idea how great. By Saturday, 25 October 1952, ten weeks had passed without a race or even a timed trial. In his training he had run over five hundred miles, many at near race pace, and he was slowly reducing the recovery time between fast laps to increase the pressure on his body. He knew how he compared against his friends on Central Park's gravel path, but not against the clock.

In the first mile race of the outdoor season between Victoria's amateur athletic clubs, Landy crossed the finish line for Geelong Guild in 4:17. He looked back to see his nearest competitor over a hundred yards behind. The *Argus* reporter Ken Moses believed Landy had held back and could have run at least five seconds faster. Moses predicted Landy would break Don Macmillan's Australian mile record of 4:09 by season's end. The following week he ran a three-mile race, beating the Australian cross-country champion Neil Robbins by some three hundred yards and trimming Les Perry's record by sixteen seconds. On 8 November he drew away from his competitors, including Perry, in the second lap of a 2,000m race, winning easily and setting another record. During the week, Landy continued to train, harnessing more strength with each session. It was clear he was on the verge of something extraordinary.

On 15 November, he 'spread-eagled the field', as Moses put it, in the mile at Olympic Park. Landy led from the middle of the first lap and finished half a lap ahead of his competitors in 4:14.8. After the race, he entertained questions from the small herd of Melbourne's athletics reporters. He said that he'd run in his oldest pair of shoes because he wanted to save himself for a really good time in early December. 'Two- and three-mile events are my objective at the moment,' he said. 'I am out to build up stamina, and only racing in those events will help me. It was stamina that beat me when I was away at the Games, and I do not want it to happen again.' Three days later he entered one of those two-mile races and broke another record. Keenly aware of Landy's early-season success, the Melbourne press sensed more records would soon fall. Athletics reporters made the rounds of his friends to see what they expected to happen. Perry commented that there was 'nothing surer' than Landy breaking Macmillan's record, and that he might even get his mile time down to 4:06. Steve Hayward of the *Herald* suspected that in a couple of years Landy could equal Gaston Reiff, who had recently run a 4:02.8 mile, the first sub-4:03 mile since Haegg and Andersson had competed over seven years ago. Hayward would not have to wait that long.

On 12 December, Landy attended a reunion of Australian Olympians held at Bob Prentice's house. It was a Friday night, a chance to let off some steam from training and to relax with friends. They drank Fosters lager, ate sausage rolls, and reminisced about Zatopek and other stars they had met. They also joked about Cerutty's behaviour in London and Helsinki. They avoided talk of their defeats by much more capable European and American runners, though these would always colour their time together. At one point in the evening the conversation shifted to Landy and his season to date. Many knew of his increased training, but they were unaware of the specifics and certainly had no idea of the full scale of effort involved. They were simply excited about how much he had improved, and they guessed that once he had someone to give him chase in a race a good mile time was inevitable. Landy shrugged off the suggestion, preferring not to be the focus of attention. 'I can only do what I can do,' he said.

The next day brought a welcome break from a week-long summer storm that had flooded highways throughout Victoria. Tales of families marooned by the floods led the news. John Landy put in his half-day filing land titles and finished at noon, feeling a bit queasy after the long night and a lack of food. After grabbing his bag with his track clothes, he decided to get some fresh air and walk to Olympic Park. He had a race at half past two. On his way he stopped for a chocolate ice cream sundae. When that failed to satisfy his appetite, he ate a pair of meat pies to hold him over until after the race. It wasn't the diet Cerutty or the Greeks would have suggested, but for Landy, this day was no more special than the next. He then strolled down the banks of the Yarra River for a few kilometres until he reached the track.

Though Melbourne had come a long way from its foundation in 1835 as a British outpost, the city remained mostly a collection of villages connected by tram lines. Car traffic was seldom a problem, and church steeples still ranked as the tallest buildings on the skyline. Bars closed at 6 p.m., television had not yet invaded living rooms, and short of barbecues, town hall dances, and private parties, local sport was one of the main entertainment outlets.

The athletes who belonged to Landy's Geelong Guild and its competing clubs ranged from students to opticians, accountants, hairdressers, and milkmen. Few Melbourne athletes, let alone Melbourne itself, ever made international news, and among the stories in the morning papers – about potato prices dropping, city budget improvements, a thwarted gold heist, and a mile race at Olympic Park – nobody could have expected the latter to launch Melbourne onto front pages around the world, least of all Landy himself. It was too absurd to imagine.

Olympic Park was the centre of the city's amateur athletics and the site of one of the two international-standard tracks in Australia. The flat stretch of land next to the river on which it stood had been used over the years for everything from farmland and army training to motorcycle races. In the 1920s, a local businessman had upgraded the grounds, installing a track which he laid with crushed scoria (a porous rock cinder produced from volcanic eruptions). The track was set within a natural bowl surrounded by grass-covered hills on three sides and concrete tiers of seats on the fourth. At best, the place was unremarkable, and despite its name it had never hosted an Olympic Games.

By two o'clock Landy had switched into his Geelong Guild singlet and the white European track shoes he had brought back with him from Helsinki. They had served Landy well on his previous runs that season. He warmed up on the grass oval track adjacent to the main track, a routine involving a few stretches, some jogging, and a couple of sprints. Since the previous week's three-mile race had been rained off, he felt as though he had some nervous energy to burn off. In the back of his mind he thought he might have a fast run in him today. Nevertheless, he planned to wait until halfway through the race to decide whether or not he should make an all-out effort. It depended on his rhythm and how he was feeling. There was no sense going into the race weighed down by the expectation of a good time.

'I think they called your race,' another athlete said.

Lost in thought, Landy had missed the track official's announcement for the mile event. If late to the line, he would be disqualified. He raced over the hill towards the track and hustled into the pack of milers getting into their places for the start, making it just in time. There were enough milers in the race to warrant a line two men deep. Landy was placed in the second row. The starter gave his usual instructions: 'Nobody will cross over in front of another, unless you're two clear yards in front ... We have a mile race, four laps, you'll get the bell with one lap to go.' The runners jockeyed into position.

Each club team stood together alongside the track. The stands were lightly scattered with family and friends, including Landy's parents. Only a few reporters were on hand. There were no programmes, concession stands, or banners. Many spectators chose to sit on the hill along the finishing straight. They had spread woollen rugs over the grass and sipped from flasks of cordial or tea. Rarely through the afternoon had they broken out in more than subdued applause. The meet, like many others, felt like a 'country picnic', as Cerutty gang member Trevor Robbins described it.

'On your marks ... set ...' The starter's gun fired.

Les Perry went out fast, faster than normal. Without Landy's knowledge, Perry had decided to pull his friend around the track for as long as he could. A sixty-second lap was flat out sprinting for him, and three-quarters of the way through the first lap he was still in the lead, but fading. There was no way he could keep it up much longer. As Landy passed him on the straight before the end of the first lap, Perry whispered to himself, 'Do it, John,' hoping that he would break Macmillan's record.

Landy was on his own. He ran on the outside of the first lane because the track to the inside edge had been chewed up by prior events and a week's worth of heavy rain. He finished a very good first lap in 59.2 seconds. He was running easily. In the lead, with the rest of the field behind him, he relaxed into the rhythm of the run. For him, relaxation came from the fingers; he liked to keep his hands soft, almost open as he strode around the track. Once in the rhythm, he could then increase his tempo, if needed.

As he finished the second lap, he heard a time called out: two minutes. Trevor Robbins and Malvern Harrier half-miler Len McRae, who studied agricultural science with Landy, had positioned themselves on the straight to call out times so their friend knew how fast he was going. Fast. Landy thought the time was either wrong or he was about to run an incredible mile. The time *was* wrong, but only by one second. Landy finished the half-mile in 2:01.

For the past ten weeks he had run countless laps at a hard pace and was nearly immune to the pain caused by exertion. He continued to run in a relaxed manner, despite the blistering pace. As the bell for the final lap rang, Robbins shouted out, 'Three minutes and three seconds!' No way would he run a sixty-five-second last lap, Landy thought, no way. His mile would be good, at least good enough to break Macmillan's record. He was hardly exhausted and he felt he had a fair bit of acceleration still in his legs.

'Then I went,' Landy later said of the start to his fourth lap. He put every gain from his months of training into that last lap. The crowd of a few hundred people rose and cheered as he entered the back straight. He increased his tempo, but maintained rhythm.

He pressed harder and harder, his stride lengthening in the final turn. McRae and Robbins rushed down to the head of the straight to get a closer look. They knew Landy was about to run an incredible time. When he passed the 1,500-metre mark in a little over 3:45, they shouted themselves hoarse for Landy to go faster as he tore down the straight. Robbins sensed that history was about to be written in Olympic Park. Trailing far behind, Perry urged Landy on in his mind.

In full stride, Landy broke the tape and slowed to a jog. His breathing was heavy, but he was nowhere near the point of collapse. Turning, he saw the timekeepers huddled together. Landy thought there was something wrong.

Half-miler Len McRae ran towards him. 'You ran 4:03,' he said.

'What?' Landy exclaimed.

'We've been timing it.'

Within moments, before he had regained his breath, reporters crowded around Landy, asking questions. The loudspeakers announced the time: 4:02.1. Everyone in Olympic Park gave Landy a standing ovation. It was the third fastest mile in history. Reporters' pencils flew across notebooks while he came to terms with what he had accomplished: he had brought his best mile time down by eight seconds and approached Haegg's long-standing world record, just seven-tenths of a second shy. Landy told reporters about his new running style and how for the first time in his athletics career he had had the confidence in his conditioning to lead from the front. 'Most of the credit must go to Perce,' Landy added, generous despite his split with his former coach. 'Had it not been for him I would not have got anywhere near my time today. Only hard work gets results. Perce has been telling us that all the time, and our trip to the Games confirmed what he said.'

While Landy explained the genesis of his run and the timekeepers and track officials nervously followed protocol to secure the record time, Percy Cerutty entered the stadium with his wife for the first time since arriving back in Australia. He couldn't understand why crowds of people were bustling about the track and infield. Events should be taking place. Something had happened. He spotted Les Perry by the stands.

'What . . . what's going on? What's all the excitement?' Cerutty asked.

'Landy just ran a 4:02 mile,' Perry said.

Cerutty registered the time like a blow. His face fell. Then he exploded. 'Here's a bloke who's come home like a whipped dog from the Olympics – couldn't qualify for a final in 4:14. And then he comes back and does this! After all the effort to get the money together to get him over there, he's bloody well wasted the fare!'* Sitting in the stands, Landy's parents heard what he said and stepped away so they wouldn't have to listen to any more of Cerutty's remarks. Only later would they tell their son. He deserved to enjoy his moment.

After Landy signed the necessary forms to ratify the record (which included verification that the track distance and official watches were accurate), the festivities continued in the bar underneath the stands. Landy and his friends had some beers and talked more about the race. This was the best race of his life, the most unexpected and therefore the most rewarding as well. Landy was overjoyed.

When he went home to have dinner with his parents, it was clear that his 4:02.1 run had changed everything for John. Winning the Australian championships and owning the Australian mile record were minor in comparison to what was possible now, and to what would be expected from him. From the most unlikely of places by the most unlikely of athletes, the world was put on notice that the mile barrier was very much in play.

7

An average man's body weighing ten stone is constructed of enough water to fill a ten-gallon barrel; enough fat for seven bars of soap; of carbon sufficient for 9,000 lead pencils, and of phosphorus to make 2,200 match heads; enough magnesium to provide one dose of salts; iron to make one medium-sized nail; lime to whitewash a chicken coop; potassium to explode a toy cannon; sugar to fill a shake; and sulphur to rid a dog of fleas. The whole could be purchased for the few shillings that accord with contemporary prices.

Sir Adolphe Abrahams, 1956

On 14 December 1952, Norris and Ross McWhirter passed through Victoria station in London and stopped by the newsstand to pick up a copy of *L'Equipe*, the Parisian-based sporting paper that collected wire services from around the world and had correspondents of their own in many countries. The twins were newspaper sportswriters themselves, who were also beginning to make a small publishing industry out of their fascination with facts and figures, not only in athletics but in fields that stretched from archaeology to zoology. To them, *L'Equipe* was a necessity. When they opened its pages and saw the news from Australia, they called Roger Bannister's flat.

'The Australian John Landy just ran 4:02.1,' Norris McWhirter said.

Bannister was stunned. He had met John Landy through his countryman Don Macmillan in England and then run against him in the first round of the 1,500m in Helsinki, and certainly he was no 4:02.1 miler back then. Not at all. This kind of progress was difficult to imagine. And Bannister wasn't alone in his surprise. In the days that followed, British and American newspapers doubted reports that a miler who had failed to qualify for the Olympic 1,500m final had dropped eight seconds from his best mile time in the span of a few months. Arthur Daley of the *New York Times* wrote, 'Never in the history of footracing have strangers come up from nowhere to shatter or approach marks. They always bore credentials first, a background of other high-class performances ... [Landy's] either one of the seven wonders of the age or something's wrong somewhere. It would indeed be nice to hear that Landy's 4:02.1 is a completely legitimate performance. For the present, please pass the salt.' Three weeks later, when Landy clocked a 4:02.8 in a stiff wind, *mea culpa*s were offered by his doubters, Daley included.

Bannister continued to follow the Australian's progress as he entered race after race through the early part of 1953. It would have been hard to ignore him, given how much media attention was focused on the acclaimed 'Meteor Miler'. Melbourne papers started the fervour by headlining how there was 'no hope of catching him, even in taxis'. The *Sydney Morning Herald* followed by profiling Landy and publishing his photograph across several columns. The wires picked up this story from Australia's flagship newspaper, and suddenly Landy was a lead item in sports pages around the world.

Still, Bannister didn't have to read the papers to stay up to date on Landy's progress: the McWhirter twins provided everything he wanted to know, and more. They wanted an Englishman to be the first to break the four-minute mile, and Bannister was their best hope, not to mention a close friend of theirs. Having recently launched the track and field publication *Athletics World*, the twins made it their business to get as much on Landy as they could. These future founders of the *Guinness Book of World Records* were adept at culling information, their interest dating back to the age of 7 when they'd begun systematically to gather facts through newspaper clippings. In December 1952 they detailed Landy's 'brutal assault' on the record and announced: 'Ever since Irving and Mallory in 1924 got ninety-six percent the way up Mount Everest, and the year before Paavo Nurmi went within 10.4 seconds of the Four Minute Mile, these two goals have fired men's minds. The year 1953 is going to see the greatest assault ever made on either.' They published fractional times of Landy's mile runs and wrote to him, asking about his training methods. Landy dutifully sent them the details, and the McWhirters published his letter for Bannister and all to see. Every week, one of the twins stopped by to see Bannister, apprising him of the latest Landy news and urging him, 'There's no good being second to run the four-minute mile.'

How the Australian miler had run the weekend before and his chances for the weekend to come were far from being Bannister's only concerns. He had a ward of patients to examine, lectures to attend, cases to study, and books to read. His days as a second-year intern at St Mary's Hospital started at 8.30 a.m. and sometimes lasted through the night. In between, he shoehorned in some time to prepare for the season's first race in May. But studying medicine took a gargantuan effort in its own right. Doing so while trying to accomplish the impossible in athletics was asking too much – for most.

Bannister's days started in a small basement flat in Earls Court, London, where he lived a self-described 'chaotic' existence, cooking for himself (usually a quick meat stew as well as pickled herring for protein) and trying to find spare moments for laundry and the like before heading to St Mary's near Paddington station. Originally founded in 1845 to serve the impoverished 'stinking Paddington' area, St Mary's had evolved into one of England's finest medical schools and research facilities, noted most famously for Alexander Fleming's discovery of penicillin. To study at the small teaching hospital, Bannister had won the scholarship established by Lord Moran, a decorated First World War medical officer who later served as Winston Churchill's doctor. While dean of the school,

Moran was known for recruiting amateur athletes because he believed sport taught character and made for good doctors. In the middle of interviews with prospective medical students, Moran would bend down below his desk and retrieve a rugby ball, which he then threw at his interviewee. If the interviewee caught the ball, he was admitted; if he threw it back, he earned a scholarship. Those days had long passed, but St Mary's remained committed to recruiting students with well-rounded interests, and Bannister had the undergraduate marks, seriousness of purpose, and athletic pedigree to warrant admittance on scholarship. Shirking his studies for the sake of athletics was out of the question.

When Bannister arrived at the hospital each morning by Tube, he was besieged with responsibility. He oversaw a ward of forty beds, interviewing patients and prescribing treatments, while under the guidance of consultants. This clinical training was supported by lectures and post-mortem examinations. Bannister rarely had the chance to sit down. Every few months he went on a different rotation that offered new challenges to manage on little sleep: junior medicine, junior surgery, gynaecology, obstetrics, and emergency medicine, among other specialities. During lunch – his only break in a day of rounds, studying, and writing papers – he hurried from the hospital with his running gear and took the underground train two stops to Warwick Avenue. There it was a quick walk to the Paddington Recreation Ground where he trained throughout the week amid a group of overweight middle-aged men who panted around the track in order to trim off a few pounds during lunchtime. He paid his sixpence, changed, and within a few minutes was into his routine of fast laps on the poorly kept, black cinder track. No time to waste with stretches and a jog. He had just thirty-five minutes in which to train before showering, grabbing a bite to eat, and returning to the hospital.

From the day Landy burst onto the scene with his 4:02.1 mile, Bannister had stepped up his training. Clearly the ambition he had held since Helsinki, to break the four-minute mile, was in jeopardy.

With a year and a half left of medical studies, his running days were numbered, and an Olympic gold was simply never going to be his. Moreover, his failure in Helsinki had left him with a need for redemption, to deal with 'unfinished business', as he said. The more he thought of the mile barrier, the more he recognised its significance. Since Landy had revived interest in it, Bannister was bombarded with questions from the press and public about whether or not it was possible. Could it be done? Bannister was certain it could be done; there was no physiological reason why not. Yet, as he later wrote, 'To say, however, "Four minutes is only a time" was presumptuous, unless I had an answer for the inevitable follow-up question – "Well, if it's possible, why don't you do it?"'

The 'Dream Mile', as the Scandinavians termed the achievement, had a mythical enchantment. Until broken, it would stand as a limit to human endeavour. The idealist in Bannister wanted to break the barrier to show that no such limit existed. More importantly, he wanted to demonstrate that an amateur athlete was capable of the effort. And the defeated Olympian in him wanted to be the one to do it first.

Bannister hit the track in late February 1953, but since the middle of the previous December he had been developing his stamina in earnest, mostly on the cricket field at Harrow School near his parents' house. After jumping a fence to get into the school grounds, he would set off on his run. There was no strict method to his routine as the fifteen acres of fields and hills gave him the freedom to run at will. He liked to train at night, when the trees and other static objects were out of sight. Then he had the feeling that there was no ceiling to his speed. His running had no measure other than the energy exerted. But the darkness was not without perils. The year before he had run into some concrete blocks left in the grass and gashed his leg down to the bone. Only after climbing back over the fence and flagging down a car was he able to get to a hospital.

Nonetheless, the sessions on the cricket field were exhilarating. 'Fartlek' best described them, as he ran fast at times, slow at others, up hills and down slopes, judging for himself when to force his legs or when to hold back, and not using a stopwatch. But it was more involved than that. At certain moments he projected a finishing line fifty or a hundred yards down the field and sprinted to break through the imaginary tape. At another moment, there seemed no end point to his running, just a feeling of pushing himself to exhaustion. After twenty minutes he had usually worked himself up to a peak where he ran 800 yards at near maximum speed. When he ascended hills he focused on gaining strength in his legs; on descent, he focused on his balance. Some nights the sessions were so hard that it took several days to recover; other nights he held back.

Two months later he was ready for more severe training on the track, and by early March he began to see some results. He didn't enjoy track work: the grind took much of the thrill out of running. Ever since he had begun training at Oxford University in 1946, Bannister had become indoctrinated with the idea of 'effortless superiority'. This was the *modus operandi* of the gentleman amateur: one never gave the impression that one had worked for one's success. Oxford sprinter Bevil Rudd illustrated this when he arrived at a quarter-mile race with a lit cigar in his mouth, put it down on the track's edge, won the event in record time, and picked up the still smoking cigar when finished. For six years Bannister had steadily reduced his mile time without abandoning the principle that running should be one part of a much larger life. But to continue to improve his fitness while balancing his studies he needed to get more from each training session without lengthening its duration. This meant grinding out harder and harder sessions on the track.

Bannister trained on his own, without coaching, convinced that he alone could get the best out of himself. His track time was limited exclusively to interval training. It was a method he had used previously to develop his speed, but he had never applied it with such pressure. His theory of training was simple: he needed to run the same distances faster each week. He had speed, but not the kind of enduring speed he would need to break four minutes. Helsinki had shown him this. In one session he ran as many as ten laps at sixty-three seconds each with only two to three minutes' rest in between. Occasionally one of the McWhirter twins would show up to time his laps; mostly, though, Bannister carried a stopwatch himself.

Each day was a test against the one before. Although the track work stole the joy from running, Bannister was fascinated by the daily adjustments in speed and effort he made to get the most from his body. He liked the intellectual challenge of determining for himself what was needed in each session. His approach to training was decidedly scientific: 'Does it work? Does it not? You learn by your mistakes. It's so subtle. If you run so hard that you can't recover, you haven't done any good. It's stressing the machinery to the point where if you had a graph and plotted performance against stress, the line at first will proceed smoothly upwards, but there comes a point when more stress becomes counter-productive and the line falls.'

In addition to his gruelling life as a medical student and the rigours of hardcore athletics training, Roger Bannister had a third job: finishing his research scholarship at Merton College, Oxford, where he was investigating the physiological effects of running. Bannister said that running the mile was an 'art of taking more out of yourself than you've got'. He first based this art on science, and few had examined the human body's capacity to withstand punishment to the extent that Bannister did.

Arterial pCO_2, blood lactate, pulmonary ventilation, carotid chemoreceptors, oxygen mixes, hyperpnoea, and gas tensions – these were the terms Bannister used to describe the effects of training on his body. In March 1953 it was the language he used to prepare two papers: 'The Carbon Dioxide Stimulus to Breathing in Severe Exercise' and 'The Effects on the Respiration and Performance During Exercise of Adding Oxygen to the Inspired Air'. Atypical expertise for your average miler. Bannister was aswim in a sea of lactate counts, carbon dioxide readings, and oxygen consumption levels from his experiments. His task was to make sense of the numbers.

Over two and a half years had passed since he'd begun the postgraduate research project supervised by two Oxford professors, and Bannister had learned as much about the impact of exercise on the body as it seemed possible to know. 'The efficient integration of the human body, in order to achieve something like the four-minute mile,' he said, 'is way ahead of our capacity to measure how much is breathing, how much is heart or how much is circulation.' This understanding of knowns and known unknowns had come at the expense of a lot of sweat, and blood, from Bannister and his test subjects – or guinea pigs, as Norris McWhirter referred to them. He knew from experience.

'Do you think you could come along and help me with an experiment?' Bannister had asked.

Without much reflection or investigation, McWhirter had replied, 'Oh, yes.'

McWhirter found himself in a small room crowded with a motorised treadmill and a frightening array of attachments: gas bags, meters, valves, pipes, tubes, and pumps. It looked thrown together on a tight budget and a prayer. The door closed swiftly behind him. Stripped down to a pair of shorts and running shoes, McWhirter winced as the assistant took his hand and shot a spring gun attached with a scalpel blade into his finger to draw blood. His singlet was already stained with blood before the experiment began. He stepped on to the treadmill and secured his mouth around a rubberised tube that jutted out over the front of the adjustable platform. From what he understood, the experiment measured the effects different oxygen mixes (from a normal level of 21 per cent to as much as 75 per cent) had on the body when running to ex-haustion. By using the mouthpiece he would inhale enriched air. His exhalation would then be measured for a variety of factors too complicated to explain to every guinea pig.

Wearing a white lab coat, Bannister fired up the 'diabolical machine', as McWhirter called the treadmill, and the sprinter began to run. The whole contraption made a terrible clatter, but the noise was the least of his worries. From what Bannister had told him, the treadmill had a gradient steep enough to ascend the nearly thirty thousand feet of Everest within six hours. Bannister had even tested the team members of the latest Everest expedition and discovered their fitness wanting. After a couple of minutes, McWhirter was hurting as well. Granted he wasn't a distance runner, but the treadmill's speed and gradient were ridiculously harsh. His difficulties were worsened by the fact that he was running with a rubber mouthpiece attached to his face, and the lab assistant repeatedly took his hand mid-stride and shot the blade into another finger to draw more blood. Oxygen-enriched air or not, he was struggling, badly. Wooden bars to his left and right kept him from pitching over the side, and a strategically placed electric fan prevented over-heating.

Five minutes into the experiment, McWhirter was weakening. He was out of breath, his legs felt like they were buckling, and he experienced what one runner called the 'black waves of nausea' from too much effort. At six minutes he was finished. His spine went to rubber, his chin fell to his chest, and his knees went up to his face. Suddenly he was shot from the treadmill into a pile of blankets and duvets positioned behind him. He was in a total state of collapse, barely able to lift his head. The assistant then set upon him once again with the spring gun. Breathless and splattered with blood, McWhirter finally pulled himself back together after ten minutes. His 'friend' needed him for three more 'damn near terminal' sessions. That was all.

In the course of his research, Bannister put himself through this same experiment on fifteen separate occasions. He managed to stay on the machine for at least three times as long as his other subjects, driving himself into a state of collapse again and again. His results were to be included in the papers as well. Afterwards, in the laboratory, he analysed the exhaled gas to see what elements influenced breathing during exertion. This analysis required painstaking exactness, the kind that made everything else in the world drift into insignificance while he worked. Under his professors' guidance, he began to make sense of the results, noticing that he and his subjects sustained themselves longer on the machine by breathing 66 per cent oxygen rather than 100 per cent. Then he tried to deduce why, in the process reading scores of physiology papers and research reports, some on such esoteric topics as carbon monoxide and oxygen uptake by sheep's corpuscles.

Oxygen was the key. A distance runner was limited by his ability to uptake and then use it, but this limit could be extended through training. Bannister knew from studies done on him that he had natural gifts. Based on body types first categorised by Hippocrates, individuals could be measured by three components: ectomorphy (thinness), mesomorphy (muscularity), and endomorphy (fatness). Like many middle-distance runners, Bannister enjoyed high degrees of ectomorphy and mesomorphy with no endomorphy. One scientist, who used these components and several others including height, weight, and heart size, scored Bannister 18,869 points in terms of potential athletic prowess, a number relevant only when it compared most favourably to others. But natural gifts could only carry him so far. In the mile's history, success had come from athletes of all shapes and sizes. Good distance runners had to be made. In contrast, sprinters were born with their talent; training helped simply to economise their movements. If Bannister wanted to run the four-minute mile, he had to harness his potential by tuning his body to best handle strenuous effort. After all, running in a bubble of enriched air wasn't an option.

His experiments and secondary research showed how once the body suffered from a lack of oxygen, muscles stopped using oxygen for energy and switched to a mechanism that could only be sustained for a narrow window of time, and which caused the release of lactic acid into the blood. Too much lactic acid resulted in withering pain and ultimately seized up muscle contractions (a self-defence mechanism). Since oxygen was the problem, there were two require-ments for Bannister: to reduce the amount of oxygen consumed by eliminating unnecessary movements and running at an even pace; and to increase his uptake, delivery, and efficient use of oxygen.

For the first, Bannister had long since perfected his stride so that no movement was wasted, or restricted by tension. A few awkward and clumsy strides stole momentum, and to regain it a runner needed to use oxygen for more energy. To keep his head poised and level, he had accustomed himself to looking at a point fifteen yards ahead of him on the track; to maintain evenness of stride he had practised accelerating while staying relaxed. Natural body lean and arm lift were individual to the runner, and he had found his groove over many years of training. Voluntary action was now reflex. As to even pace, Bannister knew this was critical for his mile attempt. He lost more energy by accelerating at one point in a race than he saved by running slower at another point. In the mile, more energy was used running laps of 58, 62, 64, and 66 seconds than for successive minute-long laps. The difference was slight, but critical in order to break a record by a few strides.

For the second element, the uptake of oxygen, Bannister knew that his body was already functioning at a level equalled only by few – from first inhalation, to the lungs' diffusion of oxygen into his blood, to his heart pumping this blood down into the capillaries of his legs, to the cells in his muscles converting digested food and oxygen into energy, to the firing of his muscle contractions, and finally to the elimination of the by-products of these reactions. In 1953, Bannister had an at-rest pulse rate of fifty beats per minute, twenty-two beats lower than the average man. His lungs absorbed 5.25 quarts of oxygen a minute, twice the standard. In other words, when he ran, his body was operating nearly 50 per cent more efficiently than the average man's. But with every year his training reaped diminishing returns: the capacities of lungs, heart, and muscles were almost fully extended. In order to improve his mile time, he needed to focus his training exclusively on the demands of running one mile and no more. His Fartlek-like training had increased the stamina he needed for the distance, which was mostly a factor of aerobic capacity. At Paddington he worked on his endurance of speed, which at a certain point was about fighting against the body's anaerobic limits. Pushing through the tape in fewer than four minutes demanded balancing and utilising both types of energy to their breaking points.

Bannister's understanding of this was incomplete. Many decades would pass before science could show how fast-twitch muscles (those used for speed) operated on anaerobic energy and slow-twitch muscles (those used for endurance) operated on aerobic energy; how both could be developed on the cellular level; and how the lungs, heart, blood, and capillaries were also adapted into enhancing this whole process. Yet from what Bannister understood – which was still much more than most – the body could manage a four-minute mile. His physiological investigations had led him to this conclusion, and coupling these with his experiences as a miler he was able to dissect the way the race needed to be run, not only in terms of training but also in manner and style. Although he hesitated to admit it, he had learned first-hand the punishment his body could withstand by using himself as a guinea pig in his experiment. He, too, had shot out of the back of the treadmill like McWhirter, so he understood about endurance. His friend explained, 'Psychologically, the rest of life is an anti-climax. People make a fuss about physical pain, but everything [after these experiments] was a breeze.'

When Bannister finished his typical day by falling into bed, having crowded into it caring for his ward, puzzling over patient histories, taking notes during lectures, fitting two hours' worth of effort into a thirty-five-minute workout, boiling down two years of lab research into cogent results, serving as secretary of the Medical Society, and trying to sustain a social life that included inviting dates to dances such as the Achilles Club Ball, acting as Lord Darlington in Oscar Wilde's *Lady Windermere's Fan*, and enjoying drinks out with friends to discuss politics and art, he was tired. This was the life he had chosen, hectic as it was. He was nothing if not well rounded.

By March 1953 the British 'experts' who had wanted to send Bannister to the gallows after Helsinki were already beginning to opine on the singleness of purpose required to break the mile barrier. A columnist at the *Athletic Review* warned that Landy had 'his eyes firmly fixed' on the prize himself and had devoted his time to training over fifty miles per week. 'Our own milers,' he wrote, 'who think a few fast quarters or halves, with an occasional 1½ to 2 mile over-distance spin, totalling around eight miles per week, should note what is required to bring back the bacon.'

As with his Helsinki preparations, Bannister continued to follow his own counsel and ran mostly alone. He refused to train for hours every day to the exclusion of everything else. At the first race of the season two months later, he planned to show that it was still possible to have a life – a full life – outside sport and achieve one of its greatest ambitions at the same time.

8

You can't flirt with the track. You must marry it.

Bill Easton

While the Third Infantry Division fought hand-to-hand combat in Korea, President Eisenhower made nice with Soviet officials after Stalin's recent death, and scientists detonated another atomic bomb in the Nevada desert, Des Moines, Iowa, was filled with floats, parades, dances, and young women hoping to be made queen of the 1953 Drake Relays. Hotels were sold out, restaurants packed out the door, and streets congested with fresh-off-the-lot Fords and Chryslers. The weekend was centred on competitions between athletes from around the Midwest, both at the high school and college level. These were happy, carefree days in an America insulated by a booming economy and a feeling of invincibility. Yes, there was the scare of communism, but optimism abounded. After all, Norman Vincent Peale's *The Power of Positive Thinking* was the country's top-selling book and people were mostly concerned less with politics and the world stage than they were with outfitting their new homes with Bendix automatic laundry machines and GE electric ranges.

On 25 April, at the height of the relays, ten thousand people jammed the stands on both sides of the stadium, many carrying placards for their favourite athlete or team, including Wes Santee and the Kansas Jayhawks. Instead of overalls and boots, the men dressed in slacks, pressed shirts, and loafers. The women wore spring dresses and coiffed their hair perfectly before donning wide-brimmed hats to keep off the sun. Flags encircled the stadium and the football field's wide swath of deep, evenly cut grass was sunk several feet below the track itself, making the oval look as if it had been elevated for the occasion.

At the moment, however, Wes Santee was oblivious to everything but his coach. In only a couple of minutes, Santee would anchor the distance medley (440–880–1,320–mile), a race in mid-progress. His team-mates had fallen behind Georgetown, again.

'Coach, let's drop out,' he shouted over the cheering fans.

'Oh, no-no,' Bill Easton replied, clutching a clipboard to his chest. The words 'Property of Coach Bill Easton' were stamped on the clipboard's top. He was a commanding presence during a track meet, looking like a general on the field of battle. Set behind his glasses, his dark brown eyes were determined. 'We can't do that. No way.'

'I'm going to be too far behind. It's silly for me to just run.'

Easton shook his head. 'No, I don't want to drop out. We're at Drake.'

Santee stepped away. He wanted to run the open mile race instead of anchoring his team in another losing bid. What was the sense of wasting energy if they didn't have a chance to win? As he watched his team slip further behind in the race, his frustration grew. He knew this was an important meet for Easton, who used to coach Drake's track team, but Santee was sick of taking the baton seventy or eighty yards back and trying to win. Yesterday's embarrassing loss in the four-mile relay against Georgetown proved there was only so much he could do. This was his third race in nearly twenty-four hours, and he wanted to focus on the mile.

With the third leg of the medley still in progress, Santee again approached Easton on the side of the track. 'Come on, coach. Let's drop.'

'No,' Easton said, barely even glancing at him. 'You're going to run.'

Santee walked away and positioned himself for the hand-off from

Lloyd Koby. Georgetown's anchor Charlie Capozzoli had already sprinted off. Santee waited, waited, and waited. Finally Koby neared and Santee began running. They exchanged the baton, and Santee settled in for the mile. With Capozzoli over half a lap in the lead and striding well, there was no way to catch him. It was over before it started. The best Santee could do was claim second place, a hundred yards behind Georgetown. He stormed off the track to avoid a repeat of the previous day's drubbing when Capozzoli had shaken his hand and said, 'Hiya, ya bum.'

When Santee marched past his coach, Easton called for him to stop.

'I don't want to talk to *you*,' Santee said, turning briefly before continuing forward. His team-mates and a host of others watched astonished as Santee kept walking. For the first time in three years he had disobeyed his coach and retreated to the locker-room. That had been his final race of the meet, and he was fed up.

It was the height of the outdoor track season. Santee was in the best shape of his running career. At the Texas Relays in March he had run his fastest mile to date – 4:06.7 – in the anchor leg of the four-mile relay, setting a new record in the event. After leading his team to triumph in the sprint medley, distance medley, as well as the two-mile relay, he was named the meet's outstanding performer. Whispers that Santee was the one to claim the mile record quickly strengthened into downright statements of fact. Although at the time still only 21 years old, young for middle-distance runners who typically peaked at 24 or 25, Santee had tongues wagging about his potential. After the Texas Relays, a *New York Herald Tribune* reporter wrote, 'It was a season-launching performance that has never been surpassed ... Any day, now, they'll be expecting Santee to go for the four-minute mile.' Another witness to his domination at the meet said, 'The guy has a lot of poise, a lot of self-assurance. He'll tell you what he can do, and you think maybe he's bragging a little, and then he goes right ahead and does it. You remember the old story about how Babe Ruth took two strikes and then pointed to the spot where he was going to sock a home run on the next pitch? And you remember the Babe went ahead and did it? Well, that's the way Santee is.'

Weekend after weekend, however, his coach neglected to give Santee the opportunity to step up to the plate. He understood that winning meets wasn't an individual affair. Usually he was the loudest supporter on the side of the track, rooting for his Jayhawks. He certainly contributed to their success, running in nearly every distance event held to score points. But when was he going to be able to concentrate on the mile, without being worn down by four races every week?

He was churning this question around in his head, pacing the locker-room, when his team-mates entered. They told him that Easton had shuffled the mile relay roster and wanted Santee to put his spikes back on and race.

'I don't want to run with you guys, none of you want to do better,' Santee said. 'You're all out there just running.'

His statement shocked them: Santee had never refused a race or complained about their performances before. They couldn't believe he was saying no to Easton. The coach's word was law. He set down strict rules, and his boys followed them or they were disciplined. Once, their team-mate Bill Nieder forgot to wear a tie for a meet, and Easton stopped him at the door of the bus.

'Where's your tie?' Easton had asked.

'Oh, Coach, I left it at home,' Nieder had replied.

'Okay, get off the bus and get your tie,' Easton had said, then turned to the driver after his star shot-putter had stepped out. 'Okay, go on to Des Moines.' The door closed and the bus rolled away.

If an athlete cursed, he had to contribute money to the 'flower fund'. If late to a training session, even by a couple of minutes, he paid in sweat. If one broke curfew on a trip away from Kansas, Easton sent him home immediately, whether or not it meant losing the meet. If one dishonoured the team, the coach had the ability to yank his scholarship – and he would. Track and field was serious business to him.

But Easton's athletes listened because they respected him, not because they feared punishment. As a team-mate pointed out, 'When Easton told you something, you believed it was going to happen.' Because usually it did. A disciple of the great Indiana University coach Bill Hayes, Easton was systematic about his approach to running. He loved his schedules and took detailed notes on his athletes, including how much they trained and the changes in their weights before and after a run. He gave written instructions on everything: how much sleep to get (a solid eight hours), what to eat before races (fruit, and definitely no fried eggs, sausages, or potatoes), which clothes to bring to meets (sports coat, white shirt, tie, and top hat – 'You are college men and are representing a university . . . Don't be different!'), and when his athletes should study (when not training or sleeping). Easton dedicated nearly every waking hour to his athletes. He earned the respect his athletes gave him, and he required it. His record spoke for itself: by 1953 he had claimed numerous dual meet, relay, and Big Seven championships plus three National Collegiate Athletic Association (NCAA) titles.

And yet here was Santee, refusing him. Speechless, his team-mates filed out of the locker-room and returned to Easton to tell him the news.

He stuck his hands in his jacket pockets, and with a no-nonsense expression said, 'Go get him to run.'

Only a few minutes before the mile relay was to begin, they rushed back to Santee and pleaded with him. 'We think we can win . . . if you get off your ass and run with us.'

Santee had by now cooled off enough to realise he was playing with fire by disobeying Easton. Easton was more than a coach to him, plus Santee had a strong sense of loyalty to his team. If they promised to start running with all their heart, he told them, he would run. They agreed.

Back on the track, Easton was cool with Santee. They barely

looked at each other, and the coach's only words to him were that he was to run in the third leg. When Santee was handed the baton in the race, he channelled his frustration into a scorching 440-yard lap of 47.4, fast enough to give his anchor Don Smith the lead to take home the win for the Kansas Jayhawks.

After the race, Easton told Santee, 'We need to talk.'

At the University of Kansas, Santee lived in a world defined by running and study, and Bill Easton was its ruler. Santee lived in the Acacia fraternity house. His small room overflowed with the newspaper clippings he'd collected of his latest exploits. He woke early, usually at six o'clock, and was out of the house within a few minutes, taking a fast walk before the sun rose. The university was set on a steep hill called Mount Oread, and his hour-long stroll around the footpaths lined with trees and rustic stone buildings was a pleasant way to get his blood going. He then reported to the Pi Phi sorority house where he laid out breakfast for the students. The job supplemented his athletics scholarship. By eight o'clock he was in class, fulfilling the requirements for his physical education degree, which Easton had suggested Santee major in during his freshman year.

The coach had arranged his schedule and had spoken to his professors before the start of each semester, as he did with his other athletes to ensure his boys were free to train at two o'clock and that they were not falling behind in their studies. If the latter occurred, the class's professor sent Easton a note. Once, when Santee was doing poorly in English, Easton told him he had two choices: improve his grade or miss the upcoming meet. 'Do whatever it takes,' Easton advised. Santee visited his professor, asked what was required to better his scores, and then worked day and night until he was finished. Easton never received another note.

At lunchtime, Santee returned to the sorority house where he cleared the dishes from the tables to the kitchen. Afterwards he attended another class before heading down to Memorial Stadium to begin the day's training session. In the locker-room, he and the other athletes undressed and one by one sat on the examining table where Easton checked their body alignment and adjusted their backs. Then each athlete would weigh in and receive the details for the day's session. They usually trained for two to four hours a day.

In high school, Santee had trained for only forty-five minutes a day, usually during his library period, but since he had run two miles to his girlfriend's house and back nearly every night – not to mention the countless miles he ran on the ranch – it was hard to know how much distance work he used to do. When he was a senior in high school, the talk in Ashland was that he risked getting an enlarged (or 'athletic') heart because of all his running. At the time, this was considered dangerous. His heart was scoped and found to be very muscular, narrow and long. This concerned him when he went to KU, but Phog Allen, the basketball coach and a certified osteopath, administered a step test and gave Wes a physical, after-wards assuring him that he was perfectly healthy. From that moment on he ran as much as Easton instructed. Santee felt as if he'd been given a licence to get stronger with each day.

Easton's training sessions changed throughout the week. On Mondays, they warmed up with a five- to six-mile cross-country run along the dirt roads leading from Mount Oread. There was the occasional hill, but mostly it was flat land that stretched for miles, perfect for farming and long-distance running. The pace was about 50 per cent of top effort. This pace was heated up by quarter- or half-mile dashes, usually prompted by Santee sprinting ahead of the others. During these faster portions of the run, the team split off in packs based on ability.

Santee always ran with Art Dalzell, Lloyd Koby, and Dick Wilson, the 'Four Horsemen' as they were called. They had arrived at the University of Kansas together as freshmen on scholarship and were the core of Easton's track and field team. Dalzell, who was well liked by the girls and could talk his way out of everything, was the second fastest miler on the team. He and Santee roomed together on the road, and it was assumed that Dalzell would forget his track clothes before a meet and Santee would have to bring them in his bag. Lloyd Koby was from the same kind of small-town farm as Santee when he arrived at KU. Dick Wilson was the 'foreigner', the only one of the four not from Kansas. He and Koby were quiet, intelligent and solid, but not extraordinary, milers.

Throughout their cross-country runs the mood was light and they bantered about the girls they were dating or how they were going to run the spikes off their opponents in the next week's meet. They often played practical jokes, like the time they lifted a Volkswagen parked outside someone's house and set it on his porch. By the time they returned to campus, Easton had usually discovered what they had done. On that particular occasion he made them return the car to its proper spot – and repeat their run.

Normally, when they returned to the stadium they changed into fresh singlets and exchanged flat shoes for spikes. Immediately afterwards Easton had them do a quarter-mile as fast as possible. Santee ran his against Dalzell and rarely lost. Easton believed if a distance man had a good quarter-mile time, he could run any event. After a short rest, they ran wind sprints barefoot on the grass infield, usually twenty 100-yard dashes. Once finished with these, they revisited the training table where Easton examined them again and noted their weights. He kept his athletes under constant watch. He knew whether or not they had given a full effort for the day, if one of his boys had been out too late the night before, or if he'd eaten the wrong kind of meal (especially their favourite donuts at Joe's Bakery). 'You're not running the way you should be running,' he would say. Nothing got past him. Whenever he asked what the problem was, it was wise to tell the truth.

On Tuesdays, they warmed up with a two-mile cross-country run, then came back for track work that normally included step-downs from a mile to three-quarters, to half, to a quarter, and then back up again, jogging in between each. On Wednesdays, they ran two miles cross-country then alternated between fast half-miles followed by sprints or doing step-downs again (but over shorter distances, from a half-mile to 600 yards to a quarter-mile to 220 yards). On Thursdays, they concentrated on speed work. This usually included eight quarter-miles or twelve to sixteen 220s. No matter how difficult the session, Easton told them at the start that 'We're gonna have some fun today. Relax and enjoy it.' They raced on Fridays and Saturdays. On Sundays, the team got together for a ten- or fifteen-mile endurance workout, easing out the strains and tensions from racing.

After a typical session, Santee hightailed it back to the sorority house to serve formal dinner. He then grabbed some food for himself and came back to the stadium to clean the locker-room – another scholarship obligation. By eight o'clock he returned to the Acacia house to study for two hours before bedtime. The opportunity to see his girlfriend, Danna Denning, was usually limited.

They had met the year before at the football stadium where Santee was selling programmes. Several of his fraternity brothers were dating her sorority sisters, and they urged the two to date. At the time Santee was still seeing his high-school girlfriend, returning to Ashland on occasion for visits. After Helsinki, he decided to take Danna out on a 'Coke Date' to test the waters. They went to the Rock Chalk Café, a block from his fraternity house, for a soda and half an hour of conversation before she had to return to her sorority house by the time they flickered the lights at 10.30 p.m. curfew. Danna came from a wealthy, established family in Elkhart, Kansas – the hometown of Glenn Cunningham. She had entered KU at the early age of 15. She was attractive in a serious, bookish kind of way, and in many areas the two were polar opposites. Danna cared about her studies in accounting, rather than sport. She was as much an introvert as Wes was extrovert. While Santee had to work to scrape around for spending money, she had a generous allowance and drove around in an Austin Healey her father had given her. Yet they found they worked together. One date turned into two, and then many. They went to church on Sundays, attended formals together, and she would stop by the track to watch him train. By April 1953, talk of marriage and having children was already on the table. As it was, Wes Santee's table was already fairly full.

Easton frowned on his athletes getting too serious with their girlfriends, but Santee had managed to get close to Danna without losing focus on his sport – not that he had much spare time to lose focus. Even in his sleep he dreamed of running. Many of those dreams involved scenes where he surged past his competitors as he turned into the final bend of the last lap and then distanced himself from them to the finish line.

Only one month after his return from Helsinki, Santee had started the cross-country season. He travelled throughout the Midwest for dual meets and championships. The Jayhawks strung together six straight meet victories, including the Big Seven championship in November. Easton motivated his team with speeches about 'KU against the World', but his boys were far from underdogs with Santee winning every three-mile race he entered. Before the holidays, Easton sent each of his athletes a letter detailing how they should balance their training with studies for final examinations. They were also advised to run every day at home over the break 'so that you will be ready for hard workouts upon your return to the campus'. The letter was headlined 'Merry Christmas!'

The indoor season began in January 1953, and Santee was equally dominant there. The papers called him the '1-man record demolisher' and the 'Menace of Mount Oread'. In late February, this 'running machine' led his team to another Big Seven title. There was hardly a break before the outdoor season, which saw him running in races every single weekend from March until late May.

This was his life. Even when he ran for fun – his version of fun – Easton was there to lead him along. In the winter, Santee had challenged his Acacia brothers to a race after being ragged for all the press attention he had received: he would run the thirteen and a half miles from Tonganoxie to Lawrence, Kansas, against twenty-seven of his fraternity brothers, each one taking a half-mile of the course. He claimed he'd whip them all to the finish line. What started out as a fraternity stunt quickly captured the imagination of the town. Before the race, Easton told reporters, 'Knowing how determined he can be, I'll wager he makes it. Matter of fact, I think I'll go out and ride along the road just to time him for each mile. Might as well get some good out of this, you know.' Santee's fraternity brothers were confident as well. The Acacia president was quoted saying, 'We can take him if we can get a three-minute or better half-mile out of every guy who runs in the race – and we're practicing.'

On a frigid 22° December morning, with highway patrol cars and fans lining the highway, Santee quickly went into the lead over freshman football player Ralph Moody and finished his first mile in 4:41. He then eased into 5:36 average mile pace, wearing a heavy blue sweatsuit and using woollen gym socks to protect his hands from the cold. Halfway finished, his opponents far behind him, he ribbed one of his waiting fraternity brothers, 'I'm more than halfway there, how about you guys?' At three miles outside Lawrence, a north-west wind bit into Santee. His muscles tightened, his side hurt, and he feared he might not be able to continue. When he turned back south, though, his body warmed and he continued on pace to whip his fraternity brothers by over four hundred yards. Throughout, Easton was positioned in the back of a station wagon driven by his wife, calling out his mile times on a jerry-rigged public address system and heckling the waiting runners as Santee passed them.

Stunts aside, Easton told Santee – and the press gobbled up the coach's every word – that he was on course to become the best miler in the United States, perhaps the world. He just needed more time to develop. Santee knew, however, that time wasn't on his side. The Australian John Landy had demonstrated that the four-minute mile was in serious contention, and with European milers such as Roger Bannister and Gaston Reiff starting their seasons soon, the barrier might fall within months. Training to win meets for the University of Kansas was great, but it shouldn't have to mean the sacrifice of his greater ambition: to run the four-minute mile first.

*　　*　　*

When the University of Kansas team returned from the Drake Relays, Easton summoned Santee. At three o'clock, Santee made his way across campus to Robinson Gym where Easton had his office. Santee was the only one on campus to wear jeans, cowboy boots and western-style shirts. He walked quickly and with purpose, always, passing other students before they even knew he was coming.

Of the many top athletes in America, Santee embodied better than most sport's changing landscape. Playing to the spectators and generating excitement was now the name of the game, and he loved doing both. The days of quiet achievement and quieter heroes were over. People wanted athletes who were confident and colourful. And they wanted to see records broken. In the 1950s, sportswriter Gerald Holland heralded this sea-change: 'For world-wide interest and participation, for huge crowds and vast audiences, for smashed records and astonishing performances by outsiders and underdogs, this new golden age in scores of ways outstrips and outdazzles them all. As if no other world existed, the world of sport is crowded with action and excitement and filled with high sports spirits.'

The exuberance in American sport reflected the age, a time that brought big Cadillacs with swooping tail fins, 'New Colorama Styling' Frigidaire ranges, bright pink dresses and buttondowns, hi-fi stereos, Disneyland, Dean Martin and Jerry Lewis, and the hope of a television in every new home. Almost alone among the peoples of the world at this time, Americans had money in their pockets and time on their hands, and sport reached a fever pitch as a consequence. Children flocked to baseball diamonds, golf courses, soccer and football fields, swimming pools, running tracks, tennis courts, and boxing rings, dreaming of becoming the next great star. Their parents encouraged these hopes, and schools boosted intramural sports programmes to meet the demand. This rise in participation was dwarfed, however, by the skyrocketing number of spectators crowding stadiums and tracking every movement of their favourite athletes. The 1952 Olympics had shown that sport had political ramifications, but who performed better, the United States or the Russians, was a minor theme compared to the sheer amount of money there was to be made from impassioned fans. With the rise of television, athletic competition was brought into living rooms across the country. New promise was bestowed in dollar signs. Families hurried to buy this new black box, perhaps at first to watch Lucille Ball and Desi Arnaz in *I Love Lucy*, the antics of Milton Berle, or the news anchored by Walter Cronkite, but soon they found it enthralling to watch sports from the comfort of their couches. In their lamp-lit rooms, they could root for Ben Hogan to continue his streak of golf major championships, marvel at Native Dancer thundering to victory in another stakes race, shudder at the punching power of Sugar Ray Robinson and Archie Moore, and love (or hate) to see Mickey Mantle lead the Yankees over the Brooklyn Dodgers on their way to five straight World Series titles. If radio in the 1920s had built a sporting economy out of gold leaf, television in the 1950s replaced it with solid gold.

As sport became serious business, its landscape was completely altered. Since hundreds of millions of dollars went into sponsorship deals, it paid to win. Naturally, this changed the nature of professional sports: there was more pressure than ever to achieve results, and failure came at a much higher cost. But amateur sports were also fundamentally affected. High schools and colleges were fast becoming farm teams, producing players for professional leagues. Sporting success could well mean a lucrative career upon graduation. Gradually, commerce was moving amateur athletics away from its original vision.

Santee understood that the pursuit of the four-minute mile had the power to fire imaginations and pack stadiums. And were he to achieve it, he knew he would win more than headlines. He enjoyed the attention he received just for commenting about the possibility. 'I don't know when it will be,' he told one journalist, 'but I'll run it, you can be sure of that. I'm as certain I can run the four-minute mile as you are that you can drive your car home. There's always the chance of an accident, but barring that, I'll do it.' Santee bathed in the media's limelight, and comments like these only heightened its intensity.

As an amateur college athlete, Santee knew that the only ones getting rich from his efforts were the race promoters urging him to attend their events. He could, however, make a few dollars later as a professional, especially if he had been the one to claim this Everest of sport. The money could wait, but the barrier would not last for ever. Easton needed to grasp this and give him his chance.

Santee climbed to the gym's third floor, taking the steps two at a time, ready to face Easton and answer for what had happened at the Drake Relays. He also needed to convince his coach of the necessity of concentrating on the mile. Easton was waiting for him behind his old wooden schoolteacher's desk, scattered with newspaper and magazine clippings. The small office was crowded with filing cabinets, trophies, and pictures of his athletes and teams through the years.

Easton went straight to the point, as usual. 'I didn't think you acted in a professional and appropriate way yesterday.'

'Yes, sir,' Santee said.

'You were insubordinate and rude.'

'Those guys didn't hold up their end. I was mad.'

'Well, I know that, Wes, but that's part of life. You can't always have what you want.' Easton was calm, his voice even. 'I didn't want to be a drop-out from the race, even though you had to run like the dickens to get second. Do you understand my position?'

Santee nodded. He knew how much pride his coach took in his former success at Drake and that he wanted the same for his Jayhawk team. Easton led Santee outside where they sat down on the steps. It was one of those brilliant Kansas afternoons when the blue sky looked to stretch to the ends of the earth.

'We may have many days that they won't produce,' Easton said.

'I don't mind running for the team,' Santee urged. 'But when do I get to run for myself?' He meant his shot at the four-minute mile.

'Well, I've been thinking about how we mesh these things together.'

Ever since John Landy had run his breakthrough mile in December 1952, Easton had tracked his progress. He'd clipped out newspaper articles about the 'No. 1 World Mile Runner' and broken down the lap times Landy was running directly onto the page, studying how the miler paced himself through the race and how difficult it was for him to maintain his speed in the final lap after leading throughout. Easton registered every detail and formulated what Santee needed to do. The scene at the Drake Relays had shown Easton that Santee couldn't be held back any longer.

'I want you to run for the team,' Easton continued. 'But when we get down to certain meets, I want you to enter the open mile event only.'

These were the words Wes Santee had been waiting to hear for months.

'You're the one to run the four-minute mile,' Easton said confidently. 'But you still need to improve. You're going to have to do different workouts than everybody else. You need to put more pressure on yourself.'

Over the next two hours they talked about how Santee would ratchet up his training by reducing the interval he took between repeat 440s; they spoke of trying to arrange for a rabbit (Easton's term for a pacemaker) to pace him through at least the first three-quarters of his record mile attempts; they discussed Roger Bannister and John Landy and others who might have a chance at breaking the barrier. It was finally clear to Santee that Easton wanted it as much as he did. Of course, his coach was always looking to help his athletes achieve their best. Santee had seen this with Bill Nieder, the former high-school football star who had hurt his knee during his first season at KU and given up on sports when Easton convinced him to master the shot-put – and turned him into a world record holder. He had seen it in the day-to-day adjustments he made in the training of his athletes, spending long hours at the track, the first to arrive and the last to leave. But Santee was unconvinced until that afternoon that Easton would be there with him in an ambition that had nothing to do with the Jayhawks.

After they'd exhausted talk of running, Easton turned to Santee to discuss his future, namely what kind of job he planned to do after graduating and finishing his Reserve Officers Training Corps (ROTC) stint with the Marines (in which he had enrolled on Easton's direction to avoid the draft for the Korean War). Although Santee was studying physical education with an eye on a coaching career, Easton suggested he was better suited for something else.

'Why don't you do something in the business school?' Easton asked. 'Your temperament is much better suited for the sales side of things.'

'I was thinking the same,' Santee said.

'You're going to have to make the change quickly.' And then Easton told him he'd help. By the end of the meeting, Santee felt protected and supported in a way he had not felt since Mr Molyneux died. It was the longest conversation Easton and Santee had ever had, and one he never could have had with his own father. They shook hands, and then Easton put his arm around Santee.

His first serious bid for the mile barrier would come in early June 1953 at the Compton Invitational in California. In the meantime, Easton planned on contacting Al Franken, the meet's promoter, about getting a pacemaker to help push Santee. Wes couldn't wait for his chance.

9

Whatever you can do,
Or think you can, begin it.
Boldness has power, and genius,
And magic in it.

Goethe

At the height of John Landy's athletics season in 1953, Percy Cerutty invited the *Argus* sports columnist Max Crittenden into his cluttered South Yarra study. The coach loved the press Landy was earning him, and he was his usual bombastic self.

'Will man ever run the mile within four minutes?' Crittenden asked.

'I'll live to see it!' Cerutty declared authoritatively, because *his* athlete John Landy was going to be the one to do it.

Statements like these were typical of Cerutty throughout the summer. He continued to assert that he was still the miler's coach. Landy simply ignored him. Since his breakthrough 4:02.1 run, when Cerutty had shot off at the mouth in front of his parents, Landy wanted nothing to do with the man. By April 1953, autumn in Australia, he was finished with 'record' runs as well, at least for the next eight months. He looked forward to escaping all this talk of a four-minute mile for a while.

He was hard at work in his final year at the University of Melbourne where thirty-four hours a week of lectures and practical work in agricultural science took up the lion's share of his days. He had only just begun training for the next athletics season, which was likely his last, since he had to give consideration to his future career, whether farming or teaching, a decision he was still weighing. He had chosen agricultural science because there were no specific courses in entomology at his university, and whatever job he chose he wanted there to be the opportunity to travel and work outdoors. His father, who was self-made, having by the age of 25 already launched his own accountancy firm in Melbourne, advised that it was unwise to engage in sport at the sacrifice of one's career prospects, particularly past the age of 24, which John turned the following April. 'There are more important things in life,' he told his son, and John agreed. In eighteen months' time, he planned to retire from athletics.

But that did not mean his focus waned. If anything, it increased because of the little time he had left. Beating Macmillan's record and winning the Australian championship, his two goals after Helsinki, had already been reached. Now he wanted to break the world mile record and claim victory at the British Empire Games mile in August 1954 before putting away his running spikes. Although by doing so he would win renown as the world's best miler, this was not his ambition. Running had become more a competition to draw out the best that was in him, as if he was plumbing the depths of his will.

Nonetheless, since his stunning run the previous December he had become a public spectacle in Australia. He received attention normally reserved for his country's star cricketers and football players. He was photographed racing, eating lunch, studying at the university library, and jogging around local parks – everywhere 'but having his morning shower', as one journalist wrote at the time. There could be no more underplaying his pursuit of running, as he had before the Olympics. One day a lecturer at the University of Melbourne stopped him between classes.

'I say, John, do you run at all?' the lecturer asked.

'A bit,' Landy replied.

'You know, I saw a fella who looked just like you with a mob of blokes with bloody spears or something, running down St Kilda Road last Saturday.'

'No,' Landy replied, his face flushing with colour. 'Couldn't have been me.'

No doubt most of his embarrassment had to do with his association with Cerutty at the time. Landy was proud of what he had been able to accomplish on his own since Helsinki. He had dominated every mile race, leading from the front and dictating the pace throughout by running flat out from the start. World record or not, he had run the fastest mile in seven years. He had taken affront to the claim by Arthur Daley in the *New York Times* that there was no way an unknown from Australia could have increased his speed so dramatically. Some joked that his mile had been timed by the big Bryant & May clock visible in the distance from Olympic Park. But when one of their correspondents attended his next mile on 3 January 1953, Landy had delivered another fast time, earning a welcome apology from Daley that read, 'Maybe too much salt was taken here ... When this old-timer started to attend track meets, the 4-minute mile was considered an utter impossibility. It is that no longer.'

Soon, every race Landy entered came with the expectation that he would break a record, and in most cases the four-minute mile. In the *Sydney Morning Herald* on 18 January, athletics writer Frank Tierney delivered an itemised list of conditions Landy needed to go about it:

✓ A relaxed mental outlook towards the race.
✓ A certain amount of nervous energy to be released.
✓ Skilful pacing, assistance.
✓ A level track with 'life' in it.
✓ A temperature not more than 80 degrees.
✓ Atmosphere free of humidity.
✓ No winds.

These were the conditions Gundar Haegg had enjoyed when he set his world mile record of 4:01.4 in 1945. The tracks and weather in Malmö, Sweden, were ideal, and Haegg had benefited from prearranged pacing by Lennart Strand.

Landy was not as fortunate when he showed up for the Australian Championship mile in Perth on Saturday, 22 January. The day before, he had withdrawn into a 1,000-acre park near the city, his butterfly net in tow. He needed to escape the intense scrutiny he was under in order to run a good time; winning the event was already a foregone conclusion. When reporters cornered Les Perry to ask when the miler might return, Perry simply said, 'If he feels hungry.' On race day, the temperature was nearly 80° and the humidity high. Landy had raced each of the previous three weekends; he was not particularly relaxed because of the enormous pressure from the press; and Les Perry was not fast enough to set the pace, though he would have loved to help his friend. Finally, track officials had neglected to arrange for the calling of lap times, which was usually standard, so he was running blind in terms of his pace. Despite these factors, Landy finished some seventy yards ahead of the closest runner in an impressive 4:04.2. But the crowd greeted the announced time with silence, shrugs, and a disappointed early departure. It was the sort of disheartening response Landy was beginning to expect. Before the race he had told a local reporter, 'I'll do my best. If it comes, it comes; but, if it doesn't, for Hec's sake [*sic*], have the gate open. This crowd will lynch me.'

Landy continued to compete every weekend through the summer, though at times he could barely see the track from the perspiration stinging his eyes. Blunders by officials continued to plague him as well. In late February he was predicted to break the 1,500m record on an oval track in Melbourne. The track was roughly 330 metres around, which meant that it would take four and a half laps to complete the distance. Feeling good, Landy set out at a fast clip. At the finish of the first half-lap, an official called out 'Three to go.' Landy knew that was wrong, and as he ran past he yelled out, 'You mean four.' He circled the track again, but the official said, 'Two to go,' when it should have been three. It couldn't be right, Landy thought, but he continued to run. Maybe the track was longer than he figured. Landy completed two more laps and broke through the tape. He was told he had run 3:55.4, which again he doubted since the fast pace he had been running would have given him a time of at least 3:45 in the 1,500m. Landy returned to the dressing room, thought through the situation, then figured out he had indeed run a lap short. He stormed onto the track, confronting the official. His elapsed time was actually 2:55.4; the official had been mistaken.

At another mile race he had so dazzled the officials with his speed that they failed to stretch the 'tape' completely across the finish in time. As they were uncoiling the wool string from its stick, Landy dashed across the line, having to angle to catch the four feet of string they had managed to unwind. With little tension on the string, it did not break, and the official lost his grip on the stick. Showing the agility of his former football days, the miler caught the stick mid-air and held it over his head for the photographers.* Landy might have been ready for world record miles, but the atmosphere in which he was running was hardly conducive.

By the conclusion of the athletics season in mid-March 1953, Landy was exhausted. For his last seven mile races he averaged 4:11. 'About this four-minute mile business – I guess I'll need another 10 years. For the present, I have had it,' he said after one of the runs. If he was going to break any records in the next Australian season, he would have to do so without the ideal conditions Tierney had outlined in the *Sydney Morning Herald*. At least until then he would not have to suffer the glare of publicity. He could study and train without distraction.

On 2 May, with Landy starting his workouts for the 1953–4 season, Roger Bannister crossed Magdalen Bridge in Oxford, the waters of the Isis flowing below. He was heading towards the Iffley Road track. The university was in spring's full bloom, a time of year when the trees shaded the narrow, meandering streets and the scent of blossoms filled the air. Hauling stacks of books, students filed in and out of the gateways of their colleges. Behind their Cotswold-stone walls generations of England's privileged had lived and studied. Bannister had fond memories of his time at Exeter, its garret rooms, its dining hall lined with stained-glass windows and oil paintings, and its quadrangle where students lounged on the grass or pored over lecture notes. His university days were over, but he still felt a strong attachment to Oxford, particularly to its track, where he hoped to make history.

In 1946, as a first-year student, Bannister had found the track in shameful disrepair. At some 600 yards per lap (three laps to a mile), the oval was misshapen and suffering from poor drainage. Rounding one bend, runners used to vanish down a steep bank behind some tall grass, only to reappear moments later before heading to the finish. In places, old brick was exposed, a hazard for those in spikes. This was where former British middle-distance champions such as Colonel Strode-Jackson and Jack Lovelock made their names, running *clockwise* around the track. 'It was just a clinker,' said Norris McWhirter of the track before Bannister was elected president of the Oxford University Athletic Club in 1948. He decided to have it bulldozed and replaced with a new cinder track 440 yards around and six lanes wide to meet international specifications. Bannister raised the money to hire contractors, and during the two years of headaches and near disasters to see it completed he promised himself that the Iffley Road track would be the site of his greatest efforts.

He wanted to break the four-minute mile in Oxford not only because he had helped build the track, but also because his university was deeply steeped in the approach to sport he considered his own. Early in the nineteenth century, Oxford dons had begun organising athletics competitions in an effort to match strong minds with strong bodies. These efforts gathered momentum when Victoria became the Queen of England in 1837. This began a new era during which the country would set about curing the ills of the years before when loose morals, corruption, idleness, and political scandal reigned. Pursuing a strong education and an appreciation for the arts, England's youth learned the Victorian values of clean and purposeful living, independence, self-control, and strenuous effort through sport. In part this was an amateur ideal, as historian Allen Guttmann contended, that 'traced back to the Renaissance, to the world of Baldassare Castiglione's *Il Cortegiano*, to the courtier who danced, wrote sonnets, played the lute, and commanded armies on the field of battle, who was, however, neither a dancer nor a poet nor a musician nor a soldier.'

During this period of Victorian reform, athletic clubs began to form in London, Oxford and Cambridge. They restricted members from competing in professional running events because they had been brought up to believe that sport was an ennobling effort, not to be pursued for something as mundane as cash. In 1879, three Oxford students brought together the leaders from the disparate clubs for a meeting, followed by dinner at the Randolph Hotel. There they decided to create the Amateur Athletic Association, a governing body for the country's amateur athletics. Its purpose, as Montague Sherman, one of those three Oxford students, wrote a few years later, was to assure the true amateur that 'wherever he goes to run under AAA laws he will find competent management and fair play – a fair field and no favour'. It proved to be the example the world would follow.

By 1953, however, Bannister knew that the gentleman amateur was fast becoming a dinosaur. The Helsinki Olympics had shown that how and why one participated in sport was losing its lustre, that victory at any price was becoming the new ruling principle of sport. In many respects, the Americans were leading the way. Their athletes were exciting, brash, well trained, and hell-bent on success. In a post-Second World War world, the United States reigned as the pre-eminent power, expecting England and other nations to follow in their path. This included the US's approach to sport. But

Bannister was not yet ready to relinquish the values he had learned at Oxford. As Winston Churchill once said, 'We have not journeyed all this way across the centuries, across the oceans, across the mountains, across the prairies, because we are made of sugar candy.'

Because of his medical studies, Bannister didn't have the time to devote three or four hours a day to training. Had he been willing to do so he could probably have raced every week, as his body would have been able to recover from the strain better. But instead of racing every week, the four-minute mile was his goal. Unfortunately, this made him appear distant and aloof to some athletes and newspaper editorial writers. But for Bannister, breaking the barrier would be the best affirmation that the gentleman amateur was still capable of realising athletics' most coveted prize. And for him to do so in the place where this ideal was in part forged would make the victory even sweeter.

The annual AAA versus Oxford University meet was the first opportunity of the 1953 season for athletes to make their mark after months of training. Given the limited number of runners in the mile race, there would be an absence of the jostling and elbow work that characterised larger competitions. In other words, it was a fine set-up for breaking records. Only a few knew of Bannister's intention as he walked into the grounds and made his way alongside the track towards the stands where the locker-room was located.

Those in the know included Chris Chataway, who had succeeded Bannister as president of the Oxford University Athletic Club. The stocky, red-headed runner was two and a half years his junior. They had met when Bannister was doing his postgraduate work at Merton College. Chataway had considered the miler a distant, senior figure, much as one viewed an Oxford don. Bannister was not known for visiting the Iffley Road track often, and initially he gave Chataway the impression that he never trained, despite rumours that Bannister was often seen running on distant playing fields around Oxford. Only after Chataway roomed with the miler in Helsinki did he become friends with Bannister and learn how seriously he took his running efforts.

Chataway had agreed to pace Bannister through to the three-quarter-mile mark, regardless of the headlines of the previous few days' newspapers that predicted 'Chataway Should Avenge Mile Defeat by Bannister'. Chataway was better suited for three miles, and having recently travelled to Morocco with Bannister for a series of races, Chataway knew that Bannister was in better shape. Victory was not on the cards for Chataway, so he chose to help. Plus, there was nobody else in the field who had the ability to push Bannister through the entire race, particularly the critical last lap. He knew it. Bannister knew it. Being paced through the first three laps was the only way Bannister had a chance at the four-minute mile. There was a precedent for the plan: in 1937 Sydney Wooderson had claimed his mile record of 4:06.4 when R. H. Thomas paced him through the first three-quarters at Motspur Park. If it worked then, it should work now. There was no time to spare with the likes of John Landy running such good miles.

In the two months since Bannister had begun his intense track work, his fitness had improved dramatically, despite a rough period of irregular hours caused by midwife duties at St Mary's. After an Easter break spent hiking in Wales, where he drank from fresh mountain streams and dashed down steep screes as fast as his legs could carry him, he ran a three-quarter-mile trial in one second over three minutes. More importantly, his pacing for each quarter was even. Two weeks later, on 13 April, he ran a 880-yard trial in 1:52.1, showing how well tuned his speed was. He had reached his peak, just at the right moment.

By three o'clock on 2 May, fifteen minutes before the mile race was to start, the stands and surrounding banks of grass around the Iffley Road track were filled. The AAA versus Oxford University match always drew a crowd, but the press had boosted the turnout by announcing that the meet would prove the 'most intensive start [to the athletics season] in sport's history'. Having consumed only a glass of orange juice mixed with glucose for lunch (his own special concoction), Bannister took his usual twenty-minute warm-up jog in his sweatsuit and readied himself for the race. His focus on an all-out attempt was clear. Over the last week he had gradually become more and more excited about this day. Soon he would channel this focus and excitement, as he later said, 'to release every ounce of mental and physical energy I possessed over four minutes'.

After the race was called, the field, including Olympic steeple-chasers Chris Brasher and John Disley, and milers Derek Burfitt and John Bryant, lined up at the starting line to the left of the stands. They tensed as the starter raised the gun. Bang! They were off. Chataway jumped into the lead within a few strides. It was an unusually fast early pace and it left the rest of the field trying to keep up. Chataway finished the first lap in 62.1 seconds with Bannister just a few yards behind him.

Chataway increased his pace, unsure of how fast he had run the first lap having got no information from the timekeepers, despite shouting at them. Bannister remained second, sure in his rhythm. Disley moved into third place, but the rest of the field was being left behind. Chataway crossed the half-mile mark in 2:04.1 – too slow. Battling against a strong wind, he spent himself completely in the third lap, struggling to finish it in 60.9 seconds for a three-quarter-mile time of 3:05. Only a few strides later, he bowed out of the race, almost veering into the long-jump pit, dizzy from fatigue. 'Only the silky-striding Bannister was still in contention,' Norris McWhirter wrote in his *Athletics World* account of the race. 'Serene and now alone, Bannister sailed on. Wearing the sad relaxed mask reminiscent of the great Manelote as he delivered the *coup de grâce* in the bull ring.'

Into the last lap, Bannister still had speed in reserve. His training had given him the endurance to follow Chataway at a harsh pace without exhausting his final kick. He delivered it now, pushing through the pain that was beginning to seize his legs. At the 1,500-metre mark, Bannister registered 3:47, only 1.8 seconds slower than his Olympic final time against the best in the world. The remaining 120 yards he sprinted, using everything he had to complete the mile in 4:03.6. It was his best time by over four seconds, it was a new British record, and it was the fifth fastest mile ever recorded. He finished seventy yards ahead of Disley, who came second, followed by Bryant and then Brasher. A crowd circled around Bannister to congratulate him. A few hours later he boarded a train to London, knowing he needed to get back to his studies.

By the next morning, he was the talk of the town again. 'Roger Made It Look Easy' proclaimed the *News of the World* after the race. 'Amazing Mile by Bannister' read another. The *Daily Telegraph* praised him as 'a hard-working medical student who between writing theses and delivering babies, turns his brain to the technique and theory of running. Bannister has a fine, though by no means an inordinately strong physique. Many others must have been as richly blessed as he. His running is a triumph of technique . . . and his success is the result of applying his intellect to the job.' The British press followed with predictions of when, not if, Bannister would break the mile record. In *Athletic Review*, Bannister was placed side by side with the British mountaineers who at that moment were 'poised high up on the frozen, precipitous slopes of Everest ready for the final assault on the world's hitherto unconquerable high mountain'.

Bannister expected the media frenzy. His 4:03.6 might have put him back in their good graces, but he cared little for their forecasts. He knew for certain after this race that 'the four-minute mile was not out of reach. It was only a question of time.' But he also recognised that he would need two pacemakers to help him make the attempt: the first to carry him to the half-mile mark under two minutes and the second to lead him through the third lap in roughly sixty seconds. He had diagnosed what was needed as if it was a medical case study. Summoning will or emotion did not seem important.

Until he could arrange these pacemakers and improve his speed,

Bannister would have to wait helplessly to see if another miler got to the record before him.

In mid-May, at Bill Easton's two-storey house in Lawrence, Kansas, Wes Santee and his coach sat on the couch in front of a grainy black-and-white television set. While they waited for the replay of an interview with Finnish miler Denis Johansson, Easton ran his small terrier mutt through a series of tricks, such as balancing a biscuit on his nose before tossing it back and catching it. Looking on, Santee thought Easton's dog as disciplined as his athletes. Finally, Johansson appeared on the screen. Reports had it that the miler, who smoked twenty-five cigarettes a day and was known as much for his good looks and ease with women as his skill on the track, was shooting his mouth off about his upcoming race against Santee and the Belgian Gaston Reiff at the Compton Invitational in June. Wes and his coach wanted to hear it for themselves.

'I think Santee will some day be a great miler,' Johansson said to the camera. 'But he still has to develop more physically and mentally. He's too unstable, flighty and cocky.'

Santee could hardly believe his ears. Who was this guy? His best time in the mile was 4:08.3, and Santee had bettered that on an indoor track this year. Sure Johansson had seen him fail miserably in the 5,000m in Helsinki, but that was some time ago.

Johansson continued, 'It may be some years yet before he really blossoms, and his mental attitude could do more to hold him back than his physical development, which hasn't far to go. I think that Santee is good enough to set a fast pace, but lack of experience in big-time competition is against him.' He finished by saying that the 31-year-old Reiff was the man to beat, given his world records in the two-mile, 2,000m, and 3,000m.

Santee boiled over. 'I'll get you!' he shouted, shaking his fist at the television.

Easton tried to calm him down, but he didn't try very hard. He *wanted* Santee fired up for the race, and Johansson was stoking the flames nicely. The Compton Invitational was Santee's best chance at the four-minute mile that season. The clay track was fast, the weather typically good, and the competition the best he would see that year. This meet was important since Easton's attempt at getting a rabbit to pace Santee at Compton had hit a brick wall with the Amateur Athletic Union, the same group that had kept Wes from representing the USA in the 1,500m in Helsinki.

The AAU was founded in 1888 by a group of private athletic clubs led by the New York Athletic Club. Their mission was to help promote and codify the rules of amateur sports, as they had done in England ten years before. By 1912, the AAU ruled US track and field, most significantly by controlling eligibility for the Olympics. Since then the organisation had carefully tended to its power, working under the fiat that 'since it was a voluntary organization, athletes had no rights . . . only privileges'.

Its leader was Avery Brundage, albeit by 1953 more in influence than title. A former decathlete who was often beaten by the American decathlon champion Jim Thorpe, Brundage had retired from competition in 1912, worked as an engineer, and eventually become a millionaire in the construction business. His first love was amateur sports. At one time or another he had held almost every position in the administration of amateur athletics, and in 1952 he was elected the first American president of the International Olympic Committee (IOC). He believed devoutly in sport as recreation, not work. In his opinion, professional athletes were 'a troop of trained seals' while amateurs lived up to the 'highest moral laws'. In particular, the Olympics became his obsession, so much so that when Jewish groups tried to get the United States to boycott the 1936 Berlin Games, Brundage became a vocal anti-Semite. Nobody dared mess with his Olympic movement, or his hold on the reigns of power.

Brundage refused to accept the changing face of sport by the 1950s, particularly the rise of sports stars, commercialism, and the pursuit of records. He was aided in his fight against these changes by

Dan Ferris, the secretary-treasurer of the AAU, who had held tightly to his administrative job for forty years. Ferris was a short, fleshy-faced man with the demeanour of a school principal whose first instinct was to punish, not help. Any decisions made by the AAU crossed his desk first, and although he knew the pursuit of the mile record could draw enormous attention to US amateur athletics, it did not merit any rule-bending. Ferris made it clear to Easton that if pacemaking was even suspected to have occurred at Compton, or any other meet for that matter, Santee's time would be disqualified. Since the AAU provided no avenue for appeal, the decision was final, just as it had been when Santee was removed from his Olympic trial the year before. These AAU officials – or, as Santee called them, 'Transatlantic Oceanic Hitch-hikers' because of their tendency to travel around Europe and the United States, eating fine dinners and staying at nice hotels on the backs of their athletes – were increasingly looking as though they had it in for him.

If plans for a paced attempt had been blocked, competition from the likes of Denis Johansson, particularly after his remarks about Santee's maturity, was the next best thing. Bannister had just recently posted his 4:03.6 mile, which Easton had broken down into split times the moment he saw the Associated Press article. Meanwhile, according to the athletics bible *Track & Field News*, Landy was already training hard for his next season. Santee had to have a go now, and Compton was his best shot. Johansson would be striving to win the race on his own, so he would make almost as good a pacer for Santee as a rabbit. If Johansson was near enough to him in the final lap, he would provide Santee with the inspiration to push harder.

On Sunday, 24 May, Santee gave the Finnish miler a preview of what he could expect in California. At the Big Seven conference championship in Ames, Iowa, Santee blazed the mile in 4:06.3, taking the national collegiate record from Glenn Cunningham, who had held it for eighteen years. After the run, he said, 'I caught my quarters right on time and the race went exactly as Uncle Bill and

I had planned.' Forty minutes later he won the half-mile in 1:50.8, prompting the crowd to shout 'Break up, Kansas!' as his team romped home to an overall victory. A week later he ran a 4:07.4.

'Nuts to Denis. We'll see who's immature Friday night,' Santee said to reporters before he left for California. 'I hope he read what I did at Ames and in the Valley AAU and choked on it. I'm going to have a score to settle with that guy.' Easton was only slightly more diplomatic when he told the press that his runner was the favourite to win. 'That's okay by us. We never run a race we don't figure we can win. If you don't feel that way, why run?'

At the Kansas City airport, Santee and his coach were ushered into the first-class cabin of the TWA Super Constellation airplane, the Waldorf-Astoria of comfort travel at the time. The pilot came through to say hello and to wish Santee luck in California. Drinks and a gourmet meal were then served. The young miler was fast learning that when he competed in an Al Franken-promoted meet, everything was first class. The AAU might not allow their athletes to get paid, but no rules forbade Franken from treating his star attraction well. After all, Santee was the reason people were buying tickets and companies had enlisted as sponsors to the meet. It was this influence, however, that the AAU was beginning to fear, whether Franken or Santee knew it yet or not.

When Easton and Santee arrived in Los Angeles on Thursday, 4 June, Franken picked them up in his Ford convertible. The day was all sunshine. Franken was six foot two and rail thin, no doubt due to the energetic excitement that punctuated his every move. He had the salesman's touch of making one feel he was the most important person in the world, and after he checked Easton and Santee into the posh Beverly Hills Hotel, Franken went to work. He escorted Santee around town for a series of television and radio appearances and arranged for the gab-about-town Hedda Hopper to interview him. He drove the miler to Hollywood movie sets where he met Kathryn Grayson and Howard Keel, two of Hollywood's biggest stars. In the middle of a shoot, Howard spotted

Santee and called 'Cut!' The actor shot towards Santee and told him what a big fan he was. There was even a brief encounter with Marilyn Monroe. Franken appeared to know everybody, and Santee was dazzled by the attention and glamour of it all. 'I was all eyes,' he later said. Afterwards, when Santee went out to train, Franken arranged for the press to watch, fuelling even more excitement for the following day's race. Santee was the promoter's dream. To the reporters he declared his confidence in winning – and yes, the mile barrier was decidedly a possibility as well.

Over the past week Santee had refined his speed, doing fast quarters instead of long runs in training. He and Easton had already gone over their tactics on a blackboard back in Kansas. The plan was for Santee to hold back for the first two laps, then to take over in the third. Reiff and Johansson wouldn't see him coming. Santee was ready to show what he was made of.

On Friday morning, while Santee went for a walk after his pre-race breakfast of oatmeal, hot tea and honey, Easton read the morning papers back at the hotel. 'Santee Set to Teach Finnish Runner Lesson' predicted one; 'Santee Choice in "Miracle Mile"' said another. The *Los Angeles Herald & Express* published a large cartoon showing Santee racing around a clock with Reiff and Johansson pushing him ahead. The quote read: 'The Kansas Cyclone, Wes Santee, prodded by Reiff and Johansson, could well be the boy to break through the 4 minute barrier!' Easton knew his runner had the confidence and ability to rise to the occasion of the biggest race of his life. Franken had obviously done his job in drumming up interest.

Easton and his athlete arrived at the stadium in the early evening. The race was scheduled for ten minutes after nine o'clock. The Compton Invitational programme, written by Franken, featured the mile event as 'The greatest ever to run on the West Coast. That is not a publicity man's pitch but a statement of fact.' Each of the five milers was briefly profiled: Gaston Reiff, 'one of the world's all-time distance stars'; Denis Johansson, 'he's loaded with class, and is the favorite of many in tonight's chase'; Bob McMillen, 'he is the mystery man in the field'; Russ Bonham, 'the longshot in the class'; and Wes Santee, 'America's greatest four lapper of all-time'.

While Santee prepared for the race, he put all the hype aside. Four hours earlier he'd had some toast and more hot tea and honey. This was his ritual, and before a race he never deviated from it. An hour before the mile, he put on his 'Kansas Olympic Team' sweat-suit top and went outside the stadium to do some light running and stretching. Then he returned to the infield, the crowd of nearly nine thousand preoccupied by the 880-yard relay. There he ran wind sprints, working up a sweat. He finished by running at race speed for the last bit. After that he returned to the locker-room, changed into a dry singlet and shorts, and lay down on the training table for fifteen minutes, hands on his stomach, eyes closed. Fifteen minutes before the race, he rubbed his lips and gums with mentholatim to prevent cotton mouth from nerves. He left the locker-room with a towel draped over his head like a boxer and wearing his specially made Japanese track shoes. Whenever he needed a new pair, he sent an outline of each foot on a piece of paper to a shoemaker he had met while competing in Japan after his freshman year. They were particularly light.

Santee spoke to nobody before the race, not his competitors, not even Easton. They had already worked everything out between them. It was up to Santee now. Only moments before the gun was set to go off, Santee stepped up to the starting line. His one thought was of crushing Johansson. The packed stands were edged up very close to the track, giving the stadium more of an indoor than an outdoor feel. Santee faced straight ahead as he waited for the gun. He was oblivious to the noise around him, but he knew the fans would inspire him during the race. They were the equivalent of another runner breathing down your neck.

Reiff went into an early lead. His best mile time was 4:02.8, but a foot injury had disrupted his normally smooth gait. Still, he finished the first lap in first place, followed within a few yards by Santee, then

Johansson, McMillen, and Bonham. When Santee heard the lap time – 62.7 – he knew it was slow, but his moment to strike had to wait. Reiff continued to set the pace for the field through the second lap, registering a half-mile time of 2:05.2. The crowd sighed, resigned to a slow race. Franken yanked on his hair; he hadn't brought all these mile stars together to run a mediocre race. One official, sitting next to a *Track & Field News* reporter, sighed, 'It's going to be a 4:10.' Santee was equally anxious; the first half-mile was too slow for a record time. He had to do something soon.

In the third lap Johansson sped quickly past Reiff and Santee followed, but as they rounded out of the turn the pace was still not fast enough for him. The crowd continued to groan and boo. Into the back straight, Santee lost his patience. He charged, nearly into a sprint, fuelled by pure emotion. He swept by Johansson before the end of the straight. The Finnish miler couldn't believe it. What was this kid doing going into a sprint fully seven hundred yards from the finish? He had made his move too early. Santee didn't think so. He had to 'go for broke' if he was to have a shot at the four-minute mile.

The crowd loved Wes Santee for his boldness as he opened up a five-yard gap. Johansson increased his tempo, knowing that if Santee put too much distance between them the race was over. Reiff followed suit. By the end of the third lap the Finn had won back a yard from Santee, with the Belgian miler six yards back from the lead. Santee had run an incredible 58.2-second third lap and the scoreboard read an elapsed time of 3:03.5. Cheers erupted from the stands. This might be a fast race after all.

McMillen and Bonham had all but thrown in the towel by this stage. This was a three-man race. Santee continued driving furiously, somehow maintaining his pace to the bewilderment of Johansson. Reiff passed the slowing Finn. By the start of the back straight Santee boasted a lead of fifteen yards over Reiff. Santee's last 440 yards, from the middle of the back stretch in the third lap to the middle of the back stretch in the fourth, was run in a heart-stopping fifty-five seconds. He was tiring, though, and Johansson began to regain ground as Reiff slowed. As the three strode into the bend, the Finn passed Reiff. Santee struggled to maintain pace. It was obvious his legs were giving out, but his lead was too great. He couldn't hear Reiff's or Johansson's breath behind him – a sure sign he was far in the lead. Johansson couldn't catch him. The crowd roared again as Santee approached the tape. Drive to the finish line, he told himself. Don't let up. At last he leaned forward into the tape, breasting it twelve yards ahead of Johansson in 4:02.4, the fastest mile by an American. The crowd chanted his name as he slowed into a walk.

The Finn approached Santee. Easton was already by his side. 'You guys are crazy,' Johansson said, barely able to talk. 'I never had anyone sprint seven hundred yards before the finish.'

Santee smiled and shook his hand, as he often did with his competitors after a race. He could always tell how tired they were by the strength of their handshake. Johansson was exhausted. In a rare display of humility, the young Kansan had to be pulled back on to the track by the meet director for a victory lap, and Santee agreed to do it only after the public address system urged him on. He took the lap barefoot, holding his shoes in his hand to wave at the crowd. They had served him well. Afterwards, he autographed race programmes pushed into his hands by kids pressing against the railings at the bottom of the stands. It was a moment of a lifetime. His immodesty returned when he responded to a reporter about how he ran. 'I didn't think it was so fast,' Santee said. When Easton was asked what he thought of the race, he simply said, 'We're getting closer.' Everyone knew what he was talking about.

News of the race made headlines from Los Angeles to New York to London to Melbourne. Johansson was the first to express how great Santee was, followed by something of an apology: 'He taught me not to pop off so much.' Gaston Reiff predicted that if Santee was to go head to head with Bannister, Santee would win. 'Santee runs the last five or six hundred too fast,' he said. Most reports, however, talked of the mile record. Easton was quoted saying, 'This was the ultimate. We'll wait a while for the next ultimate . . . But if that first half had just been faster . . .' The banner headlines spoke for themselves: 'Santee Sees Magic Mile'; '4-Minute Mile? Santee Vows He'll Run It Faster'; 'Santee Admits Getting Closer to Phantom Four-minute Mile'; and, 'Jet-Propelled Santee Flirts with 4:00 Mile'. If some had yet to hear that Santee was out to break the barrier, they most certainly knew now.

10

Still as they run they look behind,
They hear a voice in every wind,
And snatch a fearful joy.

Thomas Gray,
'Ode on a Distant Prospect of
Eton College'

In the small community of Melbourne's athletes, news of the latest exploits by international milers was traded like good gossip. The local papers carried only the sparest of reports, so those few who subscribed to magazines such as *Track & Field News* and *Athletic Review* were sought-after purveyors of information. Les Perry was one of those who shared his magazines with his friends, including John Landy. Occasionally the two would get together for a lunch of meat pies at a restaurant overlooking the railway station near the water board where Perry worked as a clerical officer. Perry, having already devoured the issues, would give them to Landy to read. It was understood that they would be passed around to Geoff Warren and others. Somehow the dog-eared copies eventually found their way back to Perry.

The recent headlines were startling: 'Oh, That Compton Meet!' and 'Bannister Runs 4:03.6!' topped the most recent issues. The write-ups told of how Bannister and Santee were nearing Haegg's record and were setting their sights on the four-minute mile itself. Landy had to wait out their seasons, despite receiving invitations to compete in the United States and England. Their summer was his winter, and he was in the middle of his studies. This was a great disappointment to track promoters, who were conspiring to bring these three milers together. The closest Landy came to being on the track with them was when one of the theaterettes around town showed a brief segment of a race in the United States or England among the hour-long mix of cartoons, newsreels, and short films. Geoff Warren, with whom Landy had roomed in Portsea, had an inside connection with one of the theatre owners and was alerted whenever there was a new clip of athletics, but they were always a couple of months behind. Although eager to see or hear news of others' runs, Landy felt that their progress was almost inconsequential: he had a course to follow, and he wouldn't let himself be rushed by others. The pursuit of the mile record was about proving how good *he* was, not about a desire to cross the four-minute threshold first. He was running for himself, not national honour.

At the end of his last season, Landy had made it clear he wouldn't be taking much of a rest. 'It won't be any good my dropping training until next spring, if I want to run fast miles [next] December and after,' he told reporter Joe Galli. 'My idea is to carry through this heavy training program right through the winter.' The details of his programme were listed on a sheet of paper tacked to his wardrobe door. His theory of training was a rather simple adaptation of the previous year: he planned on working one and a half times harder. To see that he did, he marked down each session. The listings from the past few months read like a diary of torture.

Between 18 March and 24 May he ran over three hundred miles, primarily endurance runs on roads leading out of Melbourne. Then he began timing his runs, as opposed to the previous year. This way the effort he expended in each session was more stringently defined. On 25, 27 and 30 May he ran seven miles in forty minutes, followed by half an hour of weightlifting to strengthen his upper body; on 1 June he ran six miles in five minutes each, three miles in sixteen minutes, and finished with thirty minutes of weightlifting; on 3 June he alternated 880 yards' 'fast striding' with 880 yards' jogging for a total of eight miles. He spent so much time training in Central Park that he joked that he knew every magpie in the surrounding trees, particularly the ones that 'bombed' him.

Instead of listening to Cerutty's thoughts on what it took to run a 3:53 mile, which his former coach was propagating widely in the athletics press, including advice on how to run 'OVER THE GROUND' and when to abandon racing conditioning to 'go to the hills, the sand track or the bog lands and do steady running up to 10 miles every day', Landy felt convinced that a more intense regime would produce better times than before, regardless of the slow tracks and lack of competition in Australia. In late June 1953, with frost on the ground and the transplanted oak and elm trees having lost their leaves, he stuck to this approach, not giving in to the urge to take a rest. On his long runs along the Dandenong Road, which was the start of the coastal road that linked Melbourne to Sydney, he listened to the rhythmic sound of his footfalls, sinking into a near trance. He knew that come his first race in December, when the nervous energy had expired after the first lap and the momentum from that first lap had carried him only as far as the half-mile point, he would need the conditioning from these training runs to sustain his speed to the very end. In order to run a record time, every mile of the seven he ran that day, and the day after, and the one after that, was necessary.

Although his studies and training limited his social life to time spent mostly with his family, at home or at their South Gippsland property at weekends, planting trees or walking around the farm, Landy didn't see his running as a sacrifice. He liked the discipline it required. He liked the feeling of his body learning to tolerate ever increasing levels of stress. And he was comfortable being alone to test how far he could push himself.

In the third week of that same June, Australian miler Don Macmillan was studying quietly in his London student hostel when someone down the hall shouted, 'Hey, Don, you're wanted on the phone.' It was surprising for him to get a call, so he hurried downstairs. After Helsinki, Macmillan had decided to attend a teaching college in Britain for a year while continuing to run competitively. He would have preferred to be in Australia racing against his good friend Landy, each pushing the other to faster times, as Haegg and Andersson had.

He picked up the phone.

'Roger here,' came a voice. 'Roger Bannister.'

It took Macmillan a moment to register that it really was Roger Bannister on the other end. 'G'day, Roger.'

'Jolly good news about the climbing of Everest, isn't it?'

Strange that he should be calling to talk about the news. 'Yeah, it is, isn't it?'

'Great Empire effort,' Bannister continued.

'I suppose it was.' Macmillan couldn't understand why he had phoned to tell him this. They hadn't spoken in a while. 'Marvellous,' he finally added.

'Did you enjoy the coronation?'

'Oh, yes.'

'How are you running?'

'Not too good at the moment. I have a sore leg. How are you?'

'I'm going very well. What do you think about Wes Santee?' Bannister asked.

News of the American's Compton Invitational win and his proximity to the mile barrier would have been hard to miss. The British papers covered the event, as well as Santee's announcement that he would make another attempt on 27 June. Gundar Haegg had even written to the young Kansan, urging him on in a widely publicised letter. 'I think you can be the first man under four minutes,' the Swede had penned, 'but you must hurry on.' Bannister was cited as the reason to hurry.

'Do you think he could do it?' Macmillan asked.

'I think he might be able to, but I want to beat him to it.' There was a pause. 'Would you be prepared to help me?'

'I'll do what I can, but I'm not very fit.'

'The idea is, we go down to Motspur Park on Saturday morning [27 June]. Wes is running on the same day.' Bannister explained that he could beat Santee to the punch because of the six-hour time difference. It had to be that weekend, though. Norris McWhirter had convinced the director of a schoolboys meet (the Surrey Schools AAA Championship) to include a special invitation mile in their schedule. 'I'd like you to run as far as you can at sixty seconds a lap. Chris Brasher will be there, and he'll drop back and time it so when we're starting the last lap Chris will have been jogging around and he'll be a lap behind us. He'll then be fit to take me around the last lap.'

'All right, I'll do my best. I'll go as far as I can,' Macmillan said. If he could not push Landy to a four-minute mile, it was better to have Bannister, an Empire man, run it than an American, he thought.

'On Saturday morning you'll be picked up in a black car by one of the McWhirter brothers,' Bannister continued, his tone indicating that this was to be kept quiet. 'He'll meet you at the corner of Tottenham Court Road and take you to Motspur Park.'

Macmillan agreed, and they exchanged goodbyes. Bannister had his hare.

Since the 4:03.6 mile highlighting his potential as the first four-minute miler, the pressure to do so had intensified. Obviously he was in good form. He had performed well in a series of races during the early summer and as a result the press hounded him at every turn, asking whether this day would be *the* day. 'It's becoming quite a tyranny,' he chided a reporter. On 23 May at White City stadium he had run a slow race, and a group of fans booed and harassed him for not breaking the barrier, though he easily beat the rest of the field. The next day the newspapers had Bannister 'disappointing a big crowd' and 'scarcely fulfilling the expectations of the 20,000 people present'. On 30 May, when he ran a record-breaking 1:51.9 half-mile through a blustery wind, he barely warranted a mention in the papers. The British public wanted another big achievement –

four-minute-mile big – to match the recent conquest of Everest and the coronation of Queen Elizabeth. Anything less wasn't enough.

'We know the race might not be the way you would wish, but I can organise it,' Norris McWhirter had told him in mid-June after a training session at the Paddington track. This was when the McWhirter twins had begun to put together the Motspur Park race. The clandestine nature and overt pacing of the race were not optimal. Plus, Bannister had torn his left thigh muscle in a quarter-mile race on the same day Santee had run his 4:02.4 in Compton. For a few days afterwards Bannister felt as though he'd been kicked by a horse in the back of his leg, and he was still not confident that it could take the punishment of a fast mile attempt. Nonetheless, Norris urged him onward. 'Santee's going to do it ... And you simply wouldn't want to let him do it.'

Bannister was as swept up as anyone by the exuberance his country was experiencing. Throughout May the country had been able to talk of little else besides the details of Queen Elizabeth's ceremony in Westminster Abbey and the progress of the British expedition on Everest. Himalayan weather reports and procession routes were pored over. On 2 June, Coronation Day, he and his fellow Britons had swelled with a pride they hadn't felt in almost a decade. The celebrations reminded the world of Britain's reputation for grandeur and greatness. That same day, news reached London that a member of the British expedition team, Edmund Hillary, along with Sherpa Tenzing Norgay, had reached the summit of Everest, the rooftop of the world. *The Times* said the achievement matched Sir Francis Drake's circumnavigation of the globe in terms of historical greatness. Historian Richard Holt explained the significance:

It was the manner of this triumph as much as anything else that pleased the British. There was a charming amateurism and eccentricity about the expedition. Umbrellas had been carried up to 13,000 feet. [Expedition leader Colonel] John

Hunt played the part of the cultured, competent, phlegmatic Englishman reading the *Oxford Book of Greek Verse* while organizing supplies and technical support with a minimum of fuss. There was still hope for Britain.

Editorial writers and historians aside, the feeling that had overwhelmed the country on 2 June was best summed up by an English father telling his son that day, 'The British are the best in the world. We are the only ones who could have done it.'

Bannister had closely followed the Everest expedition both in the papers and on the radio. He knew several of its members from his physiology experiments, and he had even compared his progress with the mile that summer as being at 'Camp Six'. With Santee fast approaching the record, it was critical for Bannister to get there first, and to claim the same honour Hillary had when staking the Union Jack on the world's tallest peak. Compared to Landy, Bannister had a greater appreciation of the historical significance of being the first to run under four minutes, and he was not going to let anything stop him.

By the morning of 27 June, everything was organised for the attempt. From London, Norris McWhirter drove Bannister, Macmillan, and steeplechaser Chris Brasher to Motspur Park. Brasher was not a particularly fast mile runner, but he wouldn't have to be, given their pacemaking arrangements. Chris Chataway could not participate because he was studying for his Oxford finals in politics. They arrived at 1.15 p.m., half an hour before the race was due to start. The two official timekeepers the McWhirter twins had arranged were on hand to validate the time – if it was record fast. Norris himself would serve as the third timekeeper. AAA officials Jack Crump and Harold Abrahams were also present. There were few others, apart from the thousand-odd schoolboys in attendance for the meet.

While the schoolboys broke for lunch and the three runners warmed up on the adjacent cricket field, head groundsman

J. McTaggart rolled and then lightly watered the cinders in preparation for the mile race. At 1.50 p.m., with the sky clear, temperature fair, and only a slight breeze blowing into the finishing straight, the three runners lined up at the start, Bannister wearing a new pair of German spikes. His pulled muscle felt completely healed. The 190lb, six-foot-four-inch Macmillan, whose best mile time was 4:08.8, turned to Bannister and said he would try to run a 4:05. Brasher was silent, knowing exactly what he needed to do, and typically enthusiastic to get started.

'Hope for the best,' Bannister said, and the race was on.

As planned, the Australian led from the beginning, Bannister tethered closely behind him. Brasher, who wore thick dark glasses and had an unnatural gait on the best of days, moved purposefully slowly, as his job didn't come until the end of the third lap. Although he looked like 'an amputee getting used to a new limb', as McWhirter described it, his minute-and-a-half laps would keep him fresh for the end. In comparison, Bannister and Macmillan were flying. The Australian proved a superbly even pacemaker for the first two laps, crossing the 220-yard mark in 29.5 seconds, the first 440 in 59.6, the 660 in 1:28.8, and the 880 in 1:59.7. Perfect. Brasher was over half a lap back at the halfway point. Macmillan didn't have the legs to maintain his speed. His thighs burned and his bruised heel shot pain up his leg as he struggled to finish the next 220 at a good clip. When Bannister yelled, 'Wide open, Don!' – meaning full throttle – Macmillan stalled. He was exhausted. Bannister hesitated, costing him a precious second, before shifting past the Australian to finish the third lap in 3:01.8. From trackside, McWhirter called out the time. The schoolboys in attendance chewed quietly on their sandwiches, not sure why these men were running in the middle of their meet.

At the ringing of the bell, Brasher, having run only two laps, was in position to bring Bannister around the last 440 yards. Over his shoulder Brasher yelled 'a stream of expletives' at his friend to hurry. Bannister crossed the 1,500-metre mark in 3:44.8 – a time that would have earned him gold in Helsinki. In the last 120 yards he started to 'climb the ladder', as Macmillan described the moment when exhaustion took over and the head tilted up, the knees lifted, and the arms swung higher and higher to get every inch out of the stride. Brasher shouted back again, 'Come on, Roger!' Bannister fought mightily to the tape, but it was not fast enough. He clocked a 4:02. The thousand schoolboys erupted in cheers, more from believing that Bannister had caught Brasher in the last straight to win than from the fact that the third fastest mile in history had just been run.

Although an incredible time had been clocked, the mood was sombre afterwards. It had taken a lot to arrange this event, yet it had been for nothing. There was now a sense of helplessness in having to wait to hear about Santee's performance in six hours' time. In the locker-room, Bannister thanked Brasher and Macmillan for their help, despite the failed attempt. Everyone had given of their best.

'Only five yards outside the world record,' Bannister mused, though he was still fourteen or fifteen yards away from the four-minute mile, a distance that seemed much longer than the few strides it would take him to span it.

The three quickly changed and headed to the cars. Macmillan was off to Wimbledon, courtesy of tickets provided by the McWhirters. Bannister and Brasher crammed themselves into an Aston Martin driven by Dr John More, ready for a weekend's climbing in North Wales. They would have to wait until after they arrived in Snowdonia to learn that Wes Santee had also failed in his bid. They heard from McWhirter by telephone that he had run 4:07.6 in Dayton. That night, as Bannister rested in a hay loft before the following day's climbing, he knew he wouldn't be able to summon the energy to make another attempt against the clock that summer. He desperately hoped that Santee wouldn't either. Regardless of his competitors, however, Bannister was concerned about what it would take for him to shave two more seconds off his time, considering how much he had improved, the sacrifices involved, and the limited time he had left in his running career.

'Maybe I could run a four-minute mile behind one of my father's ranch horses,' Santee replied when asked what he thought of the Motspur Park paced race, 'if that's what you want.'

By the time Santee reached Europe on 1 July for a summer tour sponsored by the AAU, there was a groundswell of reaction to Bannister's 4:02. Some called the race 'fixed' and 'unsporting'. Jesse Abramson in the *New York Herald Tribune* opined, 'The world obviously would like to see a 4:00 mile, but let's keep it kosher in a regularly fixed race.' Many in the British press felt the same: the *Daily Mail* declared the race not 'bona fide', and the *Daily Mirror* called the miler a 'clock-runner' who was 'brilliant at running against that rhythmically moving second hand on the clock face, but has little relish for the cut-and-thrust of flying spikes and jolting elbows'. Furthermore, British amateur officials were considering whether or not the record time should be ratified. Given the AAU's stance on paced races, Wes Santee thought the barrier should fall in a real race – preferably one won by him.

His European trip was supposed to provide the opportunity. The fast tracks and top-class competition had many thinking that during his travels Santee would 'beat the rest of the world to the Mount Everest of trackdom', as Abramson wrote in the same article in which he derided Bannister. The previous month had brought many things to Santee – little rest, a lot of travel, bad food, disgruntled track officials, meagre prizes, and day after day of racing – but not a mile record. The tour started in Finland where Santee lost a 1,500m race to the hometown boy Denis Johansson. Afterwards Johansson took Santee to a sauna where it was so hot that the Kansan had to use his towel as a mask through which to breathe before the Finn led him unsuspectingly into a pool of ice-cold water. And that was the peak of hospitality shown to Santee during his trip.

After a grinding schedule of races across Finland, he and his AAU team-mates, including close friend Mal Whitfield, flew to Sweden where Santee managed to break the American 1,500m record. Two days later he was entered in a 800m event, which he also won, before flying to continental Europe for more races. In total, his two-month tour schedule had him running in twenty-two races. Santee was either at the track or in transit the entire time he was away. He missed Coach Easton, and he particularly missed Danna, to whom he had given his fraternity pin to in a sure prelude to a marriage proposal. In his suitcase he had packed an eight-by-ten-inch photograph of her. He removed it at each hotel and stared at it whenever he wrote to her, which was almost every day. At one point during the tour he wanted to cut short his trip and go back to Kansas to be with her, but AAU officials demanded that he stay.

In Berlin on 3 August, Santee decided he was finished with being treated like a one-man dog-and-pony show. For weeks he had packed stadiums with tens of thousands of fans. Meanwhile, amateur officials in each country (who worked closely with the track promoters selling tickets) were providing him and his American team-mates with spartan meals. If they wanted dessert or a second cup of coffee, they had to pay. Expense money was almost non-existent, and if one of them didn't perform to the expected standard, reprimands were handed out. When Santee came first in a race, a common occurrence, he was given a plaque, mechanical pencil, or inexpensive watch for a prize. What he should have been doing was conserving his strength for one or two good races such as the mile at the British Games a few days later, but instead he was working day in and day out for no reward. 'It was work,' he later said. Having laboured many long hours for his father on the ranch without any pay, he knew when someone was taking advantage of him.

A few days earlier he had approached a German official to ask if he could pool several of his prizes for an Agfa camera. At the time it was the Rolls-Royce of cameras, and before Santee had left Kansas Easton had even suggested he should try to get his hands on one when he was in Europe. The official told Santee that he would take care of it. On the morning of 3 August, Santee called the official at his house to ask if he had arranged for the camera. The official put Santee off, saying he was looking into the matter. At lunch Santee handed his unopened prizes to the official and asked for his camera. The official said the camera was more expensive than the amateur rules allowed, and 'they could not consider any such demands'. This set Santee off. After all the money they had made on him, and the sacrifice involved on his part, they could at least provide him with a camera.

Santee pounded his fist on the table and yelled, 'You're a damn liar!'

The official insisted there was nothing he could do, but, regardless, 'We want you to stay on and run another race.'

'To hell with you,' Santee replied. 'I'm not staying here.' He then stormed from the room, slamming the door behind him. He was finished with that kind of treatment.

He left West Germany immediately for his next race in Finland. The rest of the team followed him there after they'd finished competing. Little was said of the affair, but everyone knew Santee would have to pay for his outburst one way or another. Amateur officials did not suffer these kind of actions from their athletes.

From Finland, Santee went to London for the British Games, hoping to compete against Roger Bannister. However, on his arrival he learned that Bannister was busy with his medical exams and had backed out of the international mile event. Still, the race was a big affair: they paraded Gundar Haegg, Sydney Wooderson and Paavo Nurmi around the track before the event. With Johansson and several of Britain's best middle-distance men in the event, including Chris Chataway, Bill Nankeville, and Gordon Pirie, this would have been a prime chance for Santee to get the competition he needed for a record attempt, but he was simply exhausted from the travelling and the constant competition. By the fourth lap, when most expected the American to explode to the finish line, he had nothing left to give. Pirie sprinted past him in the back straight to win by three yards in 4:06.8. 'I've run seven races – one every other day,' Santee told reporters afterwards. 'I'm more than a bit tired.'

When he returned to the United States, news of his defeat caused the pundits to declare that at the age of 21 Santee risked burning out before he reached his prime if he continued to compete so often. Santee discounted the claims, but privately he knew he wasn't being given the support necessary to break the mile barrier. Like his counterparts, he needed the ability to enlist pacemakers, he needed events featuring top-class competition, and most of all he needed enough breathing room beforehand to prepare and focus properly. But he had ignited a firestorm with his confrontation with amateur officials in Berlin, so his chances of receiving this support were now almost non-existent. Plus, his cross-country season loomed. Nonetheless, he felt that the four-minute mile was his to run first.

11

We must wake up to the fact that athletics is not, nor ever can be perfected; there will always be more to learn.

Arthur 'Greatheart' Newton,
legendary long-distance runner (1949)

Wearing jackets and ties, Roger Bannister and Norris McWhirter exited the Tube at Holborn in central London on their way home from a dinner party. It was eleven o'clock and the station was nearly deserted as they made their way through the labyrinthine tunnels towards the escalators. At their base, they decided to attempt to run up the one that led down. Holborn was one of the city's deepest underground stations, and it would require some effort to reach the top. Both knew the attempt was childish, but they found it no less compelling – nothing wrong with a little harmless fun. Halfway up, the attempt became less simple than either had imagined. It was a long way, and to ease off only an instant meant having to double the effort required. They couldn't let up now. To those few ascending on the proper escalator, they looked like lunatics. Still they continued to drive up the steps, urged on by the embarrassment they would suffer at being shot back down to the bottom. At the top, winded and legs burning, they revelled in their triumph.

Neither young man drew much of a lesson from the late-evening escapade, but if Bannister was ever to achieve the four-minute mile he knew he couldn't let up with his training. It was unlikely Landy or Santee would. But by September 1953, Bannister needed a change from pursuing this uphill battle on his own. He had started his final year at St Mary's, and was to take his medical board exams the following summer. He would have to hang up his spikes in August 1954 after the Empire Games in Vancouver and the European Games in Berne. Bannister wanted to finish his running career on a high by winning these two championships and breaking the mile barrier. For the first time, though, he wasn't sure he could do it alone.

The previous season had ended badly. On his return from his North Wales hiking trip he'd suffered a terrible thrashing by the press for the secret Motspur Park attempt, followed by an embarrassing announcement by the British Amateur Athletic Board rejecting his 4:02 mile at Motspur Park as a British record:

> [The Board] has been compelled to take this action because it does not consider the event was a *bona fide* competition according to the rules. The Board wishes it to be known that whilst appreciating the public enthusiasm for record performances, and the natural and commendable desire of athletes to accomplish them, it does not regard individual record attempts as in the best interest of athletics as a whole.

The decision was based on the fact that the two other runners had failed to complete the race and that the event was not advertised prior to its being held. Bannister accepted this decision without appeal, though the rebuke from amateur officials stung. In hindsight, he knew it was wrong to have attempted the record in conditions so far outside those of a normal race, but at the time there had seemed to be no other choice if he was to be the first to break the mile record.

In the AAA Championship mile Bannister ran a 4:05.2 but was overshadowed by Gordon Pirie, who broke the world record in the six-mile race. Pirie was unabashed about training for hours each day. Many considered him the future ideal of British athletics, though it was rumoured that he was almost a professional given that his employers at a paint sales company allowed him as much time off as he needed to train and race – his name association with the company presumably the benefit of their arrangement. In August, Bannister managed to participate in a world record four-mile relay event and ran his best half-mile time, but Pirie was the man of the hour, particularly after beating Santee at the British Games.

Bannister appreciated having the limelight shift to another runner, but he had to wonder if Pirie, who boasted that the mile barrier was in his sights, might be more fit to do it. After all, Joe Binks, a long-time Bannister supporter, declared after the British Games that 'Pirie is the most extraordinary runner the world has known, bearing in mind his amazing type of training and the distances over which he seems to be able to beat records.'

For seven years Bannister had followed his own advice and methodically improved his times. He hadn't relied on others to help him train or to sustain his level of commitment. Although his list of race championships and record times was pages long, he found himself coming up short when it came to his greatest athletic ambitions. Now, in the autumn of 1953, he took his first step away from his press-decreed 'lone wolf' approach by running with Chris Brasher at the Paddington track during lunchtime.

Born in British Guinea into a family at the top end of the social ladder, Brasher had been educated at the esteemed Rugby public school and at St John's College, Cambridge. He took nothing in life for granted, however, and his achievements were won with a fierce drive, great energy, and a never-say-die attitude. When he discovered he did not have the natural talent to be a miler (he was asthmatic and he wheezed around the track), he took to the steeplechase, which required more strength and determination than anything else. He intended to make it to the 1956 Olympics. Outside athletics, Brasher was an avid climber and just missed the 1953 British expedition to Everest. What he lacked in technical skills as a climber he made up for by demanding the impossible from himself, and from others. 'Enthusiasm was the feature you noticed about him right away,' said one friend. 'He was a thrusting sort of person ... You had the feeling that he wanted to master what he was doing and literally forced himself to do it,' said another. By the autumn of 1953, Brasher was balancing his athletics and climbing while working for Mobil Oil in a management trainee programme.

For the past year Brasher had trained with the Austrian Franz Stampfl, a man of equal immoderation who coached athletes in the grounds of the Duke of York's Barracks in Chelsea on Friday evenings and in Battersea Park over the weekend. Stampfl had given Brasher a training schedule, and part of it he fulfilled by running with Bannister at the Paddington track. On occasion, Chris Chataway also joined them. He had lately started training with the Austrian coach as well.

Like Brasher, Chataway wasn't the type one would immediately identify as a runner. His stout build was better suited to rugby than fast miles, and he enjoyed a less than healthy admiration for smoking and drinking, particularly after a good hard race. Furthermore, he never seemed to like running very much, particularly when it came to hard training, which he abhorred. Of the regimes endured by the likes of Landy and Zatopek, he said, 'For me and many others, it is simply more than we could stand.' That said, Chataway had always excelled at running, loving the thrill of competition. At 18 he'd clocked a 4:27.2 mile; in 1950, while fulfilling his National Service as an officer cadet, he set an inter-Services record with a 4:15.6 mile; and at the 1952 Olympics he might have won the 5,000m event (his best distance) had he not fallen at the last turn. It was the mettle he showed by finishing the race that distinguished him as a runner. Norris McWhirter·wrote that he was 'a man of spirit – the right spirit'.

Two years younger than Bannister, Chataway was the eldest of four children whose father was slowly dying from angina. He had graduated from Oxford that summer and had since taken a job as an under brewer with Guinness. He had all but given up on running in order to earn a living when Stampfl got hold of him. 'He invested with magic this whole painful business of trying to run fast,' said Chataway of his new coach. 'He made you feel that this would be the most wonderful thing. It would put you along with Michelangelo, Leonardo da Vinci, if you could do it, and he was quite convinced you *could* do it.'

After a few weeks of running with Bannister, Brasher and Chataway convinced their friend to meet with Stampfl. 'Come and join us, because it's fun,' they said at first. Bannister resisted. It had been a long time since he had taken a coach (or 'rubber' as they were called, from Victorian times when masseurs used to be the ones who gave advice). Training for distance events was about getting the best out of oneself by making minor adjustments in how much to push the body. How could a coach read this better than the athlete himself? Although Bannister was finding training with others helpful and he liked the companionship, this was taking it too far. But surely Stampfl could help, Brasher and Chataway pressed, just as he had them. Brasher was most insistent. He believed taking a coach was essential. 'It is absolutely necessary to have some-one to whom you can turn, who is entirely honest with you,' he said. 'Who you know will not give spurious advice . . . it wasn't so much how to lift my arms or legs up, but when I felt that I had had it, he came on, reassured, showed me the goals ahead . . . I don't think anyone can be so self-sufficient that they don't feel the need for somebody else.'

For a very long time Bannister had admittedly followed a solitary path, one that did not allow him the comfort or insight of others. But his failure to break the mile record the previous season had finally brought him to the point where he decided to open himself up to others. He had come as far as he could on his own. In October, after a day at the hospital, he went to meet Stampfl at the Duke of York's Barracks to listen to what he had to say. Chataway and Brasher were with him. The training ground was just off Sloane Square, an upmarket area in south west London. Adjacent to the barracks housing Territorial Army soldiers was a cinder track. It was in poor shape and smaller than standard – roughly five laps to a mile. In the early evening the track and a drill hall in the barracks were not used, so Stampfl had arranged with the army to use the facilities to coach athletes. He charged one shilling per session.

When Bannister entered the large hall, Stampfl was leading a group of forty athletes through warm-up exercises, mostly push-ups and callisthenics. His thick Austrian accent echoed throughout the large room as he urged his athletes on. Stampfl was barrel-chested, almost six feet tall, but as he approached them he looked even bigger, his stride strong, features sharp, and eyes alight with power. Despite being in a room full of athletes in sweats and shorts, he wore a Savile Row blazer, corduroy pants, and polished shoes. He looked more like an intellectual (albeit a sizeable one) than a coach.

Born in Vienna, Austria, in 1913, Stampfl was the son of an Austrian general and had studied writing and painting in his native city. A talented skier and javelin thrower, sport had always been part of his life; he was good enough at the javelin to participate in the 1932 Olympics. In 1936, sensing the inevitable rise of Adolf Hitler, he moved to England to study at Cambridge University. Two years later, when Hitler marched into Austria, the British government demanded he leave the country unless he showed a unique, necessary skill. Having taught skiing back in his homeland, Stampfl pitched AAA officials to coach their athletes in the latest training methods. His overpowering presence won him a job in Northern Ireland. When Britain declared war on Germany, Stampfl returned to join up with the RAF but was interned immediately as an 'enemy alien'. He went on hunger strike to protest against his confinement.

Early one July morning in 1940 he was shipped to Australia on the liner ship *Arandora Star* with a host of other prisoners of war. In the middle of the North Sea, a German U-boat torpedoed the ship. Explosions ripped through the *Arandora Star*, and within thirty minutes, amid screams of fear, the ship flooded with water and eventually sank to the bottom of the Atlantic. To survive, Stampfl forced a steel plate aside to get to the surface of the ship and then jumped into the cold, oil-slicked sea. For eight hours he swam, warding off shock from the cold and struggling to keep his head above the water, before a rescue boat sighted him. Hundreds died in the disaster, but those who survived were interned and shipped once again to Australia. There, Stampfl was sent to an internment camp in Hay, and to ease the desperation plaguing the prisoners he organised athletics, boxing, wrestling, and football matches. 'It was not just a job for me,' he said. 'It was an inner desire to survive and remain sane for myself and my friends in camp.'

When the war ended, Stampfl married an Australian woman he'd met in Melbourne and moved back to London. Although he had suffered terribly over the previous years and continued to have trouble sleeping under linen or far from an open window because of his long confinement, he still admired the English, particularly their love for amateur sport, and he felt their athletes could use his help. He reconnected with amateur officials and arranged for a number of coaching posts, including part-time ones at Cambridge and Oxford University. Still he was not asked to aid the British Olympic team in 1952 – evidence that amateur officials never brought him fully into their fold because he was an outsider. Instead he assisted the Pakistani team.

Coaching was not a well-paid profession, and on occasion Stampfl needed to work in a sports shop for additional income, but he loved helping athletes, whether they were talented or otherwise. By the autumn of 1953 he was training athletes in everything from field events (including javelin, hammer and discus) to distance running. Although he knew a great deal about interval methods and racing techniques, his most valuable insights came from an understanding of what it took to get the most out of an athlete. His experiences during the war, many too terrible to recall, had taught him a lot about will power. In his opinion, the best coaches had 'the ability to make a man go beyond the point at which he thinks he is going to die'. Anything short of this neglected to use fully an athlete's potential.

Stampfl was unlike anyone Bannister had ever met. Aware in part of his history, the miler sensed this coach truly knew of courage and determination. They were not long into a conversation when Stampfl said quite simply, 'You have to train harder.' When Bannister said he had medical school to think about, Stampfl replied, 'Do both.' In his opinion, nothing was impossible. An athlete was restricted only by what he thought he was unable to do. The four-minute mile? Easy. One could run a 3:52 or faster if one truly wanted to. It was not about spending endless hours training – an option not available to Bannister given his commitments to medical school – rather the quality of the effort.

The way Stampfl spoke, his certainty and passion, fascinated Bannister. By the meeting's end Bannister had agreed to come the following Friday to run. No other commitment was made.

One September night, at 2 a.m., John Landy was running alone along the Dandenong Road. The sodium vapour lights above the road were nearly lost in the fog and they cast an eerie orange glow onto the pavement. Landy was ascending a straight uphill stretch on the road when he saw a pair of headlights coming towards him. The car was swerving left and right, the driver obviously drunk. Landy slowed a little and waited for the car to pass when suddenly it stopped a few feet ahead of him. Although Landy made a habit of running this road, he understood that most people would be suspicious seeing someone there in the middle of the night. Apparently, this driver was one of them. He rolled down the window, and Landy stepped up to the side of the car.

'Who do you think you are, mate?' the inebriated driver asked. 'Bloody Landy?'

Better than admit he was indeed, the miler headed off down the road. Although not every Australian could recognise him, they had most certainly heard of him. Most of the time the reports spoke of his rigorous training. 'While you were at the pictures, or square dancing, last Saturday night,' wrote Harry Hopman in Melbourne's *Herald*, 'John Landy was doing a 10-mile training run.' Word was that the miler had missed only two training sessions since the previous May. Few had any idea of the nature of these sessions, and only those closest to Landy would have believed them had they known.

Daily from 21 July to 30 September, Landy averaged ten 600-yard fast runs at roughly sixty-six-second quarter-mile pace. In between each, he jogged 600 yards. Since he was studying for his final exams in October and November, he decided to train double his normal session on alternate days. On the off-days he jogged at a five- to six-minute-a-mile pace for half an hour, leaving him more time to study. On the hard days in October he ran twenty 600-yard fast laps with a jog in between each (approximately fourteen miles a night). Every other day in November, having measured out a quarter-mile grass lap on the inside of the Central Park gravel path, he ran twenty 440-yard laps at sixty-two-second pace, further developing his stamina. Night after night he pushed himself a little bit harder. If his body was a rubber band, he was stretching it just to the point before it snapped. Sometimes he even amazed himself with what he put himself through in a session.

Throughout this training he received letters from Cerutty advising him on how he should train. Landy refused to answer, let alone listen to his former coach's advice. The outburst the previous year had completely severed their relationship, but still Cerutty wouldn't let it go. He showed up at Central Park, running behind the miler as he trained, shouting that he was an 'impostor' and didn't have the 'killer instinct' to go anywhere. Landy laughed off the remarks and sped away. Cerutty was having difficulties. His marriage was deteriorating and his Stotans were leaving him one by one, many because of his behaviour at the Olympics and his attitude towards Landy. Still, Cerutty hoped his former Stotan would claim the mile record. At the start of the new season, Cerutty wrote in his diary that his coaching method would be in great demand if Landy succeeded.

Landy's former coach wasn't the only one with expectations of him. Before his first race on 21 November, the headlines cried out 'Landy Back for Big Mile Series' and 'Crack Miler Resumes at Olympic Park'. In Landy's mind, this race was only an early-season tune-up run, and he had repeatedly to deny claims that he was gunning for the 'magic mile'. Regardless, when he ran a 4:09.2, over seven seconds faster than his first race the previous year, the public smelled the blood of a four-minute mile. Of these expectations Landy remarked, 'The only thing of which I am certain is that I have a greater capacity for punishment this season.' A few days later he received a call from Ken Moses at the *Argus* informing him that he had been selected as a 1953 winner of the Helms Trophy, an award given to the best athlete from each of the six continents (not including Antarctica). Of the honour, also awarded that year to Gordon Pirie of Europe and Mal Whitfield of North America, Landy said, 'Gee, is that true? That's great news,' before quickly escaping for a training session. The constant attention, acclaim or not, was beginning to get to him.

After the completion of his finals and two more tune-ups at Olympic Park, Landy was ready to make his season's first fast run. He was in self-described 'top condition', and it was exactly one year ago to the day that he had surprised the world with his first spectacular mile. News of his expected challenge to the four-minute barrier reached Bannister with the *Athletics World* headline 'Landy's "D" Day', and Santee with a *Track & Field News* report: 'Landy has the best chance of all men today, because he is not dependent on pacemaking. He makes his own, which gives John an advantage over US, British and European milers.'

When he arrived at Olympic Park on 12 December, it was a different world to the previous year. The Prime Minister of Australia was in attendance, and all that week the papers had drum-rolled the event. The *Age* published a cartoon with Landy racing towards the finish while carrying on his back a man with the face of a clock who was shouting '4 Min Mile – Faster!' The immense pressure was palpable, and Landy knew that if he felt too tense he wouldn't run well. He had trained for this day, though, and he understood that he had the speed, as long as he didn't force it.

At 3 p.m., Landy lined up with three other runners. As he looked out at the crowd and then down at the track, he was obviously edgy to those who knew him. But with the limited field and the track in perfect condition (the inside lane had been specially reserved for the race), he still had a good shot.

From the start, Landy raced into the lead. After just two hundred yards it was clear he was out for the record. John Marks tried to push him through the first half-mile, hanging as near as he could to Landy's shoulders as the 'Meteor Miler' clocked a 58.2-second first lap and followed that up with a 60.4. At this point Marks dropped out of the race, unable to continue, and Les Perry then struggled through the next lap behind Landy, doing what he could to force competition on him. But it was no use. Landy might as well have been in the race alone. In his mind, he was. The clock was his only competition.

Perry stumbled off the track at the three-quarter mark. The bell rang at 3:00.2. Having heard the time, Landy thought he could at least beat Haegg's world record of 4:01.4. It was in the last lap that his hard training would bear fruit. The crowd was on its feet, clapping loudly. Landy felt pulled along.

Those unofficially clocking him – and there were quite a few who had brought their own watches to the meet – took his split time at the end of the first furlong of the last lap. He had run it in 29.2 seconds, which meant that he needed only to run the last 220 yards in less than 30.6 seconds to break the four-minute mile, and if not that, less than thirty-two seconds to break the world record. Landy continued to run well, maintaining his pace through the back straight and into the last turn, but when he came into the straight it suddenly felt as though the finish line was miles away. A cruel gust of wind seemed to stop him flat, though his legs kept moving. The wind ruined the rhythm of his stride, making it uneven. Five yards from the tape he slowed noticeably, and when he crossed the line he had to lean against a Victorian AAA official to keep from falling. His time was 4:02, only one-tenth of a second faster than his best mile last year, despite his increased training. His last furlong was run in a slow 32.6 seconds.

Landy shook hands with the Prime Minister and smiled for a few photographs, then retreated to the locker-room where he was physically sick. But Landy quickly came back out to speak with the reporters, his frustration clear in his words:

> No one outside of sport can imagine the grind of years of continuous training. I feel I could go on for 10 years, but I don't think it's worth it. Frankly, I think the four-minute mile is beyond my capabilities. Two seconds may not sound much, but to me it's like trying to break through a brick wall. Someone may achieve the four-minute mile the world is wanting so desperately, but I don't think I can.

No doubt some of this statement was made to reduce the amount of pressure on him. Privately, Landy felt he could still lower his time in subsequent races. He had finished his exams only two weeks before, and with some more race preparation he was sure he could run faster.

The next day Landy left for the bush in Tallarook, an area sixty miles north-east of Melbourne, to forget about running for a while. He and several others devoted to butterfly collecting were interested to find a Stencilled Hairstreak (*Jalmenus ictinus*), a butterfly that had not been captured in Victoria for over half a century (they had a museum record of its presence in Tallarook). Landy savoured these trips, net in hand, spying for a particular wing pattern and colour. It was a solitary, fulfilling pursuit, one that running had taken him away from more and more.

When reporters asked him about his hobby, he was spare with his answers. Their stories usually characterised him as running hell-bent through the trees swinging a net. The reality of collecting butterflies was that the process was much more slow and deliberate, and it was his passion, separate from running. He preferred to keep it private. Landy rarely spoke about his hobby with his friends in athletics either. The most Les Perry knew of his interest was when Landy came into his room once to find a butterfly framed in a glass case. Perry had served in New Guinea during the Second World War and had brought back the butterfly because he thought it beautiful. Amazingly as far as Perry was concerned, Landy immediately identified its taxonomical classification. The discovery of a Stencilled Hairstreak, with its dark brown wings with a patch of metallic blue in the middle, was a triumph that gave Landy, as he later said, 'equal pleasure as running 4:02 for the mile'.

A blanket of snow lay over the ground and hung heavy on trees throughout Mount Oread at the University of Kansas. The campus was quiet; most students had not yet returned after the winter break, and only a few footprints disturbed the snow-laden paths threading through the campus. On the path leading to Memorial Stadium, the falling white flakes were just beginning to cover the marks left there by Santee and his coach. From the stadium, there was the muffled sound of a fog horn.

Underneath the concrete stadium stands, in a half-lit corridor only a few feet wide, the miler burst down the home straight. He ran at full speed on a dirt track that was twelve laps to a mile and which banked around the corners. The corridor was cold and dank with condensation. Easton timed his laps in the middle of the straight. When Santee ran past him and disappeared around the corner, heading towards the back stretch on the far side, Easton readied his fog horn. Along the far side, several doors, behind which students lived, opened on to the tracks. If anyone had stayed for the holiday, Santee risked a collision. He was going too fast to react in time.

The horn's cry cut through space, the sound reverberating under the low concrete ceilings. Santee ran unconcerned, feeling strong as he took each stride. One lap to go in his three-quarter-mile trial. He passed Easton at the starting line where the track was four lanes wide. Santee sensed the time was good. Usually he could judge his pace over a quarter-mile within a second of the stopwatch. When he went out of sight around the corner, the horn sounded again, drowning out the patter of his feet on the dirt. Seconds later, he reappeared, sprinting to the finish line. Strong, very strong.

After crossing, he slowed and turned back to Easton, who held out his stopwatch. The miler's face was flush, and the electric heaters placed around the track only made the sweat sear to his skin.

'Man, look at this. You're ready. You're ready,' Easton said. 'If you can run two fifty-eight in this rat hole, you could have walked it on a real track.'

Santee knew he was right. It was early January 1954, two weeks before his four-minute mile attempt during the half-time break in the Pro Bowl, to be held in the Los Angeles Coliseum. He was hot and ready to roll, and Al Franken, who had organised the race for Santee, was expecting great things.

Easton had ratcheted up his training yet again. The goal was for Santee to accustom himself to running a 4:04 to 4:06 mile, so that doing so was more a matter of habit than strenuous effort. The year before, Easton had him regularly at a 4:08 to 4:10 mile. He explained to reporters, 'The process of running a lot of miles between 4:04 and 4:06 will put Wes in the proper mental state for his major efforts outdoors. A great miler has to feel himself capable of cutting two or three seconds off his time, should the necessity arise.' Given the right factors, namely good competition and fine track conditions, Santee would have a shot at four laps in the record time.

Over the past months, in addition to his training with the team, Santee had included numerous extra quarter-mile runs throughout the week. Some days he ran five quarter-miles in fifty-two seconds each. The type of break he took between quarters made these workouts particularly tough, but Wes Santee knew all about hard work. 'This is chicken feed,' he later said of training compared to the back-breaking labour of his youth. 'This background was the difference that I had from all the other athletes in the world at that time.' Instead of slowly jogging a lap before the next fast quarter-mile, Santee finished the quarter, jogged the 110 yards around the curve, sprinted the 110 yards back straight, and then started another fast quarter. 'My break between quarters', Santee observed, 'was no break.' After these he did wind sprints from sideline to sideline on the field, putting to shame any workout by the Jayhawks football team. Other times he ran eight to ten quarters in a session, starting the first two at sixty seconds each, and then increasing the speed for the second two at fifty-eight seconds each, then the fifth at fifty-five seconds. If he had trouble getting down to this latter time, he shortened the distance run, usually to 220 yards, and speeded up. 'This keeps you going harder,' he said. 'Otherwise you can get slower, slower and slower – all your life.'

As the weather had worsened through the autumn and into winter, many of these sessions had been held alone inside the stadium on the makeshift track. This was in stark contrast to Santee's cross-country sessions, which he ran regardless of weather. Lately he had been accompanied by Sarge, a reddish-brown German Shepherd he had befriended, who met him on the track and followed him along the roads leading from the campus.

The pay-off from all this training was obvious. In November 1953 Santee had led his Jayhawk team to victory by placing first in the Big Seven and NCAA cross-country championships. On the last day of the year at the Sugar Bowl in New Orleans he dashed to a 4:04.2 mile, which was amazing not only because the track was soggy from rain, but also because he ran the final lap in a stupefying fifty-five seconds. After the race an Associated Press reporter hit the wires with the following question: 'Wes Santee . . . John Landy . . . Roger Bannister . . . Who is going to be the first to reach the end of the rainbow and run the fabled four-minute mile?'

According to the press, the only person able to catch Wes Santee was Danna Denning, his newly announced fiancée. Their picture together, wearing matching cowboy shirts, was plastered across papers under the headline 'The Girl That Finally Caught Wes'. She had travelled down to New Orleans with him, which made for some uncomfortable arrangements: Santee slept in a room with Easton, Danna with his coach's wife Ada. But it was wonderful to have her watch him race. Danna gave him all the more incentive to do well.

Now, with this fast time trial under his belt, Santee was set for the Pro Bowl run. Just as he was about to leave for Los Angeles, however, Dan Ferris hit him with two major pieces of bad news. First, the AAU ruled him ineligible for the 1954 National Collegiate Athletic Association track championship because Easton had mistakenly included Santee as a member of the 'varsity squad' at the NCAA championship in his freshman year. It was a technicality, as Santee had the right to participate as a member of the University of Kansas 'K-Club'. Easton had been fighting this judgement for the last two and a half years, since it was literally a matter of having ticked the wrong box on the form, but Ferris was not to be swayed, not now. Second, Ferris decided to continue his investigation into Santee's European trip and reports had it that Santee risked losing his amateur status. The investigation had already cost him the Sullivan Award, the prize for the year's best amateur athlete, though no evidence of his misdeeds was presented. Ferris simply explained to reporters 'Something is hanging over [Santee's] head ... This award is based on sportsmanship and character as well as ability.' The situation looked to be getting worse. It was a constant item on the sports pages, equal in coverage to his mile attempts.

Santee and the AAU were heading for a collision. Increasingly, Santee was a threat to their hold on power. Because he sold out meets he attended, particularly with his penchant for publicity and the mile barrier looming ever nearer on the horizon, he had power. The confrontation in Germany had scared AAU officials. Santee might be out of control. Then the *Saturday Evening Post* published a profile of Santee by Bob Hurt headed 'Sure I'll Run the Four-Minute Mile'. In the article Santee was quoted as saying, 'I'd like to run for about ten more years. But I'm not going to run unless I can make it pay. I wouldn't want to waste ten years.' Also, Hurt wrote that Santee was hoping to earn enough 'expenses' from his track meets to buy a farm. Brundage must have read the article and gone ballistic. No amateur under his watch would boast of such a thing. Ferris had approached Santee after the article hit newsstands, but the miler denied saying these things. Regardless, the AAU appeared bent on bringing the miler down, at least by a notch or two.

When Santee arrived in Los Angeles and met Franken, he was weighed down by concerns over the AAU probe. But with some of the best American milers set to race against him, including Charlie Capozzoli and Bob McMillen, he had a great chance at the record, AAU investigation or not. Franken was upbeat. 'I hope we've set it up so you can do it here,' he said.

Early on 17 January, the day of the Pro Bowl, Santee left the Ambassador Hotel to take his morning walk. But when he stepped out on to the grass, his foot sank into six inches of water. It had rained through the night. A few hours later Franken came by to take him to the stadium. He was shaking his head, obviously distraught. 'I'm really sorry, Wes. It hasn't rained like this in five years. The track is flooded.'

As they drove to the Coliseum, the sun finally appeared in the sky, but it was too late. The track was under water and the race was cancelled. Santee was devastated. He was in perfect form. Landy was at the height of his season, and Bannister was sure to run well as soon as he started. Santee's outdoor season didn't begin for several months, and if the AAU had their way his prospects of competing in any more top-flight races were in serious jeopardy. During half-time he ran a few laps around the football field with Capozzoli and McMillen, waving at the packed stands. If only the AAU officials shared in the enthusiasm for what he was trying to accomplish. Some good luck wouldn't have hurt either.

12

Yet that man is happy and poets sing of him who conquers with hand and swift foot and strength.

Pindar, Greek poet, 500 BC

At four o'clock in the afternoon on Thursday, 21 January 1954, a clear, windless summer day in Melbourne, they started to come – first in pairs, then in their dozens, then in their hundreds – to Olympic Park. Men in suits and hats left work early to attend, crowding the trams and streets. Women in seersucker dresses joined their husbands, and schoolchildren their parents. Bars emptied of their patrons, and shopkeepers shuttered their doors to get to the track on time. The whole city looked to be descending on the stadium for the special twilight meet featuring miler John Landy. This was to be the race.

'A Perfect Night for John's Mile' headlined the *Sun*. 'Flat-out Attempt on 4.0 Mile' said the *Age*. Landy was on the front or back page of every city newspaper, taking up inches of column space. Reporters consulted the Weather Bureau and pronounced the season's weather 'hoodoo' no longer a threat to Landy. Dick Crossley, the venerated groundsman at Olympic Park, had personally rolled the track and declared it in perfect condition. As for Landy himself, he felt good to go. Since his 4:02 mile six weeks before, he had run in two mile races and in neither did he make a record attempt. Surely, people felt, he was saving himself for a specially arranged event.

With his university exams completed, he now trained during the day in Central Park. He was doing a lot of speed work on the 440-yard grass path inside the gravel path. At weekends, half-miler Len McRae, who was now teaching at a school outside Melbourne, ran quarters with him. They trained for an hour and a half in the 90° heat, rarely speaking. Landy timed himself, and McRae felt that his friend would have been just as happy to have been training alone. Occasionally, runners who competed in professional sprint races such as the Stawell Gift came by the park to watch Landy run. Their response was generally, 'Why would you train like this?' and 'You're going to kill yourself.' After they left, Landy and McRae used to joke about how much more advanced the professionals were, what with their ridiculous technique of running with their hands out flat to reduce wind resistance. Short of these moments, however, Landy was serious and purposeful in his training. This twilight race was to be his judgement day.

Three days earlier Landy had gone to Gippsland, taking a much-needed break from his training by stalking through the bush for butterflies he had yet to add to his collection. The night before the race he slept for twelve hours, and throughout the big day he relaxed by reading Nehru's *Discovery of India* at his East Malvern home. His only interruptions were calls from reporters and a batch of telegrams delivered to his door, wishing him good luck.

Of his attempt on the mile record, he told the press, 'I'm not a bit worried. It's just a big gamble. It might come off and it might not . . . This four-minute mile business is more than just beating opponents. It is trying to achieve something that nobody else has ever done.' Story after story praised the miler for his intelligence, work ethic, charm and modesty. One reporter described Landy as the 'most retiring world-class performer' he'd had the fortune to meet, yet he also found the miler a good talker with 'boyish laughter' and a 'studious analytical mind'.

By six o'clock the ticket sellers had run out of specially made programmes. The police transmitted an SOS to headquarters, requesting reinforcements to handle the unexpected snarl of traffic.

Over a thousand cars sat bumper to bumper on Batman Avenue, some not having moved in over an hour. More and more people poured into the stadium. Tickets could not be sold fast enough. Lines formed hundreds of yards long behind the booths.

Landy arrived at the stadium near the height of this bedlam with Len McRae and quarter-miler Ian Ormsby. McRae had picked Landy up at his house in his red Singer Six convertible, but because of the traffic they had to park the car on a nearby hill. He was astonished at the mass of people in attendance – ten thousand, maybe twenty. The atmosphere seemed more appropriate for a football match than a track event, which typically drew three or four hundred fans at best. The three athletes forced their way through the crowd, but it looked impossible to get to the front. They worried that they might miss their races.

'How are we going to get in?' McRae asked.

The crowd was becoming rowdy, anxious to get inside.

The three then fixed their eyes on the eight-foot-high wire fence surrounding Olympic Park and, after a brief conversation, decided to scale it. They tossed their gym bags over and climbed the pickets, making sure not to get stuck on the sharp points at the top.

As they cleared the fence, a highly regarded South Yarra doctor, waiting with his son at the back of the line, shouted, 'Look at those louts, getting over the fence and not paying. They're trying to gatecrash.'

'Dad,' the boy said. 'That's John Landy.'

By the time the miler had changed and begun to warm up, the crowd had swelled to such proportions that they knocked down the fence and rushed inside the stadium. Some climbed on top of the tin roof over the grandstand. Others threaded their way through the bushes and tall grass on the surrounding hills until they found a clear vantage point. By race time, a wall of people encircled the track, many standing on the outside lane. At one point, a chicken found its way into the grounds, and a mêlée of men chased it around until one of them caught his dinner. The place was total chaos.

26 July 1952. Helsinki, Finland. Josey Barthel seizes gold in the Olympic 1,500m final. Bannister in fourth place.

The 'human locomotive' Emil Zatopek grimaces his way to another Olympic gold medal.

Percy Cerutty, in typical attire, holding forth on his running theories.

At Portsea, Percy Cerutty times his two fastest milers, Don Macmillan and John Landy.

Landy relaxing at his East Malvern home with a book.

Coach Bill Easton holds the stopwatch for Wes Santee during a time trial.

Santee grins at the finish at the 1952 National Championship in California, earning the right to qualify for the Olympic 1,500m trials.

On a cold winter's afternoon in Lawrence, Kansas, Wes Santee challenges his fraternity brothers in a 13½ mile race.

6 May 1954. Chris
Brasher sets the pace
for Bannister in his
attempt at the four-
minute mile at Iffley
Road, Oxford.

7 May 1954. The
day after Bannister
runs his 3:59.4 mile,
fellow students at St
Mary's Hospital
School in London
celebrate his victory
with him.

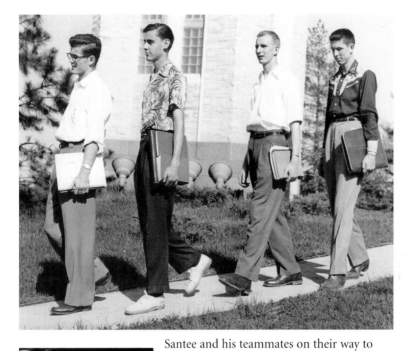

Santee and his teammates on their way to class at the University of Kansas.

Santee and his many fans, young and old alike.

Bannister's coach Franz Stampfl on the left, speaking with famed British journalist John Macadam.

Chris Brasher, Roger Bannister, and Chris Chataway
arrive in Vancouver for the Empire Games. A herd of
journalists are there to greet them.

7 August 1954.
John Landy (pole
position) and
Roger Bannister
(fifth position) at
the starting line
for their great race
at the Empire
Games in
Vancouver,
Canada.

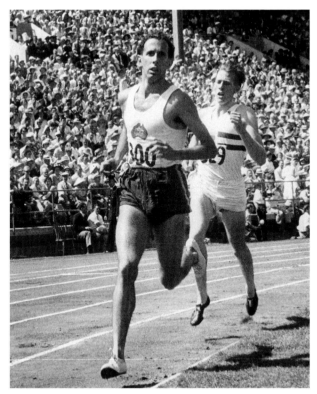

7 August 1954. A packed stadium in Vancouver watches Landy dominate the early stages of the race.

7 August 1954. Bannister approaches the finish line in Vancouver, Landy nowhere in the picture.

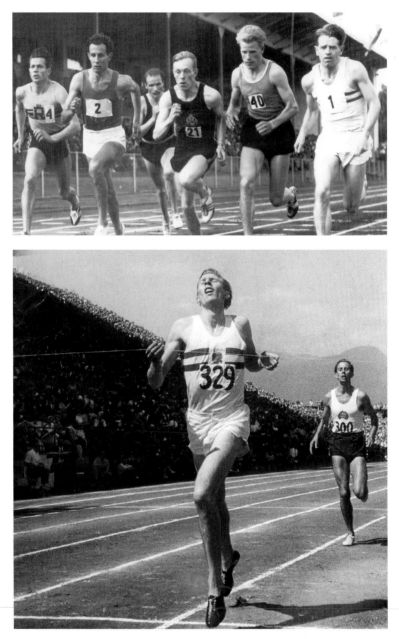

21 June 1954. In Turku, Finland, John Landy bursts away from the starting line in his world mile record bid. Chris Chataway is to the right. In the background, Denis Johansson is the last from the line.

7 August 1954. Roger Bannister wins the Mile of the Century.

When Landy took to the track minutes before the race at 7.30 p.m., the fans cheered wildly. Newsreel cameras spun, and the runners were momentarily blinded by camera flashes. A horsecaller had been brought in to announce the race on radio. More than ever, Landy felt obligated to deliver a record. The pressure was intense. At the starting line, he shook the hands of his competitors and then settled down in a crouch in the third lane from the inside, waiting for the gun. Les Perry and Geoff Warren were by his side, hoping this was the day for their friend. But there was little they could do to help. For a moment, the crowd silenced as twenty thousand pairs of eyes stared at Landy, eager to see him break the barrier for the glory of Australia.

As usual, Landy went into the lead by the first turn and never looked back. Nobody could keep up with him. He had refused pacing before the race, having told the other runners that if he suspected they weren't running to win, he would step off the track. If he broke the mile record, he wanted to be able to say that he'd done it on his own. Landy ran the first lap in fifty-nine seconds and the second in 61.3, but because of the crowd he couldn't hear his times called. He had a good sense of his pace, much like a seasoned golfer knows how far he will hit a ball by the force applied to his swing. Yet it wasn't an exact science. He knew there were conditions – his level of relaxation, wind, temperature, track condition, pressure of competition, and a favourable crowd – that affected his speed. It was impossible to know the difference between running a 59.5- and a 60-second lap, just as the crowd could not tell simply by watching him. The only thing Landy could do was run at 100 per cent effort and hope it was enough. If the other factors aligned, he might break the record.

When the bell for the fourth lap clanged, the timekeepers read 3:02.1 on their watches. Landy was far in the lead. The crowd urged him forward. They were on their feet, their applause deafening. Landy responded, looking to push faster, harder, around the track. Two hundred yards from the finish, however, Landy felt as if someone had pulled the 'master power switch', draining the electricity from his legs. He willed himself on nonetheless, fighting against the fatigue to keep driving to the finish line, trying to refuse the temptation of slowing. But it was difficult. He had run alone from the beginning, unaware of his times and without push of competition.

Not long now. The tape was in sight. He stretched to the finish, hoping it was enough. As he broke through the tape, the spectators threw programmes, handkerchiefs, and hats into the air. They followed with a standing ovation. Landy waited for his time, uncertain if he had broken the record or turned in another 4:02 performance. He rolled his head around, as if working out a kink in his neck. Finally the official time was announced on the loudspeakers: 4:02.4.

Shot through with disappointment but unwilling to show it, he jogged forward, waving at the crowd who continued to clap.

'I thought I had it,' he told the *Sun*'s Jack Dunn.

Later, after he had recovered from the effort, he explained to reporters that he hadn't been able to hear his lap times because of the cheering crowd, but the true problem was otherwise: 'I am convinced I must have someone to grind record figures out of me. I must have someone behind me to push me out.' That was the condition that would make all the difference.

When he returned to East Malvern with McRae and Ormsby, his mother had organised a party for him. Although he had not broken the mile record, none of his friends or family bemoaned the fact. After all, he had won the race. But McRae knew Landy was frustrated with not having brought his time down again. They shared a few beers instead of talking about it, though. Landy was ever reluctant to open up to anyone about his disappointment. That evening Landy suspected that he would never be able to run faster unless he went overseas where the tracks and competition were better.

The next day his run was characterised on the front pages as a

'Magnificent Failure!' The Finnish miler Denis Johansson, who was in attendance in preparation for a race against Landy the following month, had a different viewpoint: 'Landy is magnificent – the greatest mile runner I have seen. On a first-class cinder track with solid opposition he'll run 3:55 for the mile.' Johansson promised to help him see it happen, raising the possibility of Landy travelling to Scandinavia at the end of the Australian season.

On 10 February, Coach Easton and Wes Santee made one last effort to stop the AAU from punishing the miler. Santee's amateur status was at stake, and they had little recourse to overturn any judgement the AAU sent down from their New York offices. So they sent letters to Lloyd Olds, the chairman of the Track and Field Committee. They vehemently denied reports from West Germany that the miler had thrown a chair at the foreign official who'd refused to give Santee the Agfa camera. They also made it clear that Bob Hurt from the *Saturday Evening Post* had misquoted Santee about trying to make money from his running. In his correspondence to Olds, Santee included the two notes he had previously written to Dan Ferris explaining these matters. Neither had stopped the AAU official from continuing the investigation. Easton discounted each of the allegations in a typed letter to Olds, then appealed personally to the AAU official in a handwritten note on the last page that said, 'This boy is a worker and not looking for a soft job. Also, he's had to work his way in college because his Dad is not for higher education, so won't help Wes.'

A week later, Hurt wrote to Ferris saying that he had made inferences rather than directly quoted Santee in his article. Moreover, Ferris had no evidence that Santee had broken any amateur rules in West Germany and had scant corroborating proof that the miler had done anything more than raise his voice at the foreign official and slam his fist on the table. Still, the AAU issued an edict that banned Santee from competing internationally for one year. The only explanation they released to the public was that the miler had broken training while in Europe the previous summer. Bitter at the AAU's decision, Santee declared to reporters:

> The restriction is nothing – absolutely nothing – and Bill and I take it for exactly what it is, a token action to satisfy some higher-ups . . . It's why they imposed the ban, or the reason they gave, that makes us so mad. Breaking training, my foot! I no more broke training than I flew the Atlantic without an airplane.
>
> Why don't they show some courage and nail me, if they have to nail me, for what they're really sore about – the fact I told off some of their foreign officials . . . but instead of saying so they tab me with this 'breaking training' deal. That's what makes me mad, not the restriction. That's a pretty nasty way to go about it, I'd say.

Soon after that, Santee told reporters that he didn't need any competition to push him to run the mile record. He could do it anywhere, track and weather permitting, as long as his legs felt all right. But privately he later admitted, 'For me to drive myself . . . I could do it up to a point, but there was something about competition that raised the bar . . . It's like someone pulls you along. I loved to be behind . . . I judge my pace against his pace, and I'm coming on him. When I catch up and pass, it's great.' With this ban in place, good competition was going to be hard to find.

On Friday, 26 February, Roger Bannister finished his last round in his hospital ward, reviewing charts, checking on blood tests, and enquiring after his patients' well-being. After hanging his half-length white coat in his locker down in the underground pass between the medical school and hospital, he grabbed his gym bag and left St Mary's, heading for Sloane Square. He was to meet with Chataway and Brasher at the Duke of York's Barracks. The weather was no better than it had been during the past two weeks. A bitter wind from the west threatened more heavy showers, the occasional bit of hail, and a deep, pipe-bursting frost at night.

Throughout the winter, regardless of the weather, the three had trained together every week since Bannister had first met Stampfl. They started with callisthenics in the drill hall, working alongside scores of other athletes, including shot-putters and discus and javelin throwers. Stampfl ran them through a series of press-ups, stretching, and resistance exercises, increasing their upper body strength but also fostering a sense of belonging to a much larger group. On occasion, he even had them wrestle one another. After twenty minutes, they took a brief rest and then hit the track.

While training his other athletes, Stampfl kept his eye on the three men as they went through their interval training together, yelling out to them from time to time. 'Do it again! Harder!' and 'Faster! It is only pain!' The programme they had worked out was only a slight variation on what Bannister had been doing on his own. It was simply more regimented. In December 1953 they had commenced with ten quarter-miles in sixty-six seconds, with a two-and-a-half- to three-minute recovery lap in between each one. The aim was to increase the lap speed gradually over several months. They carried their own stopwatches to ensure they were running to pace. They often ran through fog, rain, and cold, and after three months they were down to a sixty-three-second average. Although they exercised throughout the week – doing the same kind of interval work, repetition half-miles, and Fartlek sessions – Friday at the Duke of York's provided 'the focus of the week', Bannister said. That was when they measured their progress to date, strengthened their sense of working together, and soaked up Stampfl's enthusiasm.

The Austrian coach had eased his way into Bannister's confidence slowly, knowing that the miler was uncomfortable taking direction from a coach. Instead of imposing a regimen, Stampfl offered suggestions and guidance. He tried never to push too hard. From the start, he knew that Bannister needed three things if he was to run the four-minute mile: pacemakers to carry him through the first three laps; more strength in his legs; and, finally, complete belief in himself. Over the past three months Stampfl had worked hard to realise these for the miler, motivated not only by a passion for helping an athlete who was impassioned himself ('They've got to love it,' he always said), but also because if Bannister broke the barrier under his guidance, no matter how overt that guidance was, more athletes would come to him for coaching.

Pacemaking was an obvious factor, but the question was how best to arrange it. Stampfl had seen Bannister at the Olympics and had watched him compete in England innumerable times. Like many milers, particularly British milers, he stayed in the pack for most of a race and then delivered a lightning-fast finishing kick at the end. Stampfl knew that Bannister would have trouble running alone through the first three laps at a fast pace. Two pacemakers were necessary, as the Motspur Park race had shown: one to take Bannister through the first half-mile, the second to the three-quarter mark. They had to be able to maintain even sixty-second laps as well as finish the race. This was the only way to comply with amateur rules.

From the beginning, Bannister made it clear that he wanted there to be no possibility of dispute as to whether or not his next attempt was bona fide. The arrangement could not be made on the spur of the moment either. Bannister needed to be able to rely on his pacemakers, to know that they would deliver the goods. Chataway and Brasher had already enlisted the previous November. Their contribution was not entirely selfless: the sessions were good training for their events, the steeplechase (Brasher) and the three miles (Chataway), and they wanted to be part of the potentially historic feat. Stampfl made sure that the team was cohesive and that Chataway and Brasher were ready.

Physically, Bannister was already very close to being capable of the achievement when they met. Stampfl just needed to push him a little further. The systematic, gradual increases of speed over the 440-yard laps promised to better adapt Bannister's body to the stress. It was a plan that appealed to the miler's methodical approach to running. At his level, improvement was difficult to discern. Running with Chataway and Brasher relieved the monotony, and Stampfl encouraged him week after week to keep at it. Ultimately, though, it was up to the miler. As the coach wrote, 'Training is principally an act of faith. The athlete must believe in its efficacy: he must believe that through training he will become fitter and stronger . . . He must believe that through training his performance will improve and continue to improve indefinitely for as long as he continues to train to progressively stiff standards.' Stampfl simply helped to set these standards.

But Stampfl's greatest contribution to Bannister's attempt to make history was his ability to inspire the miler. Although Bannister had the scientific understanding to refute the notion that the mile barrier couldn't be broken, believing you were the one to do it was altogether different. 'The great hurdle was the mental barrier,' Stampfl said. The Austrian's experiences as a coach and survivor of great hardship had proved to him that no obstacle was insurmountable. His unwavering belief in this was infectious. He loved sports and what they symbolised in life as a whole: the ability to overcome. Stampfl invested their efforts with a degree of heroic struggle. In a very real sense, he made running fun again.

After their sessions at the Duke of York's track, Stampfl would join the three for dinner near Sloane Square, where they took refuge from the cold, enjoyed a bottle of wine, and relaxed. He dominated the conversations, which usually started with a discussion of their training and how they were advancing. They spoke of Landy and Santee and how close they were coming to the four-minute mile themselves. But as the dinner progressed, the conversation would shift to politics, art, philosophy, whatever. The Austrian coach read widely and he could take every side of an argument, which made for lively dinners the three runners looked forward to after an exhausting session.

At dinner in the last week of February, aside from potential discussions of a new Tate Gallery exhibition of French impressionist paintings and Churchill's stance on the 'Sovietisation' of a divided Germany, there was much talk about their pursuit of the four-minute mile alone. Week after week they nervously waited for the latest news from the United States and Australia. The McWhirter twins continued to be their main source of information. Ross and Norris drove over to see Bannister when he trained in Paddington. They brought a watch, timed his laps, and then delivered updates of Landy's and Santee's progress over lunch at a nearby café before driving their busy doctor friend back to St Mary's. Only three days earlier the twins had brought news that Landy had run another sub-4:03 mile, the fifth in his career. They knew the kind of training sessions Landy was running, yet the Australian miler was coming up short again and again. Somehow he was stuck, but with reports confirming that Johansson was taking him to Finland to compete on that country's fast tracks, anything was possible. As for Santee, his threat was obvious. He had recently clocked a 4:02.6 mile on an indoor eight-lap-to-a-mile track. A meagre forty-one minutes later, he ran a 1:51.8 half-mile. It was the 'greatest double in American track history', as the latest issue of *Track & Field News* put it, evidence that 'the honor of running the first four-minute mile will be lodged in the USA'. Santee was likely to better his time once the outdoor season began. As the McWhirters reminded Bannister, the mile barrier was becoming 'an almost uninsurable risk' and 'obituary notices' about it were being prepared by newspapers around the world.

Their earliest opportunity to make a bid was at the AAA versus Oxford University match in early May. Bannister understood that, like scaling Everest, his goal would require not just ability and hard work, but also luck, teamwork, and a dose of inspiration. This had not always been so clear to him. When he had invited Edmund Hillary to take his treadmill test a few months after he returned to England from his Everest climb, Bannister discovered that the mountaineer wasn't in the kind of otherworldly shape he had expected. After the tests he had approached Hillary, shaking his head, and exclaimed, 'I don't know how you did it.'

Over the past sixteen months, the mile barrier had withstood the greatest assaults ever. Bannister knew he needed to throw every advantage he had at the 'brick wall' to have a chance of breaking through it. Two seconds had never seemed so long a time, but at least now he was part of a team, one that encouraged him when the training became tedious or his confidence faltered. It was making all the difference.

Most weekend mornings at the University of Kansas passed in a tranquil calm; students sleeping late, streets empty of cars, and shops keeping their doors closed. Every spring, though, the university played host to athletes from around the country for the Kansas Relays. It was a great excuse for a party.

On Saturday morning, 17 April, preparations were in full gear. Since dawn, fraternity and sorority members had been finishing off the construction of their floats for a grand parade. Hammers banged, saws cut, chicken wire was stretched, and paint sloshed, drowning out the songs of Glenn Miller and Johnnie Ray playing on the radio. High-school students, many of whom had never been out of their hometowns, ran about the campus wearing varsity letter sweaters and feeling the rush of college life. Cars jammed the streets around Mount Oread, and hundreds began to line the sidewalks for the big show. From Memorial Stadium, tinny loudspeakers announced the start of the discus event for the decathlon. A few spectators dotted the stands for the morning field events, but this was nothing compared to the thousands that arrived for the 3.05 p.m. start of the Glenn Cunningham Mile. The sun shone brightly, and the Kansas Relays looked to be staged on 'one of those first-day-of-spring, glad-to-be-alive' days.

Wes Santee didn't let the beehive of activities disturb his pre-race ritual. He had his breakfast of oatmeal, hot tea and honey, and then a few hours later walked down to the stadium to warm up. His calm exterior belied the fact that this was a big weekend, perhaps the biggest of his life. He intended to claim the four-minute mile on Saturday, then to marry Danna on Sunday.

Three months to the day had passed since his disappointment at the Pro Bowl, where the only running he did was around the stadium to burn off some nervous energy while the Eastern All-Stars football team led by Paul Brown beat Buddy Parker's Western team 20–9. Since then he had scorched around the tracks week after week, keeping fit while fuelling the four-minute fever with every stunning performance. His team waltzed away with the Big Seven indoor championship for another year, thanks in large part to Santee. At the first outdoor meet of the season in Austin, Texas, Santee arrived wearing a royal blue suit, copper tie, and orange boots. He dazzled with his running that day, too, earning his team a world record in the sprint medley with an anchor half-mile in 1:48.3 and leading the Jayhawks in the distance medley as well as the two- and four-mile relays. Santee was earning so much press that it was almost a chore for him to stay up to date with pasting into his scrapbooks the clippings fans sent him from around the country. A herd of reporters attended his every race, some from local papers but many also from major national publications such as *Time*, *Newsweek*, the *Saturday Evening Post*, the *New York Times*, and the *New York Herald Tribune*. Santee liked their headlines: 'Super Sonic Santee'; 'Santee the Lure – May Hit Magic Number'; 'Mile King in Relays Here'; 'Santee is Star'. The stories read even better: 'Some night Santee's going to travel around that course like the wind and then he'll not only run the four-minute mile but he'll cut three or four seconds off that goal.'

Despite the flood of prognostication, Santee was yet to have a good chance at the mile record because of his team obligations. At the Kansas Relays, however, Easton had set those obligations aside to give Santee a shot at a fast mile. Throughout his senior year, Easton had treated his athlete almost as an assistant coach. They sat in the stadium stands after a workout, discussing how his younger team-mates were running or who they were competing against in the next meet, and which Jayhawk runner should compete in what event. Together they had decided the team was in a strong enough position to risk Santee competing in the open mile, rather than in his usual four team events.

With Landy heading to Finland and reports that Bannister was preparing for a paced attempt in early May, it was critical that they go for the four-minute mile straight away. Santee was also running out of time because his Marine officer training began in July. He was supposed to have done his twelve weeks of boot camp in his sophomore year, but he'd gone to the Olympics instead. After his junior year, the AAU arranged for another year's reprieve because they wanted him running in Europe. Further delay, however, appeared impossible. It did not help that the AAU had banned him from competing internationally. With that restriction in place and the Marines demanding he report for duty, the Compton Invitational was the best competition he would get for the four-minute mile. Apart from that meet, his home-field advantage at the Kansas Relays was the next best thing.

By two o'clock on Saturday afternoon the parade was over and the floats (bearing themes that included the 'Easton–Wes Express' and 'Joy Through Effort') idled outside Memorial Stadium where over sixteen thousand people had gathered. It was hot and sultry, and the concessions stands quickly sold out of soda, followed by ice, and then cups. Spectators sheltered themselves from the sun with umbrellas and fanned themselves with Kansas Relays programmes that featured a picture of 'The Kansas Flyer – Wes Santee' on the cover. He was the star attraction, and many had filed into the stadium early to get the best seat for the show.

As part of his ritual preparations, an hour before the race, Santee jogged outside the stadium, and then came onto the infield for a few wind sprints. Back in the locker-room he changed, and the trainer rubbed him down. Easton was outside watching the two-mile relay, a race Santee would normally have entered. The two had said everything they needed to say to each other the night before.

'Let's try to break it,' Easton said down at the track after a brief workout. 'Do you have any questions?'

'No,' Santee replied, and they were done.

After nearly two years of planning and dreaming about how to run the mile in less than four minutes, there was no new territory to cover.

Fifteen minutes before race time, Santee taped a four-inch square of cotton dipped in Kramer's analgesic hot rub to the base of his spine. It was believed to stimulate the nerves and stir the legs. Then he left the locker-room with a towel draped over his head. Underneath it his face was a mask of cool determination. Outside, a bank of dark clouds hung in the sky – and then suddenly erupted in a torrent of rain. Umbrellas, used moments before as shields against the sun, were now deflecting pelts of rain, then hail, from a flash storm. Gusts of wind blew across the field. Those exposed ducked for cover. Then, as suddenly as the storm came, it passed. The clouds broke, and the sun returned. Short of a few upended umbrellas, everything was just as it was, except for the track. Puddles covered it, and there were divots in the cinders from the hail.

Santee was stunned. The track was wrecked, and so, it seemed, were his hopes of a fast mile. It was hard not to think that the world was conspiring against him, that nothing was on his side. Then Coach Easton went into action. Hands buried deep in his pockets – a sure sign that he meant business – he called a group of his athletes together and told them they needed to get the track ready for the open mile. With military precision, he organised a crew of freshman athletes to shovel off the water. Then he had one of his boys go over the track twice with a power-driven roller to level it off. Easton also arranged for what amounted to a propane-fuelled flame thrower to further dry out the track.

Jogging off to one side, Santee tried to keep warm as his coach and team-mates did everything they could to give him a shot. The largest crowd in Kansas Relays history waited in silence, holding their collective breath with the hope that enough could be done to make the difference for Santee. As the young Kansas miler looked around him – Easton pointing to one section, then another, guiding his athletes frantically to the areas of the track that needed attention – he felt how much he was supported. Of course, he had made sacrifices in his efforts at the mile record for them, but he now realised what kind of friendships he had earned in the process. Those friends were still working on the surface seconds before the race was to begin.

When Santee moved to the starting line the track was still heavy underfoot, but at least Easton's efforts had given him a chance of a good time. Santee planned on making the best of it. Opposing him in the race was Oklahoma A&M's Bjorr Bogerud, a freshman who had placed third in the Texas Relays; Drake's Ray McConnell, winner of the Drake Relays open mile the previous year; and Oklahoma's Bruce Drummond, a graduate student and defending champion in the Cunningham Mile. None in the small field could challenge Santee, he knew that, and with the crowd already on their feet and shouting his name, he felt charged up. He just needed to stick to the pacing he and Easton had carefully calculated. First lap, fifty-nine seconds. Second lap, sixty seconds. Third lap, sixty-one seconds. Fourth lap, go for it. His strong kick would carry him under the wire. Watching from the stand was his bride-to-be. She had wished him luck before the start of the race and now simply had to hope for the best. She knew how important this day was for Wes. These big races were difficult for her. 'I just can't talk,' she said. 'There's no use trying to be objective, because I can't. I get all tied in knots.'

Just before the gun sounded, Santee drew in a breath and held it. The gun fired, and he burst forward. Bogerud started slightly quicker, but by the end of the first turn Santee had taken the lead. Bogerud tried to catch up, but there was nothing he could do – and he knew it. By the start of the second lap Santee was only half a second off pace. Easton was calling out his times, and despite the cacophony from the stands, Santee heard him. No matter how noisy it was, he always heard him. His ear was tuned in to Easton's voice.

The miler was still uneasy though. The track was soft and wet in patches, and when he drove forward he lacked traction. And there was a strong cross wind. Nonetheless, he continued to push, extending his fifteen-yard lead over the others. The crowd spurred him on. For the second lap he ran a second and a half over pace, and for the half-mile he clocked 2:01.2. It was very good, given the conditions. Better than he'd expected. He began to settle into his stride. To keep his arms relaxed, he kept his index finger on his thumb in each hand, making sure not to make a fist. The crowd shouted 'Go, Wes, go!' when he passed the stands. They knew he was close, too. Into the third lap, Santee was gripped by the desire to run the mile record. To do it this very day in front of Danna and his home crowd.

At the bell, Santee was a hundred yards ahead of Bogerud. His three competitors looked to be running in an altogether different race. But the third lap was slow, much slower than he wanted: 63.3 seconds. The wind and traction might have affected him more than in the two previous laps. It was hard to say what had caused the slowdown – certainly not a lack of desire. He could still do it though. He had run a fifty-five-second final lap in the mile before, and that would give him a 3:59 mile.

Easton yelled from the side of the track, 'Go! Go! Go!' The crowd cheered. 'They want it,' Santee thought to himself. Everyone wanted him to be the one.

The last lap was always the hardest. He stepped up his pace. With 220 yards to go he felt the charge from inside in his chest to keep going. He was fighting against the pain and exertion. He was running with all his heart.

'Go, Wes, go!' boomed the crowd.

His training had prepared him for this finishing burst. He increased his arm action, looking almost to strike the air as one would a punch-bag. His legs followed his arms. His exhalations were heavy. By the last hundred yards he was working on sheer emotion and the enthusiasm of the crowd. The timekeepers waited at the finish line. A mass of athletes on the infield pressed forward at the edge of the track to get a better look. Many held their breath.

Santee took one last stride, driving with his right leg as he broke through the tape, mouth wide. It was a remarkable last lap given the conditions, but not remarkable enough: 58.6 seconds. The official time flashed on the scoreboard: 4:03.1. He had come short again. The brief downpour had stripped him of confidence in his chances, and the competition had not been able to provide the jolt of adrenalin he needed.

After seeing the time, the crowd deflated for a moment before shifting to applause, followed by chanting: 'Santee, Santee, Santee.' The disappointed miler accepted his trophy from Glenn Cunningham, who offered to hold on to it until Santee had finished his distance medley relay. Santee politely declined. He passed the trophy to a policeman, who walked it up to Danna. Had the weather been better, Santee was sure he could have presented her the gift of the four-minute mile instead.

At two o'clock the next afternoon, Easter Sunday, he and Danna were married in a quiet ceremony in Lawrence. Easton and his wife stood in for Santee's parents, who had not been invited. After the ceremony a small party was thrown in their honour at a friend's apartment, then Danna's parents and the newlyweds drove to Kansas City. Santee honeymooned for fewer than twenty-four hours. By Monday afternoon he was back at the track for training. Bets had been made that he wouldn't show; those who doubted his conviction to break the barrier first, lost. Anyway, Easton would not have permitted his missing practice. The *Kansas City Star* was there to report to their readers that 'Wes Santee isn't going to let a little old thing like matrimony disrupt his plans for fast running ... Santee still eyes mile in four minutes.'

13

Care I for the limb, the thews, the stature, bulk, and big assemblance of a man? Give me the *spirit* . . .

Sir John Falstaff in *Henry IV Part 2*

The stopwatch told the whole story. By mid-April 1954, Roger Bannister felt drawn out and spent. After four months of the most difficult training he had experienced in his running career, coupled with the intensity of his last days at St Mary's before taking the medical board's exam, he was in need of a break. Chataway and Brasher needed the same. All three were tired and feeling as though their efforts on the track, no matter how strenuous, had stopped returning gains.

Since December 1953 they had improved their lap times in their typical workout – ten by 440 yards with a two-minute rest interval – from sixty-six seconds to sixty-one. But in the past several weeks they had not been able to get down to the magical sixty-second mark, the point where they could feel confident that the mile barrier was within range. Each attempt brought failure, each failure a sense that they had reached their bodies' limits. Perhaps sixty-one seconds was indeed the best they could do. They tried again and again, but their time never improved. As Chris Brasher said, they were 'bogged down'.

Bannister had always been afraid that by overtraining he would become stale and reach a state where more running brought only worse results, and where he would be overcome by feelings of listlessness. This was how his hero Lovelock had described the condition of staleness. Its cause was unknown. Some thought it entirely physical: the muscles were worn out and overstrained, incapable of taking any more punishment. Others thought it entirely mental: the mind was tired of willing the body to work hard day after day; it could not translate the desire for more speed into action. Whatever the cause, the effects of staleness were very real. An athlete experienced appetite loss and overwhelming physical and mental lethargy. It was almost as if one was living in a kind of waking sleep.

Stampfl didn't believe that overtraining led to staleness. He wrote, 'It is a belief that finds no support in other fields of endeavour. The child learning to write, the pianist who practises for six hours a day, the bricklayer laying bricks – the work of these people does not deteriorate as a result of constant repetition of the same movements.' In his view, staleness resulted from a lack of competition and losing sight of one's objective.

Whatever the reason, the three athletes risked sinking into lethargy if they continued to run sixty-one-second laps in their interval training. The Oxford versus AAA meet was fast approaching and Bannister knew that feeling jaded was no way to approach the four-minute mile. Stampfl advised the three to relax by getting away from training for a few days. Brasher suggested rock climbing. 'I'll get my friend to drive us,' he said confidently. Most coaches would have withered at the suggestion of his athletes taking such a trip, but Stampfl thought it a fine suggestion. Chataway declined the offer, choosing to take his rest in the comforts of London. Soon enough, Bannister was crouched in the luggage space behind the seats of an ex-Le Mans Aston Martin, speeding towards the Scottish highlands. Brasher and his friend Dr More (whom Bannister described simply as a 'risk-taker') shared the driving. Legs wedged against his chest, Bannister listened to the hum of the engine as they drove for ten hours, through the night, to reach Glencoe, a small Scottish town nestled in the hills.

Several times before, Bannister had escaped from running in

order to return to it. He found he needed to breathe different air in order to refresh himself. Throughout the summer and the early autumn of 1950 he had lost a series of races and had grown so tired of travelling and competing that he had begun to think losing was okay. One time, after a meet in Paris, he had decided suddenly to leave the city to go hiking. He'd purchased a pair of boots at a local shop, jotted a note to friends, and taken the earliest train to the countryside. He'd hitch-hiked across the south of France, then into Switzerland and Italy, loving the freedom and the sense of not quite knowing where a driver's destination would be. Some nights he'd spent in fields, others in barns, and many, like the one on Friday, 16 April 1954, on a dark highway trying to catch a few minutes of sleep between stops for petrol. The entire experience was like a shot of adrenalin.

At dawn on Saturday morning, the Aston Martin cut through the Pass of Glencoe. Light began to edge over the horizon, softly at first. Slowly but inexorably, the night lost its hold, and colours spread across the sky. As the sun rose, the thick mist that had settled over the land gave way as well, and the mountains Bannister knew were surrounding them finally appeared. With the windows rolled down, he felt the cool, crisp air on his face, and felt renewed.

Then the adventure began. They got into it straight away. Brasher and More were experienced climbers; before they started a particular ascent they would tell Bannister, 'We'll go up this first.' That was little solace, as Bannister knew he would have to follow. They were roped together, and the climbs took a fair bit of skill. On occasion, Brasher helped Bannister up with the rope, but the miler was strong and limber enough to handle most of the faces himself. It was stressful, muscle-numbing activity, requiring the kind of jerking and pulling his body wasn't used to handling. A couple of times they ascended routes with mountain streams pouring down on them; water soaked their shirts and spilled out of their trousers, often leaving them frozen to the bone. For three days they climbed, sustained on little more than fishcakes and a few hours of sleep in a local inn while their boots and woollen sweaters dried out. There was little time to talk of record miles, or of anything at all except the next day's route.

On Monday morning Brasher led the ascent up a steep face called Jericho Wall, and slipped. Before he could get a grip, he was falling. He was saved from the twenty-five-foot fall by the belay of his nylon rope, which took most of the speed out of his fall before breaking. Before their luck truly ran out they decided to call it quits, realising that the least they risked was a sprained ankle. Ten hours later they were back in London, uncertain as to whether or not the long, strenuous weekend had left them worse for wear. At least it had taken their minds off running for a while.

After a couple more days' rest from the track, on 22 April the three runners met Stampfl at the Duke of York's. It was time to have another go at reducing their lap times to sixty seconds in their repeat ten by 440 interval regime. They all knew that achieving this would prove their readiness. After warming up, they ran the first 440 in 56.3 seconds. A very good pace. They jogged around the unmarked cinder track in two minutes, then started the next 440, then the next. Bannister ran the tenth lap in exactly the same time in which he had run the first, making the average for the entire session 58.9 seconds. They had knocked two seconds off what had earlier seemed like a wall. It was a moment of exultation after months of training. It almost felt as if they had run the four-minute mile itself. The team was finally ready.

Later they gathered at the Lyons Teashop in Sloane Square. The four men stood out among the host of women who congregated in the simple teashop for a decent cup of tea and a gossip. In the upstairs section, they talked quietly of the race to come. Stampfl drew an oval on a scrap of paper to illustrate his plan.

'You, Chris' – he looked at Brasher – 'should take the first two laps. Fifty-seven or fifty-eight seconds for the first lap, sixty seconds for the second lap. No faster – but no slower, mind you. Can you do that?'

'Yes, I think I can guarantee that,' Brasher replied confidently. His speed had improved dramatically under Stampfl's watch. In his own mind, he had always felt that his coach saw him as the weakest link in their pacing plan. Brasher respected Stampfl so much that he'd felt it necessary to prove him wrong – and he had.

'And you, Chris' – Stampfl turned towards Chataway – 'must take over and complete the third lap also in sixty seconds.'

Chataway nodded.

'And after that it's up to you, Roger,' Stampfl said. 'You're on your own for the last lap.'

It was agreed. The Thursday, 6 May attempt was to go ahead. Bannister had fewer than three weeks to fine-tune his speed for the big day. With Landy competing in Scandinavia as early as May and with Santee looking towards the Compton Invitational in early June – as the McWhirters had made him painfully aware – he knew the race at his Iffley Road track might be his last chance.

On the tarmac of an airport outside Melbourne, John Landy ascended the steps of the four-engine Qantas Constellation that would take him first to Sydney, then by connection to Singapore, and onward to Helsinki. It was 28 April, and he was looking forward to leaving Australia. He could run 4:02 miles in his sleep, but he couldn't seem to improve. Scandinavia promised the best tracks in the world, as well as a release from the weight of expectation. He was excited about the prospect. After reaching the top of the stairs, he turned and allowed a bank of photographers to snap his picture as he waved down to his father who had driven him to the airport. His parents' support throughout these many months of training and racing had been unwavering. His mother's last words to him before he left were simply, 'Enjoy yourself.' Before ducking into the airplane, Landy smiled again for the photographers, then disappeared inside. As the door closed behind him, he settled back in his seat for the long series of flights ahead.

Expectations were still high. This trip to Scandinavia was

supposed to bring him the four-minute mile. His send-off had been quite an affair. A few nights before, a dinner had been held in his honour at the Danish Club. It was hosted by the former chief justice of the High Court, and Landy was given a gold watch for his athletic achievements – and perhaps good luck as well. His countrymen might have wanted him to break the barrier on this trip, but Landy simply hoped he would be able to knock off Haegg's record. His times since the late January twilight meet at Olympic Park, even though they had been disappointing, had nonetheless qualified him – in the opinion of New York Times columnist Arthur Daley, a former sceptic – as the world's strongest miler. On 11 February in Sydney, while suffering from strained ligaments in his left ankle, not to mention battling 15mph gusts and a spongy track, he had beaten Denis Johansson in a time of 4:05.6. Two weeks later he ran 4:02.6 through semi-darkness and a slight rain in Melbourne. On 5 March he clocked a 4:05.9 mile. And just the previous week, the day after Santee competed at the Kansas Relays, Landy made a devastatingly courageous effort at the mile record on a grass track, despite getting a leather football spike stuck on his right shoe during the first lap. Though his stride was affected because the spike made each footfall awkward, Landy tore around the Bendigo Showgrounds in a time of 4:02.6.

Throughout the first half of 1954, the Australian and inter-national press were relentless in their coverage. They heralded every race as a historic attempt. 'Landy Likely to Achieve Impossible' and 'Landy Should Do It Tonight' were only two of many such head-lines. Landy had to bear the cross of these expectations, knowing that the four-minute mile had become bigger than athletics, that his attainment of it was increasingly a matter of Australian pride in the world arena. In the days before a race, he would read the papers to see what was expected of him. 'I had an obligation to per-form,' he remarked. He would have preferred to make his record-breaking attempt in an empty stadium save for some timekeepers and officials.

Whenever he had failed to break the barrier in front of a cheering crowd, it was never held to be his fault. Instead, the Australian press floated a bunch of reasons, blaming the blinding rain, the sweltering heat, the gale-force winds, a loose track, pathetic competition, and on occasion all of the above. Landy rarely uttered a word about why he had failed in a particular race. In his mind, if he were capable of running under four minutes he would have already done so. As time went on, however, he was accused of being an 'alibi-artist' because of the excuses constantly put forward by his native press, which set off a firestorm of attacks elsewhere. The *New York Post* asked, 'Do the winds blow differently "Down Under" than they do here?' *United Press* bit too: 'A great runner, the young Australian unfortunately has proven even faster to date when it comes to second guessing the results recorded on the stopwatch . . . You can take it from John that his failures were not due to the lack of four-minute muscles, but because it was too hot or too cold, his feet hurt, the crowd applauded so loud that he could not hear his lap times.'

The trip to Finland would provide an escape from this madness. But more than anything, Landy just wanted to improve upon his fastest time. He hated the thought of continuing to run the same times, and if it took travelling to and running on two continents to make a difference, so be it. He deserved at least to better Haegg's world record. The plan was to spend two and a half months racing in Scandinavia, enjoying the fast tracks and crisp weather, and then to travel to Vancouver for the Empire Games. After that, he had decided, he would call an end to his running career. He hoped that Johansson was right when he said, 'If you can run 4:02 consistently here, you can run a couple of seconds faster no problem in Finland. You'll break the record there.' It could well be his last chance.

Nearly a day later, when the plane arrived in Singapore after his connection in Sydney, Landy went out for a training session, not wanting to lose any of his fitness during the long series of flights. Through the sweltering heat he ran for an hour and a half, burning off several pounds in the process. Meanwhile, back in Melbourne, newspapers rolled off the presses with pictures of Landy at the airport and stories about how 'in one slimly built young Victorian lies the world's best prospect to conquer athletics' Mount Everest'. At last Landy was far enough away to be unaffected by this constant bombardment, free to focus on training and running fast times. In a few days' time he would finally arrive in the place where he stood a chance of getting the best out of himself, which was the only thing he had ever wanted since he first began to aim for the world record in the mile.

On Saturday, 1 May, Wes Santee, accompanied by his new wife, descended out of a thunderstorm in a single-engine plane to land on a thin ribbon of runway in Ashland, Kansas. As the plane taxied, the local high-school band fired up their march for 'Wes Santee Day'. Ashland's most famous son had come home.

The previous weekend Santee had been in Des Moines for the Drake Relays, the scene of his first coming out as a world-class runner three years before. The meet was business as usual, with Santee participating in four events to lead his Jayhawks to unchallenged victory. In the four-mile relay, Santee was almost lackadaisical about his role as the anchor. When his team-mate Art Dalzell was running the third leg of the relay, Santee visited his wife in the stands for a brief chat, still wearing his sweats. Then he ran over to speak to Easton as Dalzell began his fourth lap. Some in the stands worried whether Santee was even going to run. He looked unconcerned. Finally, when Dalzell neared the finish, Santee jogged back to his starting position, peeled off his sweatsuit, and collected the baton just in time. He strolled a 4:24 mile, just fast enough to win the race.

The next day Santee exerted himself a bit more in the distance medley, reeling off a 4:07.4 mile to cap the fine quarter-, half-, and three-quarter miles by his team-mates and setting a new world record of 9:50.4, six seconds faster than the previous mark. Fifty-five minutes later, Santee anchored the two-mile relay in 1:51.6, giving his Jayhawks another crown. The journalists covering the Drake Relays focused mostly on the fact that Easton had benched five athletes for breaking curfew. The coach explained his decision: 'Under our system, the team comes first. Any man – any man – is expendable. If he doesn't put the team and its goal above himself we'd just as soon not have him in a K.U. uniform.' He might as well have been speaking of Santee, who many would have preferred to see run in the open mile to break the four-minute barrier.

His Ashland hometown fans, however, could not have honoured him more fervently, even had he claimed one of sport's greatest prizes the weekend before. The local newspaper was awash with good wishes. The Stockgrowers State Bank took out an advertisement welcoming him home while plugging, 'Pay by Check. It will travel as swiftly and as tirelessly as our great miler!' The Heat 160 Highway Café, Crosby Oil Company, Earl Haelsig Clothier, and a host of others also paid for ads congratulating him on his success. The mayor gave him the town keys, a parade led him down Main Street, and a dinner was held in his honour. It was joked that since his arrival had brought nearly an inch in rain, the 'best soaker' in two years, the town planned on holding a 'Wes Santee Day' every weekend.

His old coach J. Allen Murray was on hand, recounting how the first time he saw Santee he'd thought, 'That boy is a runner!' His first-grade school teacher told of the day the fire alarm rang by accident, and by the time the classroom had cleared she found Wes halfway down the street and up a windmill ladder. Though not mentioned, everyone in the room understood what kind of hardship Santee had endured at the hands of his father, and it made the evening that much sweeter that he had achieved so much in spite of that. Santee's parents and siblings were there, but they were mostly quiet. Wes could hardly stand more than a couple hours around his father, and Danna, knowing more than most what David Santee had wrought upon his son, had little time for him too.

At the end of the night, Wes thanked those who had helped him throughout his childhood, particularly his coach, and he promised that one day soon he would break the four-minute barrier. For the five hundred people in the grade school auditorium who had just finished watching a twenty-five-minute newsreel of his best races, one after the other evidence of his breakneck speed and dominance on the track, this promise must have seemed as good as delivered.

In the two weeks before 6 May, Bannister trained for speed and nothing else. He had to tune up his body so that in the space of four minutes he could spend the same amount of energy that he typically used during a long interval training session. At Motspur Park on 24 April he ran a three-quarter-mile time trial with Chataway. As with the trial in anticipation of the Helsinki Olympics nearly two years before, only a few people were there to watch. Two of those were English miler Bill Nankeville and AAA national coach Geoffrey Dyson.

From the start, Bannister took the lead, and throughout the trial he sensed how keenly tuned he was. His running had reached a kind of apotheosis. He felt strong and full of energy. As he described it, 'There was no longer any need for my mind to force my limbs to run faster.' Every muscle and fibre on his lean six-foot-one-inch frame was attuned to an effortless stride. He did not have to think about how best to move his arms or kick out his legs to economise energy. It was as natural for him to shoot around the track with seven-foot strides at Motspur Park as to cross the length of a room. His judgement of pace was deadly accurate as well. 'It was as if all my muscles were a part of a perfectly tuned machine.' When he crossed the three-quarter-mile mark in three minutes flat, Chataway at his side, Bannister was delighted. They had run an even pace, and he still felt energetic. It was a far cry from his 2:52.9 in July 1952, but he knew how much more strength he had in his legs now, enough to go the full distance of a mile with the same kind of speed.

After watching the trial, Nankeville was shaken by how well Bannister was running. Dyson, also amazed by the ease with which they had run, left the track soon after to get to White City stadium for a London Athletic Club meet. There he ran into George Smith, an AAA staff member. Bubbling with excitement, Dyson said, 'The world's one mile record is doomed. I have just come from Motspur Park; Bannister and Chataway, finishing together, ran a three-quarter mile in three minutes dead, and both were as fresh as paint at the finish. Believe me, my friend, great things are about to happen in the near future.'

Bannister would have likely discounted the claim, but one thing was certain: in his many years of athletics he had never experienced such freshness and pleasure in his running. On 28 April he went to Paddington track at lunchtime for another trial, this one to be run alone. Norris McWhirter met him there with his stopwatch. This was the critical test. If Bannister could get in just under three minutes, then he felt strongly that he had a 3:59.9 mile in him; if not, if he was over three minutes by even a second, his mile time would probably translate into a 4:01. This was how close to the razor's edge his training had brought him.

The strong wind made Bannister hesitate at the start. He would have preferred to have the best conditions possible for this trial. If he failed to run the first three laps under three minutes, it might shake his confidence. Finally he decided to go for it, and when McWhirter stopped his watch as Bannister crossed the line, the time showed 2:59.9. For a moment, Bannister was overwhelmed with nerves. His mouth went dry. The time meant that he had a good shot come 6 May. McWhirter believed the same. The next day the young publisher gathered his *Athletics World* staff in their garret office at 15 Great James Street to make their predictions for Bannister's mile. On his office door, three times were written: 4:01.8, 4:01.2, and 3:59.5. The last prognostication was from Norris himself. He knew his friend was in four-minute-mile shape, and just in time as well. Landy was due to arrive in Helsinki on 3 May and Santee was preparing for the international competition and fast tracks at the Compton Invitational. Now or never. As he wrote in the May edition of his track and field magazine, 'It is not the doing of it that really counts, but doing it FIRST.' He had continued to make this clear to his friend.

On 30 April, Bannister ran a half-mile to polish his speed one last time, then put away his running spikes until the AAA versus Oxford race. He and Stampfl agreed that the best thing the miler could do now was build up his nervous energy. This had the unfortunate consequence of leaving Bannister with nothing to do with a surfeit of anxiety about the approaching day, the culmination of two years of effort and focus. He was a well of emotion with no way to sweat it out. For the next five days he worried that he was getting sick or that hurricane winds were certain to descend on Oxford on 6 May. Every night he envisioned himself at the starting line, waiting for the sound of the gun. While picturing the race in this way he literally shook; it took some time before he could relax enough for sleep. Only twenty-four hours before the big day he lost his footing on the polished, ice-like hospital floor and hobbled around the wards for the remainder of his shift. A long night of restful sleep after that was barely a possibility. All in all, he was a bit of a wreck.

As for Brasher and Chataway, in the days before the race they were busy with their jobs. Still, they spent long hours on the telephone with Bannister, who was convinced there was no way the attempt was going to come off. They let him vent his concerns and tried to reassure him. As Chataway told him one evening, 'You can do it. If you've done 4:02 and 4:03, the training you've done has been better this time. There's absolutely no reason you shouldn't do it.'

Of course, they had their own worries. The week before, Stampfl had approached the two, over tea at Lyons, about changing the pacemaking. Instead of Brasher leading for the first two laps, Stampfl thought it better that he try to make it two and a half laps round, after which Chataway would take over to the three-and-a-half-lap mark. This way Bannister would have to take alone only the final half-lap instead of a full 440. That was fine and well, but the two doubted they were in good enough shape to hold fast through another half-lap. As Brasher explained, however, 'Stampfl had a way of exorcising such doubts from the mind of an athlete.' Their coach had them so fired up that each runner daydreamed that not only would he manage the extra effort, he would somehow find a way to kick past Bannister in the final turn and seize the record himself.

The evening before the Oxford meet, Franz Stampfl was in his one-bedroom flat off King's Road, as nervous as his athletes. He knew it was going to be a big day and he felt certain that Bannister could do it but, as he told his wife Pat, 'you have to have luck in everything'. His small flat was littered with athletics journals detailing the latest exploits of the world's great milers. Stampfl was certain that someone was going to run the four-minute mile soon, so Bannister needed to do it straight away. If he didn't, Stampfl was sure, the British athletics community would blame the coach.

Across town in north London, Norris McWhirter was practising for his role as public-address announcer at the Oxford versus AAA match. The day had been hectic, one spent fielding phone calls and making sure that everything was ready for Bannister's attempt, including good media coverage. To this end he had written a 5 May story in the *Star* headlined 'Aim May Be Four Min Mile'. Yet when he'd called BBC producer/presenter Peter Dimmock, McWhirter had learned that they weren't even planning on attending.

'It's not a very important match and it's not really international,' Dimmock had said. 'Can't spare the camera or crews.'

'Well, I'm just warning you that you'd be extremely unwise to miss it,' McWhirter retorted plainly.

'Are you telling me something?'

'I'm not telling you anything really, but if the weather is propitious ... Bannister is understandably anxious about the priority of Landy and Santee.'

'Oh, right,' Dimmock replied. He agreed to have someone there for the event and then hung up.

In the bath that evening, McWhirter prepared his announcement should Bannister successfully break four minutes, more concerned with this than his expected participation in the four by 110 sprint relays. He wanted his tone to be measured, but his words full of suspense. It would start with something like 'Ladies and gentlemen, here is the result of Event Number Nine, the One Mile . . .'

14

I felt at that moment that it was my chance to do one thing
supremely well.

Roger Bannister

On Thursday, 6 May, Bannister woke up in his Earls Court flat.
When he glanced outside, his hope of a nice day disappeared. The
wind swayed the treetops violently and clouds of slate grey promised
rain. Swallowing the fear of having to reschedule the attempt, he got
ready to go to the hospital for the morning. After breakfast he went
outside and the wind buffeted his shirt like a sail. Trying for the mile
record in these conditions was certain to be futile. If they did go
ahead and he failed – and he would most certainly fail on a day like
this – then he would waste his nervous energy and find psyching
himself up for another time doubly difficult. Putting off the attempt
until the next opportunity, 17 May at the White City stadium,
would mean bearing over a week more of anxiety and strain. Neither
option was very appealing.

With these thoughts in his mind, he arrived at the hospital.
Distraught, he had nothing to do but continue with the day as if
the attempt would go ahead, all the time feeling certain it was
hopeless. At eleven o'clock, Bannister went down to the hospital
laboratory to grind his spikes and rub them with graphite. Given the
likely conditions, this would keep the cinder ash from clumping
on the bottom of his shoes, which could mean a few yards over the
mile. In the battle over tenths of seconds and half seconds, this was a
big deal. When someone peering into the laboratory to find him at

the grindstone asked, 'You don't really think that's going to make any difference, do you?', Bannister knew very well that it would. In addition, the shoes in which he was planning to run had been ordered from a specialist London cobbler. 'They should be light,' Bannister had said to the man who had once supplied Jack Lovelock with his shoes. 'I need them only for three races, for twelve laps.' The resulting pair weighed four ounces, two fewer than his normal shoes. He factored this into his carefully calculated plan. Every advantage counted.

Once finished with his spikes, Bannister decided to take an early train alone to Oxford so that he could gather his thoughts and come to some resolution about whether or not the attempt was worth making. The mile event was not scheduled until six o'clock, which left plenty of time for the weather to change, but Bannister was already leaning towards putting off the attempt altogether. On his way to nearby Paddington station he waded through pavements full of people wearing raincoats and carrying umbrellas. The station was dark, noisy, and left one choking for breath. With the sun absent from the sky, the sooty veneer on the arched glass ceiling let in very little light. Whistles blew and 'all aboard' announcements were shouted down the platforms, while smoke coughed out from train engines. After finding his platform on the information board, Bannister hurried to his train, ready to settle in for the sixty-three-mile journey he had taken so many times before.

While looking for an empty seat, he unexpectedly spotted Franz Stampfl sitting in one of the compartments. Bannister pulled aside the door, surprised at how glad he was to see him. He needed to lay bare his fears, and there was nobody better than Stampfl to help deal with them.

Bannister wasn't alone in his worries over the weather. Stampfl too had looked out of the window that morning in despair. His wife Pat, a short, kind-spirited woman who helped support them by working as a book-keeper, sensed his concern, but Stampfl told her that he believed everything would be all right. He barely spoke through breakfast and left early to take the underground train to Paddington. Nonetheless, when Bannister found him Stampfl conveyed nothing but complete confidence. To have shown anything else would have been disastrous to his athlete.

The doors slammed closed and the train jarred into movement. The dull tremor of the engine reverberated through the compartment as the two sat opposite each other, not speaking of the race to come. When they cleared the cover of the station, rain slapped against the windows, and as the train gathered momentum, cutting north out of London past rows of dilapidated Victorian houses with laundry lines strung out behind them, Bannister hesitated to ask for Stampfl's advice. At this critical moment in his athletics career he disliked the idea of needing to depend on a coach.

The train sped past warehouses and factory smokestacks under the gloomy sky. As Bannister watched the trees being buffeted by the gale-force winds, he finally began to talk about his concerns. He explained to Stampfl that the weather might ruin any chance of breaking four minutes. The wind would add a second to each of his four laps. This meant he would have to run the equivalent of a 3:56 mile in ideal conditions. A 3:56 mile. Given how much he had invested in today being *the* day, future attempts looked less hopeful. He was at his best *now*, mentally and physically. It was too difficult to keep himself at this peak, whether for the race at White City in ten days' time or for even later ones.

Stampfl knew the damage doubt could cause an athlete. He assured Bannister that on a calm day he *could* run four seconds under the barrier. He had the legs for it. 'With the proper motivation – that is, a good reason for wanting to do it,' Stampfl said in his usual bellowing Austrian voice, 'your mind can overcome any sort of adversity. In any case, the wind might drop. I remember J. J. Barry in Ireland. He ran a 4:08 mile without any training or even proper food, simply because he had the will to run . . . In any case, what if this were your only chance? Sure it'll be painful, but what's pain?' Bannister considered the question, knowing well what

Stampfl had endured. The Austrian coach continued, absolutely convinced in his own mind that the miler was capable of the effort, no matter the weather. 'If you forgo this chance, would you ever forgive yourself? Nobody knows what the future holds. Wes Santee or John Landy may do it first. You might pull a muscle. You might fall under a bus. There may never be another opportunity.'

As the train rumbled over the rails towards the black cinder track at Iffley Road, Oxford, Stampfl spoke of other runners and their times, but Bannister scarcely heard his words. He stared out of the window as they wound their way across the rolling green hills, past blurred trees. The miler steeled himself to the realisation that despite the weather, this was his best opportunity. Stampfl had faith in him. His running partners, Chris Brasher and Chris Chataway, had faith in him. And somewhere underneath the fear and doubt, Bannister had faith in himself.

When they arrived at the Oxford station, coach and miler went their separate ways. Bannister's close friend Charles Wenden was waiting for him, and they drove together to the Iffley Road track so that Bannister could test his shoes on the cinders. He needed to see how well the graphite-rubbed spikes entered and released from the track's sticky ash. Wind blew in gusts across the wet track, and once again he lost hope in the attempt. His friend invited him for lunch with his family, and Bannister accepted, knowing that it would be a good place to relax and get away from his thoughts.

Wenden was an Oxford lecturer in education studies and had won the Military Cross during the war. They had first met at an Oxford cross-country race years before, when a young Bannister had turned to Wenden after the other competitors had shot quickly off the mark and asked, 'Are they going to run like this?' – implying that he was not capable of the pace. Wenden had replied, 'Well, they are, but we don't have to.' Bannister was close to Wenden's family, his wife and two daughters, having stayed with them during his postgraduate research, and his friend knew him well enough not to ask any questions about that afternoon's record attempt. For several hours the miler lost himself in domestic routine, enjoying a lunch of ham salad and prunes with custard, and playing with the children.

Bannister left the Wendens in the late afternoon to visit Chris Chataway, who had arrived in Oxford early as well. At Magdalen College, Bannister found his running partner reclining by a window, calm and cheerful as ever. Magically, the sun had appeared in the sky at last. Chataway said, 'The day could be a lot worse, couldn't it? Just now it's fine. The forecast says the wind may drop towards evening. Let's not decide until five o'clock.' Until that time, Bannister stared out of the window, praying the wind would stop rustling through the treetops.

When they finally went down to the track, Bannister bumped into reporter Joe Binks. 'The wind's hopeless,' Binks said. They found Brasher in the wood-panelled changing rooms under the stands. There they debated whether or not to go ahead with the attempt. Through the narrow slit of the window, Bannister stared at the red-cross flag of St George over the square tower of a church on Iffley Road. It whipped strongly in the wind. Stampfl suggested that they decide nothing until closer to the race time. So, forty-five minutes before the race was due to start, the three runners went out to the rugby fields adjacent to the track to warm up. While they jogged on the grass, a bank of dark clouds rolled across the sky. A few minutes later, a quick shower burst over them. They scrambled back to the locker-room. The capricious English weather had struck again.

But at 5.45 p.m. precisely the clouds cleared and a rainbow arced over the square tower where the St George flag flew. Stampfl approached the three runners to see if they would try for the mile record. The first vote was: no (Bannister), neutral (Chataway), and yes (Brasher – always one to say yes to anything). As it seemed unlikely they would go ahead, Brasher tracked down AAA team manager Leslie Truelove, who was dressed as if he'd come straight from a business meeting, to see if he could switch to the two-mile event. Truelove declined, saying that it was too late. With five minutes until the start, Stampfl noticed the wind was dying down and reminded the three runners, 'There's nothing a man can't do if the spirit's there.' Brasher agreed, saying, 'We've done all this bloody work, we might as well go.' They took a second vote: no (Bannister), yes (Chataway), yes (Brasher). Bannister then took another 150-yard warm-up sprint, moved to the starting line, and saw the flag over the church go slack. This was the only sign he needed. 'Yes,' he told Brasher and Chataway. They were going for it.

A crowd of some twelve hundred, many of whom were under-graduates who had just arrived on their bicycles, waited anxiously for the start. Although the meet had been under way for over an hour, most had come to see the mile race. Many wore heavy coats and scarves wrapped around their necks, despite the fact it was May. Only a few days earlier the *Oxford Mail* had headlined 'Bannister at Oxford – May Make Attempt at 4-Minute Mile'. In the centre infield, two men from the BBC television programme *Sportsview* had set up a 35mm camera on top of its leather box case. They planned to shoot the race in a continuous take, 360 degrees around. Norris McWhirter, who had arranged for them to be there, had also convinced American journalist Milton Marmor to be on hand, saying he would be 'ill advised' not to attend as he would be the only one of his countrymen there. Begrudgingly, Marmor had agreed. Unbeknown to Bannister, his parents had also arrived in Oxford to watch the race. They hadn't told him so as to avoid adding any more pressure. Regretfully, his elder sister Joyce couldn't come from Bristol, though Roger had written in a letter to her a few weeks before, 'By the way, I may be trying for the four-minute mile at Oxford soon.'

The moment had arrived. The six runners approached the starting line for Event Number Nine, the One Mile. Alan Gordon and George Dole (an American studying theology at Oxford) repre-sented the university; Brasher, Chataway, Bannister and William Hulatt represented the AAA. As they settled at the mark, the sun reappeared in the sky. Bannister, wearing a green, gold and blue striped singlet with the number 41 pinned to his chest, looked down at the track, arms loose by his side, right foot slightly forward. The air was wet and cold on his skin. He was fourth from the inside, with Chataway directly to his right and Brasher a man away to his left. The crowd grew silent. Bannister coiled and readied to spring.

Before the starter gun shot, Brasher jumped – a false start. After he received an official warning from the starter, the runners returned to the mark, Bannister upset that they might have wasted valuable seconds of the lull in the wind, which could pick up again at any moment. Again the crowd silenced. Bannister waited, shifting his spikes on the cinders to get better traction. He took a long breath. This might be his last chance to be the first through the barrier. His pacemakers were ready. The plan was set. Thanks to his training he had the endurance and speed to manage the pace. And thanks to Stampfl he more than knew that a sub-four-minute mile could be run; Bannister *believed* he was able to do it, no matter the conditions. He was as prepared as he would ever be for the attempt.

The gun banged, and Brasher shot forward as arranged, quickly passing Dole who was on the inside lane from the start. Bannister followed closely behind Brasher, and Chataway moved up steadily through the field as they made their way around the turn. At last, Bannister was free of the thoughts that had plagued him throughout the previous week, free to run, and run fast. His whole body felt electrified, as if he could move around the track without expending any effort. Six days of not running had left him with a bundle of energy. Now, finally, he could put that energy to good use.

As they neared the first half-lap marker, Norris McWhirter read off the time on his stopwatch into the microphone. 'Twenty-six. Twenty-seven. Twenty-eight . . .' He had hired an electrician to wire two speakers to the microphone, one pointing down the home straight and the other on the back straight. Since he was the public-address announcer, it was entirely permissible (albeit seldom arranged) for him to give the half-lap time. This would help with the pacemaking. Bannister, however, didn't hear him correctly and felt so fired with energy in that early part of the race that he thought Brasher was setting too slow a pace.

In the back straight, Bannister yelled, 'Faster, Chris! Faster!'

Brasher heard the call but refused to react. He was running smartly and believed the pace was right. Plus, he was going as fast as he could without getting up on his toes and sprinting, which would have meant the end of him by the start of the second lap. He maintained his speed and Bannister, despite remaining anxious over the pace, was forced to hold steady behind him. Bannister was so restless that he was unaware of how fast he was running.

As they reached the end of the first lap, McWhirter's voice boomed out of the loudspeaker: 'Fifty-four. Fifty-five. Fifty-six. Fifty-seven—' Brasher crossed the line first, Bannister half a second behind him in 57.5, and Chataway third. The three were evenly spaced and already well ahead of the rest of the field. The crowd began to sense that something very special was afoot, particularly given how quickly and purposefully the three runners were striding.

Into the second lap, Brasher sustained the pace. Bannister continued to run on his nerves and had not yet settled into an easy stride. When they turned into the back straight, Stampfl shouted, 'Relax! Relax!' He was wasting energy by running so stiffly. Whether consciously or unconsciously, Bannister heard Stampfl and began to get into his rhythm. If they were running too slow, it was too late in the race to adjust. Calm descended over him, and his legs began to move as if on their own. He felt free of exertion.

'One twenty-five. One twenty-six. One twenty-seven . . .'

Brasher passed the 660-yard mark and began to feel the strain. He was running less easily than the other two and was starting to chug around the track like a freight train, arms coming across his chest as he ran. Behind him Bannister strode smoothly, beating a steady cadence on the cinder track as they approached the half-mile mark. Chataway kept to the strong pace in third position.

'One fifty-six. One fifty-seven. One fifty-eight . . .'

Bannister scarcely heard the time. His body was running within the groove he had trained many months to shape. He was in the zone. Brasher continued to lead, making a mighty effort to maintain the pace. To his mind, the bend lasted an interminable amount of time. Around the stadium the crowd clapped louder and louder. They whispered among one another that this might be the big day. Athletes on the infield stopped their warm-ups to get to the side of the track for a better view. The time was fast for the half-mile, and the officials responsible for making sure everything went according to the rules began to realise they had a reason to be especially careful.

As they approached the two-and-a-half-lap mark, Brasher was struggling. His mouth was wide open, and he looked ready to fall over at any moment. Bannister sensed that his friend was about to stall and called for Chataway to take over. 'Chris!' Bannister yelled. Chataway was tired, but on hearing Bannister he found the strength to spring forward. With his short but powerful strides, he quickly overtook Bannister, then Brasher. The three other men in the race had been long forgotten.

'Two twenty-seven. Two twenty-eight. Two twenty-nine . . .'

Stampfl checked his own stopwatch, reassuring himself that they were on pace. Brasher had always been the question mark in the pacemaking scheme because of his lack of natural speed, but he'd fought mightily through the first two and a half laps. They were on schedule. The steeplechaser had a giant heart. Now it was up to Chataway, then Bannister himself. Stampfl knew the moment would soon come for both when their fatigued legs would cry out for them to stop. The coach only hoped he had helped them enough to know they could push back this pain, convince their legs to keep striding, and will themselves onward.

Rounding the bend, Chataway focused on maintaining his speed, his lips pursed as he ran. Bannister still felt good. He allowed the motion of his arms and legs almost to lull him into a trance. It would be in the final lap that he would have to earn his chance at immortality.

'Two fifty-eight. Two fifty-nine. Three minutes.'

At the sound of the bell for the final lap, Bannister had run a 3:00.4. The crowd had been steadily clapping with the occasional cheer, but it now stood to its feet and let loose. Their voices raised into an uproar. This might very well be it. Chataway made his way around the turn, his flushed cheeks swelling with breath. At 350 yards out Bannister considered bursting past him, but he waited. He needed a fifty-nine-second last lap or the attempt would fail. It was too early to begin his finishing kick. When Chataway turned into the back straight, even his world-class endurance was finally giving out. From the sidelines, Stampfl shouted, 'Go all out!' Chataway tried to hold on as long as he could, but at the 230-yard mark Bannister swept past him on the outside, his great stride devouring the track.

'Three twenty-eight. Three twenty-nine. Three thirty . . .'

Bannister had to finish the final half-lap in fewer than thirty seconds. He forced himself to move faster, feeling as if his will to break through the tape under the four-minute mark was outpacing his feet. He heard the crowd shouting his name, their support urging him forward, stronger, faster. His great stride lengthened. He accentuated the drive of his arms to keep balance. As he passed the 1,500-metre mark his face drained of colour and contorted with effort. Ross McWhirter took the time: 3:43 – world-record fast. He dashed over to his brother Norris to tell him. The twins were convinced Bannister was about to make history.

From over seventy yards back, Brasher gasped, 'Come on, Roger . . . Roger . . . Roger!'

Bannister was beyond tired. Just fifty yards from the finish, he had exhausted himself completely. There was no pain. He was simply used up. Yet he forced himself ahead, drawing deep upon a reservoir of will only few ever discover. Twenty-five yards. Ten yards. Five yards. The distance from the tape appeared to lengthen.

He began to push his chest forward. His legs were still moving. Two strides. His chin went up, his arms drove higher. Keep going. One stride. Keep going. He flung himself at the tape, a tortured yet glorious expression of abandon on his face.

When he crossed the finish line, his legs buckled and he collapsed into the arms of former Olympic sprinter Nicholas Stacey. Leslie Truelove stepped in and draped his arm around Bannister from the other side. The crowd spilled on to the track as the other runners finished their miles. After a few steps, Bannister tried to stand again but his legs gave out. He could barely understand what was going on around him.

'Give him air!' someone shouted.

Stampfl moved forward and held Bannister up, his powerful shoulders a ballast. Meanwhile, Chataway and Brasher struggled for breath on the grass infield, unable to get to their friend because of the stampede of people surrounding him.

Bannister was barely conscious and overwhelmed with pain. For a moment he could see only in black and white. His system was completely taxed from a lack of oxygen. His legs and arms felt as if someone was gripping them tightly. He felt certain that he had broken the barrier, although the time had yet to be announced. Chest swelling with deep breaths, he closed his eyes and rested his forehead in the crook of Stampfl's neck. The coach supported him as they took a few careful steps forward.

'Did I do it?' Bannister coughed out his first words, his face still pale.

'I think so,' replied Stampfl, concerned for his runner.

Two minutes later, the timekeepers handed Norris McWhirter the official time of the race. It was his responsibility to give the result. Trying to keep his voice from breaking, McWhirter spoke into the microphone, resolved to lend his announcement the tone he had practised the previous night. The pandemonium on the track silenced as the words came over the loudspeakers:

Ladies and gentlemen, here is the result of Event Number Nine, the One Mile. First, Number Forty-One, R. G. Bannister of the Amateur Athletic Association and formerly of Exeter and Merton Colleges, with a time which is a new meeting and track record, and which subject to ratification will be a new English Native, British National, British All-Comers, European, British Empire and World's Record. The time is three—

The rest of the announcement was drowned out by the joyous cries of the twelve hundred people who had just witnessed history in the making. Roger Bannister had run the mile in 3:59.4. At last the barrier was broken.

'Three cheers for Roger Bannister!' a young undergraduate shouted.

The crowd responded. 'Three cheers! Three cheers!'

Hundreds swarmed around Bannister, pressing closer and closer. His parents broke through the crowd and threaded their way towards him. 'I knew you would do it one day, Roger,' his mother said, throwing her arms around him. He embraced her as newsreel cameramen, photographers, journalists, undergraduates, and children tried to get his attention.

Bannister finally recovered enough to stand on his own and raised his arms over his head in triumph, calling out for Chataway and Brasher. He hurried towards them. After so much effort and time spent together, he wanted to share the moment with them. He vigorously shook their hands, his usual reserve replaced by a warm smile. 'Without them, I could not have done it,' Bannister said to all around him. The three then took a victory trot around the track, a group of well-wishers following in their wake.

While officials tried to get the meet running again, Bannister signed autographs, spoke to the press, and thanked the head groundsman Walter Morris. Meanwhile, Chris Brasher, who had a talent for getting straight to the point, told the *Daily Mail*'s Terry

O'Connor what many were thinking. 'Well, we did it,' he said. 'That means Landy and Wes Santee can never break the four-minute mile first.'

After a quick shower, Bannister went to Vincent's Club for a glass of water mixed with table salt (chased with a shandy) and was then shuttled off in a waiting blue car to appear on BBC evening television. It was a far cry from the manner in which he had quietly come to Oxford earlier in the day. His great celebration was about to begin. With a covey of journalists fluttering about to file their stories, one finagling a desk and telephone at the local police station, another bribing a pub owner to monopolise his phone, life promised never to be the same again for Roger Bannister.

It was a humid afternoon on 6 May at the University of Kansas, one threatened by thunderstorms, when Bill Mayer, athletics writer for the *Lawrence Journal World*, read of the broken barrier. His office's ticker tape relayed the news amid word of a Willie Mays home run in Cincinnati and Sam Snead losing his lead in a golf tournament in New York. Before he knew it, he was kicking the machine. The four-minute mile was supposed to have been for Wes Santee. Moments later, Mayer left his office to find Santee. He had to move quickly since other local reporters were bound to be fast on the hunt for the miler. His reaction was sure to be flavourful. Mayer knew that at that time of the day the surest bet was to head for Memorial Stadium.

Santee was finishing his workout when the newsmen rushed towards him. He was sweating and still short of breath when he heard what Bannister had done. Instantly he went numb, feeling physically as he did whenever he lost a race. Easton, who was stunned as well, tried to shield Santee from the questions, but he would have had as much luck trying to hold back an avalanche.

'What do you think of the news?' one reporter asked.

'I am not exceptionally disappointed,' Santee replied. 'Of the milers capable of doing it, Bannister is the one I'd just as soon have seen break it. There still is the challenge to see who will be the first American to break the four-minute mile. The time is still not as low as it can be run.'

'Why were you beaten to the punch?'

'Having to compete for the university, I've had to run everything from soup to nuts. I haven't been permitted to concentrate.'

'Would you like to run against Bannister?' asked the *University Daily Kansan* reporter.

Santee was clear. 'Yes, and I think I could beat him if I had the chance.'

Once the reporters had got their quotes, Easton talked with Santee alone. He knew Wes was stung by the news. 'We tried,' he said. 'But we have to keep on. You still have more running to do.'

Santee agreed, although it would be several days before he was convinced of it. More than anything, he wanted a chance to compete against Bannister in a real race, one man against the other without pacing. Then the world would see.

The young miler walked alone back to the locker-room. He didn't want to talk about Bannister or running for a while.

At a restaurant in Turku, the ancient capital of Finland and a far cry from the shores of Melbourne, Denis Johansson strode towards Landy holding a cable in his hand. They had been together since Landy arrived on 3 May, and for the first day since his arrival the Australian had not trained, perhaps wanting to see first how Bannister ran in Oxford.

'Look at this,' the Finn said, passing him the cable across the table.

Bannister had done it: a 3:59.4 mile. It was a surprising perform-ance, Landy thought at first. He knew the English miler was about to make another attempt, but Landy had thought Bannister would break Haegg's record at best. Unbelievable – Bannister had knocked two seconds off the record. At least this meant an end to all the talk of the barrier, and Landy would be able to run without the 'four-minute mile' punctuating his every stride. Then the disappointment began to settle over him. After so much sweat and strain, he had been beaten to the record. Reporters would want his response, Johansson told him. Landy didn't feel up to it. Not now. He asked the Finn if he would reply to the cable with his reaction, then told him, 'Well, let's have a go [for the record] on May thirty-first.'

Johansson sent back the following quote to reporters: 'It's great, great, great. He's a great runner. I think the brilliant achievement will be bettered.'

The next day Landy planned two workouts, one in the morning and one in the afternoon. He still believed he had a good chance, on these beautiful Finnish tracks, of running faster than anyone before. If Bannister had been able to break four minutes, Landy felt he should be able to as well. He had run many more miles under 4:05 than Bannister, or anyone else for that matter. His training was more intensive as well. It was just a matter of all the right elements coming together.

And fast times weren't everything either. He also had the Empire Games to look forward to, when he and the English were likely to face off against one another. Landy had been waiting a long time to see how he would fare against the best in the world. In Australia, even in Finland, he was finding that nobody could test him in the mile.

III

THE PERFECT MILE

15

I see you stand like greyhounds in the slips,
Straining upon the start.
King Henry in *Henry V* (III.i.31–2)

As evening fell on 7 May, twenty-four hours after the triumph at Iffley Road, Bannister and his two pacemakers, Chataway and Brasher, climbed Harrow Hill, an isolated elevation of land 345 feet high in north-west London. The sun had set and a cool breeze rustled the leaves in the trees overhead. At the top of the hill stood St Mary's Church, whose foundations dated back to 1087. In the surrounding churchyard a weathered assembly of mossy tombstones sprang up from the landscape. The poet Lord Byron, who, with Winston Churchill and Lord Shaftesbury, was one of the most famous Old Harrovians, had as a young boy spent many hours leaning on these tombstones, dreaming of future adventures. The three runners looked out on the view as Byron might have seen it. They could see the proud stance of St Paul's Cathedral and the twisting shape of the Thames, a seam of darkness that threaded through the glittering cityscape.

None of the three had slept more than a few hours in the past two days. After leaving Oxford, Bannister had been driven quickly to London by the BBC crew. In the car, he'd sat quietly, pride overcoming him. 'No words could be invented for such supreme happiness,' he later wrote. His Helsinki defeat had been vindicated. He had finally achieved a great athletic ambition.

That evening on *Sportsview*, he appeared on television screens across his country, many of whose owners had bought their sets only a year before to watch Queen Elizabeth's coronation. Bannister was later praised for his 'adroit modesty' during the interview, despite his excitement. He explained how bewildered he felt to be sitting in front of a camera in London only a few hours after his run. When Peter Dimmock, the honoured statesman of British broadcasting, asked him why it was they had finally decided to make a go for the record, despite the bad weather, Bannister said, 'There comes a moment when you can't go on waiting indefinitely. You just have to accept an all-out effort.'

'And your plans for athletics?' Dimmock continued.

'Naturally we all wanted to achieve the honour of doing the four-minute mile. But it is in fact only a time. And in athletics, the main essence is races, races against opponents more than against the clock . . . And those will be what I shall set my main sights on.'

Dimmock neglected to pursue that answer by enquiring whether that meant Bannister intended to race against John Landy and Wes Santee. Instead, he concluded the interview, congratulating the miler for 'putting Great Britain back on top of the sporting world again!' It was a time for celebration, not more questions.

Once Bannister had left the studios in Lime Grove, he met Brasher and Chataway for dinner at Clement Freud's cabaret club over the Royal Court Theatre in Sloane Square. They drank champagne, enjoyed four-minute steaks (appropriately), and danced with their dates, Bannister's 'a tall fair girl in an off-the-shoulder green gown', as a *Daily Express* spy reported. The McWhirter twins stopped by the club to share in the celebrations.

In the booth, Bannister turned to the twins. 'I can't believe I did it,' he said.

'You gotta believe it. It will be in the papers tomorrow,' Norris replied.

At 2.30 in the morning, Bannister, Brasher, and Chataway wedged themselves into the latter's pre-war Austin 8 and tried to find the Sunset Club in Piccadilly Circus. When they pulled up alongside a policeman to get directions, he gave them the once-over and said, 'You gentlemen are no gentlemen if you take these ladies to that club.' He then took out a notebook from his top left-hand pocket as if to write them a ticket, but instead handed it to Bannister. 'Perhaps I can have your autographs, gentlemen?'

In the dark, smoky basement club off Carnaby Street, news of the feat was announced and Bannister was called to the front to say a few words. He pulled his two pacemakers into the light with him and said, 'I've got two better boys.' Gesturing to Chataway, he said, 'He's the one who makes me work – and keeps me amused. He will soon run a four-minute mile himself.' After more champagne and dancing, Bannister took the microphone and sang 'Time on My Hands'.

At 4.30 in the morning newspapers were delivered to the club's door. A photograph of Bannister breaking through the tape was plastered across the front pages. 'The Triumph of R. G. Bannister' read *The Times*; 'This Magnificent Man' swooned the *Daily Mail*; 'Wonderful Bannister!' headlined the *Daily Mirror*; 'At Last – The 4-Minute Mile' crooned the *Daily Express*. Amid details of the race, Bannister was praised for restoring honour to British sport after so many years of defeat and ignominy. He was heralded as a national treasure whose name would be on the lips of millions of people throughout the world once they read of his achievement on their front pages. 'The Empire is saved,' claimed one editorial. 'Roar, Lion, Roar! There's been nothing to compare with this since the destruction of the Spanish Armada. Let the Aga Khan take such satisfaction as he may from his Epsom Derby winners. Let Ben Hogan have the British Open title and welcome. England has the four-minute mile.'

As dawn grew nearer, the day's events finally took their toll on Bannister, and he called his celebration to an end. National hero or not, he had to show up at the hospital that morning and needed to catch at least a couple of hours' sleep. Chataway dropped him off at Brasher's house in Highgate. Brasher left his mother a note that the miler would be down for breakfast, then he and Chataway quickly jumped back into the car with their dates and headed off to Beachy Head, some two hours away, to watch the sunrise.

When Bannister arrived at St Mary's in the late morning, he was given a royal welcome. His fellow students paraded him through the front entrance on a chair and showered him with the hundreds of telegrams that had been sent to the hospital. In the afternoon, he travelled to Oxford to escape the attention and spent some time with the Wendens. Then he returned to visit his parents in Harrow, carrying a suitcase full of congratulatory notes and telegrams. Press from around the world had been cordoned off in front of the house. Reporters had been tracking his movements throughout the day. To avoid their flashbulbs and demands for more interviews, he climbed a series of fences leading to the back of his house.

Later, when he left to meet with Brasher and Chataway on top of Harrow Hill, he used the same route. With London unfolded before them, they had a moment of peace together. They had not expected such an uproar. Bannister had won headlines in literally thousands of papers, and he was credited with demonstrating that in life 'the impossible is no longer out of reach'. Together they had achieved the ultimate in sport, but it was just that: sport. They were amateurs; this was not supposed to be their defining moment. There was much more to the world than running. There was real work with real consequences to be done. 'Now life in earnest was beginning,' Bannister remarked, and there was much they wanted to do: Bannister in medicine, Brasher in business, and Chataway in politics. They believed their pursuit of the four-minute mile had shown the way. Their single-minded focus was the reason Bannister had beaten Landy and Santee through the barrier. As Brasher said later of their conversation, 'We honestly believed that if you have a dream and you work to make it come true, then you really can change the world. There's just nothing you can't do.'

As Bannister walked around the old graveyard with his friends, he realised that before he turned to medicine full-time, there was still one thing he needed to prove to himself as an athlete. Since the Helsinki debacle, he had been accused of being incapable of winning a race against the best in the world. Sure, he ran well against the clock, but did he have the ability to win in heated competition? He had yet to answer this question, not only for his critics but for himself. Until he had, he would not be content.

In Turku, Finland, on 10 May, after a light half-hour jog in the morning, John Landy sat down in his hotel room to write to Len McRae. Of his many friends, McRae knew better than most how seriously Landy took his running and the pressure he had been under since running his 4:02.1 mile in December 1952. In the letter, Landy described his trip to Scandinavia, how on his flight the person next to him had had a bit too much 'grog', and that on his arrival his hosts had been kind enough to fit him out in a new tracksuit and spikes. Of Bannister's record, which his running mates back in Australia thought was a dishonest effort because of the pacemaking, Landy had only a few words to say: 'Heard a rumour that Roger ran 3:59.4, which makes a guy look rather slow!!! However, I am not unduly pessimistic. In fact, I am reasonably confident of recording my best figures for one mile on 31st May.'

Even to one of his closest friends, Landy didn't want to promise too much, but he was feeling very good about his chances in the days ahead. There was no better place in the world to train and race. Turku was a quiet, old city at the mouth of the Aurajoki River. The surrounding seven hills had paths cut through them on which he could run. They were bedded with pine needles and banked with virgin forest, rivers and lakes. The air was cool and had an inspiring freshness to it. In the hometown of Paavo Nurmi, whose feats were spoken about in the whispers of legend, running was revered, and the city stadium's track was cared for in the way a mother dotes on her dearest child.

When Landy arrived, the black cinder track was dimpled and

uneven as a result of the ice that was still frozen underneath. Over the intervening two weeks, the ice had melted, and the groundsmen had rolled and smoothed out the cinders. Landy found it electrifyingly fast, though he had to shorten his stride a little because the bounce from the track tended to tire his legs out more quickly than before. Once he had adjusted to the bounce, however, he easily ran fifty-seven-second laps. Once he'd reached the proper pace, maintaining his speed required less effort than it did in Australia. He was so impressed with the track that he took a core sample of it to be examined back in Melbourne.

In the three weeks leading up to his first race in Turku, Landy trained every day, sometimes twice a day. The newspapers had detailed how Bannister's interval session of ten by 440 at a 58.9-second average was a key marker that he was ready for his attempt. Landy was regularly running the same session over a second faster. On occasion, he ran repeat 440s with only a half-lap interval jog in between and was still a tenth of a second faster than Bannister's average. If hard training sessions were the only factor, Landy was sure to beat the Englishman's time. Denis Johansson, who often trained with Landy as well as timed some of his trial runs, felt it would take more than superior fitness, however. 'Running is not only physical,' he explained. 'If it were, you could put a great bull-like guy to it and he'd break every record ... You must have some greater thing than yourself to push it.'

Landy believed the track conditions and his running form were enough to give him the edge he needed. Two days before his race, Wes Santee provided some extra incentive by running a 4:01.3, the second fastest mile in history. He had the pacemaking help of his two team-mates Lloyd Koby and Art Dalzell through the first three laps. Now another miler had beaten Landy past the long-time mark held by Gundar Haegg, and the Kansan was likely to better this time in early June against tough competition at the Compton Invitational once he'd recovered from a leg muscle strain.

When Landy arrived at Turku's stadium on 31 May, meet posters

tacked to the walls had a banner running across the top that read
'Come and See the World Record Broken'. He hoped to live up to
the advertising. With ten thousand people in the stands, Landy
stepped up to the line with three Finns: Denis Johansson, Urho
Vaharanta, and Olavi Vuorisalo. Much had changed in the two
short years since his last overseas race. The spectators now knew his
name, for a start, and expected a mile time out of him that none of
their countrymen could equal. Landy was as charged and confident
as he had ever been. Although he would have preferred to run the
mile record in his hometown, doing so in front of Finns, who were
the most devoted track fans in the world, was a close second.

Vaharanta bolted from the start into an early lead, but Landy
kept close. In the back stretch he overtook the Finn and took charge
of the race, finishing the first lap in a blazing fifty-six seconds. His
time was read over the public-address system in English, but Landy
couldn't make out the words. He thought his first lap was fifty-eight
seconds. In the second lap, Johansson tried to stay close to Landy,
attempting to spark a little competitive struggle to help him. The
Australian was maintaining too fast a pace, however. He finished the
second lap in fifty-nine seconds, giving him a half-mile time of 1:55.
Landy still thought he was two seconds slower than that, but so
eager was he to be racing that his legs were fooling his head.

By the bell, Landy's time was 2:57, a second and a half faster than
he had planned to run the first three laps, and he began to pay for
his lack of pace judgement. In the back stretch he began losing
momentum, and his face contorted into a mask of torture. The
effort to continue was enormous. The encouragement from the
stands glanced off his leaden legs, and over the last hundred yards
he looked altogether finished. Still, when he broke through the
tape the stopwatches registered his best time ever: 4:01.6. Johansson
finished next, ten seconds behind him.

Landy was unusually candid about what he thought of the race
and his future chances. Yes, he had poorly managed his pace, but he
considered himself at a level as good – and in terms of training,

237

probably better – as Bannister or Santee. 'I'm not a four-minute miler yet,' Landy said after the run, 'but I soon will be.'

'If you hooked Bannister onto the Twentieth Century Limited [train], he couldn't beat Santee.' The young Kansan referred to himself in the third person in his statements to a crowd of reporters before he boarded a plane to Los Angeles for the Compton Invitational. He explained that he had never felt in better shape.

'Why do you think you could defeat the first four-minute miler?'

'Bannister ran his super mile without pressure . . . I am confident that I can beat any and all comers in a mile foot race.'

Would he set a new record on Saturday?

'California weather and track conditions are just right for championship running. I intend to run extra fast on the coast.'

It was Thursday, 3 June, and Santee felt the noose tightening around what remained of his running career. He had graduated, and real life loomed. He needed to report for Marines officer training day in Quantico, Virginia, in ten days' time. He had only two races left: the Compton Invitational, which Bannister would not make because of his medical board exams, and the open mile at the Southern Pacific AAU meet, where Olympic 1,500m champion Josey Barthel would challenge him. Santee still desperately wanted to break the four-minute mile, and he also wanted to have the chance to run against the Briton and the Australian, perhaps even at the Empire Games in Vancouver if it could be arranged with the AAU and British Empire officials. Bannister and Landy had been his rivals too long for there not to be a showdown. If Santee did not run a record mile, this was not likely to happen. Easton was engaged in a letter campaign to get the Marines to allow him further leave, and if Santee had a sub four-minute mile to his name the publicity he would earn for the military by racing against Bannister and Landy might be worth it. With milers Ingvar Ericsson (the Swedish champion) and Russ Bonham (the Whittier College star) slated to challenge him that Saturday, he was hopeful that he might get that chance. It might be his last.

The month of May had been defined by endings. On 6 May, of course, his dream of being the first to break the four-minute barrier was finished. In the days that followed he had to suffer endless reports of Bannister's run. It was emblazoned on theatre signboards thanks to Fox Movietone News, who had distributed the BBC film footage across the country. At his next meet, he set a new collegiate two-mile record and then led his Jayhawks to their third straight, and his last, Big Seven outdoor track and field championship. Two days before the month's end, he represented the University of Kansas in his final race as a student, clocking his best mile time of 4:01.3. Because Easton had made an error on his application for the NCAA championship during Santee's freshman year, the AAU had banned the miler from competing in the championship in his senior year. No doubt Santee would have won, but his collegiate athletics career had to conclude without that victory.

But none of this would matter to Santee if he managed a record run in Compton. When he arrived in California, Al Franken gave him the star treatment once again. There were numerous television and radio appearances, and time was spent on the set of a Mitzi Gaynor and Ethel Merman picture. But Santee had a single focus: being the first American to break the mile barrier. It would not quite be the first ever, but sadly there was nothing he could do about that now. Although none of his countrymen was as close as he was, an unknown runner could burst on to the scene – much as Landy had almost eighteen months before. Santee would not rest easy until he had run under four minutes himself.

On the afternoon of 5 June, he sat in the locker-room at Ramsaur Field, ten minutes before his race. He had already done his warm-up jog and sprints, and Easton was taping up his shoes for him, pulling the tape from the outside step, over the spikes, and tight around the instep. This added strength to the arches of Santee's feet.

'How do you feel? Everything okay?' his coach asked. Santee

nodded, quiet as ever before a race. Easton patted him on the shoes and said, 'Go, get 'em.'

It was, for California, a cool June afternoon, barely 60°. In the stands, Santee's wife and her parents were watching him through field glasses. They had driven through the night from Kansas to be there. Santee left the locker-room and arrived at the starting line just as the race was about to begin. Easton had followed him out to find a place to stand on the back straight. Track officials, timekeepers, photographers, and television cameramen crowded the infield by the starting line. The timekeepers were reminded to start their watches at the sight of smoke out of the gun, not at the sound of the bang itself, to account for any delay between the shot and its sound reaching them. Everything had to be right for his attempt.

The runners positioned themselves along the line, Santee in the inside lane, his left arm up, his right foot back, facing straight ahead. His former high-school rival Billy Tidwell, who had beaten him in his senior year, was ready to help pace Santee for as long as he could, but they certainly had no strict lap schedule planned out as Bannister had done. They shot off from the line, Marty Montgomery from South California moving into an early lead in the first lap. Montgomery knew he needed to give it everything he had in order to challenge the Ashland Antelope. He stayed back in third position, Bonham just ahead of him. The crowd of eight thousand, at least one in five of whom were waving the Jayhawk symbol, were quiet.

By the end of the first lap, Montgomery had run himself out. Tidwell strode past Santee, then Bonham, then Montgomery, taking the lead a few yards into the second lap. Santee continued to hold back, having decided with Easton that he would wait until the second half-mile before he really took off. Still, his first lap was run in 58.1 seconds – pretty quick. As they moved into the back straight, however, his coach yelled out, 'It's not fast enough! Not fast enough!' Santee heard him, but wanted to ride Tidwell out as long as he possibly could. By the start of the third lap, having run the first half-mile in an impressive 1:58.2, Santee knew he would have to take the lead. Tidwell simply couldn't keep the pace fast enough. As Santee made his way into the turn, he was already past his former rival, alone now against the clock. He felt a surge of energy. He was going for the mile record.

The crowd began to chant his name. 'Santee – Santee – Santee!' Applause started to mount. Danna and her parents sensed that this could be it.

Santee stormed around the track, pushing himself to clock a good time in this third lap. It had always been his most difficult. At that point Ericsson and Bonham were barely clipping at his heels, and it was unlikely they would challenge him. Coming out of the first turn, Santee heard Easton again: 'Faster! Faster!' At the ·bell, Santee was under three minutes by a second and a half. He had managed the third in 60.3 seconds.

'Santee – Santee – Santee!' the crowd called in unison.

One more lap. He just needed to run it in sixty-one seconds. This was the moment to kick, to put aside the pain and give it everything.

In the back straight, Easton shouted, 'Go! Go, Wes, go!'

As the miler went into the last turn, he was tiring badly. Each stride was harder than the one before. He was pumping his arms higher to keep up his speed. His breathing was heavier in his chest. He could barely hear the crowd now; it felt as if he was running in a tunnel. With only a hundred yards to go, he suddenly felt cold. His hands were clammy, and his shoulders seemed to shake. He sensed himself losing feeling in his arms and legs. Still he drove on, past the 1,500-metre mark at the top of the curve where a timekeeper was stationed. Now he just had the straight, and it would be over.

'Santee – Santee – Santee!' The stands were thundering.

He was long past exhaustion as he neared the tape. His legs continued to drive, almost with their own will. This was everything he had. At the finish, he pushed his shoulders forward, and the timekeepers punched their stop buttons. Santee continued down the track, slowing into a jog. His first thought was, 'Have I done it?'

He turned back to the timekeepers. Easton rushed to his side. 'I think we're close,' he said. 'We're really close.'

Finally, the crackle of the public address system quietened the stands. They were going to announce his time. 'Wes Santee has set a new world record in the 1,500 metres with a time of 3:42.8.' Easton and his miler shared a look. That was good, but they wanted the mile time.

'Santee – Santee – Santee!' went the crowd again.

Then the stadium went silent as the announcer came back over the speakers. 'Now the mile time . . . A new stadium record of four minutes and six-tenths of a second!'

It was agonisingly close. Six-tenths of a second close. It was nothing. A flicker of time, an instant of a faster jump at the start, a slightly more favourable breeze, a half-stride, a deeper lean into the tape. Nothing. But still it was everything.

Santee waved towards Danna, who came hurrying down to the edge of the track. He hugged and kissed her before he had to turn to the bustle of reporters, eager to know what had happened. He had broken the world record for the 1,500m, but true greatness in the public eye had escaped him. He was six-tenths of a second shy.

A few days after the race he learned from Easton that the Marines had denied his request for summer leave. He wouldn't get the chance to race Landy and Bannister.

On the evening of 20 June, John Landy walked around the track at Turku's stadium with Chris Chataway. Twilight was darkening the clear sky, and the air was warm and crisp. The weather promised to be much the same for the mile race the following day. The English runner had flown into the city's small airport earlier in the morning, where Landy and Johansson had greeted him in the simple wooden terminal building.

Only a week earlier Chataway had won a 1,500m race in Amsterdam and afterwards had sat down with a *News Chronicle* journalist to declare, 'I should very much like to race against Landy some time in the next fortnight . . . I would not go [to Finland] just as a pace-maker. I would prefer to make a real race of it.' After the Iffley Road triumph, Chataway had asked Bannister and Brasher to help pace him in a world record two-mile attempt. On 6 June, in front of forty thousand fans at White City stadium, Chataway had failed in his bid by a mere three-fifths of a second. Both Brasher and Bannister, tired from competing the prior day in mile and half-mile races respectively, had not been able to assist him as much as they would have liked. After the race, Chataway said, 'I much prefer racing against men than against the clock. It is much more fun.'

Prompted by Denis Johansson, the Turku Athletic Association almost immediately issued Chataway an invitation through the British AAA. Coincidentally, Bannister's world mile record was ratified on the same day. Before Chataway accepted the offer, he made one request: he wanted the 1,500m race on 21 June changed to a mile. Everyone agreed. It was obvious to most that Chataway might prove the missing ingredient in Landy's pursuit of a record mile. If Landy managed to beat Bannister's time only weeks later, and without the help of pacing, the achievement at Iffley Road would be diminished in many minds, including Bannister's. Before Chataway left England, Bannister told his friend, 'If you do go, it makes it certain that he will break the four-minute mile.' Chataway had retorted that there was no such certainty about it; he simply wanted to see how he would fare against the Australian. Although bothered by Chataway's participation in the race, Bannister said nothing else, knowing he had no right to tell another athlete, let alone a friend, when and where to compete.

In the four races Landy had run since arriving in Scandinavia, he had yet to find what he needed to break any world record. In Stockholm, a week after his 4:01.6 mile in Turku, Landy ran the same time again, despite having the added support of his father (who was travelling through Europe with John's uncle and aunt). Perhaps this was the best Landy could do; perhaps Bannister's widely reported prediction that others would soon follow him into sub-four-minute mile territory was simply not true. On the after-noon of 11 June, on the same day that Landy tried and failed to claim a 1,500m record in Helsinki, Wes Santee was agonisingly short again, clocking 4:00.7, despite the fact that Josey Barthel was there to challenge him. With his Marines commitment, it looked like the American might not get another shot. Landy didn't have much time left himself to keep cracking his head against his own four-minute wall. On 16 June, although feeling tired from too much racing, Landy managed a 5:12.6 in a 2,000m race, eleven seconds faster than his best, but this hardly helped his mile chances.

While walking with Chataway during the evening before their race, Landy stopped at the side of the track and looked at the British miler. The Australian knew Chataway had come not in an attempt to pace Landy, as some in the press had said. Chataway was there to beat him. 'I could change into shorts and spikes now,' Landy said, 'and run a mile in 4:02 with nobody watching and with no com-petition.' Chataway believed that Landy could do exactly what he said. Unlike he and Bannister, Landy had trained hard enough to run good times week after week without much strain. This gave him a toughness, physically and mentally, that Chataway felt he simply didn't have. The English runner would have to run the best mile of his life if he was to have any chance of winning, particularly since his fastest mile was 4:07.2.

The next afternoon, Landy had a late lunch with Johansson, enjoying a beer with his Finnish host and feeling confident. Before Chataway had arrived in Turku, Landy had run three time trials – 200 metres in 23 seconds, 300 metres in 37 seconds, and 400 metres in 49 seconds – showing how sharp his speed was. As he later said, he was as 'fit as a trout'. With the British miler threatening him, Landy believed that in his seven o'clock race he might well make his own bit of history. Johansson agreed, having timed Landy in his trials. The Finn offered to arrange for a pacesetter in the race, but Landy declined. He wanted to do it on his own.

At seven o'clock, forty-six days after Bannister broke through the barrier that had withstood decades of assault, Landy wished his competitors good luck and settled into his lane at the starting line. He wore white shorts and his Geelong Guild singlet with the number 2 pinned to his chest. Chataway was number 1 in all white, Johansson number 3 in all black. Three other milers, including the young Finnish ace Antte Kallio, were lined up alongside them. It was the longest day of the year, and the sun was still bright in the sky. The weather was ideal: 70° and no wind. Eight thousand Finnish fans had jammed themselves into the small stadium, anticipating a great race, particularly with this red-headed Chataway fellow who had served as hare for the first four-minute miler. A number of journalists, many of whom had flown in for the event, were also in attendance.

As the gun trailed smoke from its barrel, the six runners bolted from the line. Kallio, who started third from the post, quickly angled his way towards the inside line past Chataway. Moving into the first turn, Landy positioned himself a stride behind Kallio's right shoulder, letting him take the lead. Landy wanted to run as even a pace as possible, in contrast to his 31 May race. Three-quarters of the way through the first lap they maintained this position, with Chataway in third place, two strides back, and Johansson in fourth. Landy finished the first lap in 58.5, Kallio ahead by half a second. The Australian was running smoothly, his form ideal – high knee lift, eased shoulders, centre of gravity balanced, heel-to-toe roll as his shoes hit the track. He was a very different runner from two years before.

At a lap and a half, Landy decided to take the lead. He had waited longer than usual, but Kallio looked to be tiring from such a strong early pace. Nearing the halfway mark, Landy was decidedly in control, Chataway ten feet behind him. Kallio, Johansson, and the rest of the field were forgotten. It was a two-man race. Chataway thought that if he held close to Landy he could dash ahead of the Australian in the final straight. At the start of the third lap stop-watches registered an average 1:57.9 – ideal pace. Landy thought he had the race in hand. He had been in this position many times before, and his competitors had always folded by the first turn in the final lap.

The third lap was steady and sure. His rhythm was good, and he continued to run relaxed. The sound of his feet striking the cinder track had the steady beat of a metronome. This was the pause before Landy gathered the focus and determination he would need to maintain a fast pace through the last lap. The lead did not change, and the two milers distanced themselves further from the field. The crowd was expectant, but with Landy, they had been there before. They knew enough about middle-distance running to understand that the proof was in the final lap.

At the bell, the time was impressive – 2:56. Landy was surprised to hear Chataway so close behind him at such a late stage in the race. He was just two strides back – incredible, given the pace. Nobody had ever been able to keep up with him this far. Nonetheless, Landy did not break. Yes, the British runner was good, but he had to fail soon; another hundred yards at most. If Landy broke too fast too soon, he would not have the drive to finish strong. He had seized up around the last turn into the final straight too many times before.

Three-quarters of a lap from the finish, the indefatigable Chataway was still on his shoulder. This is it, Landy thought. If he slowed, the British runner would surely pounce. Landy had to go. He got onto his toes and said to himself, 'NOW!' As Landy accelerated away from him, Chataway never had a chance to hold. Five yards and then ten separated them in what seemed a blink of the eye. Chataway was incredulous. Bannister had needed him and Brasher to carry him around the track for over three laps before he made his kick. Landy had managed nearly the entire race from the front yet still had the reserves to drive towards the finish with such speed. It was an amazing display of self-reliance.

Suddenly, the crowd realised what was happening. They began chanting: 'Landy! Landy! Landy!'

The Australian had to be tiring, but he maintained his rhythm as he moved into the last turn. The stands boomed his name louder and louder. Timekeepers positioned at the 1,500m mark looked at their watches after he passed. It was world record fast – 3:41.8. Blistering.

Landy did not hear the crowd, or know his time. Having broken away from Chataway, he focused solely on fighting the pain and tension to sustain form. Don't fight the stride, he told himself. His legs continued to drive down the track. It was impossible to know if they were slowing. He willed himself to go faster, though the effect was only to maintain his speed. When he broke through the tape, there was no great leap forward. He looked almost as if he planned to continue down the track.

Turning, he saw Chataway finish almost forty yards behind him. Landy had no idea what he had run. It felt fast, maybe 4:01 or 4:02. The Finnish miler Vuorisalo crossed the finish line next, then Johansson. Kallio came last. The eight thousand spectators waited anxiously for the time. Finally, the announcer came on to the public address system and spoke a few words in Finnish. Pandemonium erupted throughout the stadium. Landy couldn't understand the words, but he knew he must have done something spectacular to evoke such a response. Johansson angled towards him as the stands emptied and hundreds of cheering Finns surrounded Landy.

'A new world record!' Johansson yelled to him. '3:58!'

Landy was stunned, but had only a moment to register that he had beaten Bannister's time by a second and a half before he was hoisted onto the shoulders of a mass of people. The Finns raised him up and down like a trophy over their heads. Camera flashbulbs exploded ahead of him. He was carried forward, nearly horizontal, arms above his head. He had finally done it.

Eventually, the crowd let his feet touch the track again, and Johansson told him he should run a lap of honour. Landy found Chataway, who had run his best time of 4:04.4, and asked him to come along. There was no way he could have done it without him, Landy said.

'No, no,' Chataway replied. 'It's your achievement. It's you they want to see.'

Finally, Landy threaded his way out of the crowd and began to run slowly around the track. Thunderous applause followed him, and the Australian flag was raised over the stadium. After two years of concentrated effort and countless races run well but deemed failures, the mile record was his, and by a staggering margin.

the barrier first was almost meaningless now, particularly if the Australian beat him in face-to-face competition.

'I look forward very much to racing against Landy in Vancouver in August,' Bannister explained calmly. 'But I don't expect that his time will be broken in a race of that kind with twelve men running.'

'Will you try to break Landy's record in the near future then?'

He smiled. 'I don't know.'

When Bannister finally managed to close the door on the reporters, he faced the fact that his greatest race was not six weeks in the past, but rather six weeks in the future. Beating 3:58 was, if not completely impossible, the least of his worries. Though he continued to go to the Duke of York's Barracks, he had allowed his training to lose focus; his running, as he described it, was in the 'doldrums'. Since 6 May, he had been pulled in every direction except towards the track.

A few days after his Iffley Road triumph, he'd been shipped off to the United States for what could only be called a victory tour, encouraged by the British Foreign Office. Upon landing at New York's Idlewild Airport, he was beset by controversy. The television programme *I've Got a Secret* had paid for the trip, and since the show was commercially sponsored – and by none other than a cigarette manufacturer – Bannister risked losing his amateur status if he appeared. The appearance had to be cancelled, and his expenses repaid. Still, he participated in a number of interviews, reportedly reaching a total of seventy-five million people, answering questions including 'Do you think you will be knighted by the Queen?' ('Good gracious me!') and 'What do you think of American girls?' ('They have a certain uniformity as you see them on the street, but I am sure that individually they are delightful.') Then he stumbled into another mess when the Olympic Committee of Southern California presented him with the 'Miracle Mile Trophy', which had been created years before for the first athlete to run the landmark achievement. A firestorm erupted when reporters discovered that the trophy was worth £178 – exactly £166 more than an amateur could accept in prizes. Bannister returned to England with a miniature replica valued at £12.

Once back in London, he sank himself into his medical exams. 'You sweated blood over them,' a contemporary of his at St Mary's explained. First was a series of three-hour essay tests in medicine, surgery, obstetrics, pharmacology, and several other fields. Second was the practical exam, for which Bannister was presented with a patient and had forty-five minutes to take a history and do a full examination. At the end, he had to give a diagnosis and treatment plan. If he missed something serious, he failed. After eight years of preparation, there was a great deal at stake.

His studies left little time for a social life, but during the summer he began to see a young Swedish woman named Moyra Jacobsson, a talented artist with a studio in St. Albans Grove in London. Her father was Chief Economist for the bank for Internation Settlements. She was decidedly underwhelmed with Bannister's achievements on the track. He joked, 'I am quite sure she was under the impression that I had run four miles in one minute.' No doubt she was intriguing for this reason, as well as for her striking looks and wide-ranging interests. The two had the opportunity to meet only a couple of times that summer, but Bannister wanted to get to know her better once he'd qualified as a doctor and returned from Vancouver.

When Bannister participated in races, his results were lacklustre at best. At the British Games on 4 June at White City stadium, he ran the half-mile and lost to Czechoslovakia's Stanislav Jungwirth. The next day he saw his picture on the front of the newspapers, his jersey spattered with mud while Jungwirth breasted the tape in front of him. 'Here's mud in your eye,' Bannister joked to himself about what the headline would read, knowing how fickle the press was. Two days later he tried to help Chataway claim the two-mile world record and struggled through the second half of the race, finishing sixth. As Bannister expected, the British press seized on these failures, particularly with Jungwirth, as evidence that Bannister was better against the clock than man to man. It appeared they were just as good at toppling kings as they were at making them. Some thought Bannister was scared of the infighting and jockeying for position, the type of rough competition that made mile races so appealing to fans. The *Daily Mirror* wrote, most pointedly, 'There is a world of difference between racing for time and racing to win. The white line and clear course are needed for the one; generalship, ability to change pace, and track tactics for the other. And Bannister is not strong in these latter qualities. For that he can blame his policy of keeping actual racing to a minimum.'

If the miler was going to have a chance at the Empire Games and European Championship, the pundits recommended he start running in more races to get the feel of competition. Now that Landy had claimed a new world record, a 'titanic clash' between the two milers was expected in Vancouver. Bannister had to get cracking. After all, in many circles he was now perceived as the underdog.

Typically, Bannister ignored the press's advice. Nonetheless, he started to prepare in earnest for his showdown with Landy immediately after the news arrived from Turku. He quickly reintensified his training efforts. More importantly, he also began to strategise about how to run against this miler who had crossed the finish line in 3:58 and moments afterwards, according to Chataway, had looked like he had simply gone out for a Sunday-afternoon jog.

In the evening after Landy ran the fastest race of his life, he retreated uncomfortably from the spotlight. Of the glare of publicity, he later said, 'It's not really life. You have to see it for what it is. It's not what it's all about.' His motivation had always been to excel, but it was not about acclaim or records for their own sake. The attention was simply something to cope with as best one could. He attended a celebration party thrown for him beside a lake, but after a few beers he left early, surprising Chataway and Johansson. He knew they didn't understand his lack of elation. His 3:58 mile brought him a strong sense of accomplishment, yet he had run it without much strain, and as he put it, 'It was done. Finished. Next thing.'

He was the only one to take the record with equanimity. Such was his achievement that Finland's prime minister, Urho Kekkonen, who was a former Olympic high-jumper and friend of Paavo Nurmi, presented Landy with the Kekkonen Cup, an honour never before awarded to anyone other than a Finnish athlete. His friends back home had literally cheered into their radios as they listened to the 21 June race. His family was awakened in the middle of the night with the news. The phone in their East Malvern home rang non-stop until the morning, and Landy's mother sent a telegram to her son that read, 'Thrilled with superb run (stop) Best news ever (stop) Mother.' The Australian papers revelled in their great hero, who predicted, 'I can do even better.' Landy was noted for his 'unquenchable, indomitable spirit' and how 'perseverance should be his middle name'. In the *Sun*, his 3:58 mile was shown in comparison to previous world record times, the illustration detailing how in a race he would have finished ten yards ahead of Bannister, twenty-five ahead of Gundar Haegg, and over sixty-five yards in front of Wooderson and Cunningham. In the *Age*, an editorial remarked on how Landy had bolstered national pride, and then explained how 'sportsmen, as well as statesmen, carry a heavy responsibility for our good name. So long as they are of the Landy type, they will not let us down.' Over Melbourne's town hall, the same Australian Olympic flag that had been flown at Helsinki was raised high once again, this time in honour of John Landy, and Victorian amateur officials suggested naming Olympic Park after the great miler. When reporters tracked down Percy Cerutty, he once again took credit for coaching this national treasure and also explained how 'I have always said that Landy could run 3:57. No miler in the world has covered the training miles in twelve months that John has.'

The next day Landy escaped the crush of attention, thanks to Johansson, who arranged for a trip to Naantali, a small, secluded island outside Turku, where the miler could relax and take a hike along the wooded shoreline. Over the next week, the story about the upcoming clash with Bannister at the Empire Games gathered momentum in the news. Still Landy did not want to talk about his running. When Geoff Warren, who had been competing in England and Norway prior to Vancouver, came to visit him in Finland, Landy barely let his friend utter a word about the 3:58 record before shifting the conversation to Warren's recent 5,000m race in Oslo. Landy knew about it in detail. 'It took a major effort to be able to get him to hear my congratulations,' Warren later said.

Despite his reluctance to discuss his running, in the three weeks before his arrival in Vancouver on 15 July, Landy thought about it a lot. His 'next thing', the second of his two ambitions, was winning that mile race in the Empire Games against Bannister. He knew it would be a big deal; the die was cast when he beat Bannister's time. As Landy later put it, 'The race had the ingredients for a world title fight. On the one hand they said you couldn't run four minutes and there's a guy who does it. Seven weeks later someone betters his time. They're both going to represent their countries. There was no pacing, no artificiality. I was going to try to win from the front. He was going to try to hang on. It was almost an unbelievable set of circumstances.'

Running a mile is an art form created from speed and stamina. These two can be applied very differently, and Bannister and Landy pursued diametrically opposed styles. From what Bannister had read and heard of the Australian – and he tried to learn as much as possible – Landy was, in athletics parlance, a 'front-runner', the kind of miler who set a breakneck pace from the beginning, leaving his foes choking on his dust and unable to catch him in the last lap. He relied on pace judgement and confidence in his superior fitness to crush his opponents. Bannister was a 'racer' or 'positional runner', who stayed back, letting milers such as Landy carry him around the track, making sure to stay close enough – or in 'contact' – so that by the bell he was able to strike with a fast finishing kick. Both had advantages and disadvantages, and in the mile, all decisions on how fast to set the pace, when to break 'contact', and when to start one's kick, had to be made quickly through a haze of exhaustion. But an athlete could prepare in advance to improve his chances. He simply had to begin the race in the understanding that, much like an artist, he could sketch the lines of a painting yet could not know what colours and shades of colour would best play off one another until the first brush strokes were made.

In developing his strategy, Bannister had Chataway, who had not only brought back Landy's times broken down in 100-metre splits from his races in Finland, but knew what it was to compete against him. Prior to this, the most insight Bannister had had into the Australian came from Percy Cerutty's overblown statements that he had read in athletics journals: how in Landy there was a 'ruthlessness, lack of feeling for others, and a ferocity and antagonism, albeit mostly vented on himself, that makes it possible on occasions for John to rise to sublime heights of physical endeavour'. Chataway had experienced Landy first hand. He had walked around the track with him the night before his 3:58 mile and had seen the Australian after the record, responding as Chataway later described: 'It was a solemn moment for him. All the people gathered around him were not looking at it the same way he was. He was not ebullient or over the moon. It was as if this was an entirely private achievement, something he wanted, worked for, struggled one hell [of] a lot of time [for], and suddenly it had arrived. It was almost like having the world's press descend on your wedding night. This was entirely private to him.'

The Australian was driven by a demand to push himself to the limit. He drove fast from the beginning, never looking back. A race was less about what others were doing and more about personal challenge. Part of this had to do with the fact that Landy was never threatened in Australia, therefore this was the only kind of racing he knew, but part of it came from the kind of person he was as well. In Vancouver, he would take the lead and try to run the legs out from under Bannister.

To make sure this was his strategy, Bannister decided to send a message to Landy. The Australian might be physically tougher, but Bannister had the ability to deliver a withering finish out of sheer will. At the AAA Championship on 10 July, a day after he qualified as a doctor, he ran the first three laps of the mile race at a moderate pace, staying back in the pack. One hundred yards after the bell, he burst forward into the lead and drove at flat-out pace to the finish, clocking a last lap of 53.8 seconds for a mile time of 4:07.6. If Landy had questions about Bannister's kick, they were answered now.

In the woods outside Quantico, Virginia, Wes Santee was kneeling on the dirt, fumbling with the straps of his backpack during yet another hour-long hike through the woods in the hot mid-July sun. His M-1 rifle was leaning against a nearby tree.

'Candidate,' a voice said sternly above him.

Santee looked up to see J. D. Roberts, the former Oklahoma football star, towering above him and wearing the stripes of a lieutenant. 'Yes, sir?' Santee said.

'We want you to carry that rifle. It's not to be away from your body. You sleep with it. You take it to the latrine. Do you understand?'

'Yes, sir,' Wes replied, throwing his backpack over his shoulder and grabbing his rifle as the others in his platoon began to move away. He followed quickly behind them, his shirt sticking to his chest after a long afternoon of marching. It was his third week of boot camp, but this was his first day of training. While the others in his platoon had already been taught how to fire their rifles and pack their gear in the previous two weeks, Santee had been busy elsewhere.

The past month had been a whirlwind. On 11 June at Memorial Stadium in Los Angeles, Santee had entered into the final lap of his race against Josey Barthel two strides behind. Three minutes flat had elapsed on the clock, and once again he was in perfect position to be the first American to run the magic sub-four-minute mile. Barthel then surged ahead, looking as if he wanted to break away from Santee by the back stretch. Santee knew he needed to maintain an even pace if he was going to run under four minutes, but he couldn't risk Barthel winning the race. Halfway down the back straight, 220 yards from the finish, Santee coiled and sprang past Barthel like 'a shot out of a gun'. The crowd was mad with excitement as Santee decisively retook the lead. But a hundred yards from the finish Santee lost speed, albeit only a fraction. His burst to gain the lead had tied up his legs. He broke the tape in 4:00.7, tenths of a second too slow – again.

After the race, Barthel came up to him. 'Why did you go past me? I was setting it up for you.'

It took Santee a moment to realise what Barthel had just said. He was stunned. The Luxemburger had moved past him in the final lap in an effort to pace him to the finish. Had Santee just hung on to him until the last hundred instead of running his legs out on the back stretch, he could have had his record.

Afterwards, Santee had very little to say to reporters. It was devastating for him to have come so close for the second time, but he kept that to himself. 'I'm leaving my running to the Marines this summer,' he told them. 'I hope they will let me get away for a few meets, but I certainly don't want to be a coddled athlete.'

A couple of days later, Santee and his wife packed their clothes in Lawrence and said their goodbyes. When Santee went to the ROTC centre to pick up his orders, a Marines major stopped him at the door. 'I know you think you're a big hotshot athlete,' he said, 'but you're going down there to do your basic training. Got that?'

Santee nodded his head. 'Yes, sir.'

In Quantico, only moments after arriving and while in the process of collecting his boots and fatigues, a jeep pulled alongside his platoon and the driver yelled, 'Candidate Santee?'

Wes stepped forward. 'Here, sir.'

'Come here.'

Santee was carrying his boots and an armful of shirts. 'What am I supposed to do with this stuff?'

'Leave it there.'

Minutes later, Santee stepped into the office of General Clifton Cates, commandant of the Marine Corps School – or 'God', as some called the steely-eyed, 61-year-old three-star general who had first distinguished himself at the Battle of Verdun during the First World War.

'Nice to meet you, Wes,' the general said, shaking his hand then moving back behind his desk. 'Good to have you here. We're proud to have you as a Marine. Now, next weekend we're having the All Marine Corps track meet at Camp LaJeune in North Carolina. If you represent Quantico, we can win this thing.'

'Thank you, sir. But I'm here to do my military training.'

'I know, but we have all kinds of Marines coming in for the meet. We can win this thing if you run.'

'I need to get my military duty out of the way, sir.' Santee looked to his right, where a Marines major was moving his head up and down, indicating that he should say yes or suffer the consequences. 'When I left Kansas, I was told that I couldn't do any running down here. What am I supposed to do?'

'Hey, look,' the three-star general said calmly. 'If I say it's okay, it's okay.'

An hour later, Santee was in a staff car on his way to North Carolina. He did not even have time to call Danna to tell her he was leaving. She had to read about it in a newspaper, after which she drove down to join him. At the meet, Santee raced in the mile, half-mile, and the relays. He won them all and earned Quantico a first-place trophy. That night he received a phone call from General Cates. 'Fine job ... By the way, stay down another week, because we're going to host the All-Services Championship.'

While Santee was in North Carolina, news of John Landy's 3:58 broke, and the press hounded Wes for a comment. Given how close the Australian had come the previous month, Santee was not surprised. 'People who have concentrated in the manner that Landy and Bannister have may eventually run a mile in 3:55,' the cadet said. He resented the fact that he had not been able to do the same. When he was allowed to focus himself in the same way, an opportunity that would have to wait until his three months' military training was completed, Santee advised reporters not to exclude him from the list of milers capable of the feat. He already had a plan: in the autumn he would do intensive, cross-country training mixed with short sprints on the track; in the winter he would race on the indoor circuit to sharpen his speed; and in the spring of 1955 he would be ready. 'I'm going to train as hard as I can and sacrifice everything I have to bring the mile record back to the United States,' he promised.

When Santee returned to basic training after leading the Marines to triumph in the All-Services Championship, thoughts of four-minute barriers and mile races were lost to the demands of Quantico. He had to play catch-up learning how to be a soldier, and lieutenants such as Roberts offered no special treatment to Santee now that General Cates was finished with him. Although the Kansas miler was in better shape than others in his platoon, handling the long marches as if he was out for a stroll, boot camp had other challenges. Week after week, as Santee was instructed on marksmanship, orienteering, survival skills, and hand-to-hand combat, his name disappeared from the athletics headlines, and his hopes of a great showdown with Bannister and Landy faded.

After Landy set his mile record in Turku, he began training again in earnest for the Empire Games, scheduled for a 30 July start. Mostly he concentrated on speed work, running repeat 800 metres with two laps of jogging in between. He had been in racing form since December 1953, a long period in which to keep at top pitch without a break, but his relentless training kept him going.

As for his strategy, there was never really any question of how he would run his race. Even when he read of Bannister's 10 July last lap of 53.8 – which Landy interpreted automatically as a statement from the British miler that 'You have no alternative, mate, you have to lead' – he did not think of surprising Bannister by playing a waiting game in Vancouver. Johansson advised Landy not to set the pace from the beginning as he had in his races in Finland. The Finnish miler told him that unless he was able to establish a huge lead running from the front, Bannister would be able to catch him with his kick. Although Landy binned the letter, Cerutty instructed much the same, telling him to pace the first lap as if it was a warm-up, then to run as if it was a three-lap race.

Tactically, Landy did not have much experience. He had not lost a mile race in almost two years, and every one of those he had led almost from the start. He liked running his opposition into the ground and thought that as long as he set a fast enough pace Bannister would not have enough leg in the last lap to deliver his kick. This was what he'd done with Chataway, who had finished forty yards behind him in Turku. Landy had read up on Bannister's times, and though he was fit, Landy was fitter. Tactics were fine and good, but critical only if the race was settled by a matter of yards. If Landy had his way, he would be so far in front of Bannister there would be no room for manoeuvre on his part. More importantly, Landy simply didn't want to run a slow, jockeying race. He wanted to control it from the start.

On 11 July, in response to Bannister's statement at the AAA Championship the day before, Landy decided to send a message of his own. In his last race in Finland before leaving for Vancouver, he produced a witheringly fast 1,000 metres, only half a second shy of world record in 2:20.9, despite a strong wind and a short 300-metre track. That was the kind of speed Bannister would have to contend with in their showdown. As Landy later explained, 'I felt that this might confuse the issue as to who was going to take the lead in the Vancouver race. Maybe I was going to run a quite different race [than Bannister expected] and use my speed to win tactically by lurking behind him.'

Two weeks before the Empire Games was due to start, Wes Santee was with his platoon marching with his rifle in one of Quantico's outlying camps when he was told by his commanding officer that he was wanted at company headquarters. A jeep transported him 'Mainside', and he was ushered into the office of public affairs. Santee had no idea what to expect.

He saluted the Marines captain in charge of the office and stood at attention in front of his desk. The captain went straight to the point. 'There's the Bannister and Landy race in Vancouver on August seven, and NBC wants you to go to New York and do some commentary on it.'

Santee swallowed the news. He had no choice in the matter, so he said, 'Yes, sir.'

For a competitor like him, who had spent years training to be the best in the world in the mile, this was a cruel request. He did not want to watch these two on a monitor and announce the race. He wanted to run it. But because of his military obligations and international racing ban, he had no recourse.

'Do you have a dress uniform?' the officer asked.

'No,' Santee said. He had spikes and a singlet, he wanted to say, but this was not what he had been asked.

Santee must have thought that this meeting could have been about his competing against Bannister and Landy, had he found a way to knock six-tenths of a second off his Compton Invitational mile. He had come so close. His AAU fight, his commitment to the Marines, and his Jayhawk team obligations had kept him from achieving his own ambitions.

A jeep returned him to his platoon. Crawling quickly through the mud underneath strands of barbed-wire was the only racing he would be doing in the upcoming days.

*　　*　　*

On 15 July, Landy flew into Vancouver, circling past the city of sky-scrapers and the bay's crystal-blue waters dotted with yachts before the airplane's wheels touched down on the tarmac with a screech. As the plane taxied in, Landy looked out of the window to see what some called his 'film star' welcome. It was simply a mob. Hundreds of fans, autograph seekers, journalists, and cameramen swarmed around the miler, pushing aside the four other Australian athletes travelling with him. Vancouver's mayor had also come to welcome Landy, on account of the fact that he was proving an economic boom to the city: ticket sales had spiked the day after Landy ran his own sub-four-minute mile and had since sold out. Finally, the police had to step in to escort Landy to a waiting car before he was glad-handed to death.

When the official responsible for transporting him to the village got the door closed, he discovered that only he and Landy were inside. 'Oh,' the official said. 'Where are the other Australians? Can't forget them.'

Once the others were found and herded into the car, a motor-cycle police escort led them to the Empire Village where a press conference was waiting. Everyone wanted to know what Landy thought of his chances in the race now being labelled the 'Mile of the Century'.

On Friday, 23 July, Roger Bannister knocked on the door of Franz Stampfl's flat on the King's Road and was welcomed inside. Coach and athlete sat together on the couch while Stampfl's wife made a pot of tea in the small adjoining kitchen.

The Austrian coach had ignored the hype after Bannister's Iffley Road triumph, preferring to slip away quietly and get back to London to train other athletes. He didn't need to stand around and have his picture taken by Bannister's side, nor claim that the four-minute mile had been achieved through strict adherence to his coaching. As Stampfl told Pat on the evening of 6 May, he would have liked to escape London for a few days because 'the heavens are going to open'. The only satisfaction Stampfl got from the publicity was the knowledge that it would encourage more athletes to train with him.

As Bannister was leaving for Vancouver the following day, and Stampfl could not afford to travel with him (nor did he want to be hassled about his role as Bannister's coach), this was their last chance to speak before the Empire Games. Stampfl was convinced that the confidence the English miler had gained from 6 May would hold out for his race against Landy.

Over tea and the rumble of the King's Road traffic outside, the two talked strategy. It was largely a conversation of 'what ifs'.* What if Landy played a waiting game? What if the pace was too strong to maintain contact? What if Bannister broke too early and ran out of steam before the finish? Fundamentally, the focus was on this final question. There was no doubt Landy would maintain a severe pace through the first three laps, leaving Bannister simply too tired to keep within striking distance. If Bannister started his kick from about three hundred yards out, the typical distance at which he made his move (and there would only be the one opportunity for a move), he would find it difficult, if not impossible, to keep driving to the line at that top pace. His best chance then might be to wait, to make sure he never lost contact, and to let Landy draw him around the track until the final turn, going into the home stretch. 'That's when the damage must be done,' Stampfl told Bannister. 'Not before.' Coming out of the bend, Bannister should strike, enjoy the brief psychological advantage of passing Landy ('a blow in the stomach' as Stampfl described it), and not give him the chance to make a counter-move.

Bannister could have arrived at this strategy on his own, but developing it with Stampfl helped convince him it was possible. His coach assured him that he had the strength and competitive will to 'unleash just that extra energy' needed at the end of the race to win, as he had at Iffley Road over two months earlier. Yes, Landy had run better times with more consistency. Yes, if they had to compete against each other week after week Landy would probably win more races than he lost. But for this one race, Bannister could summon the mental focus to win.

The effect of his talk with Stampfl was profound, as it had been on the morning of 6 May. Chris Chataway best explained what these conversations with their coach provided: 'It was a sort of pre-race mental callisthenics. I would say I was tired, and he would explain why he was absolutely convinced that my finishing burst would be strong. In a way, I knew he didn't know any better than I did whether or not I would win, because it was a total unknown quantity, but just hearing someone say the things . . . was useful.'

Bannister left Stampfl that afternoon certain he would win the Empire Games mile. Perhaps by less than a stride, but a stride was all he needed.

17

What happens when a 3:59.4 miler matches strides with a 3:58 miler? It is not an academic question like the time-honored poser: What would happen if Jack Dempsey fought Joe Louis? Bannister and Landy are contemporaries, and no one will have to wait long for an answer.

New York Times, 1 August 1954

At London Airport, Bannister and a large group of British athletes, including Chataway and Brasher, boarded a plane for their flight to Vancouver. Their first stop was supposed to be Montreal, but twelve hours after take-off, because of a brisk headwind, they had to stop over at Goose Bay in Labrador, an isolated patch of land usually frozen in ice, to refuel. Since the layover lasted for several hours, Bannister disembarked and began jogging around the fifty-square-yard compound to which they were restricted. Other athletes soon followed him, and, as marathoner Jim Peters put it, 'we paced backwards and forwards like convicts during their daily exercise period'. When they eventually landed in Montreal, in the middle of the night, they slept in what amounted to an army barracks whose only luxury was a Coca-Cola machine that took English sixpence coins and gave the change in Canadian money worth more than what they had paid. For amateurs dispensed only a few pounds a day in expenses, this was a windfall.

The following morning they re-boarded the plane for the ten-hour journey to Vancouver. The boredom was relieved by a pillow fight in the back of the plane, where Bannister was sitting, and by the sight of the Rocky Mountains, with the pilot pointing out the various peaks of the vast and awe-inspiring range. Bannister had procured a melon, and he sliced it into pieces for his team-mates, some of whom, never having seen the fruit before, refused the delicacy, not daring to upset their carefully calibrated diets.

Finally, on 26 July, they landed in Vancouver. Over a thousand people and a troop of bagpipe players were on the tarmac awaiting their arrival. The athletes filed out of the airplane in strict order, team captain Jim Peters the last to leave. After nearly two days of quiet anticipation, they were thrown into the carnival atmosphere of the Empire Games. As his team-mates dispersed into the crowd, the press flocked to the main and only attraction, the newly minted doctor, Roger Bannister. His salient comment before jumping into a car was, 'I will be out to win, not to break records.' One particularly observant reporter noted that Bannister was wearing a wristwatch with the twelve letters P-E-N-N-S-Y-L-V-A-N-I-A in place of numerals for the hour markings. He had earned the watch by winning the 1951 Benjamin Franklin Mile, one of his first great victories on the international stage.

After leaving the airport in Vancouver, Bannister and Chataway dropped off their bags at the University of British Columbia campus, the site of Empire Village, and headed off to take a swim at the pool built for the Empire Games. As they walked past the training track on their way to the pool, Bannister spotted Landy on the track.

The two had not met since the Helsinki Games in 1952, yet for nearly two years each had followed the other's every move. It was inevitable that they speak before their race, and Bannister wanted to get it out of the way. He was not known for befriending his rivals. Landy must have been aware of this, as it was his country-man Don Macmillan who had told Bannister years before, 'Roger, you only become really friendly with your opponents after you've beaten them!'

Bannister and Chataway walked down to the track. Landy was

running sprints on the grass, barefoot and wearing only a pair of white shorts. He saw them and came across the field. He was darkly tanned and as fit as any miler Bannister had ever seen.

'Hello, John,' Bannister said, feeling awkward.

'Roger,' Landy said. He shook his hand vigorously and hardly seemed fazed.

Thankfully for Bannister, Chataway was there to ease the tension. He greeted the Australian as an old friend.

'Seen the track at the new Empire Stadium?' Bannister enquired.

'Yes,' Landy said. 'It looks a bit clayey. If the weather gets hot, it'll get very hard.'

The three spoke of the weather (sunny and smashing, they said) and about how Landy's father would be coming to see the race (wonderful, they agreed), but nothing was said about their upcoming race. They were two prize-fighters talking about everything except what mattered most.

'Are you going to have a run tonight?' Landy asked.

'No, we're off for a swim,' Bannister said plainly. And after a few more pleasantries, Bannister and Chataway walked off, leaving Landy to continue with his training run. It was the most they would say to each other until after their race nearly two weeks later.

Before they went their separate ways, however, a pair of *Vancouver Sun* photographers slipped over to catch the two in a picture that was splashed across newspapers the following day under headlines such as 'Mile Stars in Guarded Meeting'. The great showdown had begun.

On 30 October 1891, five years before the revival of the ancient Olympic Games, the Reverend J. Astley Cooper proposed in *The Times* a 'Pan-Britannic Festival' of sport, bringing together all the countries of the British Empire. There were many who thought that Britain owed her greatness on the world stage to the ideals her people learned in amateur athletics. The concept took some time to gather momentum, but eventually, in honour of King George V's coronation two decades later, an awkwardly titled 'Festival of Empire' was held that featured, among other exhibitions, an inter-Empire sports competition between Great Britain, Australia, South Africa, and Canada.

It was not until 1930, however, that the first true Empire Games was held, in Hamilton, Canada. Teams from seven countries, all English-speaking and united under the Union Jack flag, competed in athletics, swimming, boxing, wrestling, rowing, and lawn bowls. Only male athletes were allowed to compete, and the mile race was won by England's R. H. Thomas in 4:14. Much had changed in the twenty-four years since: now women competed alongside men; twenty-four countries were represented instead of the original four; athletes arrived by airplane instead of ship; competitions were followed throughout the world by radio and television instead of in newsprint; electronic devices decided sprint finishes instead of the naked eye; and the two men competing in the mile event had already broken the four-minute mile.

The Vancouver Games opened on 30 July to a parade of athletes, a mass hoisting of flags, the release of pigeons, and the firing of guns. The focus of attention was a far cry from Cooper's original vision of unifying Empire countries under the shared principle of sport. The only thing people wanted to read, see, and hear about was what would happen when the two sub-four-minute milers raced. Henry Luce, the famed publisher who founded *Time*, *Fortune*, and *Life*, had sent his best writer and photographer to Vancouver to cover the race for the inaugural issue of his magazine *Sports Illustrated*. He had arranged for a plane to be waiting on standby at the airport on the day of the mile final to fly the colour pictures of the finish to their printers. To televise the event across the United States and Canada, NBC took the extreme measure of building a number of permanent radio relay towers between Vancouver and Seattle because the Canadian Broadcasting Company, whose first television station had launched only two years before, had yet to build a coast-to-coast relay. From Seattle, the images would then be transmitted by relay to Portland, Salt Lake City, Denver, Omaha, Chicago, Buffalo, and finally New York. Meanwhile, 560 radio stations in the United States and hundreds of others around the world had cleared timeslots on their schedules for the event's broadcast.

For the estimated 100 million people expected to tune into the Saturday, 7 August 'Dream Race', the rest of the Games was window-dressing. And John Landy and Roger Bannister knew it. Literally hundreds of journalists and radio men from over twenty countries were assigned to follow their every move, whether it be on the track, around the city of Vancouver, or in the Empire Village. Their faces were plastered on posters and newspapers everywhere they went. The media frenzy they had attracted in their respective home countries prior to this event was child's play in comparison.

In the fortnight or so before 7 August, the two milers handled the attention as differently as they had planned on running their races. In the morning, Landy walked to the training tracks, signing autographs and speaking to the press along the way – more out of an obligation to his fans than a desire for the spotlight. In front of over five hundred people who had assembled at the track solely to watch him train, he knocked off a series of quarter- and half-miles at a pace that drew the crowd's applause. As race day approached, his sessions drew more and more people. Though at one point he had to enlist several of his Australian team-mates to encircle him on the way to the track so as not to be stampeded, he continued to train in the open. Reports of his sessions reached Bannister, and they were intimidating. After one half-mile trial in 1:58, an athlete who saw Landy's run commented to the press, 'He was as fresh as when he started. He certainly is a machine.' Each session won headlines: 'Landy Claps on the Pace'; 'Landy: Speeds Up Training'. And when he killed a three-quarter-mile trial in 2:59.4, reporters speculated that the Australian planned on running faster than the 4:02 mile he'd previously predicted would win the race against Bannister.

'Where's Roger the Dodger?' Posed by an admittedly biased Steve Hayward from the Melbourne *Herald*, the question was on everyone's mind. So seldom was he seen around Vancouver that autograph seekers rated his signature to be worth four of Landy's. Bannister was indeed training, albeit in secret. Instead of visiting the public track at the University of British Columbia, he conducted his sessions with Chataway on a pine-tree-lined golf course late in the afternoons. Though he ran the risk of being struck by stray golf balls, the course was not besieged by reporters. He ran his time trials on a cinder track ten miles outside the village in Balaclava Park, which earned him headlines such as 'Bannister Stays Out of Sight'. On 31 July, Norris McWhirter, on location in Vancouver for the *Star*, wrote that Bannister, Chataway, and Brasher 'slid out of the camp with collars turned up and in dark glasses' to train. Bannister's absence led Landy to approach McWhirter to ask, 'What is Roger up to? He never comes here.' Well, if Bannister had Landy guessing, all the better. Once, on the Empire Village training track, the press mistook a British sprinter for Bannister and were amazed at the swiftness of his 220-yard sprints, which they promptly reported the next day. Perhaps Landy saw this article; Bannister certainly hoped he had. He knew that Landy could run repeat quarter-miles with better speed, shorter intervals, and more ease than he could. Still, the Englishman believed he probably held the tactical advantage.

On Thursday, 5 August, the day of the mile's qualifying heats, the anticipation over the 'Mile of the Century' reached an even higher level. The debates, whether over meals in the Empire Village dining hall or on the newspapers' editorial pages, gathered momentum. Would Bannister's stinging finish win out over Landy's astounding stamina, or would it be the other way round? Odds were posted, giving stamina a three-to-one advantage over a fast kick. On this fifth day of seven in the competition, athlete after athlete was breaking records in other events, with England leading overall in the points table. Even so, very little warranted mention apart from the mile race. The qualifying heats, normally a routine event, prompted columns of newspaper print, and on the day the newly built stadium was packed.

Bannister was set against Australia's Geoff Warren and Don Macmillan, England's David Law and John Disley, Canada's Richard Ferguson, and New Zealand's Murray Halberg, whom many considered the dark horse in the upcoming showdown. It was debatable, between track aficionados, whether Bannister or Landy had the easier heat, but Geoff Warren planned to exhaust his countryman's rival more than he would have liked. From the start, Warren took off strong, hoping Bannister would take the bait, and ran a 2:00.4 half-mile. But the English miler wasn't biting, allowing Warren to tire himself out by the third lap. Bannister ran an even race throughout and finished third in what McWhirter called a 'nonchalant' 4:08.4. Halberg was first, Ferguson second, and Law, in fourth, was the final qualifier.

Landy faced England's Chris Brasher and Ian Boyd, Canada's William Parnell, the defending champion, Northern Ireland's Victor Milligan, and New Zealand's William Baillie. This heat was slower than the previous one, with Baillie commanding the lead for most of the race, finishing first in 4:11.4 with Milligan, Landy and Boyd crossing only inches behind him. Brasher finished last, and since the Empire Games did not include the steeplechase, his competition was over.

Reporters tried to prise from Landy and Bannister what the heats meant for the forthcoming final, but neither was talking. 'Crack Milers Take It Easy' proclaimed the *Daily Mail* the next day, yet its reporter admitted at the end of the article that 'as a guide to what is likely to happen on Saturday, the heats were completely useless'. Newspapers sold off the racks, regardless.

As if the atmosphere was not charged enough, reports spread through the village that some television executives had hatched a plot to have Wes Santee run the mile race against Bannister and Landy, by satellite, in Quantico, Virginia. The scheme involved starting Santee at the exact time the gun went off in Vancouver, and by virtue of a split-screen device thirty million American viewers would watch to see if their star miler could finish first. The fact that Santee would be in New York broadcasting the race for NBC did not seem to dispel the rumour, nor halt the preparation of official protests.

No doubt the Reverend Cooper would have blushed had he witnessed the media circus and spectacle undermining his noble concept of the Games, but his principle held strong for the two milers set to face one another forty-eight hours later. As amateurs, they wanted only to represent their countries as best they could and prove they were the best. There was no other reward.

Behind a bedroom door in the Empire Village, one whose number had been switched by team-mate Geoff Warren to throw off the press, Landy was restless. It was three o'clock on Friday morning, the day before the mile final. Like the athletes' quarters in Helsinki, the room was sparsely furnished, but Landy had only one room-mate this time, high-jumper John Vernon. Vernon was sleeping easily in the next bed. Landy decided to take a walk outside to get some fresh air and stretch his legs. It was the only time of the day when he could be alone. Besides, he was unable to sleep.

Because of the heightened press attention in the past week, Landy had not been able to relax and enjoy Vancouver with the same free-dom he had on first arriving. His every appearance was chronicled the next day in the newspapers. Meanwhile, his team-mates were out touring the city and seeing movies. Knowing he was restricted, one of them usually stayed behind to keep him company, though they sus-pected he was perfectly capable of entertaining himself by reading. One afternoon a couple of Vancouver girls with a car asked Geoff Warren if he and some of his friends wanted to see the sights. Warren finally convinced Landy to join the group, and they piled into the car, but it became clear very quickly that this car was too small for all of them. The girls said they could get a bigger car, and they drove to one of their houses. When asked inside, the father seemed to recog-nise Landy, which was exactly the kind of situation he had wanted to avoid. Warren and several of the other athletes started to talk about their particular events, but the father was more interested in Landy.

'What about you?' he asked.

One of the Australians, marathoner Bryce Mackay, answered for him. 'He's a boxer. Johnny the Kid.'

The father looked over Landy suspiciously. 'A boxer?'

Landy evaded the question, but Mackay piped up again. 'Oh, John's a fine boxer.'

The father then said, 'Let's see some boxing then.'

Landy did not want to be discovered, so he started shadow-boxing. The father gave him a look that said 'I think you're John Landy', but then they made their escape. Except to go training or to see athletics events at the stadium, Landy did not venture out much again.

For all his patience with the hoopla surrounding him in these Empire Games, Landy wanted nothing more than to be left alone to concentrate on his contest with Bannister. His friendly presence on the track masked what was going on inside, where he was gathering the determination he needed to win the race. He was 'an iron fist in a velvet glove', explained Warren, or, as Landy described himself, 'I'm vicious underneath.' To him, running was more than just a sport. In the past few years, it had become an obsession. As he later said:

In any running event, you are absolutely alone. Nobody can help you. But short races are run without thought. In very long races you must go a great distance simply to be present in the laps that really count. But almost every part of the mile is important – you can never let down, never stop thinking, and you can be beaten at almost any point. I suppose you could say it is like life. I had wanted to master it.

Since he'd arrived in Vancouver, advice about how he should run the race had come from every direction. His room-mate Vernon and Don Macmillan, two friends and athletes he respected greatly, had tried to shake him from his decision to run from the front. If he played a waiting game, they said, he would have a better shot at winning.

'Roger's going to sit you . . . and then jump you,' Macmillan had said, and he had competed against Bannister more than any other Australian. 'That's all he'll do. He'll sit, sit, sit. John, you'll be a sitting duck.'

Landy appreciated the advice, but his answer had been clear and had shut down further conversation: 'I'll run it my way.'

Nonetheless, as he stepped off the veranda outside his room in the early hours of that Friday morning, he was still nervous about the race he had planned to run. He knew front-running was psychologically more exhausting. As the hunted, he would have to worry about whether he was setting a fast enough pace and would only be able to guess at how the others were running. On the other hand, the hunter, Bannister, could wait and decide when and how fast to make his strike. Until then, his only responsibility would be to stay close enough.

While jogging barefoot on the grass, trying to relax from the weight of these thoughts, Landy suddenly felt a sharp stab of pain in his left foot. He lifted it up to see a gash on his instep, and, on the grass, a broken photographer's flashbulb. As he stumbled back towards his room, blood gushed from his foot. He rested on his bed, a trail of red on the floor, flicked on a light and saw that his foot was sliced open in a two-inch-long cut. Vernon woke up and propped himself up in bed.

'I've cut my foot. It's pretty bad.' Landy grimaced.

Vernon stayed as calm as he could, knowing what this could mean. 'We'll sort something out,' he said.

'We can't tell anybody,' Landy said. Above all, he did not want to have to give an excuse for Saturday's race if it failed to go as planned. Whether he would be able to run in it at all seemed secondary at that moment.

They bandaged the cut as best they could and tried unsuccessfully to get some sleep. A few hours later, as the other athletes began to stir and pass through the corridor, Don Macmillan came into the room. Blood was smeared on the bedding and floor.

'What the hell is this?' Macmillan asked.

'Nothing, nothing,' they both said.

'Nothing?' Macmillan was obviously unconvinced.

'He cut his foot,' Vernon said. 'He stepped on a flashbulb.'

The three of them decided that the cut had to be looked at by a doctor, but again Landy was insistent that it needed to be kept secret. Macmillan and Vernon left the room and found a mounted policeman, who arranged for a car to pull up next to a side door so that they could avoid the press, who were camped outside. They drove to the University of British Columbia health centre. A doctor was called and sworn to secrecy before he treated the cut. He wanted to stitch the diagonal gash from his instep to his heel, and told Landy he could not run. But the miler was convinced the cut would not affect his running, given its location, so the doctor agreed to tape the gash instead, and Landy returned quickly to the Empire Village. For the rest of the day he remained in his room. When several team-mates enquired as to why he hadn't visited the track, Vernon said that he was resting.

That afternoon, Andy O'Brien, a reporter commentating for the National Canadian Film Board, came to interview Landy. He found a Canadian mountie posted outside the door, who told him that Landy was sleeping and was not to be bothered. O'Brien backed down, but then returned an hour later and heard the miler's voice behind the door. He insisted on speaking to Landy since he had already agreed to the interview, finally forcing his way into the room to find the Australian.

As Landy stepped away from his bed he left a smear of blood on the floor.

'I know you will think this is awful,' Landy said, 'but I cannot do what I promised.' There was no way he could do an interview.

O'Brien stared at the blood.

'I will tell you why,' Landy added, 'only on your promise not to tell a soul. Right?'

O'Brien nodded.

Landy told him what had happened, then said, 'I am determined to run. I cannot let down my team and the fans now.'

The reporter promised not to publish the news and left. Landy wanted no alibis.

Since the cut was on the underside of his instep rather than on the pad of his foot, he was convinced it would not make a difference to his stride. At dinner that night he neglected to tell even his father, who had flown to Vancouver to support his son. His father made it a practice not to interfere with his son's running endeavours, a fact that John appreciated. He was simply glad to have his father there. Anyway, Landy planned on beating Bannister, gash or not. That the accident failed to rattle his determination and confidence showed just how much iron was inside that velvet glove.

Late in the afternoon on 6 August, Wes Santee and his wife drove through the Holland Tunnel and surfaced in Manhattan. This was Danna's first trip to New York City, and as they headed uptown they marvelled together at the Chrysler and Empire State skyscrapers and the bustling sidewalks where the sun seemed never to shine. They got turned around a few times trying to find their hotel, and Santee considered negotiating his way through traffic more difficult than herding a hundred cattle through a gate, but he eventually manoeuvred onto Park Avenue and pulled up in front of the Waldorf Astoria. NBC had booked a room for them at the luxury hotel, which at $50 a night was an extravagance they never could have afforded on their own.

This was the first opportunity they had had since Santee had entered boot camp to spend much time together alone. But it was impossible to escape the feeling that they should never have been there in the first place. Santee wanted to be in Vancouver, preparing for the race of a lifetime. In his mind, and with Easton back in Kansas, he had played out how he would have run against Bannister and Landy. He felt certain he was good enough to beat them both, and more than anything in the world he wanted the chance. Instead he was in New York, and although comforted by Danna who was as surprised and disappointed as he was that it had come to this, the next day he had to face sitting in a studio to commentate on a race that should have been his to win.

The two had a quiet dinner at their hotel and went to bed early. They did not even take the chance to go sightseeing, or to listen to the Cuban band playing in the Waldorf's Starlight Room, or to take in the new motion picture *On the Waterfront* at a nearby theatre. An NBC car was expected early in the morning to take them to the studio.

The night before the race, Roger Bannister was struggling with a chest cold he had recently caught. He was producing sputum and worried how that might affect his running. During his qualifying heat he had been afraid of being overcome by a fit of coughing, but he'd managed to run his mile without much strain – a hopeful sign, but by no means convincing. In his race against Landy he would have to work his lungs much more severely. Even if his cold took just 1 per cent off the oxygen exchange, there were consequences. For the past few days he had entertained many such scenarios.

Except for participating in the mile heat, his time in Vancouver had been little more than a painful waiting game, particularly after he'd stopped training the previous Sunday. For the busy medical student who knew little, if any, free time back in London, this gave his mind unusual leisure. As much as possible he tried not to occupy it with thoughts of the impending race. Instead he toured the city and surrounding countryside in an Austin car loaned to him (and several other British athletes) by a Canadian publisher; he swam at the Empire Village pool; he read; he went to dinner with Chris Chataway and his girlfriend, a television producer; he attended parties thrown by local residents; and he used his free stadium pass to watch some of the other events. He avoided the press as much as he could.

On 3 August he went to see Chataway compete in the three-mile event. Since their arrival on 26 July, they had taken several long walks together to discuss the tactics of their respective races. One afternoon, after a session of repeat quarter-miles in sixty seconds, they ran a trial that they hoped would serve them both in their finals. The plan was for Bannister to run 220 yards in approximately half a minute, after which Chataway would stride past him as fast as possible – the moment in his race when he hoped to seize the lead. After following Chataway around the final turn, Bannister would then sprint past him at the top of the home stretch – the place where he hoped to overtake Landy. The trial went exactly as planned, and they ran the last 220 yards in twenty-five seconds. In his three-mile final, Chataway benefited from this trial, taking over the lead in his race a half-lap from the finish and breaking through the tape first, exacting revenge on Freddie Green, who had literally inched him out in a shocking upset at the AAA Championship in July. 'The great Mr. Second', as the *Evening Standard* had once labelled him for helping Bannister's and Landy's four-minute mile attempts, had finally triumphed. His 5,000m Olympic defeat had boded ill for Bannister in Helsinki; now Bannister saw Chataway's victory in Vancouver as an 'encouraging omen'.

But even with all these diversions and promising signs, Bannister still had too much time on his hands. Much of it was spent in the room he shared with Chataway, especially the last twenty-four hours before the race. Chataway was used to his friend's nervousness before a big race, and suspected that his cold was at least in part psychosomatic. He had suffered a similar one before 6 May. As much as Chataway drank, smoked, and tried to lighten the mood with jokes about how Bannister couldn't possibly be worried about being beaten by anyone other than a good Englishman, he knew his friend was revving himself up for his race and there was nothing to be said that would make much of a difference now. As he described Bannister to a reporter before his clash with Landy:

Roger hates the idea of having to beat Landy – of having thousands of people expecting him to do it. But he'll do it. Nobody gets in such an emotional pitch before a race as he does. Roger may tell you he has slept before a race, but he hasn't. When he goes out to run, he looks like a man going to the electric chair. There are times the night before a race when he actually makes involuntary sounds, like a man being tortured. But Roger is a hard man to comfort. If you try, he'll give you a look that goes right through you.

With each hour that passed, whether taking a walk, pacing his room, or lying in bed, Bannister became more and more fired up to win. He was the underdog in this race, but that was fine with him. In Helsinki he had been favoured to win, and this had done nothing to improve his chances. His focus was intense. He ran the race over and over in his head, convincing himself each time that when his muscles told him to stop in the last lap he would refuse to listen. Everything else in his life diminished and faded away. He later admitted it was an 'abnormal state of attention'. But for this brief moment in time, his race against John Landy at 2.30 p.m. the following day was the most important thing in the world.

18

Now bid me run,
And I will strive with things impossible . . .
                    Caius Ligarius in *Julius Caesar*
                                (II.i.324–5)

The sun rose over the snow-capped mountains surrounding Vancouver. The waters of Burrard Inlet lightened, and a few early-to-rise sailors pointed their boats out towards the deeper bay. Morning strollers walked along the beaches, and the towering Lion's Gate suspension bridge began to see the first cars on what would be a tough day for traffic. The flags of twenty-four competing nations from throughout the British Empire lined the streets leading to the stadium. A horseshoe-shaped wonder of steel and concrete, it had been built, along with a bicycle velodrome and swimming centre, especially for the 1954 Empire Games. Inside the stadium, the groundsmen raked the broad jump pit and took special care when rolling the six-lane clay track. The athletes for the final day of events would soon arrive to test their spikes on it. With the forecasts predicting an afternoon of sunshine and warm temperatures, the track promised to be the perfect setting for the much-heralded mile race.

On newsstands from Vancouver to New York, and from London to Melbourne, the race was headlined on front pages and it dominated sports sections. 'Landy, Bannister in Epic Clash at Games Today' read the *Sun-Herald* in Australia; 'Mile of the Century at Vancouver Today' bannered the *Daily Telegraph* in England; 'Landy, Bannister Primed for "Miracle Mile"' proclaimed the *New York*

Herald Tribune. Hyperbole was at a premium. One newspaper predicted that the 'whole athletic world will be tuned to Vancouver with eyes, ears and heart'. Another expanded this audience: 'the race the whole world is waiting for'. Landy and Bannister were profiled and compared, from their date of birth, height, and weight to their fastest half-mile, mile, and two-mile times. Images of the two running were placed next to each other. Final quotes from the two were published. Landy: 'I have reached my peak.' Bannister: 'We may get down to four minutes.' And last-minute predictions were made: Australian papers tipped Landy to win; British papers gave Bannister the advantage; the American press took the middle road, simply saying that this race was the 'supreme test' between these two milers.

When Landy woke up early that morning after a surprisingly restful night's sleep, his room-mate Vernon, who was feeling nervous for his friend, asked, 'How does your foot feel?'

Landy replied, 'Fine,' but said little else.

The dressings, though, were soaked in blood. The cut had continued to bleed through the night, and Landy knew that he needed to get it looked at again. Though his race against Bannister was only a few hours away, he returned to the university hospital, somehow managing to elude reporters. The same doctor told him he needed stitches, race or no race. Landy relented. After stitching his foot, the doctor insisted that the miler couldn't run in his condition, but the Australian was determined. He was running. The doctor dressed and padded his foot, and Landy returned to have lunch with a few of his Australian team-mates. Despite his foot's tenderness, he refused to let it affect his gait.

When he arrived at the stadium, the stands were quickly filling to their capacity of some thirty-five thousand. In the locker-room, nobody mentioned anything to Landy about his cut foot, proof that the reporter O'Brien had kept his word. Twenty minutes before the race was to start, Landy put on his spikes, carefully slipping on his left shoe so as not to disturb the dressings. His only choice was to believe the cut would not bother him. If it had been an inch over on his heel, or on the ball of his foot, he could never have raced. Before he went out on to the infield to warm up, the doctor who had stitched his foot approached Landy, offering him a local anaesthetic for the pain. Landy said he could manage without it.

All roads had led to this moment: training at Portsea with Cerutty, the lessons of Zatopek, his surprise 4:02.1 at Olympic Park, the months of uninterrupted training, his failure to bring his time down further in Australia, and then his triumph in Turku. But now, here, this was the race that mattered most. Aside from the pressure of leading from the front with Bannister and the six other runners poised behind him, just waiting to pounce, he had to deal with the hope shared by his team-mates and millions of Australians that he would seize victory in what had otherwise been an unsuccessful Empire Games for his country. He also had to contend with the fact that every stride, move, and countermove would be watched, broadcasted, reviewed, and dissected by millions. It was difficult to handle. As the race approached, however, he concentrated solely on his game plan. He would run a moderately quick first half, followed by a very fast third lap during which he believed he could break Bannister. It wasn't a complicated strategy, but he felt it was the only one that would work. There would be nobody more fit than him on the track, and he had a tremendous motivation to win.

Before leaving for the stadium, Bannister carefully packed the same track shoes he had worn at Iffley Road on 6 May. He decided to take the team bus so as not to risk an accident if he drove himself. His mind was too preoccupied. Surrounded by his team-mates on the bus, he watched the crowds of people descending on the stadium, knowing they had all come to see him and Landy race. In the locker-room with its cement-grey walls and wooden benches, he looked pasty and white, his cold less severe than the night before yet still tight in his chest. As a *Vancouver Sun* journalist later reported, other athletes in the locker-room were not much better off:

One was inconspicuously chewing his fingernails; another held his head upon his knees, as if praying to someone above for strength for the coming race; yet another was sitting stonily on a bench in a far corner, taking everything without a reply to anything; another was unconsciously turning from side to side; another just sat still, throwing examining glances around the room; and finally, one sat alone on a bench with a nervous smile affixed upon his face.

Bannister felt the same tension. The past few hours had been almost unbearable for him. He'd eaten a light breakfast and taken a short walk in the Empire Village, but all the time he'd felt as if his whole future, as he later described, was 'hanging on a knife edge'. He didn't want to endure the agony of willing his body beyond its breaking point. He feared coming under the glare of so many people again and knew that as he stepped up to the starting line he would feel weak and almost unable to stand. It was intolerable, yet there he was, a warm-up away from race time.

Bannister had never expected to be running competitively at this point in his life. Had he won in Helsinki two years before, he would have been happy to hang up his spikes and dedicate himself fully to medicine. But the sting from his devastating loss at the Olympics had driven him to continue running, to seek the four-minute mile as evidence that his approach to sport still had merit. When he ran his 3:59.4, he thought that this would have been triumph enough, but Landy went one better at Turku, and without pacing. No, this race today was the climax. He had to win it. Failure would reward the critics who called him supercilious for following his own methods and not theirs. Failure would taint his 6 May race and validate the claim a British newspaper printed that same morning that he had 'never won a really important race when the others weren't in there to help you'. He had to get in there today, spikes flying, elbows pushing, and beat Landy and the rest of the field in a race during which anything could happen. The pressures were much the same as they had been in Helsinki – expectant British public, big crowd, critics waiting to pounce – but Bannister was not the same man any more. He had a mentor in Stampfl, training partners in Chataway and Brasher, and a more complete understanding of how important it was to have faith in himself.

The question remained, however: how good was Landy? And could he change gears at the race's end to fight off Bannister's kick?

When the starter called the milers out to the track, Bannister remembered that he also had six other runners to deal with, each with his own plan to win. Unless Landy played a waiting game, he would not have to vie for position in the pack, but Bannister would. If he was blocked off by one or two of them, it might ruin his chances. English runners David Law and Ian Boyd, both Oxonians, had best mile times of 4:08 and were not likely to prove too much of a challenge. Irishman Victor Milligan, his country's team captain and mile champion, and Canadian Richard Ferguson, a strong runner whose best distance was two miles, had no allegiances to either Bannister or Landy and would be fighting for their own space in the field. The ones Bannister had to watch most carefully were New Zealanders William Baillie and Murray Halberg. Halberg, just 20 years old and winner of the Benjamin Franklin Mile in Philadelphia, had already clocked a 4:04.4 mile. Rumour had it the Kiwis might set an early pace for Landy. Regardless of that, Halberg was likely to be a risk throughout the race.

Five minutes before the race, the concrete stands encircling three sides of the track were packed to capacity. A helicopter chartered by *Life* magazine and the *Vancouver Sun* loomed at a distance, the sound of its spinning blades reverberating around the bowl-shaped stadium besieged by hundreds of parked cars and the continuing advance of trams dropping off more and more spectators outside its walls. From the helicopter's airy perch, the crowds looked like a calm sea of white shirts and hats. Up close, particularly at the entrances, it was chaos: scalpers were selling tickets for a hundred dollars; fire wardens tried to impose order on the lines still gathered at the gates; and schoolboys scaled the four ticket booths to secure a view of the race.

Everyone's eyes were glued to the milers as they jogged around the track and began taking off their sweats. The other finals held that day, including the field events and the 440 yards, might as well have taken place on the sidelines. The mile race was all consuming. The Duke of Edinburgh, who had seen Bannister race in London and Landy in Australia, had arrived to watch the final, a twenty-one-gun salute announcing his presence. He was seated in the decorated royal box, having already inspected the Seafourth Highland Regiment in their crimson jackets, kilts, and high feathered caps while bagpipes played behind him on the infield.

Under the steel roof at one end of the stadium Norris McWhirter was ready with his stopwatch to help call the race for BBC radio with journalist Rex Alston, who, McWhirter knew, had very little understanding of the intricacies of the race despite being a former Cambridge runner. McWhirter would not have made it to the stadium in time had it not been for his staying in the Duke of Edinburgh's hotel. With his brother Ross and a few others crammed into an Austin 7, they pulled away from the hotel at the same time as the duke's limousine and proceeded to follow in the wake of his police escort, cutting through the snarl of traffic descending on the stadium. In the radio commentary box next to Norris, his brother was preparing to help call the race for the Australian Broadcast Network. Adjacent to him was Chris Chataway, lured there by a Canadian broadcaster. Everyone was waiting for the race to begin.

It was late evening in England, and Bannister's parents, recently returned from a fortnight in Cambridge, were listening to the race on the radio at their Harrow home. Their daughter Joyce, who had sent her brother a 'good luck' telegram the day before, was in her Bristol home, tuned to the same station. Stampfl sat still at the kitchen table in his King's Road flat, the radio on. His wife Pat was fidgeting around, as nervous as he was, just showing it differently.

Despite receiving several postcards about Landy's extraordinary fitness from athletes he coached who were in Vancouver, Stampfl remained convinced Bannister could win, but the waiting was torture. At St Mary's Hospital, the night shift was also tuned in to the BBC to listen to the race. To many, Bannister exemplified the best qualities of a true Englishman: well rounded, masterfully disciplined, an explorer of new territory, and brave enough, as he said himself, to run 'into extinction'.

It was Sunday morning in Australia when the race was scheduled to begin. The Landy family, apart from John's father who was with him in Vancouver, had congregated at their East Malvern house to listen to the radio broadcast. Landy's mother had decided not to send John a telegram wishing him luck, thinking it might be just more pressure for him to handle. Percy Cerutty was in his Domain Road house off the Botanical Gardens, eager to hear if Landy would follow the instructions he had sent about how to run the race. So far Landy had not responded to his letters, despite news in the Melbourne press that his former miler was running the Vancouver race to Cerutty's 'Secret Plans'. Those athletes close to Landy but not in attendance at the Empire Games, including Les Perry and Robbie Morgan-Morris, were also sitting anxiously in anticipation of the broadcast. The whole country was anchored in the moment as well. 'Australia considered Landy unbeatable,' sportswriter Adrian McGregor later commented. 'He was all we mythologized about ourselves. Gallant, modest, idealistic, but beneath it all a champion equipped with [a] destructive will.'

At dinnertime in New York, Wes Santee was staring at the camera in front of him at the RCA Exhibition Center. Instead of a singlet and spikes, he was dressed in a tan Marines uniform and dress shoes. Half the age of the four other men at the table with him – Asa Bushnell and Kenneth Wilson (secretary and president, respectively, of the United States Olympic Committee), Jesse Abramson (the *New York Herald Tribune*'s lead sports columnist), and Ben Grauer (NBC's talking head) – Santee twisted uncomfortably in his seat. He felt as if he were getting ready for the race himself. He watched it unfold in his head. Danna was off the set and in the shadows, but he was at least comforted to have her there.

'Any word yet from Edinburgh?' Grauer asked into the phone, obviously having trouble coordinating the transmission delay. 'I mean Vancouver.'

Santee knew the race was about to begin, and that, like the Olympic 1,500m trials in Los Angeles two years earlier, he was on the sidelines. He also knew how it would be run. Bannister had the faster kick, Landy the ability to set a brutal pace. If Bannister failed to hang on to the Australian by the end of the third lap, he was finished.

But as Santee waited for the transmission from Empire Stadium to appear on the monitor to his side, the race he imagined on the darkened screen included him toeing the line. Landy went out first, Santee right behind him, and Bannister in third, ten yards back. Santee stayed in the middle, all the way through three and a half laps. The pace was fast, but he had the conditioning to hold. With half a lap to go, Santee struck – a Mal Whitfield technique. Landy and Bannister had expected him to make his move coming out of the last curve, not going into it. By the time they realised what he had done, Santee was past the two milers in a flash; they never had a chance. With sixty yards to home, Bannister delivered his kick, but he was too late. It was Santee through the tape first, with Bannister or Landy in second – it didn't matter who.

This was the race as it should have happened, but Santee felt he had been robbed of the chance. The closest he could get to a battle with Bannister and Landy was via radio signal from Vancouver, through Seattle, and into New York. He knew that when the screen finally flickered in the exhibition hall, showing the runners in Vancouver pacing in front of the starting line, the race would already have started in real time.

In Empire Stadium, two minutes before 2.30 p.m., the scheduled start of the mile event, the sun cleared from behind a bank of clouds and the stands and track were enveloped in light. It was 72°, with mild humidity. The faintest of breezes stirred the air in the stadium. Officials in green coats cleared the track as Bannister and several others peeled off their sweatsuits on the infield. Bannister wanted to stay as warm as possible until he had to stand, exposed, at the starting line. Landy was the first athlete ready, walking back and forth on the track, head down, rubbing his deeply tanned arms. His light jog during warm-up had proved to him that his foot would be okay, and this improved his confidence. Before the start, he returned to the infield and shook hands with Bannister, who was perspiring and appeared deathly pale as he kicked off his sweatpants. Landy stepped back on to the track, focusing on the effort ahead. He walked away from the others, for a moment on his own. He knew he needed to run so fast that nobody 'was going to be left standing'.

Bannister was one of the last on the track. He checked the bottoms of his track shoes, making sure that nothing had clumped to his spikes while warming up. It was almost time. Tense and anxious, he was seemingly unaware of anyone else in the stadium. He told himself that if Landy went off fast in a fifty-six-second first lap and then ran the next lap in sixty seconds, it was unlikely he would have the stamina to finish the next two laps in sixty seconds each. He would have to slow down a touch, and the race would come back to Bannister. As long as Bannister ran evenly, he would conserve energy and be able to win.

The eight runners settled in their lanes five yards behind the start. At last, the two great sub-four-minute milers were facing off against each other. In the inside position, Landy wore green shorts and a white singlet. Halberg was in all black next to him. Ferguson, from Canada, was in the third lane, Milligan in fourth. Bannister had the fifth lane, wearing all white with the rose of England on his breast. His countrymen Boyd and Law were in the two lanes outside him, and Baillie of New Zealand in the outside lane. The crowd produced a steady rumble of noise, punctuated by shouts such as 'Go, Landy!' and 'Come on, Bannister!', but most were cheering for Ferguson, the host country's favourite. Cameramen on elevated platforms in the infield directed their lenses at the starting line, ready to broadcast this battle to millions. Hundreds of journalists waited with open notepads to record their impressions for the following day's papers. The team of timekeepers readied their new Omega watches – worth $8,000 – which had been checked, double-checked, and verified for accuracy.

Next to McWhirter in the radio commentary box, Rex Alston spoke into the microphone, his clear, sharp voice reaching across oceans. 'There is a tremendous feeling of excitement and tension here on this beautiful summer's day, bit of a breeze.'

Down on the infield, the starter shouted over the crowd. 'To your marks!'

The eight runners moved forward to the line. Bannister ran his fingers through his hair and glanced towards Landy. They settled at the line. Landy shot his own quick look at Bannister and then crouched down, facing straight ahead, preparing to be the hunted. The surge of adrenalin made any pain in his foot insignificant. Bannister positioned himself at a slight angle to Landy. He was standing nearly erect. Nothing else in the world mattered but what he did in the next four minutes. It had all come down to this.

A track official raised his arms over his head, signalling for the crowd to settle down. A hush fell over the stadium.

'Set!'

The starter raised his pistol to the sky with his right arm and Bannister took a deep breath, bending slightly forward. His long, thin legs looked frail. Landy deepened his crouch, ready to burst ahead. The world waited for the crack of the gun.

When its sound echoed around the stadium the milers swept forward, a wave of flying arms and legs, all breaking towards the inside lane. Gun smoke and a cloud of clay dust trailed in their wake. As they went into the first turn, the burly New Zealander Baillie angled into the lead, his taller, more fair-haired countryman Halberg behind him. Landy was third, Law fourth, Bannister clawing for room in fifth. The field remained tight as they moved around the turn; strides lengthened and shortened as they fought for position. Law cut in between Landy and Halberg to move into third. As the Englishman surged towards the back straight, he stutter-stepped and his right shoe went flying off his foot, landing in the third lane. He kept running and moved into first down the back straight. Positioned at the outside edge of the pole lane, Bannister remained a few yards behind Landy, expecting him to take the lead soon.

As they approached the 220-yard mark at the end of the back straight, Landy was ready to move ahead of Baillie and Law. He looked like a man impatiently waiting to get through a narrow doorway with two people blocking his way. The pace wasn't fast enough. At the mark, Don Macmillan, who had previously arranged with Landy to call out his split times, yelled 'Twenty-eight point nine!' and 'Three yards behind!' Hearing his time and Bannister's position, Landy increased his tempo, realising he had to take the lead now and set the pace. In the inside edge of the second lane, he shifted past the two milers as if they were standing still.

The crowds bordering the track gasped as the Australian made his move. High in the stadium, Rex Alston spoke quickly into his microphone as the race unfolded. 'Landy has decided that he must crack on the pace and has taken over the lead with 150 yards to go to the end of the first lap. Landy in his green shorts for Australia . . . slim, sallow, curly dark hair . . . And he is setting out a very fast pace.'

Landy was clear into his rhythm, his arms and legs moving smoothly as he distanced himself from the field into the home straight of the first lap. Halberg was second, Baillie third, and Bannister fourth. Law, having lost his shoe, now slowed almost to a stop. Bannister didn't want to be trapped behind Baillie or Halberg when they made the first turn of the second lap, so he moved ahead, increasing his speed almost imperceptibly as he passed the two. Landy finished the first lap in 58.2 seconds with Bannister five yards and six-tenths of a second behind him. The other runners, including

Halberg in third and Ferguson in fourth, looked incapable of maintaining the pace Landy continued to set. The race between the two sub-four-minute milers had finally been joined in earnest, and the crowd cheered.

In New York, Wes Santee watched the race unfold on the monitor. He pictured himself on the track equidistant between Landy and Bannister. He would let Landy continue to set the pace, but make sure not to let the Australian get too far ahead. Bannister would continue to trail at Santee's heels, waiting for the last lap to make his move. Santee would be there to block him out and surge ahead to victory. The four men at the table with him in the studio could see in his eyes that he wanted very much to be someplace else.

In the second lap Landy turned on the heat, his cut foot forgotten. For the first quarter he had held back, conserving his strength. But now he meant to stretch his lead yard by yard until he broke Bannister. As he rounded out of the turn, the gap lengthened. He didn't want to see the English miler's shadow or hear his breath for the rest of the race. If Bannister was near him in the last lap, Landy knew he would have trouble holding off his kick.

At the 660-yard mark, the Australian, striding purposefully and smoothly, was eight yards ahead of Bannister. In the turn, Landy picked up even more speed, increasing his lead to ten yards. It was a huge distance between the two milers. Bannister knew Landy was going too fast for him. A few more yards and Bannister would lose contact. Psychologically, it would have been the end of his race. As it was, with this gap between them, Bannister began to suffer the absence of having someone to pull him around the track. In a sense, he was running as much on his own as the Australian was. He couldn't panic though. If he got up on his toes to catch Landy too soon, it would be suicide. Bannister had to believe he could still win.

'Landy comes down the straight for half-distance,' Alston told his BBC listeners, his voice edged with anxiety, 'Bannister with his prancing, high-stepping stride, ten yards behind, ready, poised.'

McWhirter, who was very worried about the size of the gap separating his friend from Landy, showed his stopwatch to Alston as the Australian crossed the starting line for the second time. 'Here goes Landy, now has passed half-distance, Bannister second, Ferguson third, Halberg fourth, Milligan fifth, Baillie sixth, Boyd seventh, and Law has dropped out and limping. Landy is doing what I think a lot of people thought he would do . . . At half distance, 1:58.2. Bannister has done 1:59.4.'

In the nearby box, Chataway was enraptured by the showdown. He knew these two milers better than anybody and chattered anxiously into the microphone. 'Dangerous gap there between Landy and Bannister. Landy is looking stronger and Roger has got to close that [gap], and soon, if he's going to be there at the finish, with his no doubt superior finishing burst.'

Santee was barely able to keep his legs still. Landy was fifteen yards ahead now, a distance the Kansas miler never would have let his competition open up. At this point in the race he would have been three or four yards back at most. And given the pace, Santee knew he would have had enough in reserve to kick past in the final lap. Bannister would still have some fire left too. He had yet to challenge, but unless he moved up, and did so quickly, he was out of the race.

Tens of millions around the world had stopped what they were doing to listen to the race or to watch it on their televisions. In homes and bars, conversations paused, children were hushed, bridge games interrupted, pool cues abandoned, forks put down, and drinks left untouched. The collective silence was profound. Those for Landy hoped he could keep to his fast pace; those for Bannister prayed he could bridge the gap.

The crowd in Empire Stadium began to cheer wildly. Both milers were under two minutes for the first half-mile. Landy heard his time called. At this pace, he expected to cross the three-quarter mark in 2:58. He had not seen or heard from Bannister, but he still needed to keep the pressure intense. This was the critical lap for the Australian.

He ran hard, yet kept his stride economical and relaxed. From the stands, he looked inexhaustible.

Two more minutes of struggle, Bannister told himself going into the third lap, then it would be over. It would all be over. He was running to his schedule but was far back, and his rival, amazingly, was maintaining his pace. Bannister felt his confidence weaken. What if Landy never slowed down? What if he was capable of a 3:56 or better? He needed to be at Landy's shoulder by the last lap or it was over, and there were fifteen yards between them. Unless Bannister adjusted his speed, unless he abandoned the pace he had planned to run for the one being forced on him by Landy, he would lose.

Into the turn, Bannister increased the tempo of his circular stride, but in such small measures that from the stands it was nearly impossible to notice that he had accelerated. He was like a ball gathering momentum down a hill. First, he took one yard from Landy, then two, then three, closing the gap gradually so as not to exert too much energy. His legs ached from the effort, but by the back straight he was only five yards back.

As they sped into the turn, Bannister felt himself connected again to Landy. He watched the Australian's stride, almost mesmerised by the steady, rhythmic strike of Landy's spikes on the cinder track. In his mind, Bannister had drawn a 'cord' around Landy, and as they moved around the turn he pulled himself closer and closer.

'Here they come into the straight,' Alston continued enthusiastically. 'Bannister is striding up to Landy . . . he's running absolutely beautifully, a much bigger stride. Fifty yards to go to the bell and Bannister is at Landy's elbow . . . Now what's going to happen?'

At the bell Landy clocked 2:58.4; Bannister was only three-tenths of a second behind him. Ferguson was twenty yards back in third place, followed closely by the rest of the field, but everyone's attention was on the two leaders. Photographers lined the infield, snapping shots. Newsreel cameras whirred. And tens of thousands of spectators jumped up and down, many shouting until their throats went hoarse. The race was everything they had expected, and more. At this pace, the two milers might break four minutes too.

Santee was witnessing a race that had played out exactly as he'd suspected. He desperately wanted to be there to take advantage of the strategy he had devised for this final lap. He could almost see himself in the monitor, running just half a lane wide of Landy so as not to step on his heels. If Bannister wanted to pass Santee, the English miler would have to step out into the second lane, and this would force him to run just enough extra distance to prove fatal. Had Santee been there – it was so hard to bear – he knew he'd be in exactly the right position to make his break on the final curve. He had as good, or better, a kick as Bannister, and Landy would have been too tired from playing the rabbit to counter. By the start of the fourth lap, Santee knew that victory would have been his for the taking.

Landy turned into the first bend, shooting a glance over his shoulder. He saw Bannister's shadow, heard his breathing. His hunter had pulled close, too close. This was the race now. Bannister was not yet run off his feet. Landy had to hope that his rival had become exhausted after drawing himself back into contention. It was time to go. Landy fought gallantly to drive down the track at a greater pace than before. This was his move. Now was the moment to crack Bannister. Out of the turn into the back straight, the Australian pulled away again from Bannister – one yard, two, three. Landy's shadow lengthened in front of him into the next lane. He could not see Bannister's.

As Landy approached the final 220-yard mark, the noise from the crowd drowned out Macmillan's call. But he could see his Australian team-mates gesturing wildly, as if to say, 'Keep it going, you've got him!' Bannister should have made his move by now. 'When is it?' Landy thought, looking back yet again. 'When's the kick going to come?' Perhaps he had finally stolen it from the Englishman. Landy began to lose momentum, knowing he had given everything, and hoping it was enough.

'Landy has got a lead of three yards.' Alston gripped his microphone. 'Two hundred and twenty yards to go – I don't think Bannister will be able to catch him. Landy is running beautifully.'

Bannister dashed into the final turn, shocked that Landy was still driving so hard. This man was a machine. Because Bannister had abandoned his even pace in the third lap he was more tired at this point than he had expected to be. They had run so fast, for so long. Bannister had to win though. He had too much to prove to himself and to others. His finishing kick had to be there in the end; it hadn't been there in Helsinki. Every hour of training, every race, every sacrifice, every ounce of his love for running had come down to this final moment, this final half-lap around the track. When they came out of this bend into the final straight, he had to be close enough to strike. Once again, he drew a bead on Landy's back. His legs had to be deadening, Bannister told himself. Stride by stride, Bannister again began to close the gap between them. If Landy only knew how much he had exhausted his competitor he might have found the strength to go even faster, but he didn't know. The front-runner never did.

As they neared the home straight, Bannister marshalled his remaining kick. This was his final chance. This was the moment in the race he and Stampfl had decided Landy would never anticipate. This was the strike he had practised with Chataway. Bannister needed to win. He *had* to win. The Australian could run as an expression of the best that was within him, but Bannister ran to be better than anyone else. This was the moment to reveal that he was.

Ninety yards from the tape, Bannister swung his arms high and lengthened his stride. He convinced his tired muscles to react. The effort took every shred of will and heart he had left. When he passed Landy, he wanted to do so at pace.

Coming out of the bend, Landy thought he had finally shaken off the Englishman. He still couldn't see his shadow. Good thing, since Landy knew he had no more strength in his legs. He looked over his left shoulder to make sure he was right.

Exactly at that moment, Bannister hurled himself around Landy on the right in two long strides, seeing the Australian glance the other way and knowing that the hesitation would cost him, if only the smallest fraction of a second. Seventy yards from the tape, Bannister seized the lead. It was exhilarating. Although the spurt was proving excruciatingly painful, this was the moment he loved most in running, when his spirit fused with the physical act of running. The roar of the crowd pushed him onward. Everything was a blur but the finish line. He sped down the track, momentum carrying him now. Landy tried to kick again down the home stretch, but he knew his legs were finished.

'Bannister has passed Landy!' Alston shouted excitedly, losing any sense of unbiased composure. 'He comes into the straight. It's going to be Bannister's race. Landy is flagging. Here comes Bannister, striding absolutely magnificently. He's got a lead of two yards, three yards, four yards. About fifteen yards to go, and Bannister . . .'

The English miler sprinted to the line, his long stride unfailing. With a last drive off his right foot, he leapt forward, head back in sheer exultation. He broke through the tape, victory his at last.

'He's done it! He's done it!' Chataway exclaimed into the microphone, tens of thousands of Canadian listeners sharing in his excitement.

A stride and a half past the tape, Bannister was in a state of collapse. The will that had held his legs up was now utterly spent. Landy finished five yards behind him. His shoulders slackened, and he closed his eyes briefly, as if he wanted to be anywhere at that moment but in the Empire Stadium. He slowed and walked forward as the English team manager, Leslie Truelove, kept Bannister, whose face was deathly pale, from falling. The track was swallowed up by officials and athletes. Ferguson came in third, Milligan fourth, Boyd fifth, Halberg sixth, and Baillie seventh, but they were forgotten. In the stands, guards held back a feverish crowd that was trying to rush the track.

Landy tried to step clear of the throng, but too many people surrounded him. He had run his hardest, done everything he could, yet Bannister had never broken. 'Hard luck, John ... Great run though, great effort.' He gave his well-wishers a smile, but there was little anyone could say to quell his disappointment.

Bannister drew in several deep breaths, still supported by Truelove. People milled around him, congratulating him, patting him on the back, shaking his hand. When his legs finally regained some strength, he only wanted to see one person. He stood upright, loosened himself from Truelove, and jogged forward, filled with the glory of his triumph. Weaving through the mass of bodies, he found Landy between two policemen and threw his arms around him.

'You were colossal, Roger,' Landy said with a smile.

'I knew that if I did beat you it would take everything I had,' Bannister replied, keeping his left arm around the Australian, knowing the anguish he must have been feeling.

Photographers herded around them to get a shot of the two together. Fans were pushing and pulling to get at them. Bannister leaned backwards to draw more breath. He nearly collapsed again, but Landy held him strong.

In the infield, away from the pandemonium, the four time-keepers who had clicked their stopwatches when Bannister broke through the tape, and the three who had clocked Landy, settled on the official time. The three timekeepers stationed at the 1,500-metre mark had already agreed that Landy, who had led the race 120 yards from the finish, had been only a tenth of a second shy of his world record of 3:41.8, set in Turku. The official times for the top three finishers, Landy, Bannister, and Ferguson, were decided and given to the announcer to read over the public-address system. Over the loudspeaker, the announcer declared what most in the stadium already knew unofficially. Nonetheless, a hush descended throughout the stands.

'Winner of event six, the mile, Roger Bannister, in a time of 3:58.8 ... Second place, John Landy, in a time of 3:59.6 ...'

Cheers and applause boomed through the stadium as Bannister

and Landy jogged around the track, waving at the stands. In the race of the century, in the contest between the first two milers ever to break four minutes, both runners had once again crossed the threshold. It was perfection in sport.

In New York, Wes Santee was alight with excitement as he spoke into the camera. 'It was a magnificent race, and I think the better man won ... Those two boys just threw everything into it, and the result was this greatest of mile races ever run. Bannister was magnificent, but so was Landy.' As the other panellists commented on the race, Santee looked off wistfully. The two milers had run tremendously, and he would call them later to say the same, but Santee still believed that had he been in the thick of the battle, he would have breasted the tape first. Sitting there in the studio, he was worn out, as if he had actually run in the race himself. As he later explained, though, 'I was more exhausted because I hadn't been there.'

In Melbourne, Landy's family was deflated by the outcome. Reporters were keen for their comments, but they held off for the moment. Les Perry, agonised by his friend's defeat, called the Landy house to say how sorry he was that John had lost. He found Landy's mother philosophical and not full of lament. They were proud of John regardless. Cerutty, who usually used these big occasions to pontificate on his insights into Landy, made no comment. Robbie Morgan-Morris, who idolised Landy and who had been given the miler's singlet after his December 1952 run, best described what millions in his country felt that morning after hearing the news: 'When Landy lost in Vancouver, the whole of Australia cried.'

In London, newspaper editors were already preparing the next day's headlines. Franz Stampfl, who had known Bannister would win from the moment Landy had proved unable to shake him loose on the last turn, was quietly satisfied. For the Austrian, the race was a triumph of the individual will, and he was simply glad to have helped in the effort. The win was testament to his methods, though he never would have admitted it.

In Vancouver, ten minutes after the race had finished and the crowd was starting to calm itself after the bedlam, Bannister donned his tracksuit with 'England' stitched across its front and moved to the winner's stand. On the results board, a green-capped official had placed the results of the mile race, including the times, below the oversized portrait of a saluting Queen Elizabeth. Bannister stepped up on to the top position – Landy to his right, Ferguson to his left – and looked out across the stadium, overwhelmed by the sight of it all.

It was his finest moment. He had beaten the best of competitors in John Landy. He had brought glory to his country. He had captured victory in a race greater than any numerical barrier. Roger Bannister had run the perfect mile.

EPILOGUE

And thick and fast they came at last
And more and more and more
Lewis Carroll,
Alice's Adventures in Wonderland

Twenty minutes after Bannister crossed the finish line ahead of Landy in one of the most triumphant moments in sport, tragedy struck when 35-year-old English team captain Jim Peters ran into the stadium for the last few hundred yards of the marathon. The favourite to win, he was more than a mile in front of his nearest competitor, and the crowd rose to its feet to cheer him around the track. But something was wrong with Peters. He looked uncertain on his feet and almost blissfully unaware of where he was. The crowd hushed.

Peters took a few steps forward, weaving from side to side like a drunk, and then collapsed. He rolled onto his side, his white singlet stained by the track's clay dust, and pushed himself to his feet. His arms were listless, his legs akimbo, his face blanched. He struggled forward another few yards and then stopped. Wavering, he took one more beleaguered step before falling again. He sat on the track, looking up at the sky before once again finding his way to his feet. His legs then buckled for a third time and he dropped back down. Everyone in the stadium watched in horror, suddenly aware of the scorching sun and thick air and seeing the effect of those conditions on a runner gallantly trying to finish his race. As Peters attempted to stand yet again, people buried their heads into one another's shoulders; they covered their faces with their hats and wept; they begged for him to stop or for someone to help him. Please, help him.

Bannister and Landy stood next to each other on the infield. For two runners who time and time again had pushed themselves to the extreme, they understood why Peters drove himself onward. At this level of competition, an athlete had to ignore the body's call to stop. After years of punishing training, it was instinct.

For almost fifteen minutes, Peters stumbled, staggered, and at times crawled forward, making his way 150 yards around the track before dropping for the twelfth time. This looked to be the end, but then he pushed himself back to his feet and zigzagged another twenty yards forward to where he thought the finish line was. Just as he was about to collapse again, the British trainer gathered him in his arms. The finish line was still a few hundred yards away, but Leslie Truelove had seen enough. A stretcher was called, and Peters was carried into the dressing room, barely conscious. 'Did I win?' were his first words to the nurse before the ambulance arrived.

To the thousands in the stadium waiting to hear of his condition, Peters was a painful reminder of how far these athletes were willing to go to capture victory. Rarely in the history of sport had tragedy and triumph juxtaposed in such a short space of time.

The next day, newspaper front pages chronicled the extraordinary climax of the Empire Games, some carrying side by side columns: 'Triumph!' and 'Disaster!' Mostly, though, editors in Australia and America followed their English counterparts and led with the dramatic mile race. 'Bannister Outruns Landy' detailed the *New York Times* on their front page, above the fold – quite a placement considering there was no American in the race. The *Chicago Tribune* and *New York Herald Tribune* gave similar prominence to the story. 'The Great Finish! One of Us Had to Crack: John' read Melbourne's *Argus*. The *Sydney Morning Herald* went with 'Bannister's Triumph in Empire Mile', but with a sub-banner that read 'Bannister Collapses!' Of the many stories from the day, the most evocative of the mile race's importance was when British marathoner Stanley Cox, delirious from the heat, ran headlong into a telephone pole in the twenty-third mile of his race. When he finally came to, he wanted to know one thing: 'Did Bannister make it?' After hearing that he had, Cox said, 'God bless him,' and then lay back down.

After the closing ceremonies in Vancouver, Roger Bannister did not return immediately to London with the rest of the team. Instead he stayed on to help tend to Jim Peters, who had been hospitalised, and to fly back with him in case there were any complications during the marathoner's journey. It was what any good doctor would have done. Peters and Bannister were scheduled to fly into London Airport a week later. A press contingent was waiting for them, but a thick fog caused their plane to be diverted, and they landed in Kent in almost complete anonymity. One of the world's most famous athletes, back from claiming glory for his country, had to wait for over an hour to clear customs. Later, when Bannister arrived in Harrow by car, he was able to enjoy a small celebration with his friends and family. The next day he ran alone around the Harrow cricket field, pleased to be home and away from the crush of media attention.

Two weeks after returning from Vancouver, Bannister travelled to Berne in Switzerland for the European Championship. The 1,500m final was almost a replay of the race he had lost two years before in Helsinki. As Bannister later said, the race promised 'a crowded field, lots of barging, twelve runners, all Europeans, and the best in the world . . . It was an act of completion that I felt I needed.' From the gun, Bannister ran a tactical race, staying back in sixth position through the first 400-metre lap, allowing Czechoslovakia's Stanislav Jungwirth, West Germany's Werner Lueg, and Denmark's Gunnar Nielsen to carry the lead. By the end of the second lap Bannister had moved into second place behind Jungwirth, with Nielsen in third place. At 1,200 metres they held the same positions, but the Czech was flagging. The Dane appeared to be the lone runner who could contest Bannister. Into the back straight, with only a few hundred metres to go, Bannister unleashed his kick – nearly in the same place he had hoped to burst ahead in Helsinki. This time he did not falter and he pulled quickly away from Jungwirth and Nielsen. The Dane tried to recover, but Bannister was unfailing. He drove towards the finish, long stride after long stride, and won easily. Nielsen, who claimed the silver medal, told reporters after the race that he was giving up middle-distance running to take up lawn tennis. Such was the devastating nature of Bannister's finishing kick. But Nielsen had no reason to fear the great English miler now, because after the final Bannister announced that he had run his last race. He was retiring from athletics to devote himself to medicine.

In the span of 112 days, Bannister had broken the mile barrier, graduated from St Mary's, passed his medical board exams, met his future wife Moyra, beaten John Landy in the 'Mile of the Century', claimed the 1,500m European crown, and won his future residency as a doctor. Frankly, he had done it all.

At the Savoy Hotel on the last day of 1954, he was honoured with the Sportsman of the Year award by Lord Brabazon, who in his magisterial voice summarised what the whole of Britain now felt for Bannister: 'I'd like to say, Bannister, we have taken you to our hearts ... in your bearing, in your approach to sport, in your modesty. You are an example to the world of our ideal sportsman ... It is given to very few people to do something in this world which will be forever remembered. That is what you have done.'

'It was the race I had to win, but I didn't,' John Landy later succinctly described his loss at Vancouver. Directly after the race, he was the consummate gentleman, praising Bannister for a terrific run and telling the press that the better man had won. A day later he told the press that he had accepted a teaching job at Geelong Grammar School and that his future as a miler was 'hazy'. But this announcement was drowned out by the report that his foot had been cut prior to the race. And that he had said nothing about it. Andy O'Brien, the sportswriter who had promised to keep Landy's gashed foot a secret, had broken his word and told what he knew on a nationwide Canadian broadcast.

At first, when a Melbourne *Herald* correspondent approached him in the Empire Village, Landy tried to discount the story.

'Did you stand on a flashbulb on Thursday?' the correspondent asked.

'How do I know if I stepped on a flashbulb?' Landy replied. 'All I'm saying is that I went to the mile start 100 per cent fit.' He then moved away, favouring his right leg over his left.

'Are you sure that limp isn't due to a cut?' the correspondent continued.

'If I can run a 3:59.6 with a limp,' Landy retorted, 'I've got possibilities as a runner.'

The story was too big to hide, however. Journalists tracked down the doctor who had tended to Landy. They confronted the Australian team manager to see what he had known (nothing). Finally, Landy admitted the truth, but remained adamant that it had made no difference in the race. His story would never change, and the fact was he *did* run a sub-four-minute mile in the final.

When Landy returned to Australia, he discovered that his zeal for racing had left him.

> Everybody beat me when I got home. A schoolboy beat me in a quarter-mile. I could see no reason for going on. Running is not a big sport in Australia, and I had run against the best in the world on the best tracks in the world. At home I faced the prospect of running badly on mediocre tracks against mediocre competition in little meets attended by three people. It was too much. Running is not a life; I had to quit some time. I decided that the time had come to scrub it.

The headmaster at Geelong Grammar, Dr J. R. Darling, provided Landy with a retreat. He had started a branch of the school in Timbertop, a secluded enclave in the Victorian Alps, where each student was required to live for a year. Darling needed a biology teacher, and Landy accepted.

The first seven months were a dark period for the miler, a time often spent hiking alone through the woods. He was away from family and friends and found himself constantly reliving that moment when Bannister passed him. Gradually, though, the desire to race took hold of him again, and he began training. In sand shoes, Landy ran along meandering trails and up and down hills, with no destination or end point in mind. He abandoned his schedules, and for the first time in a long while he began to enjoy running again.

On 4 January 1956, at the age of 25, Landy returned to Olympic Park for his first race since his defeat by Bannister. Melbourne newspapers had a heyday, announcing 'Landy to Run Next Week' in a tall linotype. Landy ran in the half-mile against the world record holder in the distance, Len Spurrier, and lost only by inches. At the month's end in the Victorian Championship he blistered the Olympic Park track, doing what he had never been able to do before in Australia: run under four minutes. He clocked a 3:58.6, the second fastest mile in history, second only to his world record set in Turku which had yet to be improved upon. The next day he won the 880-yard title in his fastest time in the distance, 1:50.4, showing newfound speed and finally besting a sixteen-year-old Australian record. A few weeks after that he beat his own record in the three-mile event by eleven seconds. Melbourne's favourite son was back, better than before, and with the 1956 Olympics set to be held in the city, a 1,500m Olympic gold was likely to be theirs.

At the Australian Championship in early March, Landy was slated to go for a mile record. A new crop of milers, including Robbie Morgan-Morris, Ron Clarke, and Merv Lincoln, all of whom had been inspired by Landy's efforts in the four-minute mile pursuit, were set against him. Over twenty thousand people showed up at Olympic Park. By the end of the second lap, Morgan-Morris was in the lead, having run 2:02, with Clarke in second place and Landy in third. The race looked to be unremarkable. Into the second turn of the third lap, however, with the entire field muscling for position to go into the bell lap, Clarke unexpectedly tumbled to the track. Landy was right behind him and tried to jump clear. The rest of the field shot ahead. Instead of continuing, Landy stopped – literally stopped – and turned back to see if Clarke was all right. Although Landy had spiked Clarke's arm with his shoe, the 19-year-old miler got back to his feet, said he was okay, then rushed past Landy to rejoin the race. At this point, Landy had lost roughly seven seconds and was forty yards behind Lincoln, who was now in first position. Nonetheless, Landy chased after the leaders, sprinting the remainder of the third lap to get within striking distance. Into the turn, he was only fifteen yards back, having already passed Clarke. By the back straight he had come within five yards, and around the last turn he burst past Lincoln and sprinted to the finish to win the race by twelve yards in 4:04.2.

The renowned sports journalist Harry Gordon wrote an open letter to Landy in the Melbourne *Sun*, summarising what many felt after seeing that race:

Dear John,
The fellows in the Press box don't have many heroes. Often they help to make them – but usually they know too much about them to believe in them. Up in the Press seats they don't usually clap . . . Mostly, they've mastered the art of observing without becoming excited. On Saturday at 4.35 p.m., though, they forgot the rules. They had a hero – every one of them. And you were it. In the record books, [today's race] will look a very ordinary run for these days. But, for my money, the fantastic gesture and the valiant recovery make it overshadow your magnificent miles in Turku and Vancouver. It was your greatest triumph.

A couple of months later, Landy flew to California to help promote the Melbourne Olympics. He ran back-to-back sub-four-minute miles, became a hero to American track and field fans, and boosted ticket sales for the 1956 Olympics. But the trip, which Landy had decided to take more out of a sense of obligation than desire, cost him dearly. At a time when he should have been resting he had to fly halfway around the world, do countless interviews, and run on hard Californian tracks. The latter aggravated the tendonitis he had developed. In the Olympic 1,500m final he placed a disappointing third; Ron Delany, whom Landy had crushed in one of his races in California, won the gold. As at Vancouver, Landy never uttered a word of complaint about his misfortune. After the Olympics he ran a few more races, but he retired in February 1957 at the age of just 26.

Wes Santee never broke the four-minute mile, nor did he participate in the 1956 Olympics, both ambitions he had set out to achieve when he finished boot camp at summer's end 1954.

In November 1954, track and field expert Cordner Nelson predicted that '1955 should be a great season for the ex-Kansan. He will not have to run two to four races every weekend. Instead he'll concentrate on the mile, and if he doesn't break 3:58, I'll be disappointed.' The Marines supported Santee in his efforts, permitting him a schedule that allowed him to enter competitions. After all, his running brought them good press. He trained as religiously as ever, and though Danna was expecting their first child, his focus remained sharp. During the winter season, he set a new world indoor record with a 4:03.8 mile. At his first outdoor meet at the Texas Relays, he shaved one-tenth of a second off his best mile time with a 4:00.5. A sub-four-minute mile looked guaranteed, and Bill Easton, who continued to coach Santee, said after the race, 'If you got this close the first time you tried outdoors this season, you can't miss. It will come.' Unfortunately, this was the fastest he would ever run the mile.

On 1 June, a *San Francisco Chronicle* article reported that in a series of West Coast meets in 1955 – including the West Coast

Relays (14 May), Coliseum Relays (20 May), and California Relays (21 May) – Santee had received $3,000 in expense money. AAU rules allowed athletes only $15 per day. The *Chronicle* article neglected to mention that Santee had recently turned down an invitation to run in a meet sponsored by the newspaper in which the miler was offered much more than his AAU limit in expenses; Santee had refused because he had a previous speaking engagement at a Catholic high school in Redding, Pennsylvania. Hypocrisy, vendetta, or not, Santee was in trouble. Dan Ferris and the AAU demanded an immediate investigation. The Missouri Valley AAU, which had jurisdiction over the matter, looked into the allegations, and determined that Santee had taken at least $1,200 in expenses. They permanently suspended him as an amateur athlete.

Santee appealed, but as he was in Quantico, Easton went in his stead to argue the case. His coach did not dispute that Santee had accepted the money, but he pointed out that the meet pro-moters, most of whom were AAU officials, had freely offered it to him. Years later Santee explained it this way: 'It was as if I handed my grandson a candy bar, he ate it, and then I slapped him for eating it.' Easton asked the simple question: if it was illegal, why were these officials giving him the excess expenses in the first place? The obvious answer to the question was that amateur officials wanted Santee at their meets to sell tickets. However, no such explanation was forthcoming. Instead, the Missouri Valley AAU simply annulled Santee's suspension by a twenty-one to seven vote. Perhaps they were unwilling to have the underbelly of what sports historian Joseph Turrini referred to as their 'underground-labor-relations system in track' exposed.

Santee considered the matter resolved and turned his attention to the 1956 Olympics. But Dan Ferris and the AAU were not finished. The miler, and those rallying around his cause including Frank Carlson, an influential US Senator, were threatening their control of amateur athletics. This would not do. In December 1955, Ferris reopened the case, even after the time allotted, according to

AAU procedures, to pursue further an investigation had already passed. Santee continued to race, but his focus was distracted by the legal wrangling.

Early in 1956, Ferris privately asked Santee to quit amateur athletics before things got even uglier, but he refused. In fact, Santee, aided by Charles Grimes, a bulldog of a former New York City district attorney who had taken on the case *pro bono*, warned Ferris that he would sue the AAU for an illegal investigation. This did not help. On 19 February the AAU banned Santee from amateur athletics. Ferris told reporters that the young Kansan would 'never run in another track meet in which the AAU [was] involved'. Only after Grimes complained to the press did the AAU turn over the evidence to support their secret investigation. They claimed that in 1955 Santee had taken $2,355 more in expenses than allowed. He was also punished for using a 'booking agent' in California, namely Al Franken. Franken denied the accusation and later said that Santee requiring 'a booking agent was like Muhammad Ali in his heyday needing someone to speak for him'. None of the AAU officials who had given Santee the expense money received more than a slap on the hand.

Santee continued to fight. On 1 March he received a temporary injunction on his ban from the New York State Supreme Court. More and more people came to Santee's defence, including Glenn Cunningham and several other prominent athletes who knew well the hypocrisy and unchecked power of the AAU. The wife of Jim Thorpe, who was the most famous American athlete to be banned by the amateur officials, asked that every American 'protect this man from the bloodsucking octopus of the AAU'. A survey conducted in California found that only one person among the 4,639 polled thought that the AAU was in the right on the matter. When Santee competed at events, the stadium cheered his name and booed the AAU. Unfortunately for Santee, this matter was about power, not popularity.

The AAU immediately went to court to have the injunction

lifted. Meet directors and athletes feared that if they invited Santee, or ran against him, they risked punishment. That same March, Santee went out to his lawyer's house in Long Island. The athlete wanted to testify. Grimes asked him what he planned to testify to, and Santee replied, 'That all of us got more money than the rule book allowed.'

Grimes, taking on the role of the AAU lawyer, asked, 'How do you know?'

Santee told Grimes that he had seen many athletes take money from the AAU over the years, some of whom were to be on the 1956 Olympic team. And then he suddenly understood Grimes's question. If Santee were to testify, he would have to name names, something that he refused to do.

In court the next day, Santee did not testify in his own defence. The AAU lawyer excoriated him in his summation, saying, 'He can run a mile, but he cannot walk twenty feet to the witness stand in his own defense. He makes a confession by not calling a single witness in his own behalf.' The judge lifted the injunction, and Santee was again banned from amateur athletics, this time for life.

Enraged at the injustice of the AAU's action, he telephoned Easton. 'What do we do now, coach?'

Easton knew the fight was over. His tone was resigned. 'I don't know what to do, Wes. There's nothing you can do.'

Though Santee was the best middle-distance runner in America, he was not going to the Olympics. As for his four-minute dreams, even though Al Franken tried to get him together with Roger Bannister and John Landy in a professional race, the idea never got off the ground. Santee had got himself tangled up in the middle of a sporting world in transition, where amateur officials were fast losing control to the rising tide of professionalism. Wes Santee was its victim.

On 28 May 1955, Dr Roger Bannister, now retired from athletics, went to White City stadium to support Chris Chataway in the

British Games mile race. Chataway's fiercest competitors were his countryman Brian Hewson and Hungary's Laszlo Tabori. At the three-quarter-mile mark, Hewson held the lead in a time of 3:02. In the back straight, Chataway and Hewson were neck and neck, with Tabori in third place. Then the Hungarian began to kick; the two British milers answered with their own increase in pace. With sixty yards to go, the three were within inches of one another. They fought to the finish, Tabori stretching out a lead of four yards by the tape to win. Chataway and Hewson crossed the line in the same time. All three ran under four minutes, and Bannister, having lost his world mile record to Landy almost a year earlier, now found that he could no longer lay claim to the fastest mile in Britain.

'Après moi, le deluge,' Bannister had said in the days after he made history at the Iffley Road track in Oxford, referring to the famous statement by Madame de Pompadour, intimate of Louis XV. And with the barrier of the four-minute mile removed, the flood did indeed begin. First Landy, then Tabori, Chataway, and Hewson. Was Bannister's prediction accurate because he had removed the psychological obstacle that the four-minute mile might not be impossible? Or had the barrier's fall simply been a matter of progress, of runners training better and more frequently? The answer probably falls somewhere between the two, but there is no doubt that the four-minute mile turned out to be little more than a stepping-stone that the fastest milers of today take on their way to greatness.

Progress on the world mile record has been steady since 1954. Landy held his record for two days shy of four years, Yorkshireman Derek Ibbotson taking it with a 3:57.2 run in London, fulfilling a promise he had made to his wife on the birth of their first daughter a month earlier. On 6 August 1958, Herb Elliott from Australia, the much-heralded new prodigy of Percy Cerutty, obliterated Ibbotson's time by nearly three seconds with a 3:54.5 mile in Dublin. Of his astounding run, Elliott later remarked, 'It was just another time, another progression.' Naturally enough, that was not how Ibbotson felt. Elliott had been staying with him before he left to go to Dublin. When the Australian returned to gather his things, he found them on the doorstep. 'What's my case doing out here?' Elliott asked. Ibbotson said, 'If you think you're staying here after taking my record, you can piss off.' In 1962, New Zealander Peter Snell, whose workout schedule included twenty-two-mile Sunday runs in the mountains around Auckland, lowered Elliott's time by one-tenth of a second. And in 1964 he lowered his own record by three-tenths of a second to 3:54.1. He was bested by half a second a few months later by Frenchman Michel Jazy (3:53.6), who then lost his crown in 1966 to Jim Ryun (3:51.3), a Kansas native and the first American to hold the record since Norman Taber in 1915. Ryun was also the first high-school student to run the mile in under four minutes. His coach Bob Timmons had inspired him by telling him stories of *Roger Bannister*.

Ryun's time wasn't bested for over eight years. Tanzania's Filbert Bayi held the record for four short months, until New Zealand's John Walker ran 3:49.4 on 12 August 1975. Then the great rivalry between the United Kingdom's Sebastian Coe and Steve Ovett saw the record pass back and forth between the two over the course of twenty-five months. Their battles recalled the days of Haegg and Andersson. Coe ended with the best time of 3:47.33 in August 1981 (records now being parsed to the hundredth of a second). His countryman Steve Cram followed him with a 3:46.31 mile in 1985; Algeria's Noureddine Morceli ran 3:44.39 in 1993; and then, on 7 July 1999 in Rome, Morocco's Hicham El Guerrouj delivered a 3:43.13 mile. Had Bannister been in the same race, he would have finished almost a quarter of a lap behind. By the time El Guerrouj seized the world mile record, almost a thousand individuals had run under four minutes.

So much for a barrier.

This progress begs the question: how fast can the mile be run? If not four minutes, then three and a half? The prognosticators of the past, those who wagered bottles of champagne with Joe Binks that the four-minute mile was a fantastical dream, those such as Brutus Hamilton who banked their reputations on a 'perfect record' that stopped at 4:01.6, have all been proved wrong. As for how far off the mark they were, one has to excuse them for not foreseeing synthetic tracks, high-tech shoe design, two-a-day workouts, engineered diets, high-altitude training, and a field of milers selected from countries far and wide, the very best of whom find a prosperous career and not a little fame in running. This is to say nothing of those who will dare to push the body's limits through performance-enhancing drugs, hormone replacement and – don't be surprised – genetic modification. The only sure bet as to how fast the mile will be run is to acknowledge the wisdom of the old cliché: 'Records are made to be broken.' The longer a record stands, the surer one can be that some ambitious young kid will place it firmly in his or her sights.

But the methods and reasons for pursuing ever faster miles have changed in the past half-century. If one is to become an elite athlete today, there is little room for anything else. The best of them train four or five hours a day, and their lives completely revolve around running. When some discover that their times, no matter the amount and kind of training they undergo, fail to improve, they turn to drugs that not only threaten their expulsion from competition if they are caught, but also have dangerous side effects.

Of course, the rewards for being a top-flight runner seemingly mitigate the sacrifices involved in becoming one. Allan Webb, the first American to break Jim Ryun's high-school mile record, dropped out of the University of Michigan after his freshman year to earn six figures a year in sponsorship deals. El Guerrouj socks away more than a million dollars a year in appearance fees, sponsorship, and prize money. Beyond a desire to be the best, that is a lot of reasons to claim the fastest mile in the world. But the steady encroachment of commerce into modern athletics over the years has taken some of the romance out of the mile record. There was more honour in pursuing it for no other reward than knowing one has pushed through the boundary of what seemed impossible.

No matter how far the record falls, people will look back to the breaking of the four-minute barrier, and the showdown between Landy and Bannister in Vancouver, as two defining moments in the history of the mile – and in sport as well. On 6 May 1954, Roger Bannister, an amateur who trained little more than an hour a day and for whom running was nothing more than a passionate hobby, achieved greatness on a cinder track he had helped build, in front of a small crowd, a handful of journalists, and a lone camera crew that had to be persuaded to attend. Only three months later, in a modern concrete and steel stadium, Landy and Bannister battled each other in a heavily promoted race covered by an army of journalists and camera teams, broadcast to millions of homes worldwide, and commentated on by their fiercest rival. The 'Mile of the Century' had all the hallmarks of a professional sporting event except that not one of its competitors earned a penny in the process. If the first race sounded the death knell of amateurism, the second race struck one of the first notes of sport's future.

Fifty years later, Wes Santee, John Landy, and Roger Bannister live only a short distance from where each ran his first fast mile. Walking around the tracks at the University of Kansas, Olympic Park, and Iffley Road, they must hear the echoes of the past: the pop of the starter's pistol, the rhythmic strike of steel spikes into cinder, the crescendo of the crowd's cheer, the crackle of the public-address system as everyone hushed for the mile time, wondering if today was the day.

Often when one thinks of his sporting heroes, they are ageless. One remembers them in their prime, faces unblemished, bodies still taut with power. If a measure of a person is how they live their whole lives, not simply their youth, then these three men deserve to be regarded for what they did after their pursuit of the four-minute mile as well. Wes Santee had a long and distinguished career serving as a Marines reservist while running his own insurance business. He remains a champion of the University of Kansas and continues to

315

support youth programmes in sport. After his teaching stint at Geelong Grammar, John Landy joined the chemical company ICI as a rural scientist and was head of their rural research and development by the time he retired. He served on the Melbourne Olympic committee, chaired a task force to promote Australian athletics, led the Australian Sports Drug Agency, and also wrote a couple of books on natural history. In 2000, he was appointed Governor of Victoria. Once retired from athletics, Roger Bannister dedicated himself to medicine, becoming a noted neurologist. He sidelined as an official on Britain's Sports Council, and led two major campaigns: the first to build recreational centres throughout the country; the second to discourage athletes from taking performance-enhancing drugs through random testing. In 1975 he was knighted for his efforts in medicine and sport. Bannister also wrote one of the most evocative books on running, and was the Master of Pembroke College, Oxford University.

Bannister, Landy, and Santee look back on their competitive running days with a blend of pride and 'oh, not that old story again'. Santee remains stung by his fight with the AAU. Landy is wistful about what might have been in Vancouver. Bannister still exudes the determination and aggression that gave power to his finishing kick. Dramatic as their efforts were to many millions of people, the three speak pointedly about what sport gave to them, regardless of four-minute barriers and miracle miles.

Landy said, 'Running gave me discipline and self-expression . . . It has all the disappointments, frustrations, lack of success, and unexpected success, which all reproduce themselves in the bigger play of life. It teaches you the ability to present under pressure. It teaches you the importance of being enthusiastic, dedicated, focused. All of these are trite statements, but if you actually have to go through these things as a young man, it's very, very important.'

Santee said, 'Hard work pays off. You have to be just as disciplined to run a business as you do to train for an athletic event. You have to eat right, still have to get up early and work more than others. Great athletes usually spend extra time in the weight room, shoot extra baskets, run extra sprints, whatever. And that whole thing translates into larger life . . . When I'm going to give a speech, like to young Marines, I will plan my whole day around that so I am mentally and physically alert. You can't separate these when you're performing, same as if I was running an event. I still eat my tea, toast and honey.'

And as Bannister learned to understand, 'Sport is about not being wrapped up in cotton wool. Sport is about adapting to the unexpected and being able to modify plans at the last minute. Sport, like all life, is about taking your chances.'

ACKNOWLEDGEMENTS

When I began *The Perfect Mile*, I was inspired by the words of Alan Hoby, who in 1954 documented the role of a good sportswriter: 'It is not simply to write a technical treatise in which the performer is dissected like some laboratory specimen . . . It is much more. It is heat and fire, drama and high excitement. It is victory and disaster. It is perspiration and the pungent whiff of liniment. It is the roar of the crowd . . . Above all, it is recapturing for the reader the supreme effort of the [athlete] – the very heartbeats of the particular triumph or tragedy the reporter is striving to word-paint.'

Recreating the events of a story that occurred fifty years ago in this manner is no small feat, and any success I have had is thanks to the patience and forthrightness of Roger Bannister, John Landy, and Wes Santee. Each of them sat through several interview sessions and responded to scores of questions; then they entertained follow-up phone calls and correspondence and provided further detail. I never could have written this book without them, and they have my heartfelt appreciation and respect.

During my travels to visit them, I also connected with their friends, running mates, and acquaintances from the time, many of whom invited me into their homes and discussed days past. Thank you to Chris Chataway, Norris McWhirter, Nicholas Stacey, Dr. Ronald Williams, John Disley, Peter Hildreth, Terry O'Connor, and Pat Stampfl for regaling me with stories of Roger Bannister. Thank you to Len McRae, Geoff Warren, Trevor Robbins, John Vernon, Don Macmillan, Les Perry, Julius Patching, Ron Clarke, Robbie Morgan-Morris, Merv Lincoln, Kev Dynan, and Murray Halberg for sharing their recollections of John Landy. And thank you to Tom Rupp, Dick Wilson, Al Frame, Lloyd Koby, Bob Timmons, Bill Mayer, Don Humphreys, and Herbie Semper for their many helpful insights and anecdotes about Wes Santee.

I would still be researching if it was not for sportswriter Dave Kuehls, who signed on at this book's inception to help me through each stage in the process. He tracked down interview subjects, guided me through the world of track and field, offered suggestions on each draft, and was truly my right-hand man from start to finish. Thanks to Liz O'Donnell, doyenne of the written word, who was my first reader and made critical edits in each chapter. I also want to acknowledge Todd Keithley, Bruce McKenna, and Joe Veltre for their early reads as well. And I would be remiss if I did not mention my friend Jim Catlin, who got me out of Dodge and housed me in his too-swank Milan flat for a month while I began this book.

Throughout, I have been enthusiastically guided by my literary agent Scott Waxman. He has a great eye, and, most importantly, he is a good man to have in your corner. Thanks also to Simon Trewin, Justin Manasek, Joel Gotler, Danny Baror, and Susan Mindell.

I have had the pleasure of working on this book with two fine publishers, Houghton Mifflin in the United States and Harper-Collins in the United Kingdom. At Houghton Mifflin, I first want to thank my editor Susan Canavan. She possesses a terrific sense of narrative flow, wields a mean line-edit pencil, and has been a great champion of this book from the beginning. Thank you also to her assistant Sarah Gabert, as well as Gary Gentel, Bridget Marmion, Lori Glazer, Carla Gray, and Megan Wilson. Drinks are on me when I come to Boston. At HarperCollins UK, I owe a great deal of gratitude to Michael Doggart, publishing director of CollinsWillow. He fired my imagination as to what this book could be and has been a great support throughout. Thank you also to Tarda Davison-Aitkins and the rest of the team in London.

This book is dedicated to Diane and her unyielding faith in what is possible.

AUTHOR'S NOTE

When an author sets out to investigate a legend, and there are few stories as legendary in sport as the pursuit of the four-minute mile, it is initially difficult to see the heroes around whom events unfolded as true flesh-and-blood individuals. Myth tends to wrap its arms around fact, and memory finds a comfortable groove and stays the course. What makes these individuals so interesting – their doubts, vulnerabilities, and failures – is often airbrushed out, and their victories characterised as faits accomplis. But true heroes are never as unalloyed as they first appear (thank goodness). We should admire them all the more for this fact.

Getting past the panegyrics that populate this history has been the real pleasure behind my research. No doubt there have been some very fine articles written about this story, but only by interviewing the principals – Roger Bannister, John Landy, and Wes Santee – and their close friends at the time does one do justice to the depth of this story. Their generosity in this regard has been without measure. These interviews, coupled with contemporaneous newspaper and magazine articles as well as memoir accounts by several individuals involved in the events, serve as the basis of *The Perfect Mile*. With this material, the story almost wrote itself.

I have included collective references for those interested in knowing the sources behind particular conversations and scenes. No dialogue in this book was manufactured; it is either a direct quote from a secondary resource or from an interview. That said, half a century has passed since this story occurred. On some occasions, dialogue is represented as the best recollection of what was in all probability said. Furthermore, memory has its faults, and in those situations where interview subjects contradicted one another I almost always went with what the principal recollected. In those instances when contemporaneous sources (mainly newspaper articles) did not correspond with memory, I primarily went with the former, particularly when there were several sources indicating the same facts. Having inhabited this world for the past eighteen months, aswim in paper and interview tapes, I feel I have been a fairly accurate judge of the events as they happened. I hope that I have served the history of these heroes well.

REFERENCES

Prologue

p. 1, 'How did he know': Roger Bannister, personal interview.

p. 1, 'seemed so perfectly round': *Sports Illustrated* (27 June 1994).

p. 2, Running the mile: 'Four-Minute Men', *Sports Illustrated* (16 August 1994).

p. 2, 'He just flat believed': Wes Santee, personal interview.

p. 2, Few knew that running: Wes Santee, personal interview.

p. 2, 'I'd rather lose a 3:58': Arthur Daley, 'Listening to John Landy', *New York Times* (22 May 1956).

p. 2, Running revealed to him: John Landy, personal interview.

p. 3, They spent a large part: *Sports Illustrated* (27 June 1994).

p. 3, If they weren't training: Chris Chataway, personal interview.

p. 4, 'tapestry of alternating triumph and tragedy': Norris McWhirter, National Centre for Athletics Literature (NCAL) interview, University of Birmingham.

Chapter 1

p. 7, 'Bannister had terrific grace': Terry O'Connor, personal interview.

p. 7, Some said he could: Peter Hildreth, personal interview.

p. 8, Bannister loved that moment: Roger Bannister, *The Four Minute Mile* (Globe Pequot Press, 1955), 59.

p. 8, He held his thumb firmly: Norris McWhirter, personal interview.

p. 8, They were three years older: Norris McWhirter, personal interview.

p. 8, 'There lies the body': Norris McWhirter, 'The Man Who Made History', *World Sport* (June 1954).

p. 9, 'At least, Norris': Chris Chataway, personal interview.

p. 9, But he knew one way: Dr Ronald Williams, personal interview.

p. 10, When Bannister was not racing: Arthur Daley, 'Listening to a 4-Minute Mile', *New York Times* (22 May 1956).

p. 10, 'Roger . . . they put in a semi-final': Dr Ronald Williams, personal interview.

p. 11, He was to be the hero: Terry O'Connor, personal interview.

p. 12, 'It is gone': John Montgomery, *The Fifties* (George Allen and Unwin, 1965), 46–7.

p. 12, 'we still bathed': Juliet Gardiner, *From the Bomb to the Beatles* (Collins and Brown, 1999), 30.

p. 12, It was so cold: Alfred Havighurst, *Twentieth Century Britain* (Harper and Row, 1966), 399.

p. 12, 'the largest, saddest and dirtiest': ibid., 35.

p. 12, 'just like Britain': ibid., 52.

p. 12, Crowds wearing black armbands: Harry Hopkins, *The New Look: A Social History of the Forties and Fifties in Britain* (Secker and Warburg, 1963), 283–4.

p. 13, 'England has owed': J. E. C. Weldon, headmaster of Harrow, 1881–95, quoted in Richard Holt, *Sport and the British: A Modern History* (Oxford University Press, 1990), 205.

p. 13, Yet even in sport: ibid., 105–6.

p. 13, 'United, Euphoric': Peter Lewis, *The Fifties* (Heinemann, 1978), 15.

p. 13, After that the country: Hopkins, *New Look*, 283–4.

p. 13, For a country that considered: Holt, *Sport and the British*, 276–7.

p. 13, He didn't come from a family: Roger Bannister, interview by American Academy of Achievement (27 October 2000).

p. 14, All Roger knew: Bannister, *Four Minute Mile*, 46.

p. 14, Only later in life: BBC Radio 4, 'A Conversation Piece with Sue McGregor' (17 May 1990).

p. 14, 'I was startled and frightened': Bannister, *Four Minute Mile*, 11–12.

p. 14, When he was 10: Bannister, American Academy of Achievement interview.

p. 14, As an awkward, serious-minded: Bannister, *Four Minute Mile*, 32–5.

p. 15, The next day Bannister: ibid., 34.

p. 15, 'You'll be dead': ibid., 38.

p. 15, His new school: ibid., 38–44.

p. 15, Bannister intended to study: George Smith, *All Out for the Mile* (Forbes Robertson, 1955), 144–5.

p. 15, 'If there was a moment': BBC, *Suspense: The Four-Minute Mile* (18 July 1954).

p. 16, 'Stop bouncing': Bannister, *Four Minute Mile*, 50–1.

p. 16, 'over-stride in a series': ibid., 51.

p. 16, The cruel winter: ibid., 56–61; Smith, *All Out*, 144–5.

p. 17, 'You mean *the* Jack': Bannister, *Four Minute Mile*, 60.

p. 17, On 5 June he clocked: ibid., 64–78.

p. 17, He had taken a coach: Roger Bannister, American Academy of Achievement interview.

p. 18, He had spent the two previous years: Bannister, *Four Minute Mile*, 88–118.

p. 19, First he flew to New Zealand: ibid., 124–9.

p. 19, 'No manager, no trainer': ibid., 136.

p. 19, In front of forty thousand: 'British Miler Beats Wilt; Gehrmann 3D', *Chicago Sunday Tribune* (29 April 1951).

p. 19, 'Anyone who beats him': Joe Binks, 'Bannister's Race My Oslo Memory', *News of the World* (24 June 1951).

p. 20, 'Go Back': Doug Wilson, 'Bannister Can Still Learn Much', *News of the World* (12 August 1951).

p. 20, To escape the attention: Bannister, *Four Minute Mile*, 149–50.

p. 20, Throughout the winter: ibid., 153–9.

p. 21, 'more sensitive': L. A. Montague, 'Why R. G. Bannister's

Training Methods Are Right', *Manchester Guardian* (9 June 1952).

p. 21, 'Don't worry': James Stagg, *Daily Mirror* (7 July 1952).

p. 21, 'No alibis': Norris McWhirter, 'Bannister will have no alibis', *Star* (3 May 1952).

p. 21, 'Victory at Helsinki': Bannister, *Four Minute Mile*, 159-160.

p. 22, 'We will not let Britain down': 'British Athletic Team Reach Helsinki', *Daily Telegraph* (16 July 1952).

p. 22, His friend Chris Chataway: 'Goggles for Chataway', *Star* (16 July 1952).

p. 22, It didn't take him long: Bannister, *Four Minute Mile*, 162.

p. 22, 'I could hardly believe it': ibid.

Chapter 2

p. 24, In the narrow concrete tunnel: Wes Santee, personal interview.

p. 24, He remembered arriving: ibid.

p. 25, 'Boy, this building': ibid.

p. 25, His countrymen had cleared forests: Red Smith, 'Red Smith in Helsinki', *New York Herald Tribune* (19 July 1952); Graem Sims, *Why Die? The Extraordinary Life of Percy Cerutty* (Lothian Books, 2003), 113–14.

p. 25, Peerless Paavo: Jesse Abramson, 'Nurmi', in Herbert Warren Wind (ed.), *The Realm of Sport* (Simon and Schuster, 1966), 629–33.

p. 26, From a distance: *Manchester Guardian* (21 July 1952).

p. 27, Had his father: ibid. This account of Santee's early life is taken largely from my personal interviews with him. Many of the details were checked against newspaper and magazine articles written about him in the early 1950s.

p. 28, 'If I was told': Bob Hurt, 'Sure I'll Run the Four-Minute Mile', *Saturday Evening Post* (26 September 1953).

p. 32, Santee did not bring his arms back: Wes Santee, personal interview; Bill Easton, 'Santee's Stride', Archives of William Easton, University of Kansas (undated).

p. 33, Led by Santee: 'KU Freshman Track Team Rated', *Daily Kansan* (February 1951).

p. 33, While some athletes: Wes Santee, personal interview.

p. 33, 'I want to make the Olympic team': Jerry Renner, 'Wes Santee, KU Track Star', *Daily Kansan* (2 October 1951).

p. 34, 'Look what it says here': profile of Wes Santee, Archives of William Easton, University of Kansas (untitled, n.d.).

p. 34, 'He's wilting': Wes Santee, personal interview.

p. 34, 'Santee's not human': Bob Hurt, 'Writers Name Santee as Drake Relays Star', *Daily Capital* (28 April 1952).

p. 34, 'Santee stuck out': ibid.

p. 35, 'Santee is the greatest': ibid.

p. 35, 'win as he pleases': United States Olympic Team Meet Schedule, Archives of William Easton, University of Kansas (n.d.).

p. 35, 'Wes, I'm sorry': Wes Santee, personal interview.

p. 36, Only the previous week: Dwain Esper, 'Four Records Fall in AAU Championships', *Track & Field News* (July 1952).

p. 36, The coach had the stocky build: James Gunn, 'Second Isn't Good Enough: A Day in the Life of Bill Easton', *University of Kansas Alumni Magazine* (May 1959).

p. 36, The three weeks: Wes Santee, personal interview.

p. 36, He ran in an exhibition: Stan Hamilton, 'Wes Santee', article in Santee's scrapbook (n.d.).

Chapter 3

p. 38, All was quiet in Kapyla: Norman Banks, *The World in My Diary: From Melbourne to Helsinki for the Olympic Games* (William Heinemann, 1953), 54–5.

p. 38, At 57, Cerutty: Harry Gordon, *Young Men in a Hurry: The Story of Australia's Fastest Decade* (Lansdowne, 1961), 18.

p. 39, Prancing around Motspur Park: Sims, *Why Die?*, 117.

p. 39, 'So, you're Bannister': ibid., 118.

p. 39, 'Others can run faster': ibid.

p. 40, Earlier that evening: J. H. Galli, 'Man of the Miracle Mile', *Sport* (August 1954).

p. 40, In London he had placed second: William T. J. Uren, 'Australian Olympic Team at Helsinki 1952' (Australian Olympic Committee, 1952), 58–9.

p. 40, 'paralyzing burst': Ron Carter, 'Sprint Star Breaks Own in Final', *Argus* (23 June 1952).

p. 40, 'had not seen a runner': Bruce Welch, 'Woman Athletes Star in Belfast', *Age* (27 June 1952).

p. 40, He had even set: 'Record 2-mile by John Landy', *Herald* (1 July 1952).

p. 41, 'Runners were oddities': Trevor Robbins, personal interview.

p. 41, The country had a long tradition: Geoff Warren, personal interview.

p. 41, 'Olympic Park': Joseph Galli, 'Landy's Mile', *Amateur Athlete* (January 1953), 17–18.

p. 42, It has been noted: Wray Vamplew and Brian Stoddart, *Sport in Australia* (Cambridge University Press, 1994), 11.

p. 42, In the early 1950s: 'Australians "Most Avid Sports Fans"', *Sydney Morning Herald* (23 July 1953).

p. 42, Total attendance: Vamplew and Stoddart, *Sport*, 11-13.

p. 42, 'world champion': 'Fastest Man in the World', *Sun-Herald* (27 June 1954).

p. 42, Landy enjoyed: John Landy, personal interview; Les Perry, personal interview.

p. 43, The young John Landy: ibid.

p. 43, 'prefects whack[ed] the boys': Paul O'Neil, 'Duel of the Four-Minute Men', *Sports Illustrated* (August 1954).

p. 43, John was part of a group: John Landy, personal interview.

p. 43, In his final year at Geelong: Joseph Galli, 'Victorian John

Landy May Soon Become Our Greatest Middle-Distance Runner', *Sports Novels* (April 1952).

p. 43, When he enrolled: ibid.

p. 44, The club captain: John Landy, personal interview.

p. 44, 'You're not fit': Len McRae, personal interview.

p. 44, The two went to see Cerutty: Sims, *Why Die?*, 100–101; Percy Cerutty, *Sport Is My Life* (Stanley Paul, 1966), 34–5.

p. 45, The first was Les Perry: Sims, *Why Die?*, 80–6; Les Perry, personal interview.

p. 45, When Macmillan: Sims, *Why Die?*, 86–93; Don Macmillan, personal interview.

p. 46, 'What did you say': Sims, *Why Die?*, 100–101; Cerutty, *Sport*, 34–5; Joseph Galli, 'Landy Will Set More Records, Says Coach', *Amateur Athlete* (August 1954); John Landy, personal interview. This scene, including the dialogue, is drawn from a combination of these sources.

p. 46, When Landy left: J. H. Galli, 'Landy Will Set More Records, Says Coach', *Amateur Athlete* (August 1954).

p. 46, It took three weeks: Robert Solomon, *Great Australian Athletes: Selected Olympians 1928–1956* (R. J. Solomon, 2000), 163. Solomon has done an extensive study of John Landy's times in this book.

p. 47, On 22 May: John Landy, personal interview.

p. 47, Landy had natural coordination: J. H. Galli, 'Man of the Miracle Mile', *Sport* (August 1954).

p. 47, Almost from the day: Keith Dunstan, *Ratbags* (Sun Books, 1979), 148–50; Sims, *Why Die?*, 7–33; Graeme Kelly, *Mr. Controversial: The Story of Percy Wells Cerutty* (Stanley Paul, 1964), 35–67.

p. 48, 'I can't heal you': Sims, *Why Die?*, 35.

p. 48, He restricted his diet: ibid. 34–56; Alan Trengrove, *The Golden Mile: The Herb Elliott Story* (Cassell, 1961), 34–7.

p. 48, 'I've come down to have a run': Sims, *Why Die?*, 49.

p. 48, The road hadn't been easy: Trengrove, *Golden Mile*, 38.

p. 48, 'Thrust against pain': ibid.

p. 49, The gate to the property: Trevor Robbins, personal interview; Sims, *Why Die?*, 105–10.

p. 49, His parents were circumspect: John Landy, personal interview.

p. 49, He had brought a sleeping bag: Trevor Robbins, personal interview; Sims, *Why Die?*, 105–10.

p. 50, 'primitive man': John Vernon, personal interview.

p. 50, 'Move your bloody arms!': Sims, *Why Die?*, 229.

p. 51, 'Realization that': Dunstan, *Ratbags*, 148.

p. 51, 'There. Did the cat do stretches?': Trevor Robbins, personal interview.

p. 52, The first night Landy stayed there: ibid.

p. 52, 'It's pretty tough out here': Don Macmillan, personal interview.

p. 52, 'He undervalues himself': Sims, *Why Die?*, 103–4.

p. 53, 'It is bad luck': 'Cheers were Mile[d]', *Argus* (14 January 1952).

p. 53, If Landy and a few others: Julius Patching, telephone interview.

p. 53, John heard the news: John Landy, personal interview.

p. 54, 'I don't know just what': Galli, 'Victorian John Landy May Soon Become Our Greatest Middle-Distance Runner', *Sports Novels* (April 1952).

p. 54, And he was very sensitive: Les Perry, personal interview.

Chapter 4

p. 55, The rain during the opening ceremony: *The Official Report of the Organizing Committee for the Games of the XV Olympiad, Helsinki 1952* (Werner Soderstrom Osakeyhtio, 1952), 247.

p. 55, Wes Santee woke up in his room: Wes Santee, personal interview.

p. 56, It was quite certain: Jesse Abramson, 'U.S. Athletes are Favorites in Ten Events', *New York Herald Tribune* (6 July 1952).

p. 56, Late that afternoon: 'U.S. Olympic Track Squad in Helsinki', *Topeka Capital* (10 July 1952).

p. 57, On the first day: Lainson Wood, 'Zatopek Storms Home in Olympic 10,000 Metres', *Daily Telegraph* (21 July 1952).

p. 57, 'mobilized to win': 'Muscles Pop Through Iron Curtain', *Life* (28 July 1952).

p. 57, No effort was spared: Alan Hoby, *One Crowded Hour* (Museum Press Limited, 1954), 41.

p. 59, When he saw Fred Wilt: Wes Santee, personal interview

p. 60, Sitting in the stands: John Landy, personal interview.

p. 60, He was in the fourth: 'Track and Field Prospects: New World's Record Probable in Great 1,500 Metres', *Manchester Guardian* (16 July 1952).

p. 61, 'There's nothing graceful': Jim Denison (ed.), *Bannister and Beyond: The Mystique of the Four-Minute Mile* (Breakaway Books, 2003), 24.

p. 61, He had failed to qualify: Solomon, *Great Australian Athletes*, 167.

p. 61, When the gun went off: Hoby, *One Crowded Hour*, 25-35; Cordner Nelson, 'Profiles of Champions – Emil Zatopek', *Track & Field* (December 1953); Raymond Krise and Bill Squires, *Fast Tracks: The History of Distance Running* (Stephen Greene Press, 1982), 119–20; Lainson Wood, 'Chataway Cracks Within Sight of the Tape', *Daily Telegraph* (25 July 1952).

p. 61, 'apoplectic fit': Hoby, *One Crowded Hour*, 25.

p. 63, Landy himself was impressed: John Landy, personal interview.

p. 63, 'mad scramble': ibid.; 'Hot Field', *Herald* (25 July 1952).

p. 64, 'No man or woman': 'Olympic Athletes Criticised: Not Fit Enough', *Age* (14 March 1954).

p. 64, When Perry first arrived: Sims, *Why Die?*, 123–5; Les Perry, personal interview.

p. 64, After his 1,500m loss: Geoff Warren, personal interview.

p. 65, 'Piped Piper of Hamelin': John Landy, personal interview.

p. 65, 'When I was in the 1950': Les Perry, personal interview.

p. 65, 'I shall learn': Frantisek Kozik, *Zatopek: The Marathon Victor* (Artia, 1954), 93.

p. 65, Roger Bannister was too exhausted: Bannister, *Four Minute Mile*, 168–80; Chris Chataway, personal interview ; Nicholas Stacey, personal interview; Roger Bannister, personal interview.

p. 66, 'While he goes for a twenty-mile training run': Bannister, *Four Minute Mile*, 171.

p. 66, 'Bannister had watched the race': ibid., 172.

p. 67, 'I will eat a pair': Nicholas Stacey, telephone interview.

p. 67, 'Don't Worry': *Daily Mirror* (22 July 1952).

p. 67, 'rarely bothered': ibid.

p. 67, But his legs hurt: Bannister, *Four Minute Mile*, 168–80.

p. 68, 'Good luck, Don': Don Macmillan, personal interview.

p. 68, When the Duke of Edinburgh arrived: A. J. Liebling, 'Letter from the Olympics', *New Yorker* (9 August 1952).

p. 68, 'There was a peculiar loneliness': Christopher Brasher, *Sportsmen of Our Time* (Victor Gollancz, 1962), 20.

p. 68, Chris Chataway was also in the stands: Chris Chataway, personal interview.

p. 68, However, though tense and sapped: Roger Bannister, personal interview.

p. 69, Suddenly, they were off: Roger Bannister, personal interview; Bannister, *Four Minute Mile*, 175–80; Chris Chataway, personal interview; R. L. Quercetani, '1,500 Meters', *Track & Field* (August 1952); Brasher, *Sportsmen*, 20–1; Liebling, 'Letter from the Olympics'; Douglas Wilson, 'Bannister's Gallant Failure', *News of the World* (27 July 1952); 'Bannister Fourth in 1,500 Metres', *The Times* (28 July 1952).

p. 69, 'He is not running': 'Commentary by Harold Abrahams – 1,500 metres', BBC Sound Archive – Helsinki Olympic Games in 1952.

p. 70, 'A disaster is something': Brasher, *Sportsmen*, 21.

Chapter 5

p. 71, 'Every morning in Africa': Bernd Heinrich, *Racing the Antelope: What Animals Can Teach Us About Running and Life* (Cliff Street Books, 2001), 9.

p. 72, 'symbolized laying claim': Edward Sears, *Running Through the Ages* (McFarland & Company, 2001), 14.

p. 72, Other early societies: John Marshall Carter and Arnd Kruger (eds), *Ritual and Record: Sports Records and Quantification in Pre-Modern Societies* (Greenwood Press, 1990); Allen Guttmann, *From Ritual to Record: The Nature of Modern Sports* (Columbia University Press, 1978). To read more about early sporting traditions and how they were recorded and quantified, these are two illuminating books.

p. 72, A Greek citizen named Coroebus: John Kieran, 'Olympic Games', in Wind (ed.), *Realm of Sport*, 625–9.

p. 72, Sporting ability: John Blundell, *The Muscles and Their Story from the Earliest Times* (Chapman and Hall, 1864), xvii.

p. 72, The Romans favoured: ibid., 24.

p. 72, Roman soldiers: George Gretton, *Out in Front* (Pelham Books, 1968), 83–4.

p. 73, By the nineteenth century: Sears, *Running*, 50–6.

p. 73, Running a mile: ibid., 80–111.

p. 73, For most of the nineteenth century: ibid., 113–19.

p. 74, It is impossible to know: Sears, *Running*, 110–213; Smith, *All Out*, 37–87. The history of the progress of the four-minute mile and the quotes in this short section are taken from these two sources. Smith's book is the best history of the mile, and the runners who achieved predominance, that I found in my research. It contains rare interviews and profiles that have never been reproduced elsewhere. As for *Running Through the Ages* by Sears, this history proved indispensable in my research of the history of running and contains innumerable anecdotes of great fun to anyone interested in running.

p. 76, 'the other side': Denison (ed.), *Bannister and Beyond*, 11.

p. 77, Andersson/Haegg chart: Smith, *All Out*, 86.

p. 77, 'Can the mile be run': Lawrence J. Baack (ed.), *The Worlds of Brutus Hamilton* (Tafnews), 64–7.

p. 78, 'When we stop this nonsense': Colonel Strode-Jackson, *Colliers Magazine* (1944).

p. 78, 'The Poles had been reached': Frank Deford, 'Pioneer Miler Roger Bannister and Everest Conqueror Edmund Hillary', *Sports Illustrated* (3 January 2000); Denison (ed.), *Bannister and Beyond*, 13.

p. 78, Fewer than forty-eight hours: Bill Brown, 'British Empire versus U.S.A.', *Athletic Review* (September 1952).

p. 78, The stadium had staged: Norris McWhirter, personal interview.

p. 78, The stadium was now used: Terry O'Connor, personal interview.

p. 79, 'every time we had stepped': Wes Santee, personal interview.

p. 80, 'I couldn't understand how': Don Humphreys, personal interview.

p. 80, 'Wesley Santee has recently broke': Wes Santee scrapbook.

p. 81, Only days after returning: Bob Hurt, 'Sure I'll Run the Four-Minute Mile', *Saturday Evening Post* (26 September 1953).

p. 81, John Landy had a different announcement: John Landy, personal interview.

p. 81, For his stride: Sims, *Why Die?*, 136–44; John Landy, personal interview.

p. 82, On the flight back: John Landy, personal interview; Len McRae, personal interview.

p. 82, 'He thoroughly deserved his success': 'Travelling Too Much', *Argus* (10 August 1952).

p. 82, Save for a horse: A. W. Ledbrooke, *Great Moments in Sport* (Phoenix House, 1956), 39–43.

p. 82, 'Hang out the crepe': Cecil Bear, 'Bravo Helsinki!', *World Sports* (September 1952).

p. 83, 'Britain was failing to win': Hyton Cleaver, *Before I Forget* (Robert Hale Limited, 1961), 176.

p. 83, 'Roger Bannister could have won': 'Give Them Some REAL Competition', *Daily Mirror* (9 August 1952).

p. 83, Not only did Bannister: Brasher, *Sportsmen*, 16.

p. 83, 'greater degree of self-determination': ibid., 21.

Chapter 6

p. 87, 'A man who sets out': Paul O'Neil, 'A Man Conquers Himself', *Sports Illustrated* (31 May 1956).

p. 87, In Melbourne's Central Park: John Landy, personal interview; Steve Hayward, 'Mile Star Shows Technique', *Herald* (n.d.), from Len McRae scrapbook; O'Neil, *Sports Illustrated* (31 May 1956).

p. 87, Cerutty had promoted: Steve Hayward, 'Run Like a Rooster, Says the White Sage', *Herald* (n.d.), from Len McRae scrapbook.

p. 88, 'They don't run on their toes': *Sporting Globe* (19 November 1952).

p. 89, 'the mind is always selling': John Landy, personal interview.

p. 89, 'It's like a car starting': ibid.

p. 89, On a typical night: Fred Wilt (ed.), *How They Train* (Tafnews, 1973), 102–3; John Landy, personal interview; Ron Clarke (ed.), *Athletics: The Australian Way* (Lansdowne, 1976), 53–7.

p. 90, On a typical day: John Landy, personal interview.

p. 9, In this schedule: 'Fastest Man in the World', *Sun-Herald* (27 June 1954).

p. 90, 'The harder, the better': 'Landy Runs 4:02.1', *Track & Field News* (December 1952).

p. 90, 'I just go out there': 'Runners are Getting Nearer the Four-Minute Mile', *Sydney Morning Herald* (10 February 1954).

p. 90, 'There is no gray': O'Neil, *Sports Illustrated* (31 May 1956).

p. 90, It was sustained: Adrian McGregor, 'The Greatest Mile of the Century', *National Times* (18 August 1979), 14.

p. 91, 'How fast is this bloke': Robbie Morgan-Morris, personal interview.

p. 91, In October: Les Perry, personal interview.

p. 91, 'I'm taking no more advice': Gordon, *Young Men*, 104.

p. 91, In the history of athletic training: Wilt (ed.), *How They Train*, 9–10; Sears, *Running*, 32–3; Blundell, *The Muscles*, 196–7.

p. 92, The ancient Romans: Walter Thom, *Pedestrianism: An Account* (1813), 221–7.

p. 92, By the seventeenth century: Sears, *Running*, 47.

p. 92, Training techniques looked like: ibid., 62–5; Thom, *Pedestrianism*, 228–31.

p. 93, 'Not all training is good': Adolphe Abrahams, *The Human Machine* (Pelican, 1956), 104.

p. 93, Some physicians thought: Tim Noakes, *The Lore of Running: Discover the Science and Spirit of Running* (Leisure Press, 1991), 670.

p. 93, 'First, I figured out': ibid., 115.

p. 94, 'Monday a mile': John Graham, *Practical Track and Field Athletics* (Fox, Duffield and Company, 1904), 41.

p. 94, The trials and the errors: Noakes, *Lore*, 135–65.

p. 95, 'it's not unusual': ibid., 449.

p. 96, 'Two- and three-mile events': Ken Moses, 'Landy Wins Easily', *Argus* (17 November 1952).

p. 97, Three days later he entered: Steve Hayward, 'Run for Record Praised', *Herald* (19 November 1952).

p. 97, On 12 December: John Landy, personal interview; Les Perry, personal interview; Sears, *Running*, 142.

p. 97, John Landy put in his half-day: John Landy, personal interview.

p. 98, Olympic Park was the centre: Trevor Robbins, *Running Into History: A Centenary Profile of the Malvern Harriers Athletic Club* (Malvern Harriers, 1996), 169–71.

p. 98, By two o'clock: John Landy, personal interview; Les Perry, personal interview.

p. 99, 'I think they called': John Landy, personal interview.

p. 99, 'Nobody will cross over': Robbie Morgan-Morris, personal interview.

p. 99, Each club team stood: Trevor Robbins, personal interview.

p. 100, 'Then I went': John Landy, personal interview.

p. 101, 'You ran 4:03': ibid.

p. 101, 'Most of the credit': Ken Moses, 'Landy Chasing Records', Argus (15 December 1952).

p. 101, While Landy explained: Les Perry, personal interview; Sims, Why Die?, 143.

p. 102, 'Here's a bloke': ibid.

p. 102, When he went home: John Landy, personal interview.

Chapter 7

p. 103, 'An average man's body': Abrahams, Human Machine, 13.

p. 103, On 14 December 1952: Norris McWhirter, personal interview; Roger Bannister, personal interview.

p. 103, Bannister was stunned: Bannister, Four Minute Mile, 184.

p. 104, 'Never in the history': Arthur Daley, 'With a Grain of Salt', New York Times (December 1952).

p. 104, 'no hope of catching him': 'Wells on the Track', Age (5 January 1953).

p. 105, 'Ever since Irving and Mallory': Athletics World (December 1952).

p. 105, 'There's no good being second': Norris McWhirter, personal interview.

p. 106, In the middle of interviews: Dr Ronald Williams, personal interview.

p. 106, When Bannister arrived: Bannister, personal interview; Dr Ronald Williams, personal interview; Anthony Carthew, 'The Man Who Broke the Four-Minute Mile', New York Times (19 April 1964).

p. 107, 'unfinished business': Roger Bannister, personal interview.

p. 107, 'To say, however': Bannister, Four Minute Mile, 188.

p. 107, But the darkness: Roger Bannister, personal interview.

p. 107, Nonetheless, the sessions: Roger Bannister, personal interview.

p. 108, Oxford sprinter Bevil Rudd: Chris Chataway, personal interview.

p. 109, 'Does it work?': Roger Bannister, personal interview.

p. 109, 'art of taking': ibid.

p. 109, Arterial pCO_2: R. G. Bannister, Dr Cunningham, and Dr Douglas, 'The Carbon Dioxide Stimulus to Breathing in Severe Exercise', *Journal of Physiology* (1954); R. G. Bannister and Dr Cunningham, 'The Effects on the Respiration and Performance During Exercise of Adding Oxygen to the Inspired Air', *Journal of Physiology* (1954).

p. 110, 'The efficient integration': Roger Bannister, personal interview.

p. 110, 'Do you think you could': Norris McWhirter, personal interview.

p. 111, 'black waves of nausea': G. F. D. Pearson (ed.), *Athletics* (Nelson, 1963), 28.

p. 111, 'damn near terminal': ibid.; Bannister, Cunningham, and Douglas, 'The Carbon Dioxide Stimulus'; Bannister and Cunningham, 'The Effects'; Roger Bannister, personal interview.

p. 111, Afterwards, in the laboratory: Bannister, *Four Minute Mile*, 120.

p. 112, Based on body types: Roger Bannister, personal interview; 'Science Predicts Athletic Prowess', *New York Times* (16 August 1951).

p. 113, For the first, Bannister: Roger Bannister, 'How to Run the Mile', *World Sports* (December 1954); A. V. Hill, 'Where is the Limit?', *World Sports* (August 1952).

p. 113, In 1953, Bannister: Carthew, 'The Man Who Broke the Four-Minute Mile', *New York Times* (19 April 1964).

p. 114, Many decades would pass: James Fixx, *The Complete Book of Running* (Random House, 1997); Charles Houston, *Going*

Higher: The Story of Man and Altitude (Little, Brown and Company, 1987); Wilt (ed.), *How They Train*; Noakes, *Lore*. These four books provide a comprehensive and in-depth investigation of the fascinating science behind running, chemical reactions and all.

p. 114, 'Psychologically': Norris McWhirter, personal interview.

p. 115, 'his eyes firmly fixed': 'Round and About', *Athletic Review* (January 1953).

Chapter 8

p. 116, 'You can't flirt with the track': James E. Gunn, 'Second Isn't Good Enough', *University of Kansas Alumni Magazine* (May 1959).

p. 116, On 25 April: Dick Wilson, personal interview; Wes Santee, personal interview.

p. 117, 'Coach, let's drop out': Wes Santee, personal interview.

p. 118, 'Hiya, ya bum': Bob Asbille, 'Prayed All Year We'd Get Revenge', *Des Moines Tribune* (25 April 1953).

p. 118, At the Texas Relays: Ed Fite, 'Kansas Runners Dominate Relays', *United Press* (28 March 1953).

p. 18, 'It was a season-launching': 'Santee Finds Short Race is His Forte', *New York Herald Tribune* (29 March 1953).

p. 118, 'The guy has a lot': Bill Moore, 'Track Experts See Him as the Fastest Mile Runner', *Kansas City Star* (5 April 1954).

p. 119, His statement shocked them: Wes Santee, personal interview; Dick Wilson, personal interview; Tom Rupp, personal interview; Bob Timmons, personal interview.

p. 120, 'When Easton told you': Dick Wilson, personal interview.

p. 120, He gave written instructions: Bill Easton, 'Letter to Athletes prior to Texas Relays', 2 April 1955 (Archives of Bill Easton, University of Kansas).

p. 120, 'You are college men': Bill Easton, 'Letter to Athletes prior to Oklahoma A&M Trip', 19 October 1951 (Archives of Bill Easton, University of Kansas).

p. 120, 'Go get him to run': Wes Santee, personal interview.

p. 121, 'We need to talk': ibid.

p. 123, 'You're not running': Dick Wilson, personal interview.

p. 124, 'We're gonna have some fun': Tom Rupp, personal interview.

p. 124, They had met the year before: Wes Santee, personal interview.

p. 125, Easton frowned: Wes Santee, personal interview; Dick Wilson, personal interview; Tom Rupp, personal interview.

p. 125, 'so that you will be ready': Bill Easton, 'Letter to Athletes – Merry Christmas', 13 December 1952 (Archives of Bill Easton, University of Kansas).

p. 125, '1-man record demolisher': 'Santee and Mates Take on Missouri', *University Daily Kansan* (19 February 1953).

p. 125, 'Menace of Mount Oread': 'All Eyes on K.U. Ace' (n.d.), Dick Wilson scrapbook.

p. 126, 'Knowing how determined': Wes Santee scrapbook (untitled, n.d.); Bill Mayer, 'Colorful Santee Whips Frat Team', *Lawrence Journal-World* (15 December 1952).

p. 127, 'For world-wide interest': Gerald Holland, 'The Golden Age is Now', *Sports Illustrated* (16 August 1954).

p. 127, The exuberance in American sport: Karal Ann Marling, *As Seen on TV: The Visual Culture of Everyday Life in the 1950s* (Harvard University Press, 1994).

p. 127, Children flocked to baseball diamonds: Holland, 'The Golden Age is Now', *Sports Illustrated* (16 August 1954).

p. 128, 'I don't know when': Bob Hurt, 'Sure I'll Run the Four-Minute Mile', *Saturday Evening Post* (26 September 1953).

p. 129, As an amateur college athlete: Wes Santee, personal interview.

p. 129, 'I didn't think you acted': ibid.

Chapter 9

p. 132, 'Will man ever run': Max Crittenden, 'A Four-minute Mile', *Argus* (6 January 1953).

p. 132, By April 1953: John Landy, personal interview.

p. 133, 'There are more important things': ibid.

p. 133, 'but having his morning shower': Solomon, *Great Australian Athletes*, 170.

p. 133, 'I say, John': Sims, *Why Die?*, 103.

p. 134, Some joked that his mile: Len McRae, personal interview.

p. 134, 'Maybe too much salt': Arthur Daley, 'Too Much Salt', *New York Times* (January 1953).

p. 134, A relaxed mental outlook: Frank Tierney, 'Landy Will Need Help in Pacing', *Sunday Herald* (18 January 1953).

p. 135, 'If he feels hungry': Steve Hayward, 'Butterflies for Speed', *Herald* (22 January 1953).

p. 135, 'I'll do my best': Ben Kerville, 'Landy Lost No Prestige in Missing His Record', *Perth Daily News* (28 January 1953).

p. 135, Blunders by officials: John Landy, personal interview; Ken Moses, 'Blunder Upsets Landy', *Argus* (18 February 1953).

p. 136, At another mile race: *Globe* (28 January 1953).

p. 136, By the conclusion: Solomon, *Great Australian Athletes*, 171.

p. 136, 'About this four-minute mile': 'John Has Had It', *Argus* (23 February 1953).

p. 137, 'It was just a clinker': Norris McWhirter, personal interview.

p. 137, Bannister raised the money: Roger Bannister, personal interview; Norris McWhirter, personal interview; Bannister, *Four Minute Mile*, 49, 73.

p. 137, Early in the nineteenth century: Gretton, *Out in Front*, 27–51.

p. 138, 'traced back to the Renaissance': Randy Roberts and James Olson, *Winning is the Only Thing: Sports in America Since 1945* (John Hopkins University Press, 1998), 3.

p. 138, 'wherever he goes': Gretton, *Out in Front*, 35.

p. 139, 'We have not journeyed': Frank Deford, 'Pioneer Miler Roger Bannister and Everest Conqueror Edmund Hillary', *Sports Illustrated* (3 January 2000).

p. 139, The annual AAA: John Disley, personal interview.

p. 139, Those in the know: Chris Chataway, personal interview; Bannister, *Four Minute Mile*, 192–3.

p. 140, 'Chataway Should Avenge': Harold Palmer, 'Chataway Should Avenge Mile Defeat by Bannister', *Evening Standard* (30 April 1953).

p. 140, Chataway was better suited: Chris Chataway, personal interview; Bannister, *Four Minute Mile*, 192–3.

p. 140, In the two months: Bannister, *Four Minute Mile*, 192–3.

p. 140, After an Easter break: ibid., 190–1.

p. 140, 'most intensive start': 'Big Start to the Athletic Season', *Daily Telegraph* (1 May 1953).

p. 140, Having consumed: Roger Bannister, personal interview.

p. 141, 'to release every ounce': ibid.

p. 141, 'Only the silky-striding Bannister': Norris McWhirter, 'Bannister Runs 4:03.6 for A.A.A.', *Athletics Weekly* (June 1953).

p. 142, 'a hard-working medical student': E. W. Stanton, 'Do Players Give Enough Thought to the Game?', *Daily Telegraph* (4 May 1953).

p. 142, 'poised high up': Bill Clark, 'High Endeavour', *Athletic Review* (June 1953).

p. 142, 'the four-minute mile': Bannister, *Four Minute Mile*, 193.

p. 143, 'It may be some years': Bill Mayer, 'Sport Talk', *Lawrence Journal-World* (1 and 5 June 1953); Wes Santee, personal interview.

p. 144, Its leader was Avery Brundage: Roberts and Olson, *Winning*, 9–11.

p. 144, 'a troop of trained seals': ibid., 11.

p. 145, Any decisions made by the AAU: Wes Santee, personal interview.

p. 145, 'Transatlantic Oceanic Hitch-hikers': ibid. This statement was ascribed to Phog Allen, the coach of the University of Kansas basketball team. In addition, I heard the name from Bob Timmons, the coach who succeeded Bill Easton as the Jayhawk track coach.

p. 145, 'I caught my quarters right': Norris Anderson, 'Santee Sets National Mark in Mile' (24 May 1953; no source), Wes Santee scrapbook; 'Santee Sets Mile Mark As Kansas Wins Title', *New York Herald Tribune* (24 May 1953).

p. 146, 'Nuts to Denis': Bill Mayer, 'Sport Talk', *Lawrence Journal-World* (1 June 1953).

p. 146, 'That's okay by us': ibid., 2 June 1953.

p. 146, At the Kansas City airport: Wes Santee, personal interview.

p. 147, 'The greatest ever to run': Al Franken, 'Compton's Meet – Best Yet!', Compton Invitational Program, June 1953 (Wes Santee scrapbook).

p. 148, While Santee prepared: Wes Santee, personal interview.

p. 149, In the third lap, Johansson: 'Oh, That Compton Meet', *Track & Field News* (June 1953); 'Fastest American Mile', *Time* (15 June 1953).

p. 150, 'You guys are crazy': Wes Santee, personal interview.

p. 150, 'I didn't think it was so fast': *Track & Field News* (June 1953).

p. 150, 'We're getting closer': 'Santee Runs Mile in 4:02.4', *New York Herald Tribune* (7 June 1953).

p. 150, 'He taught me': Maxwell Stiles, 'Denis Praises Santee', *Los Angeles Mirror* (6 June 1953).

p. 151, 'This was the ultimate': Bob Hurt, 'Santee Cracks Record', *Daily Capital* (6 June 1953); 'Santee Admits Getting Closer to Four-Minute Mile', *Wichita Eagle* (6 June 1953).

Chapter 10

p. 152, In the small community: Les Perry, personal interview; Geoff Warren, personal interview.

p. 153, The closest Landy came: Geoff Warren, personal interview.

p. 153, 'It won't be any good': Joe Galli, 'John Landy Goes Into Training', *Track & Field News* (March 1953).

p. 153, 'The details of his programme': Denison (ed.), *Bannister and Beyond*, 21.

p. 153, His theory of training: John Landy, personal interview; Wilt (ed.), *How They Train*, 102–3. The latter reference documents Landy's training sessions from August 1952 up to his race in Turku, Finland, in June 1954.

p. 154, He spent so much time: Gordon, *Young Men*, 110.

p. 154, 'OVER THE GROUND': Percy Cerutty, '3:53 Mile is Possible', *Track & Field News* (May 1953).

p. 154, He knew that come his first race: Ibid.; John Landy, personal interview.

p. 154, Although his studies: John Landy, personal interview.

p. 155, He would have preferred: Don Macmillan, personal interview.

p. 155, 'Roger here': Don Macmillan, personal interview.

p. 155, 'I think you can': 'His Faith in Santee', Associated Press (24 June 1953), Wes Santee scrapbook.

p. 156, 'It's becoming quite a tyranny': 'They All Plan My 4-min. Mile – Except Me', *Evening Standard* (15 May 1953).

p. 156, On 23 May: Smith, *All Out*, 104.

p. 157, 'We know the race': Roger Bannister, personal interview.

p. 157, 'Santee's going to do it': ibid.

p. 157, 'It was the manner of this triumph': Holt, *Sport and the British*, 279–80.

p. 158, 'The British are the best': Kenneth and Valerie McLeish, *Long to Reign Over Us: Memories of Coronation Day and of Life in the 1950s* (Bloomsbury, 1992), 103.

p. 158, By the morning of 27 June: Smith, *All Out*, 105–6; Norris McWhirter, 'The Story of Bannister's 4:02', *Athletics World* (July 1953); Don Macmillan, personal interview; Bert Johnson, 'Bannister Strikes Again', *Athletic Review* (July 1953). There was immense attention paid to this race, but these four reports are the most authoritative.

p. 159, 'Hope for the best': Don Macmillan, personal interview.

p. 159, 'an amputee': Norris McWhirter, 'The Story of Bannister's 4:02', *Athletics World* (July 1953).

p. 159, 'Wide open, Don!': ibid.

p. 160, 'climb the ladder': Don Macmillan, personal interview.

p. 160, 'Only five yards outside': Bert Johnson, 'Bannister Strikes Again', *Athletic Review* (July 1953).

p. 161, 'Maybe I could run': Jesse Abramson, 'Views of Sport', *New York Herald Tribune* (1 July 1953).

p. 161, 'The world obviously': ibid.

p. 162, 'It was work': Wes Santee, personal interview.

p. 162, A few days earlier: letter to Bill Easton from Lloyd Koby at the Amateur Athletic Union, 4 February 1954 (Archives of Bill Easton, University of Kansas).

p. 163, 'You're a damn liar!': Wes Santee, personal interview.

p. 164, 'I've run seven races': 'Pirie Beats Santee in 4:06.8', *New York Herald Tribune* (9 August 1953).

Chapter 11

p. 165, Wearing jackets and ties: Norris McWhirter, personal interview.

p. 165, But by September 1953: Bannister, *Four Minute Mile*, 203–4; Christopher Brasher, 'Christopher Brasher Recalls the Day', *Observer* (5 May 1974).

p. 166, '[The Board] has been compelled': 'Bannister's Record', *Manchester Guardian* (13 July 1953).

p. 166, In hindsight, he knew: BBC, *Suspense: The Four-Minute Mile* (18 July 1954).

p. 166, Many considered him: Roger Bannister, personal interview.

p. 167, Bannister appreciated: 'Pirie Beats Santee in 4:06.8', *New York Herald Tribune* (9 August 1953).

p. 167, 'Pirie is the most extraordinary runner': Joe Binks, 'His Mile Victory Over America's Best', *News of the World* (9 August 1953).

p. 167, Born in British Guinea: H. A. Meyer (ed.), *Modern Athletics by the Achilles Club* (Oxford University Press, 1958), 99.

p. 168, 'Enthusiasm was the feature': Chris Chataway, personal interview.

p. 168, 'He was a thrusting sort': Peter Hildreth, personal interview.

p. 168, Furthermore, he never: Norris McWhirter, personal interview.

p. 168, 'For me and many others': Norris McWhirter, 'This Man Chataway,' *World Sports* (August 1955).

p. 168, 'a man of spirit': ibid.

p. 169, 'He invested with magic': Chris Chataway, personal interview.

p. 169, 'Come and join us': BBC, 'Franz Stampfl' (BBC Sound Archives, British Library, 1994).

p. 169, or 'rubber': Norris McWhirter, personal interview.

p. 169, 'It is absolutely necessary': BBC, 'The Loneliest Place in the World' (BBC Sound Archives).

p. 169, For a very long time: Roger Bannister, interview by American Academy of Achievement (27 October 2000).

p. 169, The training ground: Chris Chataway, personal interview; Peter Hildreth, personal interview; Norris McWhirter, personal interview; Terry O'Connor, personal interview.

p. 170, Born in Vienna: Pat Stampfl, personal interview; Benzion Patkin, *The Dunera Internees* (Cassell, 1979); Merv Lincoln, personal interview; Peter and Leni Gillman, *Collar the Lot!: How Britain Interned and Expelled its Wartime Refugees* (Quartet Books, 1980); 'The Dunera Internees', *Age* (8 September 1979).

p. 171, 'It was not just a job for me': Patkin, *Dunera Internees*, 78.

p. 171, 'the ability to make a man': David Walsh, 'The Miracle Mile', *Sunday Times* (17 January 1999).

p. 172, Stampfl was unlike anyone: Roger Bannister, personal interview.

p. 172, 'You have to train harder': Pat Stampfl, personal interview.

p. 172, In his opinion: BBC, 'Franz Stampfl' (BBC Sound Archives, British Library, 1994).

p. 172, 'Who do you think you are, mate?': John Landy, personal interview.

p. 173, 'While you were at the pictures': Harry Hopman, 'Landy Training for Summer', *Herald* (22 April 1953).

p. 173, From 21 July: Wilt (ed.), *How They Train*, 102–3.

p. 173, Throughout this training: Sims, *Why Die?*, 146–7; Gordon, *Young Men*, 20.

p. 174, Before his first race: although Landy ran in a race at his former school Geelong Grammar on 17 October, this was not part of his competitive interclub athletics season.

p. 174, 'Landy Back for Big Mile Series': Steve Hayward, *Herald* (20 November 1953).

p. 174, 'Crack Miler Resumes at Olympic Park': Bruce Welch, *Age* (21 November 1953).

p. 174, 'The only thing': Jack Dunn, '"Best Ever" Mile Display', *Argus* (23 November 1953).

p. 174, 'Gee, is that true?': Ken Moses, 'Helms Award goes to John Landy', *Argus* (1 December 1953).

p. 174, 'top condition': Joe Galli, 'Joe Galli Reports', *Track & Field News* (September 1953).

p. 174, The immense pressure: John Landy, personal interview; Jack Dunn, 'Timing Error Hampers Landy in Record Mile Try', *Sun* (7 December 1953).

p. 175, From the start, Landy raced: 'John Landy Runs 4:02 Mile', *Age* (14 December 1953); Jack Dunn, 'Landy Could Be Greatest Ever', *Sun* (14 December 1953); 'Landy Plans Short Ease Up', *Argus* (14 December 1953).

p. 175, The wind ruined: Denison (ed.), *Bannister and Beyond*, 27.

p. 176, 'No one outside': 'Landy: Only 2 More Tries', *Herald* (14 December 1953).

p. 176, Privately, Landy: John Landy, personal interview.

p. 176, The next day Landy: John Landy, personal interview; Geoff Warren, personal interview; Trevor Robbins, personal interview.

p. 177, Amazingly as far as Perry was concerned: Les Perry, personal interview.

p. 177, 'equal pleasure': John Landy, personal interview.

p. 177, A blanket of snow: Wes Santee, personal interview; Dick Wilson, personal interview.

p. 178, 'Man, look at this': Wes Santee, personal interview.

p. 178, 'The process of running': Jack Clowser, 'Record Planned for Wes', *Track & Field News* (January 1954).

p. 178, 'This is chicken feed': Wes Santee, personal interview.

p. 179, Instead of slowly jogging: Bill Easton, 'Workout Sheets – December 19–31, 1953' (Archives of Bill Easton, University of Kansas).

p. 179, 'My break between quarters': Wes Santee, personal interview.

p. 179, 'This keeps you going': ibid.

p. 179, 'Wes Santee . . . John Landy': 'Santee Spurs Rising Furor Over Four-Minute Mile', Associated Press (7 January 1954).

p. 180, 'The Girl That Finally Caught Wes': 'Wes Santee Sets One-Mile Record', *The Letter from Home* (November 1953).

p. 180, She had travelled down: Wes Santee, personal interview.

p. 180, First, the AAU ruled: Bob Busby, 'Rule Out Santee', *Kansas City Times* (9 January 1954).

p. 180, 'Something is hanging over': 'Santee, Whitfield Shunned by Sullivan Award Group', *Evening Eagle* (14 December 1953).

p. 180, 'I'd like to run': Bob Hurt, 'Sure I'll Run the Four-Minute Mile', *Saturday Evening Post* (26 September 1953).

p. 181, 'I hope we've set it up': Wes Santee, personal interview.

p. 181, 'I'm really sorry': ibid.

p. 181, Santee's outdoor season: 'May Ban Whitfield, Santee', *The Mirror* (15 December 1953).

Chapter 12

p. 183, 'Why would you train': Len McRae, personal interview.

p. 183, The night before the race: Steve Hayward, 'Landy Will Run Hungry', *Herald* (21 January 1954).

p. 183, 'I'm not a bit worried': 'Man of Moment Has No Worries', *Age* (21 January 1954).

p. 183, 'most retiring world-class performer': Steve Hayward, 'Landy Will Run Hungry', *Herald* (21 January 1954).

p. 184, Landy arrived: John Landy, personal interview; Len McRae, personal interview; Les Perry, personal interview; Peter Banfield, 'Landy Goes "Over"', *Argus* (22 January 1954).

p. 185, When Landy took to the track: John Landy, personal interview.

p. 185, Nobody could keep up: Robbie Morgan-Morris, personal interview.

p. 185, He had a good sense: John Landy, personal interview.

p. 186, 'master power switch': Trevor Robbins, personal interview.

p. 186, When he returned to East Malvern: John Landy, personal interview; Len McRae, personal interview.

p. 186, The next day his run: Jack Dunn, 'Applause Cost Landy Mile Record', *Sun* (22 January 1954); '14,500 See Landy Just Miss 4 Min', *Age* (22 January 1954); Peter Banfield, 'Magnificent Failure!', *Argus* (22 January 1954); Steve Hayward, 'No Let-up in Plans', *Herald* (22 January 1954); Joe Galli, 'Landy Below 4:03 Again', *Track & Field News* (January 1954).

p. 187, 'Landy is magnificent': Steve Hayward, 'He May Go to Europe', *Herald* (22 January 1954).

p. 187, So they sent letters to Lloyd Olds: letter from Bill Easton to Lloyd Olds, 10 February 1954 (Archives of Bill Easton, University of Kansas); letter from Wes Santee to Lloyd Olds, 10 February 1954 (Archives of Bill Easton, University of Kansas).

p. 187, A week later: Wes Santee, personal interview.

p. 188, 'The restriction is nothing': Bill Mayer, 'Sport Talk', *Lawrence Journal-World* (24 February 1954).

p. 188, Soon after that, Santee: 'Who Needs Foreign Stars', *Los Angeles Times* (22 March 1954).

p. 188, 'For me to drive myself': Wes Santee, personal interview.

p. 188, After hanging his half-length white coat: Roger Bannister, personal interview.

p. 189, Stampfl ran them: ibid.; Franz Stampfl, *Franz Stampfl on Running: Sprint, Middle Distance and Distance Events* (Macmillan Company, 1955), 110–11.

p. 189, On occasion: 'Interview with Roger Bannister' in Brian Lenton (ed.), *Through the Tape* (self-published),

p. 189, 'Do it again! Harder!': John Disley, personal interview.

p. 189, 'Faster! It is only pain!': Pearson (ed.), *Athletics*, 28.

p. 189, 'the focus of the week': Roger Bannister, personal interview.

p. 189, The Austrian coach: Pat Stampfl, personal interview.

p. 189, From the start, he knew: Smith, *All Out*, 112; BBC, 'Franz Stampfl' (BBC Sound Archives, British Library, 1994).

p. 190, 'They've got to love it': Pat Stampfl, personal interview.

p. 190, Stampfl had seen Bannister: Bud Greenspan, 'Bannister's Run was for All-Time', *Montreal Gazette* (8 May 1994).

p. 191, 'Training is principally': Stampfl, *Franz Stampfl*, 37.

p. 191, 'The great hurdle': Greenspan, 'Bannister's Run was for All-Time', *Montreal Gazette* (8 May 1994); BBC, 'Franz Stampfl' (BBC Sound Archives, British Library, 1994).

p. 191, Stampfl invested their efforts: BBC, 'Franz Stampfl' (BBC Sound Archives, British Library, 1994).

p. 191, In a very real sense: ibid.

p. 191, After their sessions: Chris Chataway, personal interview.

p. 192, Week after week they nervously waited: Bannister, *Four Minute Mile*, 201–2.

p. 192, The McWhirter twins: Norris McWhirter, personal interview.

p. 192, 'greatest double in American track history': Jack Clowser, 'Santee's Relay Efforts', *Track & Field News* (February 1954).

p. 192, 'an almost uninsurable risk': 'Prospects for A.D. 1954', *Athletics World* (February 1954).

p. 192, 'obituary notices': 'Santee Blazes to 4:02.2', *Athletics World* (January 1954).

p. 193, 'I don't know how': Sir Edmund Hillary, *View from the Summit* (Pocket Books, 1999), 26.

p. 193, Most weekend mornings: Betty Lou Watson, 'The Fleet and Fair', *University of Kansas Yearbook* (April 1954).

p. 194, Three months to the day: 'Pro Bowl Won by East Stars', *University Daily Kansan* (18 January 1954).

p. 194, At the first outdoor meet: George Breazeale, '4-Minute (Maybe) Miler Strictly Team Man Here' (n.d., no source), Wes Santee scrapbook.

p. 194, 'Some night Santee's': Edgar Hayes, 'Sees 4-Minute Mile Nearing for Santee' (n.d., no source), Wes Santee scrapbook.

p. 195, By two o'clock on Saturday: Betty Lou Watson, 'The Fleet and Fair', *University of Kansas Yearbook* (April 1954); 'Track, Exposition, Parade Included in Relays Weekend', *University Daily Kansan* (19 April 1954).

p. 196, 'Let's try to break it': Wes Santee, personal interview.

p. 196, Fifteen minutes before race time: ibid.; Bill Mayer, personal interview. There are conflicting reports about the weather that day. The news reports make no mention of the rain, but do say there were strong gusts of wind and that the track needed to be rolled several times before the Cunningham Mile began. Santee and Mayer both said it rained before the meet.

p. 196, Jogging off to one side: Wes Santee, personal interview.

p. 197, Opposing him in the race: 'Santee Enters Cunningham Mile for First Time', *University Daily Kansan* (13 April 1954).

p. 197, He just needed to stick: Wes Santee, personal interview.

p. 197, 'I just can't talk': Lulu Mae Coe, 'Santee's Bride Finds Track Tour Exciting Honeymoon' (n.d., no source), Wes Santee scrapbook.

p. 197, Just before the gun: Wes Santee, personal interview; 'Next Best Mile', *Kansas City Star* (18 April 1954); 'Santee Decided Too Late for Mark', *Kansas City Star* (18 April 1954); Dana Leibengood, 'Santee Sets Record in Cunningham Mile', *University Daily Kansan* (19 April 1954); 'Santee 4:03.1', Associated Press (17 April 1954); 'Drake Relays Next Target', *New York Herald Tribune* (18 April 1954).

p. 199, 'Wes Santee isn't': Skipper Patrick, 'Wedded Wes Santee', *Kansas City Star* (19 April 1954).

Chapter 13

p. 200, 'Care I for the limbs': Norris McWhirter, 'This Man Chataway', *World Sports* (August 1955). Quotation from Shakespeare's *Henry IV Part 2*, III.ii. 253–5.

p. 200, The stopwatch told: Bannister, *Four Minute Mile*, 204–5.

p. 200, Bannister had always been afraid: Norman Harris, *The Legend of Lovelock* (Nicholas Kaye, 1964), 138.

p. 201, 'It is a belief': Stampfl, *Franz Stampfl*, 40.

p. 201, In his view: ibid., 37–40.

p. 201, Stampfl advised the three: Roger Bannister, personal interview; Chris Chataway, personal interview; Christopher Brasher, 'Christopher Brasher Recalls the Day', *Observer* (5 May 1974).

p. 201, Several times before: Bannister, *Four Minute Mile*, 113–18.

p. 202, At dawn on Saturday morning: ibid., 204–5; Brasher, 'Christopher Brasher Recalls the Day', *Observer* (5 May 1974); Brasher, 'Forty Years Ago We Ran Into History', *Sunday Times* (1 May 1994).

p. 203, After a couple more days' rest: Ross McWhirter, 'The Long Climb', *Athletics World* (May 1954).

p. 204, In his own mind: Frank Bath, 'The Loneliest Place in the World – Speaking with Chris Brasher', BBC Sound Archive.

p. 204, 'You, Chris': Brasher, *Sportsmen*, 11. The exact date of this meeting between the four remains uncertain, but in several sources it is noted to have occurred in April. For continuity's sake, the author has placed it after the achievement of the ten by 440 intervals under sixty seconds, when it can be assumed they resolved exactly how to run the 6 May race.

p. 204, On the tarmac: 'Landy Off with Big Smile', *Sun* (29 April 1954); Bruce Welch, 'John Landy at Peak in June', *Age* (29 April 1954); Peter Banfield, 'Quest for the Magic Mile', *Argus* (28 August 1954); John Landy, personal interview.

p. 205, His times since the late January twilight meet: 'U.S. Writer Says Landy Best', *Argus* (24 April 1954).

p. 205, On 11 February: 'Duke's Dash to See Landy Win Mile Title', *Sydney Morning Herald* (12 February 1954).

p. 205, Two weeks later: Peter Banfield, 'Landy Romps Home in 4:02.6', *Argus* (24 February 1954).

p. 205, And just the previous week: 'Great Run by Landy at Bendigo', *Age* (20 April 1954); John Landy, personal interview.

p. 205, 'I had an obligation': Darren Alexander, 'An Examination of the Victorian Newspapers' Portrayal of John Landy's Attempts at the Four-Minute Mile Between 1952 and 1954', LaTrobe University (1991). Alexander's essay is a very thorough record of the media attention paid to John Landy and worthwhile for those interested in knowing more about how the press at that time spiralled out of control.

p. 206, Whenever he had failed to break: ibid.

p. 206, 'Do the winds blow differently': 'Critics Storm at Landy "Alibis"', *Sun Herald* (14 February 1954).

p. 206, 'A great runner': Kelly, *Mr. Controversial*, 65–6.

p. 206, But more than anything: Peter Banfield, 'Quest for the Magic Mile', *Argus* (28 August 1954).

p. 206, 'If you can run 4:02': John Landy, personal interview.

p. 207, 'in one slimly built': Peter Banfield, 'Quest for the Magic Mile', *Argus* (28 August 1954).

p. 207, On Saturday, 1 May: Bill Murdock, 'Wes Santee at Home' (n.d., no source), Wes Santee scrapbook.

p. 207, In the four-mile relay: 'Santee Does 1:49.8 as Kansas Again Beats U.S. Mark', *Des Moines Register* (24 April 1954).

p. 208, 'Under our system': 'Easton–Santee TV Blackout, Curfew Trouble Cleared Up' (n.d., no source), Wes Santee scrapbook.

p. 209, He had to tune up his body: Bannister, *Four Minute Mile*, 205–7.

p. 209, 'There was no longer any need': ibid., 206.

p. 209, Every muscle and fibre: ibid., 205–7; Norris and Ross

McWhirter, 'Bannister Does It – 3:59.4', *Athletics World* (May 1954).

p. 209, After watching the trial: Doug Wilson, 'Stand by for a Fast Mile', *News of the World* (2 May 1954).

p. 210, 'The world's one mile record': Smith, *All Out*, 114.

p. 210, Bannister would have likely discounted: Bannister, *Four Minute Mile*, 205–7; Norris and Ross McWhirter, 'Bannister Does It – 3:59.4'; Norris McWhirter, *Ross: The Story of a Shared Life* (Churchill Press Limited, 1976), 129.

p. 211, 'It is not the doing': Norris and Ross McWhirter, 'Bannister Does It – 3:59.4'.

p. 211, On 30 April: Bannister, *Four Minute Mile*, 207; Brasher, *Sportsmen*, 12.

p. 211, As for Brasher and Chataway: Brasher, 'Christopher Brasher Recalls the Day', *Observer* (5 May 1974).

p. 211, 'You can do it': Chris Chataway, personal interview.

p. 212, The evening before the Oxford meet: Pat Stampfl, personal interview.

p. 212, Across town in North London: Norris McWhirter, personal interview; Norris McWhirter Interview (University of Birmingham).

p. 212, To this end: Norris McWhirter, 'Aim May Be Four Min Mile', *Star* (5 May 1954).

Chapter 14

p. 215, 'You don't really think': Bannister, *Four Minute Mile*, 207.

p. 215, 'They should be light': Krise and Squires, *Fast Tracks*, 128.

p. 215, The resulting pair: Larry Montague, 'Preparing for a World's Record', *Manchester Guardian* (15 May 1954).

p. 215, Once finished with his spikes: Bannister, *Four Minute Mile*, 208.

p. 215, Bannister wasn't alone: Pat Stampfl, personal interview.

p. 216, He explained to Stampfl: Bannister, *Four Minute Mile*, 208–11.

p. 216, With the proper motivation: ibid., 209–10; Roger Bannister, personal interview; BBC Radio 4, 'A Conversation Piece with Sue McGregor' (17 May 1990); David Walsh, 'The Miracle Mile', *Sunday Times* (17 January 1999). There are a number of versions of what exactly what was said during this meeting between Bannister and Stampfl. I have endeavoured to convey the words, thoughts, and meanings as best as possible.

p. 217, When they arrived: Bannister, *Four Minute Mile*, 210–11; Roger Bannister, personal interview; 'Star Man's Diary', *Star* (7 May 1954).

p. 218, 'The day could be a lot worse': Bannister, *Four Minute Mile*, 211.

p. 218, 'The wind's hopeless': ibid.

p. 218, But at 5.45 p.m.: Ross and Norris McWhirter, 'The Four-Minute Mile Story', *Athletics World* (May 1954); Brasher, *Sportsmen*, 13–14; Hoby, *One Crowded Hour*, 125.

p. 219, A crowd of some twelve hundred: E. D. Lacy, 'The Four-Minute Mile', *Athletic Review* (June 1954).

p. 219, In the centre infield: Paul Fox, 'Sport: Bannister Build-Up Begins', *Daily Telegraph* (18 April 1994).

p. 219, Norris McWhirter: Norris McWhirter, personal interview.

p. 219, 'By the way': 'The World's Most Popular Athlete', *Daily Mirror* (8 May 1954).

p. 219, The moment had arrived: the account of Bannister's run was assembled from these sources: Bannister, *Four Minute Mile*, 212–15; McWhirter, 'The Four-Minute Mile Story', *Athletics World* (May 1954); Brasher, *Sportsmen*, 11–16; Hoby, *One Crowded Hour*, 122–41; Brasher, 'Christopher Brasher Recalls the Day', *Observer* (5 May 1974); Smith, *All Out*, 112–21; 'His Day of Days', *Track & Field News* (May 1954); Syd Cox, 'Last-Minute Decision Led to Bannister's Success', *Oxford Mail* (7 May 1954); McWhirter, *Ross*, 130–5; Bud Greenspan, 'Bannister's Run was for All-Time', *Montreal Gazette* (8 May

1994); Terry O'Connor, personal interview; Roger Bannister, personal interview; Norris McWhirter, personal interview.

p. 226, 'Well, we did it': Terry O'Connor, personal interview.

p. 226, It was a humid afternoon: Bill Mayer, personal interview.

p. 226, Santee was finishing: Wes Santee, personal interview.

p. 226, 'I am not exceptionally disappointed': 'Santee Hails Great Run', *Kansas City Star* (7 May 1954).

p. 227, 'Why were you beaten to the punch?': This exact quote for the question was not detailed in the news reports on Santee's response. No doubt the thrust of the question was the same, though the syntax might have been different.

p. 227, 'Having to compete for the university': 'Santee Lauds Bannister's Performance', *University Daily Kansan* (7 May 1954).

p. 227, 'We tried': Wes Santee, personal interview.

p. 227, At a restaurant in Turku: John Landy, personal interview.

p. 228, 'It's great, great, great': McWhirter, 'The Four-Minute Mile Story', *Athletics World* (May 1954); Smith, *All Out*, 117.

p. 228, The next day Landy: 'World Record Schedule', *Track & Field* (January 1958).

p. 228, If Bannister had been able: Denison (ed.), *Bannister and Beyond*, 27.

Chapter 15

p. 231, As evening fell on 7 May: Roger Bannister, personal interview; Karl Baedeker, *London and its Environs: A Handbook for Travelers* (Baedeker, 1951).

p. 231, 'No words could be invented': Bannister, *Four Minute Mile*, 215–16.

p. 231, That evening on *Sportsview*: Peter Dimmock, 'Four-Minute Mile', *Sportsview* (6 May 1954).

p. 232, 'adroit modesty': Norris McWhirter, personal interview.

p. 232, 'a tall fair girl': 'At Last – The 4- Minute Mile', *Daily Express* (7 May 1954).

p. 232, 'I can't believe I did it': Norris McWhirter, personal interview.

p. 233, 'You gentlemen are no gentlemen': Chris Brasher, 'Forty Years Ago We Ran Into History', *Sunday Times* (1 May 1994).

p. 233, 'I've got two better boys': 'Bannister and His Pacemakers Go Dancing until Dawn', *Evening Standard* (7 May 1954).

p. 233, 'The Empire is saved': Red Smith, 'Empire Reborn', *International Herald Tribune* (8 May 1954).

p. 233, National hero or not: 'Star Man's Diary', *Star* (7 May 1954); Christopher Chataway, 'Chris Brasher – Eulogy', provided by Dr Ronald Williams.

p. 234, When Bannister arrived at St Mary's: Bannister, *Four Minute Mile*, 216; BBC Radio 4, 'A Conversation Piece with Sue McGregor' (17 May 1990).

p. 234, Later, when he left: Roger Bannister, personal interview.

p. 234, 'Now life in earnest': ibid.; Chris Chataway, personal interview.

p. 234, 'We honestly believed': Patrick Collins, 'Chris Brasher – 1928–2003', *Marathon News* (2003).

p. 235, 'Heard a rumour': John Landy, letter to Len McRae, 10 May 1954.

p. 235, Turku was a quiet, old city: Sylvie Nickels, Hillar Kallas, and Philippa Friedman (eds), *Finland: An Introduction* (George Allen & Unwin, 1973), 137–8; *Jussi Kiisseli* (Tampereen Uusi Kirjapaino, 1952), 105–9.

p. 235, When Landy arrived: John Landy, letter to Len McRae, 10 May 1954; John Landy, personal interview.

p. 236, He was so impressed: MMBW Officer's Journal (July 1955).

p. 236, In the three weeks: 'World Record Schedule', *Track & Field* (January 1958).

p. 236, 'Running is not only physical': 'Pride Not Enough', *Sydney Morning Herald* (11 February 1954).

p. 236, Two days before his race: Bill Mayer, 'Sport Talk', *Lawrence Journal-World* (31 May 1954).

p. 237, Vaharanta bolted from the start: Australian Associated Press, 'Landy 2.2s Behind Bannister', *Herald* (1 June 1954).

p. 238, 'I'm not a four-minute miler yet': 'I'll Soon Be a 4-Minute Miler', Australian Associated Press (1 June 1954).

p. 238, 'If you hooked Bannister': Skipper Patrick, 'Scorn by Santee', Associated Press (4 June 1954).

p. 238, It was Thursday, 3 June: Bill Mayer, 'Final Big Fling By Santee', *Lawrence Journal-World* (31 May 1954). 'Noose tightening' is a close reference to Mayer, who wrote in this article, 'The noose is drawing tight on Santee's freedom on the cinders.'

p. 238, Santee still desperately wanted: Wes Santee, personal interview.

p. 238, Easton was engaged: ibid.

p. 239, 'How do you feel?': Wes Santee, personal interview.

p. 240, Santee left the locker-room: ibid.; 'Wes Clips Record for 1,500 Meters', *New York Times* (5 June 1954); 'Santee Runs 4:00.6 Mile', *Chicago Tribune* (5 June 1954); 'Wes Vows to Break 4:00', *Lawrence Daily Journal-World* (10 June 1954); 'Wes Sets 1,500 Meter Mark', *Lawrence Daily Journal-World* (5 June 1954); 'Wind Stops Wes', *Kansas City Star* (5 June 1954); Ernie Klann, 'Valley Sports Corral', *Citizen-News* (8 June 1954). The account of this race is drawn from a collection of these sources. Conversational quotes are directly from the interview the author conducted with Wes Santee.

p. 242, 'I should very much like to race': Smith, *All Out*, 124–5.

p. 243, 'I much prefer racing': Harold Palmer, 'Chataway Beat British Two Miles Record', *Evening Standard* (7 June 1954).

p. 243, It was obvious to most: Bannister, *Four-Minute Mile*, 223–4.

p. 243, 'If you do go': Roger Bannister, personal interview.

p. 243, In the four races Landy had run: Solomon, *Great Australian Athletes*, 179–81.

p. 244, The Australian knew Chataway: John Landy, personal interview.

p. 244, 'I could change into shorts': BBC, *Suspense: The Four-Minute Mile* (18 July 1954).

p. 244, 'fit as a trout': Adrian McGregor, 'The Greatest Mile of the Century', *National Times* (18 August 1979), 14.

p. 244, The Finn offered to arrange: ibid.

p. 247, '3:58': in fact, Landy's time was 3:57.9, but fifths, not tenths, of seconds were accepted in official times, so his time was rounded up to 3:58.

p. 248, 'No, no': Chris Chataway, personal interview.

p. 248, the mile record was his: Chris Chataway, personal interview; John Landy, personal interview; R. L. Quercetani, 'Landy's Turn – 3:58', *Track & Field News* (July 1954); 'Butterfly Chaser Runs a Record Mile', *Life* (July 1954); Smith, *All Out*, 126–33; '3:58 – And I Can Do Better', *Herald* (22 June 1954); 'Landy: My Future is in the Air', *Herald* (25 June 1954).

Chapter 16

p. 249, 'The possibilities in racing tactics': Stampfl, *Franz Stampfl*, 20.

p. 249, Half an hour after Landy: Bannister, *Four Minute Mile*, 224.

p. 249, 'Roger, what do you think': 'Now a 3:58 Mile', *Daily Mirror* (22 June 1954); 'He Sets World Record for 1,500 Metres, Too', *Daily Mail* (22 June 1954).

p. 249, The moment Bannister heard: Bannister, *Four Minute Mile*, 224–5.

p. 250, 'Do you think you will be knighted': 'Bannister Flies Home Triumphant', *Daily Mail* (15 May 1954).

p. 250, Then he stumbled into another mess: 'Bannister Clears Trophy Obstacle', *New York Times* (14 May 1954).

p. 251, 'You sweated blood over them': Dr Ronald Williams, personal interview.

p. 251, First was a series: Roger Bannister, personal interview.

p. 251, His studies left little time: ibid.; Norris McWhirter, personal interview.

p. 251, 'I am quite sure': Carthew, 'The Man Who Broke the 4-Minute Mile', *New York Times* (19 April 1964).

p. 251, When Bannister participated: Bannister, *Four Minute Mile*, 222–3

p. 251, 'Here's mud in your eye': Roger Bannister, personal interview.

p. 252, 'There is a world of difference': Geoffrey Simpson, 'Do More Racing, Bannister', *Daily Mail* (7 June 1954).

p. 252, 'It's not really life': John Landy, personal interview.

p. 252, 'It was done': ibid.

p. 253, 'I can do even better': '3:58 – And I Can Do Better', *Herald* (22 June 1954).

p. 253, 'unquenchable, indomitable spirit': H. J. Oaten, 'Landy Heads Great Mile Trio', *Herald* (23 June 1954).

p. 253, 'sportsmen, as well as statesmen': 'Landy's Achievement Builds National Pride', *Age* (23 June 1954).

p. 253, 'I have always said': 'Coach Always Confident', *Sydney Morning Herald* (23 June 1954); 'Coach Lauded', *Age* (23 June 1954).

p. 253, The next day Landy: 'Landy Rests on Isolated Island', *Sydney Morning Herald* (24 June 1954).

p. 254, 'It took a major effort': Geoff Warren, personal interview.

p. 254, 'The race had the ingredients': John Landy, personal interview.

p. 254, Running a mile is an art form: Stampfl, *Franz Stampfl*, 28–32.

p. 255, In developing his strategy: John Landy, personal interview.

p. 255, 'ruthlessness, lack of feeling': Sims, *Why Die?*, 201.

p. 255, 'It was a solemn moment': Chris Chataway, personal interview.

p. 256, To make sure this was his strategy: Bannister, *Four Minute Mile*, 227.

p. 256, In the woods outside Quantico: Wes Santee, personal interview.

p. 256, On 11 June at Memorial Stadium: 'Wes Shy by .7', *Kansas City Times* (12 June 1954).

p. 257, 'Why did you go past me?': Wes Santee, personal interview.

p. 257, I'm leaving my running': Charles Stevenson, 'Santee Pacer is Slow', *Kansas City Star* (12 June 1954).

p. 259, 'People who have concentrated: 'Bannister Congratulates Landy, Looks Forward to Racing Him', *New York Times* (22 June 1954).

p. 259, 'I'm going to train': 'Hard Work Basic Ingredient in Santee Bid at Mile Mark', *Lawrence Daily Journal-World* (27 July 1954).

p. 259, Mostly he concentrated: 'World Record Schedule', *Track & Field News* (January 1958).

p. 260, 'You have no alternative, mate': John Landy, personal interview.

p. 260, Johansson advised Landy: Cerutty, *Sport*, 40–1.

p. 260, He liked running his opposition: John Landy, personal interview.

p. 260, Tactics were fine and good: Ron Clarke and Norman Harris, *The Lonely Breed* (Pelham Books, 1967), 118–23.

p. 260, On 11 July: John Landy, personal interview.

p. 260, 'I felt that this might confuse': John Landy, personal interview.

p. 261, 'There's the Bannister and Landy race': Wes Santee, personal interview.

p. 262, On 15 July: 'Police Rescue Landy from Welcoming Mob', *Sydney Morning Herald* (16 July 1954).

p. 262, On Friday, 23 July: Bannister, *Four Minute Mile*, 226–30; Pat Stampfl, personal interview.

p. 263, As Bannister was leaving: Pat Stampfl, personal interview.

p. 263, 'what ifs': ibid.

p. 263, There was no doubt Landy: Stampfl, *Franz Stampfl*, 104–5.

p. 263, 'That's when the damage': Adrian McGregor, 'The Greatest Mile of the Century', *National Times* (18 August 1979), 14.

p. 263, 'a blow in the stomach': Krise and Squires, *Fast Tracks*, 131.

p. 263, His coach assured him: Bannister, *Four Minute Mile*, 227–8.

p. 264, 'It was a sort of pre-race': Chris Chataway, personal interview.

p. 264, Bannister left Stampfl: Bannister, *Four Minute Mile*, 228.

Chapter 17

p. 265, At London Airport: Jim Peters, *In the Long Run* (Cassell & Company, 1955), 182–8.

p. 266, 'I will be out to win': 'Rivals Happy to See Each Other', *Age* (27 July 1954).

p. 266, One particularly observant reporter: 'Bannister, Man with a 10-Second Secret', *Herald* (August 1954).

p. 266, 'Roger, you only become': Bannister, *Four Minute Mile*, 127.

p. 267, 'Hello, John': 'Rivals Happy to See Each Other,' *Age* (27 July 1954); 'Mile Stars in Guarded Meeting', *Herald* (27 June 1954); Dick FBeddoes, 'Mile Aces Avoid Talk of Records', *Vancouver Sun* (26 June 1954).

p. 267, On 30 October 1891: 'Australia at the British Empire and Commonwealth Games, Vancouver, Canada, 1954', *British Empire Games Official Programme* (30 July 1954); John Blanch and Paul Jenes, *Australia's Complete History at the Commonwealth Games* (John Blanch Publishing, 1982).

p. 268, Henry Luce: Norris McWhirter, personal interview.

p. 268, To televise the event: 'TV Mile Thriller Seen by 40,000,000', *New York Times* (8 August 1954).

p. 269, For the estimated 100 million: Arthur Daley, 'Dream Race', *New York Times* (1 August 1954).

p. 269, In the morning, Landy: 'Crowd Sees Landy Train', *Sydney Morning Herald* (19 July 1954).

p. 269, As race day approached: Geoff Warren, personal interview.

p. 269, Reports of his sessions: Bannister, *Four Minute Mile*, 232.

p. 269, 'He was as fresh': 'Landy: Speeds Up Training', *Sydney Morning Herald* (27 June 1954).

p. 269, And when he killed: 'Fast Trial by Landy Revives Specu-
lation', *Sydney Morning Herald* (28 July 1954).

p. 269, 'Where's Roger the Dodger?': 'Roger the Dodger has not
been Loafing', *Herald* (30 July 1954).

p. 270, 'What is Roger up to?': Norris McWhirter, 'Landy is Kept
Guessing by Bannister', *Star* (31 July 1954).

p. 270, Once, on the Empire Village training track: Bannister, *Four
Minute Mile*, 232–3.

p. 271, Bannister was set against: 'Bannister and Landy Are All Set',
Star (6 August 1954).

p. 271, 'as a guide to what': 'Crack Milers Take It Easy', *Daily Mail*
(6 August 1954).

p. 271, As if the atmosphere: 'Star Man's Diary', *Star* (31 July 1954).

p. 272, Behind a bedroom door: John Landy, personal interview; Geoff Warren, personal interview; John Vernon, personal
interview.

p. 272, Because of the heightened press attention: Geoff Warren,
personal interview.

p. 273, 'an iron fist': Geoff Warren, personal interview.

p. 273, 'I'm vicious underneath': Paul O'Neil, 'A Man Conquers
Himself', *Sports Illustrated* (31 May 1956).

p. 273, 'In any running event': ibid.

p. 274, 'Roger's going to sit you': Don Macmillan, personal
interview.

p. 274, He knew front-running: O'Neil, 'A Man Conquers Himself',
Sports Illustrated (31 May 1956).

p. 274, While jogging barefoot: John Landy, personal interview;
John Vernon, personal interview; Don Macmillan, personal
interview; John Fitzgerald, 'Landy's Cuts Treated at University
Centre', *Sun* (11 August 1954); 'Landy Did Not Tell His Father',
Sun (12 August 1954); 'Landy Kept Secret From Father', *Age*
(12 August 1954). The exact sequence of events related to
Landy's cut foot is not entirely clear. Sources and interviewers
contradict one another.

p. 275, 'I know you will think': 'Landy Had Foot Stitched Before Final of Mile Race', *Age* (11 August 1954).

p. 276, Late in the afternoon on 6 August: Wes Santee, personal interview.

p. 277, The night before the race: Roger Bannister, personal interview.

p. 277, Except for participating: ibid.; Chris Chataway, personal interview.

p. 278, One afternoon, after a session: Bannister, *Four Minute Mile*, 234.

p. 278, In his three-mile final: 'English Track Triumph', *Daily Mail* (4 August 1954).

p. 278, 'The great Mr. Second': Smith, *All Out*, 130.

p. 278, 'encouraging omen': Bannister, *Four Minute Mile*, 235.

p. 278, Chataway was used to: Chris Chataway, personal interview.

p. 278, As much as Chataway drank: ibid.; Roger Bannister, personal interview; Bannister, *Four Minute Mile*, 236–7.

p. 279, 'Roger hates the idea': 'Four-Minute Men', *Sports Illustrated* (16 August 1994). In an interview, Chris Chataway said it was probably he who made this statement, though it is possible it was Chris Brasher instead.

p. 279, 'abnormal state of attention': Roger Bannister, personal interview.

Chapter 18

p. 28, 'whole athletic world': 'Landy, Bannister Primed for "Miracle Mile" Today', *New York Herald Tribune* (7 August 1954).

p. 281, 'I have reached my peak': Judy Joy Davies, 'Mile of the Century', *Argus* (6 August 1954).

p. 281, 'We may get down': 'Landy Tipped to Take in 3:57', *Sydney Morning Herald* (7 August 1954).

p. 281, 'How does your foot feel?': John Vernon, personal interview.

p. 281, The dressings, though, were soaked: 'Doctor Tells of Injury', *Age* (12 August 1954).

REFERENCES

p. 281, Twenty minutes before: John Landy, personal interview.

p. 282, Before he went out: Adrian McGregor, 'The Greatest Mile of the Century', *National Times* (18 August 1979), 18.

p. 282, He would run a moderately quick first half: 'John Landy: The First Australian to Run the 4-Minute Mile', *Australian Sport Through Time* (National Sport Information Centre archive, Canberra, Australia).

p. 282, He decided to take the team bus: Murray Halberg, personal interview; Roger Bannister, personal interview.

p. 283, 'One was inconspicuously': Skip Rusk, 'Long Wait Tests Nerves', *Vancouver Sun* (7 August 1954).

p. 283, 'hanging on a knife edge': Roger Bannister, personal interview.

p. 283, Failure would reward the critics: Peter Wilson, 'The Night Before the Mile', *Daily Mirror* (7 August 1954).

p. 284, He had a mentor in Stampfl: 'The Meaning of the Four-Minute Mile', transcript of panel discussion at Grinnell College (5 April 1984).

p. 284, When the starter called: Roger Bannister, *Four Minute Mile*, 237; 'Bannister and His Rivals', *Daily Mail* (7 August 1954).

p. 284, Five minutes before the race: 'In Their Thousands They Came to Cheer the Miracle Mile', *Vancouver Sun* (7 August 1954).

p. 285, He was seated in the decorated royal box: 'Bannister Beats Landy in 3:58.8 Mile', *New York Herald Tribune* (8 August 1954).

p. 285, Under the steel roof: Norris McWhirter, personal interview; McWhirter, *Ross*, 136.

p. 285, In the radio commentary box: Chris Chataway, personal interview; Norris McWhirter, personal interview.

p. 285, It was late evening in England: 'Lightening Round the Teapot', *Star* (7 August 1954).

p. 285, Stampfl sat still: Pat Stampfl, personal interview.

p. 286, To many, Bannister exemplified: Adrian McGregor, 'The Greatest Mile of the Century', *National Times* (18 August 1979), 13.

p. 286, It was Sunday morning in Australia: 'It's Suspense . . . And Hope for John's Mother', *Sun* (7 August 1954).

p. 286, 'Australia considered Landy unbeatable': Adrian McGregor, 'The Greatest Mile of the Century', *National Times* (18 August 1979), 13.

p. 287, Santee knew the race: Wes Santee, personal interview.

p. 287, The closest he could get: 'TV Mile Thriller Seen By 40,000,000', *New York Times* (8 August 1954).

p. 287, In Empire Stadium: *Vancouver Race* (video), NSIC (7 August 1954); Smith, *All Out*, 136–9.

p. 288, 'was going to be left standing': Adrian McGregor, 'The Greatest Mile of the Century', *National Times* (18 August 1979), 13.

p. 289, 'There is a tremendous feeling': Rex Alston, 'British Empire Games – One Mile Race', BBC Video Archive (7 August 1954).

p. 289, 'To your marks!': ibid.; 'Four-Minute Men', *Sports Illustrated* (16 August 1994); Norris McWhirter, 'Bannister Slammed in the Clutch', *Athletics Weekly* (August 1954); Erwin Swangard, 'Miracle Mile Thrills World', *Vancouver World* (9 August 1954); Bert Nelson, 'Miracle Mile to Bannister', *Track & Field News* (August 1954); Smith, *All Out*, 136–9; Bannister, *Four Minute Mile*, 236–40; *Vancouver Race* (video); Clarke and Harris, *Lonely Breed*, 118–23; Adrian McGregor, 'The Greatest Mile of the Century', *National Times* (18 August 1979), 13–18; John Landy, personal interview; Roger Bannister, personal interview; Chris Chataway, personal interview. These were the primary sources used to describe the Mile of the Century race. The author has indicated direct sources for quotes and important, specific descriptions as well. In addition, the author used as a model the race sequence described in Harris, *Legend of Lovelock*, 168–74.

p. 290, 'Three yards behind!': Don Macmillan, personal interview.

p. 291, A few more yards: Bannister, *Four Minute Mile*, 238–9.

p. 292, 'Dangerous gap there': Chris Chataway, personal interview.

p. 292, Tens of millions around the world: Ledbrooke, *Great Moments*, 57.

p. 293, Two more minutes of struggle: Bannister, *Four-Minute Mile*, 239–40.

p. 294, 'Keep it going': Clarke and Harris, *Lonely Breed*, 122.

p. 294, 'When is it?': 'Landy to Make Attempt on 2 Miles Record', *Sydney Morning Herald* (9 August 1954).

p. 296, 'He's done it!': Chris Chataway, personal interview.

p. 297, 'Hard luck, John': Clarke and Harris, *Lonely Breed*, 123; Roger Bannister, personal interview.

p. 297, 'You were colossal': 'Roger, You're Colossal', *Argus* (9 August 1954).

p. 297, In the infield: '24 Watches Time Mile of Century', *New York Times* (9 August 1954).

p. 298, 'It was a magnificent race': 'Santee Says Thrilling', *Daily Mail* (9 August 1954).

p. 298, 'When Landy lost': Robbie Morgan-Morris, personal interview.

p. 298, Franz Stampfl: Pat Stampfl, personal interview.

Epilogue

p. 301, 'And thick and fast': excerpted from Arthur Daley, 'Counting the Milestones', *New York Times*.

p. 301, Twenty minutes after Bannister: Jim Peters, *In the Long Run*, 195–207; Peter Wilson, 'Peters Cries in Delirium', *Daily Mirror* (9 August 1954); 'Bannister Wins Greatest Mile of All', *The Times* (9 August 1954).

p. 303, 'Did Bannister make it?': 'Vain Agony of Peters', *Manchester Guardian* (9 August 1954).

p. 303, 'a crowded field': Roger Bannister, personal interview.

p. 303, From the gun: Norris McWhirter, *Athletics World* (August 1954).

p. 304, In the span of 112 days: ibid.

p. 304, 'I'd like to say, Bannister': Lord Brabazon, 'Sportsman of the Year Presentation', BBC News Archive (31 December 1954).

p. 304, 'It was the race': John Landy, personal interview.

p. 304, Directly after the race: Steve Hayward, 'Landy to join Geelong G.S.', *Herald* (9 August 1954).

p. 305, 'Did you stand on a flashbulb': John Fitzgerald, 'Landy Runs With Foot Badly Cut', *Herald* (9 August 1954).

p. 305, 'Everybody beat me': Paul O'Neil, 'A Man Conquers Himself,' *Sports Illustrated* (31 May 1956).

p. 305, The headmaster at Geelong: ibid.

p. 306, On 4 January 1956: Solomon, *Great Australian Athletes*, 194–215.

p. 307, Dear John, The fellows in the Press box: Harry Gordon, 'Landy Run Back', *Sun* (11 March 1954).

p. 307, A couple of months later: Solomon, *Great Australian Athletes*, 194–215.

p. 308, '1955 should be a great season': Cordner Nelson, 'Track Talk', *Track & Field* (November 1954).

p. 308, 'If you got this close': Joseph Turrini, 'Wes Santee – The Four-Minute Mile, and the Amateur Athletic Union of the United States', *Sport History Review* (1999), 66–7.

p. 308, On 1 June: ibid.; Wes Santee, personal interview.

p. 311, 'What do we do': Wes Santee, personal interview.

p. 311, On 28 May 1955: Smith, *All Out*, 144–5.

p. 312, 'It was just another time': Denison (ed.), *Bannister and Beyond*, 63.

p. 313, 'What's my case doing out here?': ibid., 37.

p. 313, In 1962, New Zealander Peter Snell: ibid.

p. 313, By the time El Guerrouj seized: James Dunaway, 'Running a Four Minute Mile is No Longer Mythical', *New York Times* (4 May 2003).

p. 316, 'Running gave me discipline': John Landy, personal interview.

p. 316, 'Hard work pays off': Wes Santee, personal interview.

p. 317, 'Sport is about': Chris Brasher, 'Christopher Brasher Recalls the Day', *Observer* (5 May 1974).

INDEX

Abrahams, Harold 10, 69, 70, 158, 161

Abrahams, Sir Adolphe 103

Age 253

Allen, Phog 122

Alston, Rex 285, 289, 290, 291, 292, 293, 295, 296

Amateur Athletic Association (AAA) 138, 156, 170, 176, 209, 210, 218, 219, 243
  Championships 83, 156
    1948 18
    1951 19
    1952 40
    1953 166
    1954 256, 260, 278
    vs Oxford University 1953 139, 140–1
    1954 192, 201, 212

Amateur Athletic Union (AAU) Championships 1951 33, 35–6, 37; creation of 144; amateur status, rules concerning 145, 146; Santee, relationship with 161, 162, 180, 181, 187, 188, 195, 239, 261, 309, 311, 316

Andersson, Arne 8, 15, 46, 76–8, 97, 155, 313

Andrews, Harry 71

Arandora Star 170–1

Argus 96, 132, 174

Athletic Review 115, 142, 152

Athletics World 104, 141, 174, 210

Australia 41–54

Australian Broadcast Network 285

Baillie, William 271, 284, 288, 289, 290, 292

Bannister, Alice 13–14

Bannister, Joyce 219

Bannister, Moyra 304

Bannister, Ralph 13

Bannister, Roger 2–3
  AAA championship 18, 19; AAA vs Oxford University 1953 139, 140–3; Benjamin Franklin Mile 1951 19; British Games 1951 19; Centennial Games 1950 19; coach *see* Stampfl, Franz; doctor, life as 105–6, 139; early life 13–16; Empire Games 1954 283–99, 301–4, 306; four minute mile, breaks 214–28, 231–5; Hillary's Everest conquest inspires 155–8, 192–3; Inter-Hospitals Meet 1952 21; Landy, rivalry with 103–5, 174, 179, 181, 236, 238, 244, 246, 247, 249–50, 255–6, 260–4, 266–7, 269,

AAA championship – *cont.*
270–1, 273, 274, 276, 277–9,
281; mentality 7–8; 'Miracle
Mile Trophy' 250–1; Motspur
Park 27th June 1953 158–61;
Motspur Park 3/4 mile 24th
April 1954 209–10; Olympics
1952 60, 63, 65–70, 79, 82–4;
Olympics 1952, preparation
for 18–22; Oxford University
Athletic Club, role in 16, 18,
137–8, 139; Oxford vs
Cambridge mile race 1947
16–18; physique 7–8; Pirie,
rivalry with 166–7; retirement
311, 312, 313, 315, 317;
running style 7–8, 254–5;
Santee, rivalry with 126, 130,
145, 150, 155–7, 163, 242;
training 17–18, 106–15, 139,
140, 165–72, 188–93, 200–4,
209–12, 243; wife, meets 251
Barclay, Captain Robert 73, 92–3
Barry, J. J. 216
Barthel, Josey 69, 70, 23, 244,
256–7
Bayi, Filbert 313
BBC 69, 219, 226, 231, 239, 285,
291–2
Benton, Ethel 27
Binks, Joseph 75, 218, 313–14
Bogerud, Bjorr 197, 198
Bonham, Russ 148, 149, 238–9,
240, 241
Boyd, Ian 271, 284, 288, 292, 296
Brasher, Chris 68, 141, 156, 158,
159, 160, 167–8, 188, 190, 191,
200, 201, 202, 203, 211, 212,
217, 218, 219, 220, 221, 222,
224, 225, 231, 232, 233–4, 243,
246, 265, 270, 271, 284

British Amateur Athletic Board
166
Brown, Jack 29
Brundage, Avery 144
Bryant, John 141
Burfitt, Derek 141

Cambridge University 68, 74
Capozzoli, Charlie 118, 181
Carlson, Frank 309
Cates, General Clifton 258, 259
Cerutty, Percy 38–41, 44–5, 46,
47–54, 63, 64, 65, 81, 87, 88,
91, 97, 98, 99, 101–2, 132, 134,
154, 173, 253, 255, 260, 282,
286, 298, 312
Chataway, Chris 7, 9, 22, 61–2, 66,
68, 84, 139–40, 141, 158, 163,
168–9, 188, 190–1, 200, 201,
209, 210, 211, 217, 218, 219,
220, 221, 222, 223, 224, 225,
231, 232, 233–4, 242, 243, 244,
245, 246, 247–8, 249, 251, 252,
255, 260, 264, 265, 267, 270,
277–8, 285, 292, 295, 296,
311–12
Churchill, Winston 105–6, 139,
192
Clarke, Ron 306–7
Cleaver, Hyton 83
Coe, Sebastian 313
Cooper, Reverend J. Astley 267,
272
Coroebus 72
Cox, Stanley 302–3
Crittenden, Max 132
Crossley, Dick 182
Crump, Jack 21–2, 158
Cummings, William 74
Cunningham, Glenn 29, 31, 33,
75–6, 124, 145, 253, 310

Daily Express 232, 233
Daily Mail 161, 225–6, 233, 271
Daily Mirror 67, 83, 161, 233, 252
Daily Telegraph 142
Daley, Arthur 104, 134, 205
Dalzell, Art 122, 123, 207, 236
Darling, Dr J. R. 305–6
Davis, Walter 57
Deford, Frank 78
Delaney, Ron 308
Denning, Danna 124, 125, 162, 179–80, 194, 198, 199, 242, 258, 276, 277, 287
Des Moines Register 34–5
Dick, Alan 66
Dimmock, Peter 212, 232
Disley, Chris 141, 142, 271
Dole, George 219
Druetzler, Warren 35
Drummond, Bruce 197
Duke of York's Barracks 168–9, 191, 203, 250
Dunn, Jack 186
Dyson, Geoffrey 82, 209, 210

Easton, Ada 180
Easton, Bill 31, 32–2, 34, 35, 36, 58, 59, 80, 116, 117, 118, 119, 120, 121–2, 123, 124–6, 127, 129, 130, 131, 143, 144, 145, 146, 147, 148, 150, 162, 177, 178, 180, 187, 194, 195–6, 197–8, 199, 208, 226, 227, 239, 240, 242, 276, 308, 309, 311
Edinburgh, Duke of 285
El Mabrouk 63, 69
Elizabeth, Queen 3, 157
Elliott, Herb 312–13
Ericsson, Ingvar 238, 241
Evening Standard 278

Fartlek training 95, 107–8, 114, 189
Ferguson, Richard 59, 271, 284, 288, 291, 293, 286, 297, 299
Ferris, Dan 145, 180, 181, 187, 309–10
First World War 11
Fox Movietone News 239
Franken, Al 131, 146, 147, 149, 178, 181, 239, 310, 311

Galli, Joseph 41, 53, 153
George, Walter 71, 74–5, 76, 93–4
Gerschler, Dr 95
Gordon, Alan 219
Gordon, Harry 307
Grauer, Ben 286, 287
Gray, Thomas 152
Green, Freddie 278
Grimes, Charles 310, 311
Guerrouj, Hicham El 313, 314
Guinness Book of World Records 104
Guttmann, Allen 138

Haegg, Gundar 46, 76–8, 95, 97, 101, 135, 152, 155, 163, 175, 205, 206, 227, 236, 253, 313
Halberg, Murray 271, 284, 288, 289, 290–1, 292, 296
Hamilton, Brutus 77–8, 314
Harrier, Malvern 100
Harvard University 94
Hayes, Bill 120
Hayward, Steve 97, 269–70
Hewson, Brian 84, 312
Hill, Archibald 95
Hillary, Edmund 3, 157, 158, 192–3
Hitler, Adolf 170
Hogan, Ben 3, 233

Holland, Gerald 127
Holt, Richard 1578
Hopman, Harry 173
Hopper, Hedda 146
Hulatt, William 219
Humphreys, Don 80
Hurt, Bob 180–1, 187

Ibbotson, Derek 312, 313
Indiana University 59, 120
International Olympic Committee
  (IOC) 144

Jackson, Marjorie 64
Jacobsson, Moyra 251
Jazy, Michel 313
Johansson, Denis 68–9, 143, 145,
  146, 147, 148–9, 150, 161, 187,
  192, 205, 227, 228, 236, 237,
  242, 243, 245, 247, 252, 253–4,
  260
Jungwirth, Stanislav 67, 251,
  303–4

Kallio, Antte 245, 247
Kansas City Star 199
Kekkonen, Urho 253
Koby, Lloyd 24, 118, 122, 123, 236
Kolehmainen, Hannes 26
Korean War 3

Ladoumegue, Jules 75
Landy, Elva 42
Landy, Gordon 42–3
Landy, John 2, 3, 155, 315, 316
Bannister, reaction to defeat by
  304–8; Bannister, rivalry with
  103–4, 140, 158, 191, 192, 210,
  212, 217, 227–8, 232, 234,
  249–50, 253–6, 258–62, 263–4,
  265, 266, 269–70, 271, 272–9,

301, 302, 311, 312; coach see
  Cerutty, Percy; early life 42–7;
  Empire Games 1954 (versus
  Bannister) 280–9; Geelong
  Guild 96–7, 98; Helms Trophy
  174; Olympics 1952,
  preparation 38–42; Olympics
  1952 60–1, 63–5, 79; races
  96–102, 135–6, 174–7, 182–7;
  running style 87, 96; Santee,
  rivalry with 126, 130;
  Scandinavia Tour 1954 204–7,
  235–8, 239, 242, 243, 244, 245,
  246–8; training 50–4, 81–2,
  87–91, 96–8, 132–6, 145,
  152–4, 165, 168, 259;
  University of Melbourne 90,
  132; Victorian Public Schools
  Championship 1948 46
LaPierre, Joe 34
Law, David 271, 284, 288, 289, 290
Liebling, A.J. 70
Life 284
Lincoln, Merv 306–7
London Society 93
Los Angeles Herald & Express
  147
Lovelock, Jack 7, 16, 17, 18, 19, 69,
  75, 76, 94, 137, 200–1, 215
Luce, Henry 268
Lueg, Werner 69, 70, 303

Mackay, Bryce 273
Macmillan, Don 19, 38, 39, 40, 43,
  45–6, 52, 53, 63, 65, 68, 81, 82,
  91, 96, 97, 100, 103–4, 154–5,
  158, 159, 160, 266, 271, 273–4,
  275, 290, 294
Manchester Guardian 21
Marks, John 175
Marmor, Milton 219

Mayer, Bill 226
McConnell, Ray 197
McGregor, Adrian 286
McMillen, Bob 35, 60, 63, 69–70, 79, 148, 181
McRae, Len 100–1, 182, 184, 186, 235
McTaggart, J. 159
McWhirter, Norris 8, 9, 10, 22, 103, 104, 105, 109, 110–11, 137, 141, 156, 157. 158, 159, 160, 165, 168, 192, 204, 210, 212, 219, 220–1, 224, 232, 270, 271, 285, 289, 292
McWhirter, Ross 8, 103, 104, 105, 109, 192, 204, 223, 285
Metcalf, James 73
mile running:
    four minute challenge, pre-1952 74–8; history of 72–4; training, history of 91–5
Milligan, Victor 271, 284, 288, 292, 296
Milo of Croton 92
Mimoun, Alain 61, 62
Monroe, Marilyn 147
Montague, L.A. 21
Montgomery, Marty 240
Moody, Ralph 126
Morceli, Noureddine 313
More, Dr John 160, 201, 202
Morel, Rene 75
Morgan-Morris, Robbie 91, 298, 306
Moses, Ken 96, 174
Motspur Park 7, 9, 21, 76, 84, 140, 156, 158, 161, 166, 190, 209, 210
Murray, J. Allen 29, 30, 31, 208

Nankeville, Bill 163, 209

National Canadian Film Board 275
NBC 261, 268, 272, 276–7, 286–7
Nelson, Cordner 308
New York Athletic Club 144
New York Herald Tribune 19, 75, 118, 161
New York Post 206
New York Times 104, 134, 205, 265
New Yorker 70
News of the World 142
Newton, Arthur 94
Nieder, Bill 119, 130
Nielsen, Gunnar 303–4
Norgay, Tenzing 157
Nurmi, Paavo 25–6, 40, 63, 74, 75, 94, 105, 163, 253

O'Brien, Andy 275–6, 281, 304–5
O'Connor, Terry 7, 225–6
O'Neil, Paul 87
Olds, Lloyd 187
Olympic Games 72–3, 308, 311
    1924 Paris 26, 75
    1936 Berlin 17, 18, 76, 144, 170
    1948 London 13, 17, 33
    1952 Helsinki 18, 19–22, 23–6, 38–41, 54, 55–7, 60, 61, 78, 107, 115, 124, 127–8, 138, 160, 167, 171, 209, 231, 235, 253, 266, 295
Ormsby, Ian 184, 186
Ovett, Steve 313
Oxford Mail 219
Oxford University 75, 108, 109
    Achilles Club 8; Athletic Club 137, 139; history of athletics at 137–8

Parnell, William 271
People 82

Perry, Les 38, 45, 46, 52, 61, 63,
   64, 81, 91, 96, 97, 99–100, 101,
   102, 135, 152, 175, 177, 185,
   286, 298
Peters, Jim 265, 266, 301–2, 303
Phillips, Tom 67
Pirie, Gordon 57, 62, 163, 166–7,
   174
Prentice, Bob 38, 39, 97
Princeton University 75

Reiff, Gaston 61, 62, 97, 126, 143,
   147, 148–9, 150
Richards, Bob 36
Robbins, Neil 96
Robbins, Trevor 52, 99, 100–1
Roberts, J. D. 256
Rudd, Bevil 108
Ryun, Jim 313, 314

San Francisco Chronicle 308–9
Santee, David 27, 28, 29–30, 31
Santee, Henry 28, 31
Santee, Ina May 28, 31
Santee, Wes 2, 3, 4, 315, 316
   AAU Championships 1951 33;
   AAU, battles with 35–6, 144–5,
   187–8, 309–11; Bannister,
   rivalry with 155, 156, 157, 158,
   160, 161, 192, 204, 210, 212,
   217, 226–7, 232, 234, 244; Big
   Seven conference
   championship, Ames 1953
   145–6; coach see Easton, Bill;
   Compton Invitational 131,
   143–4, 146–51, 239–42; Drake
   University Relays 34–5, 80,
   116–17, 129, 130, 207–9; early
   life 27; Glenn Cunningham
   Mile 1954 193–9; Helsinki
   Olympics 1952, preparation
   for 23–7, 35–7, 55–7; Kansas
   Jayhawks, role in 34, 116, 119,
   121, 125, 131, 179, 195, 261;
   Landy, rivalry with 152, 174,
   238; Los Angeles Memorial
   Coliseum, Olympic trial 1952
   35; Marine Corps, joins 256–9,
   261, 271; Olympics 1952
   58–60, 79–81; Pro Bowl
   January 1954 178–81, 193;
   Randall's Island 1952 36–7;
   Summer tour Europe 1953
   161–4; Texas Relays 1953
   118–19; training 32–3, 119–31,
   165, 177–9; University of
   Kansas, influence on career of
   24, 31, 56–7, 58, 76, 79, 81,
   121–7, 130, 177, 193, 208, 239,
   315; watches Bannister-Landy
   race 276–7, 286–7, 291, 294,
   298, 308, 310–11
Saturday Evening Post 180–1,
   187
Schade, Herbert 59, 60, 61, 62
Sears, Edward 71
Second World War 8, 11, 25,
   76–7, 177
Sherman, Montague 138
Shrubb, Alf 94
Slijkhuis, Willi 19
Smith, Don 121
Smith, George 210
Snell, Peter 313
Sports Illustrated 87, 90, 268
Sports Novels 53–4
Sportsview 219, 231–2
Spurrier, Len 306
Stacey, Nicholas 66, 224
Stalin, Joseph 57, 116
Stampfl, Franz 168–72, 189, 190,
   191, 201, 203, 204, 211,

215–17, 219, 221, 222, 224, 262–4, 285–6, 295, 298
Stampfl, Pat 212, 215, 219, 221, 222, 223, 224, 249, 262, 284, 285
Star 10, 212, 270
Stotans 51–4, 173
Strand, Lennart 135
Strickland, Shirley 64
Strode-Jackson, Colonel 78, 137
Sunday Express 82
Sydney Morning Herald 90, 104, 134, 136, 302

Taber, Norman 74, 313
Tabori, Laszlo 312
Thomas, Bill 17–18
Thomas, R. H. 140, 268
Thorpe, Jim 144, 310
Tidwell, Billy 34, 80, 240, 241
Tierney, Frank 134, 136
Times, The 157, 267
Timmons, Bob 313
Tolgyesi 63
Track & Field News 90, 145, 149, 152, 174, 192
Truelove, Leslie 218–19, 224, 296, 297, 302
Turku Athletic Association 243
Turrini, Joseph 309

'Ultimate in Human Effort, The' (Hamilton) 77
University of British Columbia 266, 270, 275

Vaharanta, Urho 237
Vancouver Sun 267, 282, 284
Vernon, John 272, 273, 274, 275
Vuorisalo, Olavi 237, 247

Warren, Geoff 52, 152, 153, 185, 254, 271, 272, 273
Webb, Allan 314
Wenden, Charles 217, 218, 234
White City stadium 21, 78, 156, 210, 214, 216, 243, 251, 311–12
Whitfield, Mal 33, 162, 287
Wide, Edvin 74
Williams, Ronnie 7, 8, 9
Wilson, Dick 122, 123
Wilt, Fred 59
Wooderson, Sydney 15, 16, 17, 76, 140, 163, 253

Zatopek, Emil 34, 36, 39, 40, 46, 57, 60, 61, 62, 63, 64, 65, 66, 81–2, 88, 91, 95, 96, 97, 168, 282